Metacognition
in
Educational Theory and Practice
ଓ୫ଓ

The Educational Psychology Series

Robert J. Sternberg, Series Editor

Marton/Booth • *Learning and Awareness*

Hacker/Dunlosky/Graesser • *Metacognition in Educational Theory and Practice*

Smith/Pourchot • *Adult Learning and Development: Perspectives From Educational Psychology*

Metacognition
in
Educational Theory and Practice
∞

Edited by

Douglas J. Hacker
The University of Memphis

John Dunlosky
University of North Carolina at Greensboro

Arthur C. Graesser
The University of Memphis

 LAWRENCE ERLBAUM ASSOCIATES, PUBLISHERS
1998   Mahwah, New Jersey   London

Lawrence Erlbaum Associates, Inc., Publishers
10 Industrial Avenue
Mahwah, New Jersey 07430

Cover Design by Kathryn Houghtaling Lacey and John Dunlosky

Cover figures taken from the following sources:
Carver, C. S., & Scheier, M. F. (1990). Origins and functions of positive and negative affect: A control-process view. *Psychological Review, 97*, 19–35. Copyright © 1990 held by the American Psychological Association. Adaptation printed with permission by Carver.

Miller, G. A., Galanter, E., & Pribram, K. H. (1960). *Plans and the structure of behavior.* New York: Holt, Rinehart & Winston.

Nelson, T. O., & Narens, L. (1994). Why investigate metacognition? In J. Metcalfe & A. P. Shimamura (Eds.), *Metacognition: Knowing about knowing* (pp. 1–25). Cambridge, MA: MIT Press.

Library of Congress Cataloging-in-Publication Data

Metacognition in education theory and practice / edited by Douglas J. Hacker, John Dunlosky, Arthur C. Graesser.
    p. cm.
    Includes bibliographical references and indexes.
    ISBN 0-8058-2481-2 (Cloth : alk. paper). —ISBN 0-8048-2482-0
(pbk. : alk. Paper)
    1. Cognitive learning–United States. 2. Metacognition.
I. Hacker, Douglas J. II. Dunlosky, John. III. Graesser, Arthur C.
LB1067.M425 1998
370.15'2—dc21   97–38586

                                              CIP

Books published by Lawrence Erlbaum Associates are printed on acid-free paper, and their bindings are chosen for strength and durability.

Printed in the United States of America
10 9 8 7 6 5 4 3 2 1

To Margaret F. Hacker, **nee** *LaFond,*
Paul Turnitza,
and Roy K. Graesser

Contents

Foreword Metacognitive Food for Thought in Educational Theory   ix
and Practice
Thomas O. Nelson

Preface   xiii

1 Definitions and Empirical Foundations   1
Douglas J. Hacker

2 Verbalization and Problem Solving   25
Roger L. Dominowski

3 Smart Problem Solving: How Metacognition Helps   47
Janet E. Davidson and Robert J. Sternberg

4 Metacognition in Mathematics From a Constructivist   69
Perspective
Martha Carr and Barry Biddlecomb

5 Knowing How to Write: Metacognition and Writing   93
Instruction
Barbara M. Sitko

6 Test Predictions Over Text Material   117
Ruth H. Maki

7 Influence of Knowledge Activation and Context   145
on Comprehension Monitoring of Science Texts
José Otero

8 Self–Regulated Comprehension During Normal Reading   165
Douglas J. Hacker

9 Metacognition, Childhood Bilingualism, and Reading   193
Georgia Earnest García, Robert T. Jiménez, and P. David Pearson

10   Impaired Awareness of Deficits in a Psychiatric Context: **221**
      Implications for Rehabilitation
      Susan M. McGlynn

11   Training Programs to Improve Learning in Later Adulthood: **249**
      Helping Older Adults Educate Themselves
      John Dunlosky and Christopher Hertzog

12   Studying as Self–Regulated Learning   **277**
      Philip H. Winne and Allyson F. Hadwin

13   SMART Environments That Support Monitoring, Reflection,   **305**
      and Revision
      Nancy J. Vye, Daniel L. Schwartz, John D. Bransford,
      Brigid J. Barron, Linda Zech, and The Cognition and Technology
      Group at Vanderbilt

14   The Metacognition of College Studentship: A Grounded   **347**
      Theory Approach
      Michael Pressley, Shawn Van Etten, Linda Yokoi,
      Geoffrey Freebern, and Peggy Van Meter

Epilogue   Linking Metacognitive Theory to Education   **367**
      John Dunlosky

Author Index   **383**

Subject Index   **401**

Foreword

Metacognitive Food for Thought
in Educational Theory and Practice

Thomas O. Nelson
University of Maryland

This book describes the broad domain of research on metacognitive aspects of education. In contrast to earlier books, such as J. R. Kirby's Cognitive Strategies and Educational Performance (1984, Academic Press) in which the ideas about metacognition are sprinkled throughout the book without systematic attempts to integrate those ideas into coherent wholes, the present book does try to give coherence to ideas about metacognition. What are the slices in the metaphorical pie of metacognitive aspects of education, and how should the pie be cut up so that each piece can stand on its own as well as contribute in a useful way to the overall whole?

In this book, we see the beginning of some answers to those questions. The authors of each chapter were assigned the task of reviewing the current literature, discussing the theoretical implications, suggesting the educational implications, and making suggestions for future research.

How did we get to this point, where sufficient interest in metacognition has arisen to warrant a book on the status of current research on the metacognitive aspects of education? Although metacognition had its roots in research conducted prior to the 1970s, the pioneering research on metacognition per se occurred in the 1970s, primarily in developmental psychology. This pioneering research focused on global demonstrations of interesting phenomena, and even at that time, the potential applications to education could be anticipated. However, the methodology of the early research was not highly sophisticated, and rigorous theories were not available. Nevertheless, it was obvious that people who, for instance, were in self-paced learning tasks would distribute their study time in ways that were not haphazard and that varied systematically across different kinds of learners. However, because the research program was not yet analytic, researchers did not have much understanding about the specific metacognitive mechanisms that gave rise to those differences in study times.

Then in the 1980s and 1990s, researchers in cognitive psychology joined the researchers in developmental psychology and educational psychology to produce more sophisticated methodologies for assessing metacognition. Theoretical frameworks also were developed in the early 1990s that helped to suggest ways in which various metacognitive activities could be analyzed (e.g., differences in self-paced study times could be due either to differences in the monitoring of what was being learned or to differences in the control of self-paced study time, or both). One of the main kinds of metacognitive monitoring that received attention from researchers during the 1980s and early 1990s was the feeling of knowing, which pertains to people's predictions of what they know when they cannot recall an item from memory. Although the feeling of knowing is interesting for theoretical reasons (e.g., how can a system know that it knows an item without being able to recall the item?), the feeling of knowing is only of limited use in applied situations such as the learning of new information. Fortunately, however, increased interest began in the 1990s on the topic of how people monitor their ongoing learning, and this research focused on judgments of learning. Questions were investigated both about the bases for people's judgments of learning and about the accuracy of people's judgments of learning, and overall frameworks began to integrate the judgments of learning (the monitoring component) with various control components (e.g., allocation of self-paced study time, choice of strategies for encoding the to-be-learned items).

These latter developments are relevant to applications in education, especially in educational situations where learners have some control over their study activities. In the present book, you see chapters describing cutting-edge research on how learners do monitor and/or control their own learning. Several of those chapters are focused on learning in classrooms, whereas other chapters are focused on education in the larger sense, such as on the treatment and management of psychiatric patients who are trying to learn various things, and on the role of self-awareness in various clinical populations. In this book, even the learners in the classroom are not limited to typical elementary-age and high school children, but also include bilingual children, college students, and older adults. In addition to describing metacognitive activities in different kinds of target populations, this book includes chapters that focus on different kinds of content that is being learned. Some chapters explore the metacognitive strategies and metacognitive aspects of the learning of mathematics. Besides focusing on learning per se, several chapters focus on metacognitive activities during reading and during writing. There are also chapters on metacognition and problem solving and on the role of think-aloud protocols in research.

Although every chapter attempts to highlight the educational implications of recent research on metacognition, one point to keep in mind when reading those chapters is that there is simultaneously an ongoing shift from theory to practice (i.e., attempts are increasingly being made to apply theoretical ideas to various educational situations) and a parallel effort to enhance our understanding both of the theoretical aspects of metacognition and of the applied aspects of metacognition. Thus while it would be incorrect to think that the theories of metacognition are currently so highly developed that the applications to education are straightforward, it would also be incorrect to assume that our current ideas about metacognition are so fragmented and poorly developed that any applications to education would be premature. This is an exciting time for people who are interested in metacognition and education. Some potentially useful applications are already underway and yet there still is plenty of room for new developments to occur. This book will be helpful to those who are interested either in the current status of those applications or in having a statement of what the current research problems are so as perhaps to join in the attempts to solve those problems. The pie of metacognitive aspects of education contains ample food for thought both for basic researchers and for applied researchers.

Bon appetit!

Preface

Metacognition has been a topic of much interest in recent years. As a rough measure of this interest, a recent review of the literature referenced in PsycLIT for the years 1979 through 1995 indicated that 503 journal articles and 169 book chapters have been written on topics concerning metacognition. Although these articles and chapters range across a wide variety of topics, one trend is evident: A strong focus on theoretical aspects of metacognition in earlier writings has recently produced an equally strong focus on educational application. An earmark of the maturity and substance of a scientific concept is the shift it undergoes from theory to practice. Metacognition has undergone such a shift, and it is time to disseminate its educational potential to a wider audience.

The purpose of this volume is to examine ways in which metacognition has made the shift from theory to practice in education. The book is organized around four general areas relevant to education, and within those general areas specific topics have been addressed. Chapters 2 through 4 deal with metacognition in problem solving, and within that area, Roger Dominowski presents the effects of verbalization on problem solving, Janet Davidson and Robert Sternberg discuss general problem solving, and Martha Carr and Barry Biddlecomb address mathematical problem solving. Chapters 5 through 9 deal with metacognition in verbal comprehension: Barbara Sitko treats writing processes; Ruth Maki, José Otero, and Douglas Hacker discuss monitoring and control of reading processes; and Georgia García, Robert Jiménez, and P. David Pearson address bilingualism. Chapters 10 and 11 are concerned with metacognition in the education of nontraditional populations: Susan McGlynn addresses rehabilitation of impaired brain activity, and John Dunlosky and Christopher Hertzog discuss learning by older adults. Finally, chapters 12 through 14 deal with metacognition in studentship. Within this broad topic, Philip Winne and Allyson Hadwin address aspects of studying; Nancy Vye, Daniel Schwartz, John Bransford, Brigid Barron, Linda Zech, and The Cognition and Technology Group at

Vanderbilt introduce environmental supports of learning; and Michael Pressley, Shawn Van Etten, Linda Yokoi, Geoffrey Freebern, and Peggy Van Meter describe academic coping.

In each chapter, the authors pursue three objectives: They review current literature as it applies to their areas of interest, discuss theoretical implications and suggestions for future research, and provide educational applications. Each chapter, then, describes testable theory and provides examples of how theory can be applied to the classroom. Thus, the volume should have wide appeal to the researcher and student concerned with the scientific investigation of metacognition and the practitioner concerned with the cultivation of learning and achievement in his or her students.

This volume provides what we believe to be a unique contribution to the literature. At present, we are aware of only three books that overlap in some way with our volume: Schunk and Zimmerman's (1994) Self-Regulation of Learning and Performance: Issues and Educational Applications; Pressley, Harris, and Guthrie's (1992) Promoting Academic Competence and Literacy in School; and Jones and Idol's (1990) Dimensions of Thinking and Cognitive Instruction. Our volume adds to these fine works by describing the most recent research that has examined specific theoretical aspects of metacognition in domains of direct relevance to education. Many researchers and practitioners are convinced that by fostering metacognitive processes during instruction, more durable and transferable learning can be achieved. That is a major thesis of this volume.

ACKNOWLEDGMENTS

We wish to thank Robert Sternberg for providing us the opportunity to put this volume together and for supporting us throughout the process. We also would like to thank Naomi Silverman and Sara Scudder of Lawrence Erlbaum Associates for their helpful advice and direction on many aspects of this volume.

—Douglas J. Hacker
—John Dunlosky
—Arthur C. Graesser

REFERENCES

Jones. B. F. & Idol, L. (Eds.) (1990). Dimensions of Thinking and Cognitive Instruction. Hillsdale, NJ: Lawrence Erlbaum Associates.

Pressley, M., Harris, K. R., & Guthrie, J. T. (Eds.) (1992). Promoting Academic Competence and Literacy in School. London: Academic Press.

Schunk, D. H., & Zimmerman, B. J. (1994). Self-Regulation of Learning and Performance: Issues and Educational Applications. Hillsdale, NJ: Lawrence Erlbaum Associates.

1

Definitions and Empirical Foundations

Douglas J. Hacker
The University of Memphis

A diligent 12th-grade student sits attentively in her pre-calculus class trying to follow the teacher's first lesson on the fundamental theorem of integral calculus. The teacher is using the analogy of finding the area under the sinuous track of a roller coaster to instruct the concept of area under a mathematically defined curve. The steel girders holding up the track circumscribe rectangular columns whose widths can become increasingly smaller, and with increasingly smaller widths a closer approximation of the total area under the track can be obtained. Our student recalls the section in her mathematics textbook that she studied the night before, and she is beginning to make the connection between the textbook's presentation and the teacher's analogy. She knows how to calculate the area of a rectangle, and she understands how she can use what she knows to find the total area under the track by adding all the rectangular columns of area under the track. However, she has not quite arrived at how the total area would be affected by making the widths of the columns increasingly small. She realizes that she does not understand, and she tries to increase her concentration on the teacher's explanation and on the diagram of the roller coaster drawn on the blackboard. Unfortunately, her attempts to increase concentration are failing because two students sitting behind her are distracting her with whispers about what happened to a mutual friend over the weekend. And to add to her difficulties, the teacher's use of the roller coaster analogy has reminded her of last summer's vacation to Disneyland. Memories of the fun she had there on the roller coaster are further interfering with her thoughts of the problem at hand. She decides to redouble her concentration and is able to filter out the students' whispers. She then also realizes that her memories of Disneyland can be used if she focused attention specifically on memories of the superstructure that supported the roller coaster. Her insight, however, is interrupted when she hears the teacher tell the class to take out a piece of paper for a surprise quiz on the material just covered. Our diligent student is hit with a sinking feeling in her stomach because

*she knows that she did not understand the lesson, and her poor performance on the
quiz will likely bring her average for the course down to a "C."*

Many of the thoughts and feelings experienced by this 12th-grade student as she attempts to take charge of her learning can be described as metacognitive: realizing she does not understand, deliberately increasing her concentration to block out environmental distractions, and consciously using her memories of Disneyland to progress toward understanding. What makes these thoughts or feelings "metacognitive" as opposed to simply cognitive is not easy to describe (Nelson & Narens, 1990). Descriptions are difficult because metacognition is, by its very nature, a "fuzzy concept" (Flavell, 1981, p. 37), made even fuzzier by a ballooning corpus of research that has come from researchers of widely varying disciplines and for widely varying purposes.

The purpose of this chapter is to cut through the fuzziness surrounding the concept by describing the characteristics of metacognition that have remained relatively constant across disciplines and purposes since John Flavell's pioneering work helped give form to the concept and whose call for research provided an impetus for its study. In addition, greater understanding of metacognition can be gained by knowing how it has been investigated. Therefore, a brief review is given of the ways in which metacognition has been operationalized and investigated. By attempting a definition of metacognition and describing how researchers have come to know the concept, some of the fuzziness should be resolved.

FLAVELL'S CONTRIBUTION

It [memory development] seems in large part to be the development of intelligent structuring and storage of input, of intelligent search and retrieval operations, and of intelligent monitoring and knowledge of these storage and *retrieval operations*—a kind of "metamemory," perhaps. Such is the nature of memory development. Let's all go out and study it![1] (Flavell, 1971, p. 277)

---

[1]Typically, a distinction is made between metamemory and metacognition. Often, *metamemory* is defined as knowledge about memory and memory processes, and *metacognition* is defined as knowledge of cognition and monitoring and control of cognitive activities. If one does not closely scrutinize the definition of memory, this distinction can be maintained. However, if one accepts a definition of memory as "applied cognition" (Flavell, 1971, p. 273), the distinction becomes considerably blurred. In which case, the definition of metamemory becomes knowledge about applied cognition, which appears to be simply metacognition. To further blur the distinction between the two terms, Flavell (1977) described as part of metamemory, knowledge of the variables that interact to affect memory performance. These variables include person, task, and strategies. The person variable includes knowledge of oneself and others as storers and retrievers of information and the ability to *monitor and interpret* one's memory in specific memory situations. Once again, what is defined as metamemory seems considerably blurred with what is defined as metacognition. Thus, the convention adopted for this chapter is that metamemory is not distinct from metacognition; rather, it is a case of metacognition in which the object of thought is memory.

What is basic to the concept of metacognition is the notion of thinking about one's own thoughts. Thinking can be of what one knows (i.e., metacognitive knowledge), what one is currently doing (i.e., metacognitive skill), or what one's current cognitive or affective state is (i.e., metacognitive experience). To differentiate metacognitive thinking from other kinds of thinking, it is necessary to consider the source of metacognitive thoughts: Metacognitive thoughts do not spring from a person's immediate external reality; rather, their source is tied to the person's own internal mental representations of that reality, which can include what one knows about that internal representation, how it works, and how one feels about it. Therefore, metacognition sometimes has been defined simply as thinking about thinking, cognition of cognition, or using Flavell's (1979) words, "knowledge and cognition about cognitive phenomena" (p. 906).

In Flavell's description just quoted, the idea that metamemory involves intelligent structuring and storage, intelligent search and retrieval, and intelligent monitoring suggests that metacognitive thoughts are deliberate, planful, intentional, goal-directed, and future-oriented mental behaviors that can be used to accomplish cognitive tasks (Flavell, 1971). Metacognition is an awareness of oneself as "an actor in his environment, that is, a heightened sense of the ego as an active, deliberate storer and retriever of information" (p. 275). It is the development of memory as "applied cognition" (p. 273), in which whatever "intellectual weaponry the individual has so far developed" is applied to mnemonic problems (1977, p. 191).

Often, further definition of a term can be gained by considering its source. Therefore, further definition of this fuzzy concept may be gained by considering a source of, or at least a likely contributor to, Flavell's idea of "knowledge and cognition about cognitive phenomena": Jean Piaget. Among Flavell's many notable accomplishments is his work that introduced Piaget to many people in the United States. The Developmental Psychology of Jean Piaget (Flavell, 1963) has had tremendous impact on how researchers, practitioners, and the general public conceptualize child and adolescent cognitive development. Although recent advances in developmental psychology have indicated a need to modify some of Piaget's work, many of those advances in fact found their impetus in Piaget's theories.

The idea of deliberate, planful, and goal-directed thinking applied to one's thoughts to accomplish cognitive tasks is deeply embedded in Piaget's conceptualization of formal operations in which higher ordered levels of thought operate on lower ordered levels. During this stage of cognitive development, the abilities of the adolescent begin to differentiate from those of the child. Flavell (1963) wrote:

> What is really achieved in the 7-11-year period is the organized cognition of concrete objects and events per se (i.e., putting them into classes, seriating them, setting them into correspondence, etc.). The adolescent performs these first-order operations, too, but he does something else besides, a necessary something which is precisely what renders his thought formal rather than concrete. He takes the results of these concrete operations, casts them in the form of propositions, and then proceeds to operate further upon them, i.e., make various kinds of logical connections between them (implications, conjunction, identity, disjunction, etc.). Formal operations, then, are really operations performed upon the results of prior (concrete) operations. Piaget has this propositions-about-propositions attribute in mind when he refers to formal operations as second-degree operations or operations to the second power. (pp. 205–206)

Inhelder and Piaget (1958) provided further elaboration on second-degree operations: "… this notion of second-degree operations also expresses the general characteristics of formal thought—it goes beyond the framework of transformations bearing directly on empirical reality (first degree operations) and subordinates it to a system of hypothetico-deductive operations—i.e., operations which are possible" (p. 254). Thus, first-degree operations, which are thoughts about an external empirical reality, can become the object of higher order thoughts in an attempt to discover not necessarily what is real but what is possible. "Formal thinking is both thinking about thought [italics added]…and a reversal of relations between what is real and what is possible" (pp. 341–342,). Referring to Inhelder and Piaget's work, Flavell (1977) wrote: "Another way to conceptualize it is to say that formal operations constitute a kind of 'metathinking,' i.e., thinking about thinking itself rather than about objects of thinking. Children certainly are not wholly incapable of this and other forms of 'metacognition'" (p. 107).

Eight years after his call for metamemory research, Flavell (1979) acknowledged the wide interest and promise of this "new area of cognitive-developmental inquiry" (p. 906). At that time substantial work that would eventually be viewed as foundations of metacognitive research already had been accomplished by many others: Brown (1978), Belmont and Butterfield (1969), Corsini (1971), Hagen and Kingsley (1968), Hart (1965), and Markman (1977), to name only a few. And their areas of interest included such diverse topics as "oral communication of information, oral persuasion, oral comprehension, reading comprehension, writing, language acquisition, attention, memory, problem solving, social cognition, and various types of self-control, and self-instruction" (Flavell, 1979, p. 906). This work on metamemory added significantly to the information-processing paradigm that had emerged shortly before through the theorizing of researchers such as Newell, Shaw, and Simon (1958), Miller (1953), and Atkinson and Shiffrin (1968). Key to this new psychological paradigm was the conceptualization of thought as the flow of information in and out of a system of mental structures. Questions concerning how information is stored in and retrieved from those structures, how the structures develop with age, and how storage and retrieval are controlled drew the attention of many researchers.

Flavell's (1979) model of metacognition and cognitive monitoring developed from answers to many of those questions. According to his model, a person's ability to control "a wide variety of cognitive enterprises occurs through the actions and interactions among four classes of phenomena: (a) metacognitive knowledge, (b) metacognitive experiences, (c) goals (or tasks), and (d) actions (or strategies)" (p. 906). Metacognitive knowledge refers to one's stored world knowledge that "has to do with people as cognitive creatures and with their diverse cognitive tasks, goals, actions, and experiences" (p. 906). It consists of one's knowledge or beliefs about three general factors: his or her own nature or the nature of another as a cognitive processor; a task, its demands, and how those demands can be met under varying conditions; and strategies for accomplishing the task (i.e., cognitive strategies that are invoked to make progress toward goals, and metacognitive strategies that are invoked to monitor the progress of cognitive strategies). Metacognitive knowledge may influence the course of cognitive enterprises through a deliberate and conscious memory search or through nonconscious and automatic cognitive processes. Metacognitive knowledge may lead to a wide variety of metacognitive experiences, which Flavell describes as conscious cognitive or affective experiences that accompany and pertain to an intellectual enterprise.

A look at the aforementioned 12th-grade student will illustrate the components of Flavell's model of metacognition. The use of metacognitive knowledge can be inferred in at least three parts of the vignette. The first occurs when the student gains the metacognitive knowledge of how her knowledge of calculating the area of a rectangle can be used to obtain an approximation of the total area under the roller coaster by adding all the rectangular areas under the track. The use of metacognitive knowledge can be inferred again when she realizes that her memories of Disneyland, rather than being distractions from the task, can be used to accomplish it: She has knowledge of the superstructure of the roller coaster at Disneyland, and she has metacognitive knowledge of how to use that knowledge to enhance the teacher's roller coaster analogy. The third illustration of metacognitive knowledge occurs near the end of the vignette when the student assesses her understanding of the lesson and realizes that she does not know the material well enough for the quiz. In this case, she has metacognitive knowledge of what she does not know.

Metacognitive experiences also are illustrated in three parts of the vignette. Once she understands how to use her knowledge of calculating the area of a rectangle to obtain an approximation of the total area, she has the metacognitive experience that there is something she still does not understand. What eludes her is the understanding of how increasingly accurate approximations of the total area can be obtained with increasingly smaller widths of the rectangles. Another metacognitive experience occurs with the insight that her own personal experiences of the roller coaster at Disneyland can be used to enhance her understanding of the teacher's roller coaster analogy. Finally, when she hears about the quiz and assesses her lack of knowledge, the resulting metacognitive experience leaves her with the sinking feeling in her stomach that her grade for the course is going to suffer.

Strategy use is also illustrated in the vignette. In response to her metacognitive experience that she still does not understand how to obtain increasingly accurate approximations of the area, she increases her concentration on the teacher's explanation and on the diagram on the blackboard. Her use of this simple strategy may have been a nonconscious automatic response that she had acquired over years of learning, or it may have been the result of her conscious and deliberate choice. In the latter case, then, that choice likely required metacognitive knowledge of the task and of herself as a problem solver. Metacognitive knowledge of the task would be required to provide understanding of how she had previously managed the demands of tasks that she perceived to be similar to the one at hand; and metacognitive knowledge of herself would be required to provide understanding of whether she, as a problem solver, could meet those demands.

Unfortunately, her strategy immediately failed because of unforeseen environmental distractions and because the teacher's use of the roller coaster analogy created cognitive interference that further distracted her. In the face of these distractions, she continues to rely on her selected strategy and puts forth even more effort to concentrate on the task. Her strategy proves successful in filtering out the students' whispers, and it also leads to the insight about her memories of Disneyland. Once again, however, she is distracted from the task by the disturbing news of the quiz. Her metacognitive judgment that she has not learned the lesson fills her with dread of the outcome.

Thus, the vignette illustrates that metacognition involves "active monitoring and consequent regulation and orchestration" of cognitive processes to achieve cognitive goals (Flavell, 1976, p. 252). Monitoring, regulation, and orchestration can take the form of checking, planning, selecting, and inferring (Brown & Campione, 1977), self-interrogation and introspection (Brown, 1978), interpretation of ongoing experience (Flavell & Wellman, 1977), or simply making judgments about what one knows or does not know to accomplish a task. However, the vignette also illustrates that along with the ideas of "active" and "conscious" monitoring, regulation, and orchestration of thought processes is the possibility that thinking about one's thinking, through repeated use or overlearning, may become automatized and consequently nonconscious.

> ...conscious monitoring of mnemonic means, goals, and variables may actually diminish as effective storage and retrieval behaviors become progressively automatized and quasi-reflective through repeated use and overlearning. The metamemory–memory behavior link of the older child is not thereby extinguished, of course. However, the need for it to become clearly conscious may well diminish as the behaviors it once mediated become more self-starting. (Flavell & Wellman, 1977, pp. 28–29)

As already mentioned, the 12th-grade student's use of the simple strategy to increase concentration may have been a conscious and deliberate choice, or it may have been a nonconscious automatic response developed over years of repeatedly attributing learning of difficult material to greater effort (e.g., Nicholls & Miller, 1984). If nonconscious and automatic, does her strategy use illustrate a metacognitive process or is it simply a cognitive one? At one time her response may have been conscious and deliberate. Should thoughts that were once metacognitive but have since become automatic through repeated use and overlearning still be called metacognitive? Automatic cognitive processes may involve knowledge and cognition about one's own cognitive phenomena just as metacognitive processes do.

However, because people are likely to be aware of only the products of nonconscious automatic processes and not the processes themselves, it is difficult if not impossible for people to report on them (cf. Ericsson & Simon,

1980). Accordingly, it is difficult if not impossible for researchers to know whether automatic cognitive processes reflect people's beliefs in what plausible links should exist between a stimulus and a response or of what links actually exist (Nisbett & Wilson, 1977). In their own right, beliefs in plausible links (i.e., *a prior*, causal theories, or on-line constructions) are deserving of study, but they likely do not reflect veridical reports of nonconscious cognitive processes. Without accurate reports to rely on, the study of nonconscious processes is greatly impeded.

Thus, whether the term metacognitive should be used to describe thoughts that were once metacognitive but have since become nonconscious and automatic remains a debatable issue. Certainly, the nonconscious and automatic nature of these thoughts contrasts sharply with other, more prominent, features of metacognition, namely, the extent to which metacognitive processes involve an awareness of oneself as "an actor in his environment" and a "deliberate storer and retriever of information." It seems reasonable, therefore, to adopt a convention that many researchers have (e.g., Borkowski & Muthukrishna, 1992; Bracewell, 1983; Carr, Alexander, & Folds-Bennett, 1994; Davidson, Deuser, & Sternberg, 1994; Paris & Winograd, 1990) and reserve the term *metacognitive* for conscious and deliberate thoughts that have other thoughts as their object. As conscious and deliberate, metacognitive thoughts are not only potentially controllable by the person experiencing them, but are also potentially reportable and therefore accessible to the researcher. This convention will be adopted throughout the remainder of this chapter.

OTHER CONTRIBUTIONS TO THE
DEFINITION OF METACOGNITION

Building on Flavell's contributions to metacognition, Kluwe (1982) brought further definition to the concept by identifying two general attributes common to "activities referred to as 'metacognitive': (a) the thinking subject has some knowledge about his own thinking and that of other persons; (b) the thinking subject may monitor and regulate the course of his own thinking, i.e., may act as the causal agent of his own thinking" (p. 202). Furthermore, using a distinction made earlier by Ryle (1949), Kluwe linked the first attribute to declarative knowledge, "stored data in long-term memory," and the second attribute to procedural knowledge, "stored processes of a system" (p. 203).

Importantly, Kluwe helped to make a finer distinction between what is and is not metacognitive—something not always easily determined, as was suggested by the earlier discussion of nonconscious and automatic thoughts. Stored data in long-term memory and stored processes of a system can be found at both metacognitive and cognitive levels. According to Kluwe, at cognitive levels, stored data may consist simply of domain knowledge, which refers to what a person knows about "domains of reality" (e.g., knowledge about mathematics, social interactions, personal history), and stored processes may consist simply of solution processes (i.e., processes directed to the solution of a specific problem). Portions of the 12th-grade student vignette can be used to illustrate these ideas of nonmetacognitive declarative and procedural knowledge. Nonmetacognitive declarative knowledge is illustrated by the student's recollections of the textbook dealing with integration, the friend being discussed by her classmates, and last summer's vacation to Disneyland. These memories reflect stored data drawn from her mathematical knowledge and her personal knowledge domains. Nonmetacognitive procedural knowledge is illustrated by the solution process to calculate the area of a rectangle. Likely, the student had long ago mastered this process, which she can now intentionally direct to the solution of a specific problem.

By contrast, processes that "monitor the selection and application as well as the effects of solution processes and regulate the stream of solution activity" represent, according to Kluwe (1982, p. 204) metacognitive procedural knowledge. Kluwe uses the term *executive processes* to denote this kind of procedural knowledge. Executive *processes* involve both monitoring and regulating other thought processes, and therefore, correspond with Flavell's (1979) metacognitive strategies and Brown's (1978) metacognitive skills. Executive *monitoring* processes are those that are "directed at the acquisition of information about the person's thinking processes" (Kluwe, 1982, p. 212). They involve one's decisions that help (a) to identify the task on which one is currently working, (b) to check on current progress of that work, (c) to evaluate that progress, and (d) to predict what the outcome of that progress will be. Executive *regulation* processes are those that are "directed at the regulation of the course of one's own thinking" (p. 212). They involve one's decisions that help (a) to allocate his or her resources to the current task, (b) to determine the order of steps to be taken to complete the task, and (c) to set the intensity or (d) the speed at which one should work the task.

Thus, the general distinction between procedural and declarative knowledge and the finer distinctions between what is and is not metacognitive within each kind of knowledge have helped to further define metacognition and cognitive monitoring. But perhaps more importantly, Kluwe (1982) helped to emphasize the importance of metacognitive research as a way to gain greater understanding of humans, not only as thinking organisms but as self-regulatory organisms who are capable of assessing themselves and others and directing their behavior toward specified goals:

> It is important that human beings understand themselves as agents of their own thinking. Our thinking is not just happening, like a reflex; it is caused by the thinking person, it can be monitored and regulated deliberately, i.e., it is under the control of the thinking person. (p. 222)

Whether people can monitor and regulate their thinking, how and when they monitor and regulate, and whether greater chances for success are realized through monitoring and regulating depend on the task, the demands posed by the task, people's knowledge of the task, and the kinds of cognitive strategies they can bring to bear on the task. However, equally important is how people assess themselves as self-regulatory organisms, as "agents of their own thinking" (Kluwe, 1982, p. 222). For example, many people are convinced they are terrible at solving mathematical word problems. Because they assume that every mathematical word problem will forever evade them, they are little motivated to attempt a solution, and even less motivated to monitor and regulate their attempts. Also, many people are overwhelmed by stress and anxiety whenever they are asked to perform in front of a group of peers, thereby making it nearly impossible for them to monitor and regulate their performance. Thus, self-assessments of one's affective states often serve as the gateway to further assessments concerning the task, its demands, the knowledge necessary for its completion, and strategies for its completion. These personal-motivational states often "determine the course of new strategy acquisition and, more importantly, the likelihood of strategy transfer and the quality of self-understanding about the nature and function of mental processes" (Borkowski, Carr, Rellinger, & Pressley, 1990, p. 54).

The notion of *self-efficacy* is echoed by Paris and Winograd (1990) who believe that most researchers now recognize a definition of metacognition that "captures two essential features of metacognition—self-appraisal and self-management of cognition" (p. 17). Self-appraisals are people's personal reflections about their knowledge states and abilities, and their affective states concerning their knowledge, abilities, motivation, and characteristics as learners. Such reflections answer questions about "*what* you know, *how* you think, and *when* and *why* to apply knowledge or strategies" (Paris & Winograd, 1990, p. 17). Self-management refers to "metacognitions in action," that is, mental processes that help to "orchestrate aspects of problem solving" (p. 18). Focusing on self-appraisal and self-management helps in the conceptualization of learners as individuals who need to be actively involved in the orchestration of their knowledge construction.

In summary, this brief examination of the definition of metacognition was intended to provide an overall view of the kinds of thought processes that have been associated with it. Certainly, much more could be said about the characteristics and dynamics of metacognitive processes. Hopefully, this cursory synthesis of the literature has shown that what started out in the 1970s as a "fuzzy" concept embedded within developmental research has evolved over 25 years into a more precisely defined concept that can be found in many areas of psychological research. Although not all researchers will agree on some of the fuzzier aspects of metacognition, there does seem to be general consensus that a definition of metacognition should include at least these notions: knowledge of one's knowledge, processes, and cognitive and affective states; and the ability to consciously and deliberately monitor and regulate one's knowledge, processes, and cognitive and affective states.

METACOGNITIVE RESEARCH

Now that a definition of metacognition has been attempted, what will likely resolve even more of the fuzziness surrounding the concept is to move beyond the question of what it is and address the question of how it has been studied. Adopting a constructivist point of view, which is so prevalent in education today, one can argue that the realities we come to know reflect the ways in which we come to know them. Glasersfeld (1984) has provided further elaboration of this argument, "the experiencing consciousness creates structure in the flow of its experience; and this structure is what conscious cognitive organisms experience as 'reality' " (p. 38). Therefore, the knowledge that researchers have gained of metacognition can be further illuminated by looking at the ways in which they have gained it.

Most of the early investigations of metacognition were descriptive in nature in that they sought to describe general developmental patterns of children's knowledge about memory processes, particularly processes concerned with conscious and deliberate storage and retrieval of information.

However, as studies moved from descriptive to experimental, the kinds of methodology expanded, the number of studies ballooned, and the need for a scheme to classify this growing corpus of literature on metacognition arose. Several classification schemes have been used to group, analyze, and evaluate these studies (e.g., Cavanaugh & Perlmutter, 1982; Kluwe, 1982; Schoenfeld, 1987; Schneider, 1985); even though there are important differences among them, overall, three general categories consistently appear.

The first category includes studies of cognitive monitoring. These studies have examined people's knowledge of their knowledge and thought processes and how accurately they can monitor the current state of their knowledge and processes (Kluwe, 1982; Schoenfeld, 1987). Many of these studies assess prediction performance (i.e., predictions of what knowledge is stored in memory) and effort and attention allocation (i.e., allocation of study based on one's judgments about knowledge that is or is not currently in memory; Schneider, 1985). Often, subjects' verbal reports during the performance of a memory task are used to determine what memory knowledge the individual brings to the task (Cavanaugh & Perlmutter, 1982).

The second category includes studies that have focused on "regulation of one's own thinking processes in order to cope with changing situational demands" (Kluwe, 1982, p. 210). These studies typically include both a training task and a strategy transfer task (Schneider, 1985). First, people are taught a strategy to complete a specific task. Once they have demonstrated mastery of the strategy, they are given another task (i.e., the transfer task), different from the first but structurally equivalent to it. People then must decide whether to use the instructed strategy, modify it, or abandon it in favor of a different strategy that could be used to complete the transfer task.

Finally, the third category includes studies in which both monitoring and regulation are examined. In these studies, people monitor available information during the course of their own thinking and then use this information to regulate subsequent memory processes (Kluwe, 1982; Schneider, 1985; Schoenfeld, 1987). Often, these studies focus on people's organizational or elaboration strategies in memory and how strategies can be used to improve performance (Schneider, 1985). A goal of these studies is to discover what and how much people know about memory that is relevant to performance of a particular memory task (Cavanaugh & Perlmutter, 1982).

Studies of Cognitive Monitoring

Ability to monitor one's knowledge and processes is no trivial matter as far as education is concerned. Currently, educators have great interest in self-regulation of learning. "Theoreticians seem unanimous—the most effective learners are self-regulating" (Butler & Winne, 1995, p. 245). Key to effective self-regulation is accurate self-assessment of what is known or not known (Schoenfeld, 1987). Only when students know the state of their own knowledge can they effectively self-direct learning to the unknown. Therefore, knowing whether students can accurately monitor their knowledge and thought processes and whether memory monitoring of complex tasks can be taught to younger children are key concerns of teachers, researchers, and theoreticians interested in encouraging self-regulation of learning.

"Tip-of-the-tongue" experiences, feeling-of-knowing (FOK) judgments, serial recall, allocation of study effort, "seen" judgments, judgments of learning (JOL), and ease-of-learning (EOL) judgments are all metacognitive phenomena that have been used to investigate the notion that people have knowledge of their knowledge and thought processes and can accurately monitor their knowledge and processes. Tip-of-the-tongue experiences, the investigation of which can be traced back to William James (1890), concern a person's judgment that currently forgotten information is in fact recallable, that is, the memory is on the tip of one's tongue. Closely related, FOK judgments concern a person's knowledge that a currently forgotten or unrecallable item can be recognized when presented with other items. Serial recall has been used to determine how accurately people can judge whether a sequence of pictures or words they have seen for a brief period can be recalled. Allocation of study has been used to examine how accurately people can judge the current state of their knowledge and, based on that judgment, whether they allocate greater effort to study items that have not yet been learned. Seen judgments involve a person's knowledge of whether an item has been seen before; JOLs concern a person's knowledge of whether an item has been learned; and EOLs are judgments about how difficult it will be to learn new information from a particular domain, given what one knows about that domain. Four of these metacognitive phenomena (FOK, serial recall, allocation of study effort, and JOLs) serve here as illustrations of this category of metacognitive research.

Remarkably, as far back as the mid-1960s, during the early years of the cognitive revolution, Hart (1965) investigated people's accuracy in monitoring their stored knowledge. Using what has become known as the recall-judgment-recognition (RJR) paradigm, the dominant research paradigm for feeling-of-knowing judgments, Hart first asked undergraduate students to recall answers to a collection of general-information questions drawn from a variety of subject areas. Using only those items that students had gotten wrong, Hart then asked them to make FOK judgments about whether they would be able to recognize the correct answers among several wrong answers. Finally, students were given a multiple-choice test and asked to recognize each correct answer. Thus, students' accuracy in monitoring their knowledge could be determined by comparing their FOK judgments with their actual recognition performance. Hart found that feeling-of-knowing judgments were relatively accurate indicators of what is or is not stored in memory for the undergraduate students. However, similar investigations using young children (e.g., Wellman, 1977) have shown that feeling-of-knowing judgments are much less accurate. Although evidence has not always been consistent (see Butterfield, Nelson, & Peck, 1988, for a surprising reversal of these results), overall, studies examining FOK have shown a developmental pattern: With increasing age, knowledge about what is or is not stored in memory becomes increasingly accurate.

Using serial recall, Flavell, Freidrichs, and Hoyt (1970) showed young children (i.e., preschoolers to fourth graders) for very brief times successively longer sequences of pictures of familiar objects. The researchers then asked the children to predict whether they could recall the pictures in correct serial order, after which the children were asked to recall them. The children's predicted recall compared with actual recall indicated that the youngest children tended to overestimate their recall ability, whereas the older children not only could hold more pictures in memory than the younger children, but they were more accurate in their predicted recall.

Bisanz, Vesonder, and Voss (1978) showed that there are developmental differences between young (i.e., first and third grade students) and older children (i.e., fifth graders and college students) in the ability to monitor current knowledge in memory and in how the results of monitoring are used in the allocation of study effort. These authors first asked students to learn lists of picture pairs. Knowledge of the picture pairs was tested by presenting students with one picture from each pair to serve as a cued recall for the second picture. After being tested on all of the picture pairs, students were told to learn all of the picture pairs until they got them all right. Next they were shown each of the picture pairs and asked to indicate whether they had gotten each pair correct. They were then encouraged to restudy any that were incorrect. After all the picture pairs had been restudied, students were retested. This procedure was followed until each student reached a criterion. Results showed that discrimination between correct and incorrect items was accurate for all grades, although first grade subjects made more false positives (i.e., said they had gotten a pair correct when in fact they had not) than older subjects. In addition, older students utilized their ongoing monitoring judgments by allocating greater study to those items they had reported as incorrect, whereas younger students were less inclined to do so. Thus, students at all four grades could monitor current knowledge and processes in memory, but monitoring ability increased with age. Moreover, older students were more inclined than younger students to use memory monitoring information to allocate greater study to those items they had monitored as incorrect.

In the last study to be discussed, Nelson and Dunlosky (1991) used JOLs to investigate whether accuracy of memory monitoring of recently learned knowledge was affected by the amount of time that was allowed to transpire between learning and monitoring. A JOL is made after a person has studied an item; it reflects the person's confidence that a recently studied item will be remembered on a future test. Nelson and Dunlosky hypothesized that if a memory-monitoring judgment is made immediately after an item has been learned, there is a possibility that what the person is monitoring is short-term memory rather than long-term memory. Because future test performance depends on knowledge in long-term memory, a JOL based predominantly on knowledge in short-term memory will be of little predictive value. To test their hypothesis, these researchers asked college students to make JOLs either immediately after learning an item or after a filled delay. They found that JOLs made after a delay were dramatically more accurate than JOLs made immediately or shortly after learning. Thus, in determining whether people can accurately monitor their memories, it is important to consider whether long- or short-term memory is being monitored. Long-term predictions of future test performance based on monitoring of short-term memory are likely to be inaccurate.

Overall, research from the first category of metacognitive research has shown that even kindergartners can accurately monitor their knowledge. With increase in age, however, people gain not only in the amount of knowledge that can be held in memory, but also in how accurately they can monitor their knowledge. Although in judging memory monitoring ability, it is important to consider more than simply age. One must also consider the kinds of thought processes or knowledge that are being monitored. When memory monitoring tasks are simple and do not overload working memory (e.g., simple recall or recognition tasks) there is little difference between younger and older children (Schneider, 1985). But as the complexity of tasks increases, such as using strategies to allocate greater study time to more difficult items, so does the difficulty in monitoring the thought processes necessary to complete them (Schneider, 1985).

Studies of Cognitive Regulation

The second category of metacognitive research includes studies that have examined "regulation of one's own thinking processes in order to cope with changing situational demands" (Kluwe, 1982, p. 210). Many of the earliest studies from this category were focused on mentally or educably retarded children (e.g., Brown & Campione, 1977; Butterfield & Belmont, 1977); however, more recently, children representative of a broad spectrum of abilities have been studied. Typically, these studies include both a training task and a strategy transfer task (i.e., a task different from the training task but structurally equivalent to it). People are first taught a strategy to complete a task. Tasks have included sort-recall, free recall, alphabet search, word or picture association, or letter-series completion. Once mastery of the strategy has been demonstrated with the training tasks, a transfer task is given to determine whether people use the strategy, modify it, or abandon it in favor of a different one. Thus, as people learn a strategy to facilitate performance on the training tasks, researchers examine whether they develop metacognitive awareness of the utility and function of the strategy, which is essential if people are to regulate application and modification of strategies to meet new situational demands.

A study illustrative of the second category of metacognitive research is Lodico, Ghatala, Levin, Pressley, and Bell (1983). The purpose of this study was to determine whether instruction of general principles of strategy monitoring would influence children's regulation of strategies on subsequent tasks. Earlier research had shown that it is difficult to teach children to continue to use instructed strategies when presented with new tasks, even if the tasks could be efficiently accomplished by using the strategies. Lodico et al. hypothesized that for children to maintain the use of a strategy on their own, it is necessary for them to learn the value of the strategy for improving their performance. Furthermore, these researchers hypothesized that children can learn the value of a strategy through training that focuses on monitoring the relationship between strategic behavior and task performance.

Seventy-two second-grade students were assigned to one of two training conditions. In one condition, students were trained to monitor the effectiveness of two strategies designed to help draw a circle and two strategies for remembering a list of letters. In the other condition, students were exposed to the same strategies but received no monitoring training. Subsequently, half of the students in each condition were taught two strategies for learning a paired-associate word task, one strategy being more effective than the other; the other students were taught two different strategies for a free-recall word task, also with one strategy being more effective than the other. After practicing, all children were asked to assess their performance with the two strategies and to explain any differences between the two. They were then given another trial with the task, but this time they could choose the strategy they believed was more effective. After completing the task, they were asked why they had chosen their paricular strategy.

Results showed that a greater proportion of the children who were taught to monitor strategy effectiveness than of those who were not so trained (a) recognized that their better performance on the task was due to the more effective strategy, (b) choose the more effective strategy when given a choice, and (c) explained that their choice was made because they believed it would improve their performance. In contrast, a majority of the children who did not receive monitoring training either could not explain why they had chosen a particular strategy or their explanations were unrelated to performance. Thus, this study joins with others (e.g., Butterfield & Ferretti, 1987; Cavanaugh & Borkowski, 1979; Moynahan, 1978) in showing that young children can be trained to monitor their strategic behavior and performance, and that this training can enhance their regulation of efficient strategies. Moreover, if people are taught metacognitive awareness concerning the utility and function of a strategy as they are taught the strategy, they are more likely to generalize the strategy to new situations.

Studies of Cognitive Monitoring and Regulation

Finally, the third category of metacognitive research includes studies in which people monitor available information during the course of their own thinking and then use this information to regulate subsequent memory processes (Kluwe, 1982; Schneider, 1985; Schoenfeld, 1987). Paris and Winograd (1990) would probably refer to this category of research as studies of self-management, that is, "metacognitions in action" that help to "orchestrate aspects of problem solving" including "the plans that learners make before tackling a task," "the adjustments they make as they work," and "the revisions they make afterwards" (p. 18). According to Kluwe (1982), these studies, along with studies from the second category, show what "is at the core of metacognition" (p. 211).

Many of the studies from this category have employed a sort-recall paradigm in which people are asked to recall as many as possible of the words or pictures that appear on provided lists (Schneider, 1985). The task requires that people (a) monitor their processing of the lists of words or pictures, (b) understand that recall can be facilitated by strategically sorting the words or pictures according to meaningful categories, and (c) regulate their recall by using the categories as memory prompts. In some of these studies, students have been instructed to use strategies to facilitate recall; in others, students have been observed for spontaneous use of strategies. Salience of the relationships among items to be recalled has been manipulated as has salience of the relationships between the kinds of items and students' base knowledge. In some studies, metacognitive monitoring and regulation has been inferred only if people can verbalize how their recall was facilitated by using a sorting strategy.

Corsale and Ornstein (1980) provide an example of this category of metacognitive research. Third- and seventh-grade students were assigned to one of three conditions, each condition receiving different instructions concerning a sorting task that used semantically unrelated pictures. Students in one condition were instructed to sort pictures into groups that "go together," but were not told that they would need to subsequently recall the pictures; students in a second condition were instructed to sort the pictures so that they would be able to recall them at a later time; and students in the third condition received a combination of the instructions given to the other two conditions. Results showed that for seventh-grade students there were no differences among the three conditions in the amount of recall. Apparently, even the seventh-graders who were not forewarned of the recall task were able to use organizational strategies to facilitate recall on a par with those students who had been forewarned. Surprisingly, third-grade students who were told to sort the pictures for later recall performed worse than third graders in the other two conditions. Even though these younger students later indicated that they knew a sorting strategy would help their recall, being forewarned of future recall did not help them develop such a strategy. Their production deficiency could be explained by a lack of knowledge concerning the kind of strategy to use with unrelated items or when a strategy should be used. But, for whatever reason, by the time students reach seventh grade, knowledge of strategy production and use appears to develop.

In general, studies that have used the sort-recall paradigm have shown that even 6- to 8-year-old children can monitor incoming information necessary to perform recall tasks and can understand that recall is facilitated by strategically sorting information into meaningful categories. However, young children appear to have difficulties spontaneously regulating recall, either because they lack knowledge of appropriate sorting strategies, or they know appropriate strategies but lack knowledge of when the strategies should be used, or they are uncertain about the importance of the strategies. Often, young children will rely on less effective, although familiar, rehearsal strategies even when more effective strategies have been demonstrated to them. But, by the age of 10 years, children begin to use sorting strategies spontaneously to facilitate recall. However, even at this age, ability to use sorting strategies may depend on whether the child has sufficient knowledge relevant to the items being recalled (Schneider, 1985).

Other studies from the third category of metacognitive research have examined how people regulate their selection of strategies based on information they monitor while employing the strategies. People are assumed to have monitored and regulated their use of strategies if, after using the strategies, they select the more or most efficacious one. This kind of study is illustrated by Pressley, Levin, and Ghatala (1984) in which students first were taught to use sentence-elaboration and repetition strategies to learn vocabulary words. After the two strategies were learned, students were asked to choose the more effective strategy to learn a list of new vocabulary words, but before choosing, they were assigned either to a no-practice or a practice condition. In the former, students were not allowed to practice the strategies prior to choosing one; in the latter, students were allowed to practice using a long vocabulary list. Students in both conditions were further assigned to one of three recommendation conditions: Before students made their choice of a strategy, the experimenter recommended either the sentence-elaboration or the repetition strategy, or gave no recommendation. Results showed that in the absence of practice, students were more likely to choose the strategy that was recommended by the experimenter. However, after practice and testing, students were more likely to choose the more effective strategy, the elaboration strategy, despite the experimenter's recommendation. Thus, by monitoring their practice and testing the two strategies, students gained an awareness of the relative effectiveness of the two and regulated subsequent strategy use by choosing the one that had been shown to be more efficacious, even if the experimenter had made a recommendation to the contrary.

Studies Examining Metacognition in Education

More recently, a fourth category of metacognitive research has appeared. The strong focus on theoretical aspects of metacognition, which has dominated much of the metacognitive research since the 1960s, has recently produced an equally strong focus on educational application. Many researchers, convinced of the educational relevance that metacognitive theory has for teachers and students, are shifting their attention from the theoretical to the practical, from the laboratory to the classroom. For example, Borkowski and Muthukrishna (1992) argued that metacognitive theory has "considerable potential for aiding teachers as they strive to construct classroom environments that focus on strategic learning that is both flexible and creative" (p. 479); and Paris and Winograd (1990) argued that "students can enhance their learning by becoming aware of their own thinking as they read, write, and solve problems in school. Teachers can promote this awareness directly by informing students about effective problem-solving strategies and discussing cognitive and motivational characteristics of thinking" (p. 15).

Therefore, this fourth category of metacognitive research includes studies that have examined ways in which metacognitive theory can be applied to education. Broadly defined, these studies have focused on a fundamental question, Can instruction of metacognitive processes facilitate learning? The researchers who have contributed to the present volume, along with many other researchers and educational practitioners, have responded to this question with a resounding "yes." This volume contains many examples of the ways in which researchers have answered this question in specific educationally relevant domains: Davidson and Sternberg have provided answers in the domain of general problem solving; Dominowski in the domain of verbalization of cognitive processes; Vye, Schwartz, Bransford, Barron, Zech, and The Cognition and Technology Group at Vanderbilt in the domain of science; Carr and Biddlecomb in the domain of mathematics; Sitko in the domain of writing; both Otero and Hacker in the domain of reading; García, Jiménez, and Pearson in the domain of bilingual education; Maki in the domain of test prediction; Winne and Hadwin in the domain of studying; Pressley, Van Etten, Yokio, Freebern, and Van Meter in the domain of academic coping; McGlynn in the domain of rehabilitation; and Dunlosky and Hertzog in the domain of aging and problem solving.

These researchers would likely agree that to enhance learning to the fullest, learners need to become aware of themselves as self-regulatory organisms who can consciously and deliberately achieve specific goals (Kluwe, 1982). In general, metacognitive theory focuses on (a) the role of awareness and executive management of one's thinking, (b) individual differences in self-appraisal and management of cognitive development and learning, (c) knowledge and executive abilities that develop through experience, and (d) constructive and strategic thinking (Paris & Winograd, 1990). Thus, the promise of metacognitive theory is that it focuses precisely on those characteristics of thinking that can contribute to students' awareness and understanding of being self-regulatory organisms, that is, of being agents of their own thinking.

REFERENCES

Atkinson, R. C., & Shiffrin, R. M. (1968). Human memory: A proposed system and its control processes. In K. W. Spence & J. T. Spence (Eds.), *Psychology of learning and motivation* (Vol. 2, pp. 89–195). New York: Academic.

Belmont, J. M., & Butterfield, E. C. (1969). The relations of short-term memory to development and intelligence. In L. C. Lipsitt & H. W. Reese (Eds.), *Advances in child development and behavior* (Vol. 4, pp. 29–82). New York: Academic.

Bisanz, G. L., Vesonder, G. T., & Voss, J. T. (1978). Knowledge of one's own responding and the relation of such knowledge to learning: A developmental study. *Experimental Child Psychology*, 25, Journal of E 116–128.

Borkowski, J. G., Carr, M., Rellinger, E., & Pressley, M. (1990). Selfregulated cognition: Interdependence of metacognition, attributions, and self-esteem. In B. F. Jones & L. Idol (Eds.), *Dimensions of thinking and cognitive instruction* (pp. 53–92). Hillsdale, NJ: Lawrence Erlbaum Associates.

Borkowski, J. G., & Muthukrishna, N. (1992). Moving metacognition into the classroom: "Working models" and effective strategy teaching. In M. Pressley, K. R. Harris, & J. T. Guthrie (Eds.), *Promoting academic competence and literacy in school* (pp. 477–501). San Diego, CA: Academic.

Bracewell, R. J. (1983). Investigating the control of writing skills. In P. Mosenthal, L. Tamor, & S. Walmsley (Eds.), *Research on writing* (pp. 177–203). New York: Longman.

Brown, A. L. (1978). Knowing when, where, and how to remember: A problem of metacognition. In R. Glaser (Ed.), *Advances in instructional psychology* (Vol. 1, pp. 77–165). Hillsdale, NJ: Lawrence Erlbaum Associates.

Brown, A. L., & Campione, J. C. (1977). Training strategic study time apportionment in educable retarded children. *Intelligence*, 1, 94–107.

Butler, D. L., & Winne, P. H. (1995). Feedback and self-regulated learning: A theoretical synthesis. *Review of Educational Research*, 65, 245–281.

Butterfield, E. C., & Belmont, J. M. (1977). Assessing and improving the executive cognitive functions of mentally retarded people. In J. Bailer & M. Sternlicht (Eds.), *Psychological issues in mental retardation* (pp. 277–318). Chicago: Aldine.

Butterfield, E. C., & Ferretti, R. P. (1987). Toward a theoretical integration of cognitive hypotheses about intellectual differences among children. In J. G. Borkowski & J. O. Day (Eds.), *Cognition in special children* (pp. 195–233). Norwood, NJ: Ablex.

Butterfield, E. C., Nelson, T. O., & Peck, V. (1988). Developmental aspects of the feeling of knowing. *Developmental Psychology*, 24, 654–663.

Carr, M., Alexander, J., & Folds-Bennett, T. (1994). Metacognition and mathematics strategy use. *Applied Cognitive Psychology*, 8, 583–595.

Cavanaugh, J. C., & Borkowski, J. G. (1979). The metamemory–memory "connection": Effects of strategy training and maintenance. *The Journal of General Psychology*, 101, 161–174.

Cavanaugh, J. C., & Perlmutter, M. (1982). Metamemory: A critical examination. *Child Development*, 53, 11–28.

Corsale, K., & Ornstein, P. A. (1980). Developmental changes in children's use of semantic information in recall. *Journal of Experimental Child Psychology*, 30, 231–245.

Corsini, D. A. (1971). Memory: Interaction of stimulus and organismic factors. *Human Development*, 14, 227–235.

Davidson, J. E., Deuser, R., & Sternberg, R. J. (1994). The role of metacognition in problem solving. In J. Metcalfe & A. P. Shimamura (Eds.), Metacognition: Knowing about knowing (pp. 207–226). Cambridge, MA: MIT Press.

Ericsson, K. A., & Simon, H. A. (1980). Verbal reports as data. Psychological Review, 87, 215–251.

Flavell, J. H. (1963). The developmental psychology of Jean Piaget. New York: D. Van Nostrand.

Flavell, J. H. (1971). First discussant's comments: What is memory development the development of? Human Development, 14, 272–278.

Flavell, J. H. (1976). Metacognitive aspects of problem solving. In L. B. Resnick (Ed.), The nature of intelligence. Hillsdale, NJ: Lawrence Erlbaum Associates.

Flavell, J. H. (1977). Cognitive development. Englewood Cliffs, NJ: Prentice-Hall.

Flavell, J. H. (1979). Metacognition and cognitive monitoring: A new area of cognitive-developmental inquiry. American Psychologist, 34, 906–911.

Flavell, J. H. (1981). Cognitive monitoring. In W. P. Dickson (Ed.), Children's oral communication skills (pp. 35–60). New York: Academic.

Flavell, J. H., Freidrichs, A. G., & Hoyt, J. D. (1970). Developmental changes in memorization processes. Cognitive Psychology, 1, 324–340.

Flavell, J. H., & Wellman, H. M. (1977). Metamemory. In R. V. Kail, Jr. & J. W. Hagen (Eds.), Perspectives on the development of memory and cognition. Hillsdale, NJ: Lawrence Erlbaum Associates.

Glasersfeld, E. V. (1984). An introduction to radical constructivism. In P. Watzlawick (Ed.), The invented reality: How do we know what we believe we know? Contributions to constructivism (pp. 17–40). New York: Norton.

Hagen, J. W., & Kingsley, P. R. (1968). Labeling effects in short-term memory. Child Development, 39, 113–121.

Hart, J. T. (1965). Memory and the feeling-of-knowing experience. Journal of Educational Psychology, 56, 208–216.

Inhelder, B., & Piaget, J. (1958). The growth of logical thinking from childhood to adolescence. New York: Basic Books.

James, W. (1890). Principles of Psychology. New York: Holt.

Kluwe, R. H. (1982). Cognitive knowledge and executive control: Metacognition. In D. R. Griffin (Ed.), Animal mind—human mind (pp. 201–224). New York: Springer-Verlag.

Lodico, M. G., Ghatala, E. S., Levin, J. R., Pressley, M., & Bell, J. A. (1983). The effects of strategy monitoring training on children's selection of effective memory strategies. Journal of Expeimental Child Psychology, 35, 273–277.

Markman, E. M. (1977). Realizing that you don't understand: A preliminary investigation. Child Development, 48, 986–992.

Miller, G. A. (1953). What is information measurement? American Psychologist, 8, 3–11.

Moynahan, E. (1978). Assessment and selection of paired-associate strategies: A developmental study. Journal of Experimental Child Psychology, 26, 257–266.

Nelson, T. O, & Dunlosky, J. (1991). The delayed-JOL effect: When delaying your judgments of learning can improve the accuracy of your metacognitive monitoring. Psychological Science, 2, 267–270.

Nelson, T. O., & Narens, L. (1990). Metamemory: A theoretical framework and new findings. In G. Bower (Ed.), The psychology of learning and motivation (Vol. 26, pp. 125–173). New York: Academic.

Newell, A., Shaw, J. G., & Simon, H. A. (1958). Elements of a theory of human problem solving. Psychological Review, 65, 151–166.

Nicholls, J. G., & Miller, A. T. (1984). Development and its discontents: The differentiation of the concept of ability. In M. L. Maehr (Ed.), Advances in motivation and achievement, (Vol. 3, pp. 185–218). Greenwich, CT: JAI.

Nisbett, R., & Wilson, T. (1977). Telling more than we can know: Verbal reports on mental processes. *Psychological Review, 84*, 231–259.

Paris, S. G., & Winograd, P. (1990). How metacognition can promote academic learning and instruction. In B. F. Jones & L. Idol (Eds.), *Dimensions of thinking and cognitive instruction* (pp. 15–51). Hillsdale, NJ: Lawrence Erlbaum Associates.

Pressley, M., Levin, J. R., & Ghatala, E. S. (1984). Memor. Strategy monitoring in adults and children. *Journal of verbal learning and jerbal behavior, 23*, 270–288.

Ryle, G. (1949). *The concept of mind.* London: Hitchinson.

Schneider, W. (1985). Developmental trends in the metamemory–memory behavior relationship: An integrative review. In D. L. Forrest-Pressley, G. E. MacKinnon, & T. G. Waller (Eds.), *Metacognition, cognition, and human performance* (Vol. 1, pp. 57–109). New York: Academic.

Schoenfeld, A. H. (1987). What's all the fuss about metacognition? In A. H. Schoenfeld (Ed.), *Cognitive science and mathematics education* (pp. 189–215). Hillsdale, NJ: Lawrence Erlbaum Associates.

Wellman, H. M. (1977). Tip of the tongue and feeling of knowing experiences: A developmental study of memory monitoring. *Child Development, 48*, 13–21.

2

Verbalization and Problem Solving

Roger L. Dominowski
University of Illinois at Chicago

The old lady, quoted by E. M. Forster—
"How can I know what I think until I see what I say?"
                    —W. H. Auden, The Dyer's Hand, 1962

Problem solving is a difficult enterprise. Any task worth calling a problem must have an element of uncertainty as to whether the desired solution will be reached. Thus, problem solving can be characterized as goal-oriented activity where the path or means to the goal is at least somewhat uncertain. The extremes of problem solving are these: A task might be given to a problem solver who quite simply lacks some knowledge that is essential to achieving the goal. For example, if a theoretical physics problem is posed to a person who knows no physics, failure is assured. Many problems might be failed because of lack of necessary knowledge, but the failure itself is uninteresting. At the opposite extreme, a problem solver might be given a task that is extremely familiar so that the solver simply knows what to do, with no uncertainty. For example, an elementary math problem is really no problem for a mathematician who will immediately know how to find the answer. The interesting cases of problem solving lie between these extremes, where the problem solver has the knowledge necessary to arrive at a solution (in some form or another, and perhaps weakly) but will still face difficulties in reaching a solution. Many such situations occur in everyday life, in education, and in research on problem solving, where puzzle-type problems are frequently used precisely because no special training is required to possess the knowledge needed to find a solution.

Because problems often result in failures to solve or less than optimal solutions, one focus of research on problem solving is to identify ways in which performance might be improved. Notice that in such research the investigator's interests are quite compatible with those of teachers. Among the techniques that have received attention are various ways of having problem solvers verbalize while working on problems. The general term *verbalize* is used deliberately because different forms of talking have been studied, and the results depend on the kind of verbalizing that occurs.

Why should verbalizing attract attention with respect to problem solving? There are, in fact, multiple reasons for such an interest. The relation between language and thought has a long, complex, and argumentative intellectual history. Between the extremes of "language = thought" and "language and thought are independent" lies a vast range of possible relations. A question of considerable interest has been the extent to which linguistic behavior (speech) might influence performance on tasks that vary in their formal reliance on language.

People sometimes talk aloud while working on problems. These verbalizations range from relatively incoherent mutterings to articulate, problem-relevant statements. The role of mumbling might be difficult to decipher, but several effects might result from task-relevant speech. In discussing children's thought and speech, Vygotsky (1962) argued that very young children's thought and speech are largely disconnected. However, children's subsequent "egocentric" speech serves a self-regulating function; that is, children talk to themselves to guide their actions. Somewhat later, such self-directed speech becomes inner speech (quiet) or unnecessary as they gain task competence. Keeping in mind that older children and adults do not regularly talk aloud to themselves, it is nonetheless possible that, when faced with a problem, overt speech might occur for self-regulating functions. People might think aloud in an attempt to clarify their understanding of the situation and to guide their actions, at least initially.

The general purpose of language and speech is to communicate with others. One might wonder how much we are actively listening when we "talk to ourselves," as opposed to merely vocalizing. When verbalization is studied, there is typically another person in the room—the researcher. Even if one is instructed to simply "think aloud, to just say whatever comes to mind," an instruction that does not directly request communicating to the observer, it is possible that our verbalizations could be modified, perhaps more organized versions of our pre-vocalizing thoughts because of the presence of an observer. Any such slight change in thoughts, if it occurs, would seem likely to affect task performance only slightly, if at all. Requests for more complex communications, such as "describe the strategy you're using" would be expected to exert greater influence. In seeking to understand the relations between verbalization and problem solving, it is apparent that we must pay attention to the kind of verbalizing that is done. It is also important to consider the task being attempted: As task demands change, the relation between verbalizing and task performance might also change.

KINDS OF VERBALIZATION

One might verbalize in many ways while trying to solve problems. Ericsson and Simon (e.g., 1980, 1993) have provided a system for distinguishing types of verbal reports. The core of their system is that verbal reports are based on the current contents of working memory. As people work on a task, they attend to various items of information: These are the contents of working memory at any time. A fundamental question is whether verbalizing makes use of what would ordinarily be heeded or results in some change in working memory content. If verbalizing changes working memory content, the implications are that the verbal report might be in some way an inaccurate representation of task-relevant thinking and that producing the verbalization might alter task processing.

Ericsson and Simon (1980, 1993) distinguish retrospective from concurrent reports. Retrospective reports are made after a task or part of a task has been done; because they are after-the-fact descriptions of prior thinking, they virtually always involve a change in working memory content. If the task episode is very short and verbalizing occurs immediately afterward, the report might be quite accurate. But under typical problem-solving conditions, retrospective reports occur at least a minute (usually more) afterward. Trying to say what one was thinking, what one was attending to a short while ago, or how one went about solving a problem will require some retrieval from long-term memory and construction of a response. A person might not remember, or might misremember what happened earlier. Some might "invent" memories, even without knowing they are doing so, to meet a request to verbalize. Retrospective reports are likely to be noticeably incomplete descriptions of prior thinking and are subject to bias. With respect to accuracy, retrospective reports of details should be difficult to produce; reporting a strategy, which is a more global aspect of thinking rather than a feature of thought at a particular instant, might be more accurate. Of course, there is the possibility that people will describe strategies that just occurred to them when they were asked. Retrospective reports cannot change the thinking that preceded them, but they might well change the thinking that follows them. If, say, a person is working on a series of problems and is asked for some retrospective report after each of them, task performance might be expected to change as the series proceeds. Some examples of such effects are given later.

Concurrent reports are made while people are doing the task at hand. Ericsson and Simon (1980, 1993) distinguish three levels of reports. Level 1 verbalization is simply the vocalization of verbal working-memory content that is ordinarily heeded in doing the task. The idea is that the person's task-relevant thoughts are verbal in form and thus just need to be externalized (i.e., said aloud). Verbalizing should be easy to do and should not change task performance, although, to the extent that people can think faster than they can talk, Level 1 verbalizing could slow them down a bit. The possible effect would be slight.

For Level 2 reports, the person is again verbalizing content ordinarily heeded in doing the problem task, but here the content itself is not in verbalizable form and thus must be recoded. For example, visual, spatial, or perceptual-motor information would require recoding into appropriate language. So long as such verbalizing does not change what is heeded, the only effect of Level 2 reports is expected to be an increase in the time to complete a task because of the time needed for recoding. Ericsson and Simon note that Level 2 reports might be difficult to achieve, because perceptual processing might be relatively automatic or appropriate verbal codes might not be available. For example, in an experiment by Dominowski (1974), subjects were asked to think aloud while going through multiple trials of a concept-learning task. They had to learn how to categorize items, each of which consisted of one or more geometric figures varying in size, color, shape, and so on. What was often missing in subjects' verbalizations were descriptions of the figures they were looking at; clearly they were taking in this information (there was no other way to do the task) but it didn't appear in their reports. Ericsson and Simon (1993) reported that people have difficulty reporting their thoughts when working on manipulative puzzles. The implication is that Level 2 reports might be quite incomplete. Of perhaps greater concern is the possibility that trying to verbalize nonverbal information will change the person's task-relevant behavior. Subjects' attention could be biased toward features of the situation that are more easily described verbally, or they could adopt a more verbal rather than perceptual approach to the problem. Whether such changes will help or hurt task performance will depend on the specific characteristics of the task.

Level 3 verbalizing involves changes in working memory content, making inferences, interpretation, a shift in attention, or some other additional processing. Level 3 verbalizing is expected to alter task performance. As noted previously, attempts to produce "simple" think-aloud reports can result in Level 3 verbalizing. Ericsson and Simon comment that a change in level can occur in quite subtle ways. For example, when subjects are asked to verbalize while attempting a task, it is common practice for experimenters to give verbalizing reminders when subjects are silent for 10 to 15 seconds. Ericsson and Simon (1980, 1993) point out that asking the person to "keep talking" is different from asking "what are you thinking?" The latter directs subjects' attention toward their own thoughts and thus shifts the report to Level 3. Verbalizing that involves people's explanations of their thoughts is the best example of Level 3 reports and will receive the greatest attention in the research review presented here. Such verbalizing is metacognitive.

INDIVIDUAL DIFFERENCES

One reason for having people think aloud while working on problems is to allow an observer to gain information about how the problems are being approached. Thus, an experimenter might have a research participant think aloud, or a teacher could ask a student to think aloud to better understand the person's problem-solving processes. Ericsson and Simon's (e.g., 1993) treatment of verbal reports focuses on the accuracy of such reports, as mentioned earlier. In problem situations, concurrent reports are likely to be more accurate than retrospective reports with respect to the details of problem-solving processes. It should never be assumed that verbal reports are complete; rather, it is better to assume that verbalization is incomplete. When people simply think aloud while working on problems, some of what they say will be difficult for an observer to comprehend. Asking specific questions might seem preferable to the observer. For theoretical reasons, an experimenter might be reluctant to ask direct questions for fear of affecting the person's approach to the problem. Teachers need not be so reluctant; if their direct questioning changes the student's approach for the better, that would be fine (the teacher needs to assume that probing won't hurt). From the perspective of trying to diagnose an individual student's problem-solving approach, having the student think aloud and asking more direct questions when they seem needed (by the teacher) is a good idea. As will be seen, asking particular kinds of questions is an even better idea (most of the time).

People differ in their verbalizations, and one can ask whether individual differences are reliable and informative. With respect to quantity of verbalization, stable individual differences have been found. That is, people who produce longer and more complete verbal protocols on one problem also tend to do so on other problems (Gilhooly & Gregory, 1989).

Other researchers have focused on the content of what is said under think-aloud instructions and related individual differences in content to differences in problem-solving effectiveness. Kaplan and Simon (1990) examined subjects' think-aloud verbalizations produced while working on a difficult puzzle, the Mutilated Checkerboard Problem, (see Fig. 2.1). As you can see, two diagonally opposite squares have been removed from an 8 x 8 checkerboard. Imagine having 32 dominoes, each of which covers two adjacent squares either vertically or horizontally, but not diagonally. If the board were intact, the 32 dominoes would cover the 64 squares. The problem is to show, with the two squares removed, either how 31 dominoes could cover the remaining 62 squares or to prove that it is impossible to do so. You might want to try the problem before reading the solution.

When given this problem, people typically begin by trying to arrange the 31 dominoes so that they cover the 62 squares. When a first attempt fails, they try a variation, and so on. All such covering attempts will fail because the task is, in fact, impossible. At some point the problem solver might begin trying to prove that coverage is impossible. A key to finding the solution is attending to the fact that there are two kinds of squares, here black and white. Each domino covers one black and one white square. The diagonally opposite squares that are removed are the same color; their removal leaves

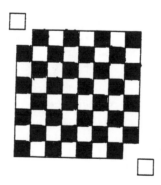

FIG. 2.1. The mutilated checkerboard problem.

32 squares of one kind and 30 of the other. Thus, after 30 dominoes have been used to cover 60 squares, one will always be left with one domino to cover two squares of the same color, which cannot be done.

Because there is a very large number of ways to try covering the squares, a person could go on endlessly trying variations of this approach. Attending to the two kinds of squares, noticing that it is always two squares of the same color that are left uncovered, noticing that each domino covers one square of each color, will lead to abandoning attempts to cover and also serve the construction of the impossibility proof. Kaplan and Simon (1990) found in subjects' verbal protocols that faster solving subjects noticed more things about the problem and more rapidly noticed perceptual invariants (that a domino always covers one square of each color, that two squares of the same color always seem to be left, and so on). In this way, the verbalizations of faster and slower solvers were different and provided clues regarding why solution speeds differed.

In a very different situation, Chi and Bassok (1989) had students think aloud while reading worked-out examples of physics problems. The students later were given a test containing a number of problems to solve. Chi and Bassok found that students who were more successful on the test had generated a greater number of "self-explanations" while reading the worked-out examples, compared to students with poor test performance. Self-explanations were statements that went beyond what the students were reading at a particular time—drawing inferences, relating the current material to the goal of the problem, and the like. In contrast, merely re-reading the text was more characteristic of poor students. In addition, good and poor students differed in the ways they monitored their under-standing of the examples. Good students referred to their *lack* of under-standing much more often than did the poor students, and their statements of this type were more specific (e.g., "Why is this value negative?"), whereas poor students' statements were more general (e.g., "What should you do here?"). Again we see that think-aloud verbalizations can provide useful information about why people differ in their problem-solving efficiency.

In these studies, everyone verbalized and the researchers examined the content of verbal reports to understand why differences occur in problem-solving success. In the remainder of this chapter, our focus is on the effects of verbalizing versus not verbalizing, and the effects of different kinds of verbalization on problem-solving performance. These studies can be used to devise techniques that might improve problem solving.

EFFECTS OF THINKING ALOUD

In Ericsson and Simon's (1980, 1993) model, thinking aloud (Level 1 or 2) should not affect task performance except that, under certain circumstances, performance might be slowed. In general, research on the effect of thinking aloud on problem solving has supported this expectation. Keep in mind that thinking aloud here refers to verbalizing in response to a general request to say what one is thinking. Also, for a proper comparison of thinking aloud with "silent" performance, other aspects of the procedure should be identical. For example, some researchers, using problems that call for a series of "moves" of some sort, have required their think-aloud subjects to tell the experimenter what move to make, whereas silent subjects make the desired move directly. The procedural change might affect performance quite separately from any thinking-aloud effect. Ericsson and Simon (1993) provide extensive discussion of the nuances of studies of verbalization that do not quite meet simple think-aloud criteria. Here we concentrate on a sample of studies that seem to meet basic think-aloud criteria.

Kellogg and Holley (1983) used a concept-identification task requiring subjects to discover how to categorize items presented over a series of trials with feedback. They found that subjects required to think aloud did not differ from those who remained silent on any performance measures. Norris (1990) found that having people think aloud while taking a critical-thinking test resulted in scores that were comparable to those for people taking the test silently. Flaherty (1974) found no difference in performance on algebra word problems between thinking-aloud and silent subjects.

The problems used in the aforementioned research are relatively analytic; that is, they tend to be approached in a careful, deliberate manner. In more theoretical terms, they tend to require executive processing. Schooler, Ohlsson, and Brooks (1993) also found no effect of thinking aloud for their analytic problems, but they reported a negative effect of thinking aloud for their insight problems. These problems typically require a change in one's representation of the problem (e.g., Dominowski & Dallob, 1995). That is, insight problems tend to elicit interpretations that cannot lead to a solution, and the problem solver must change interpretations to succeed. Schooler et. al. argued that changes in representation occur automatically rather than via executive control, and that for this reason thinking aloud was harmful. This is apparently the only instance in which simple thinking aloud appeared harmful. The idea should be considered with caution because Weisberg and Suls (1973) found no effect of thinking aloud for an insight problem not used by Schooler et al.

Relatively few studies meet the criteria for simple thinking aloud; more commonly, the request for verbalizing asks for additional processing. It would seem that, by and large, simple thinking aloud does not have much effect on problem solving. Therefore, having problem solvers think aloud will provide information about what they are doing but probably will not change their success at reaching solutions.

EFFECTS OF GIVING REASONS

Researchers sometimes have labeled their procedures as "thinking aloud" but in fact have asked people to give reasons, explain what they are doing, and so on. These kinds of verbalization are not just "thinking aloud" but call for Level 3 responses in Ericsson and Simon's (1993) scheme. We now consider what happens to task performance when people are asked to explain what they are doing or why they are doing it. Several different techniques have been employed, depending in part on the problem-solving task. People might be asked to tell what hypothesis they are trying out, what reason they have for a particular solution attempt, what strategy they are following in trying to find a solution, and the like. An important implication of labeling such techniques as "Level 3" verbalization is that problem solvers do not of their own accord focus on these aspects of problem solving. Suppose that a person is working on a problem and is asked simply to think aloud. Among the various things the person might say are statements such as "I think what's wrong is . . ." "Ok, I'll try this move to see if . . . ," or "What I want to do is simplify the expression. . . . ," These statements reflect attention to what one is doing, and such statements are made under think-aloud instructions. But, as we shall see, directly requesting such statements greatly increases their occurrence. Asking for reasons and the like is therefore likely to make the problem solver adopt a more deliberate approach. The question is how this affects problem-solving performance. Research findings will be grouped by the type of task employed, as the results change somewhat from one type to another. In a number of these studies, the effects of reason giving have been assessed both while people are verbalizing (or not) and when they are later given other problems to solve with no verbalization required. Also, it should be noted that people are not always talking in these studies; reasons or explanations might be given by writing them down or completing forms spcially designed for a particular task.

Concept Identification

These tasks require the person to determine what classification scheme is in use by observing a series of instances and being told to which category each instance belongs. The instances are often geometric forms varying in features such as shape, color, and size. The concept might be simple, based on a single feature, such as "All red things belong to the target concept, other-colored things do not." More complex concepts based on various combinations of features have also been studied, such as conjunctive concepts ("All things that are both square and small belong") and disjunctive concepts ("Things that are either circles or blue belong"). The usual measure of performance is the number of instances (trials) people require before discovering the target concept, as evidenced by their ability to classify instances correctly. Several studies have concerned the effects of requiring hypotheses. Thus, in the control condition, each trial consists of showing the person an instance, having the person try to predict its category, and then providing feedback about the correct category for that instance. Alternatively, people are required also to state their current hypotheses about the target concept.

An understandable pattern of results emerged. Byers and Davidson (1967) and Bower and King (1967) found that requiring hypotheses reduced the number of trials needed to identify the target concept. Karpf and Levine (1971) found no effect of requiring hypotheses, but they used simpler concepts. The relevance of concept complexity was shown in a study by Dominowski (1973), where requiring hypotheses had no effect with a simple concept but reduced trials to solution for more complex, conjunctive, and disjunctive concepts. With more complex concepts, subjects' learning methods are often disorganized and error prone. Requiring hypotheses encourages more careful attention to instance features and category assignments as well as more deliberate formation of hypotheses, thus improving their efficiency.

Reasoning

There are many kinds of reasoning tasks, and although all require inferences to be made in some form, their processing demands are by no means the same. Reason-giving and explanations have been studied with several different reasoning tasks, with uneven results. Evans, Barston, and Pollard (1983) gave subjects syllogisms in which the task was to decide whether a conclusion did or did not logically follow from a set of premises. They found that requiring subjects to explain why they thought a conclusion was or was not valid had no reliable effect on reasoning accuracy. Norris (1990) found that requiring people to explain why they chose their answers to a critical thinking test did not change test performance.

Berry (1983) and Dominowski (1990) used Wason's selection task, which has these general characteristics. Four (carefully selected) cards are presented, each of which has two kinds of information (e.g., letters on one side, colors on the other), with only one side of each card visible. So for example, the subject might see cards showing A, K, blue, and green, respectively. The task is to indicate which of the cards need to be turned over to determine if a rule (e.g., "If a card is blue, then it has a vowel on the other side") is or is not correct. Many kinds of content can be used in this task, and difficulty varies greatly; with abstract content (as in the example) the task is quite difficult, whereas familiar, meaningful content can make the task relatively easy.

Dominowski (1990) found that performance was improved by requiring subjects to give reasons for their decisions to turn over or not turn over each card. The improvement was greater for more concrete versions of the task. Berry (1983) found that providing an explanation of the solution to concrete versions of the task did not by itself improve performance on a more abstract version. But if subjects were required to give reasons for their decisions after receiving the explanation, they were more successful. These findings are not directly comparable, but both suggest that reason-giving has positive effects for this particular reasoning task. However, because of the heterogeneity of the tasks and results across these studies on formal reasoning, no clear statement can be made about the effects of reason giving. This is an area in which more systematic research is needed.

Multistep Problems

The effects of verbalizing with problems involving a sequence of steps or moves have been examined in a number of studies. A popular task has been a disc-transfer puzzle, (see Fig. 2.2). To start, the discs are stacked at A in order of size, the smallest on top. The goal is to get the discs stacked in the same way at C by moving discs one at a time between A, B, and C while observing the following rule: No disc may ever be covered by a larger disc. The difficulty of this problem varies greatly with the number of discs. With just two discs the solution is trivial: Move the smaller to B, the larger to C, and then the smaller to C. With, say, six discs the problem is much harder (if you are not familiar with this task, try it).

FIG. 2.2. The disc-transfer problem.

Several researchers have employed the same basic methodology: Subjects solve a series of disc-transfer problems, with the number of discs increasing across the series. The first task has two discs, the second three discs, and so on through five discs. During this practice phase, some subjects are required to give reasons for their moves, others are not. Finally, all subjects are then given the more difficult 6-disc problem with no one required to verbalize. Consistent results have been obtained. Subjects who are required to give reasons for their moves on the practice problems perform better on those problems; that is, they require fewer moves to reach the solution (Ahlum-Heath & Di Vesta, 1986; Berardi-Coletta, Buyer, Dominowski, & Rellinger, 1995; Gagne & Smith, 1962; Wilder & Harvey, 1971). Giving reasons produced more efficient solutions than doing the problems silently. In addition, transfer performance on the harder, six-disc problem, where no verbalization is required, was better for those who had given reasons during the practice phase. Therefore, giving reasons improves current problem solving and also results in better problem solving later when a difficult task is done silently. Stinessen (1985) employed a slightly different procedure but obtained comparable results. Ahlum-Heath and DiVesta (1986) also found that, for subjects who received no practice problems and attempted the six-disc problem as their first problem, giving reasons on the six-disc problem led to more efficient solutions. Indeed, people with no practice who gave reasons with six discs did better on that problem than those who had received the full training series but had never given reasons.

Berardi-Coletta et al. (1995) also studied the effects of reason-giving with a different complex task—Katona's card problem. The task is to arrange a small deck of cards so that, when the deck is dealt by alternating between placing a card face up on the table and placing a card at the bottom of the deck, a particular pattern of cards is produced on the table. For example, how should one arrange the cards "4, 5, 6, 7" so that they appear on the table in precisely that order? The answer is to arrange the cards, starting with the top card, in the order 4, 6, 5, 7. Berardi-Coletta et al. used a method comparable to that used with disc-transfer problems. Subjects attempted a practice series of card-arranging problems, with the number of cards increasing. During this phase, some subjects were required to give a reason for each arrangement they tried, while others were not. Subsequently, all subjects solved a harder problem with no one required to verbalize. The results were comparable to those with the disc-transfer problem: Giving reasons improved performance both during the practice phase and on the subsequent transfer problem. Additional aspects of these studies are discussed shortly.

Learning Complex Relations

Berry and Broadbent (1984) gave subjects the task of learning to control the output of a system for which the input–output relations were complex. In one version, subjects were asked to try to achieve and maintain a stated level of (hypothetical) sugar production by manipulating the size of the work force. An initial level of production and the desired level were given at the start of a problem; on each trial, the subject selected a work force size and was told the resulting production level. The output level was related to both the size of work force and the previous output, plus a random factor. Multiple trials were given, and performance was measured in terms of the number of trials for which the subject achieved production levels close to the desired level.

With this task Berry and Broadbent (1984) found some dissociation between task performance and subjects' verbal knowledge about the task. That is, subjects would improve their scores over trials, showing that they had learned something about the input–output relation, but they would not be able to answer questions about the task very well. This finding suggests that the task can be done on an implicit basis, using knowledge that is not in readily verbalizable form. Providing verbal instruction about how to do the task helped subjects answer questions but did not improve their task performance. Having subjects give reasons for their choices did not, by itself, increase task success. However, the combination of verbal instruction followed by giving reasons did result in better task performance. Also, McGeorge and Burton (1989), who used a more difficult version of the sugar production task, found that having subjects give reasons for choices after they had some experience with the task improved task performance.

Berry and Broadbent (1987) obtained a similar result with a task requiring subjects to select pollutants for testing in order to determine which factory was polluting a river. A total of 16 factories and 24 pollutants was involved. They found that providing an explanation of a good selection strategy at the start of a problem did not improve task performance, nor did having subjects give reasons for pollutant selections. The combination of explanation plus subsequent reason giving did improve task performance.

For these complex tasks the role of verbalization is also complex. It appears that subjects must have some minimum level of verbalizable task knowledge to benefit from giving reasons. Berry and Broadbent (1984, 1987) point out that, when no explanation was provided, subjects giving reasons talked at a very general level, in distinct contrast to the more specific, predictive statements made by reason-giving subjects who had received an explanation. Conversely, initial verbal instruction by itself was ineffective regarding task performance but became effective when it was followed by reason-giving. Berry and Broadbent proposed that verbalizing made relevant information, namely the initial explanation, available at a time when it could be connected to actions. Once a satisfactory level of performance has been attained, subjects can maintain that level without further explanations or overtly giving reasons (Berry & Broadbent, 1987).

The Importance of Metacognition

We have seen that requiring subjects to give reasons for their choices and actions often results in improved task performance. Why, one might ask, is giving reasons effective? Berardi-Coletta et al. (1995) proposed that giving reasons promotes metacognitive processing, which is focusing attention on one's task-related processes. Metacognitive processing includes monitoring solution attempts or strategies and evaluating progress. To explore this metacognitive hypothesis, Berardi-Coletta et al. employed several kinds of verbalization. As noted earlier, these researchers found reason giving to lead to better current performance and transfer than a silent control condition. The other verbalizing conditions were thinking aloud and answering either problem-focused or metacognitive questions. Problem-focused questions directed subjects' attention to problem characteristics (e.g., What is the goal of this problem? What are the rules for this problem?). Metacognitive questions focused subjects' attention on their own processes (e.g., How are you deciding which disc to move? How do you know that this is a good move?).

For the disc-transfer problem, the think-aloud and silent control conditions had nearly identical performance levels, as expected on the basis of Ericsson and Simon's (1993) model of verbalization. The reason-giving and metacognitive conditions did not differ from each other but yielded the most efficient solutions on training and transfer problems. Performance in the problem-focused conditions fell between the two groupings. For Katona's card-arrangement problem, the metacognitive condition was superior to silent, control, think-aloud and problem-focused conditions (reason-giving was not included). Overall, examination of verbal protocols confirmed that process-focused statements were made at a far greater rate with metacognitive questioning or reason-giving, compared to the other verbalization conditions. In a similar vein, Dorner (1978) reported several studies showing that requiring subjects to reflect on their own thinking after completing a problem resulted in greater improvement over a series of complex problems.

Why Does Metacognition Work?

Research shows that having subjects attend to their problem-solving efforts has positive results: The efficiency of current and transfer performance is improved. What changes when metacognitive processing is promoted? Metacognitive processing has resulted in more flexible approaches to problem solving and the use of more complex and effective strategies. Berardi-Coletta et al. (1995) examined the verbalizations and paper-and-pencil records of both think-aloud (control) subjects and metacognition-cued subjects working on multiple versions of Katona's card problem. Recall that this task requires ordering a deck of cards so that a specified sequence is produced when the cards are dealt following a rule to alternate between placing cards on the table or at the bottom of the deck. The researchers identified five strategies that might be used on these card problems. The simplest was guessing, or just randomly ordering the cards; this approach yielded solutions only for the simplest problems (small numbers of cards). Swapping referred to exchanging the places in the deck of cards that were out of order when dealt. For example, if the goal was to produce 1, 2, 3, 4 and one ordered the deck 1, 4, 2, 3, the result of dealing would be 1, 2, 4, 3; swapping would mean exchanging the positions of the 4 and 3, and trying the order 1, *3*, 2, *4* (swapped position shown in italics). Swapping would work with small- to medium-size problems but led to failure with the more complex problems. The more sophisticated strategies were representing the difference between "up" versus "bottom" cards, using blanks to represent unknown cards between known cards, and checking an order on paper before offering the card deck for dealing.

The differences between groups were striking. Control subjects used either guessing or swapping for all versions of the problem. Although a majority used blanks for unknown cards, only some represented the up/bottom difference. None ever used the checking strategy. In contrast, metacognitive subjects didn't guess; only some ever used the swapping strategy, and these abandoned it early in the problem series. All metacognitive subjects distinguished up/bottom cards, used blanks for unknowns, and employed the checking strategy. The efficient strategies are connected; preliminary checking of a card order requires constructing an effective representation of the order of the deck and the prospective effect of the dealing rule. Good representations facilitate monitoring and further refinements. In problem situations, metacognitive processing is optional; problems directly call for problem-relevant activity. Indeed, novice problem solvers are known for leaping into action—any action, one might say. Solution monitoring, analysis of problem requirements, and deliberate construction and evaluation of problem representations are effective procedures. Novice problem solvers, on their own, seldom engage in these activities. Metacognitive probing promotes a different kind of problem-solving approach, a more reflective strategy that subjects continue to use even when answering questions is no longer required.

Is Talking Necessary?

Research has clearly shown that different kinds of verbalizing have different effects on problem solving. Simple thinking aloud usually does not change task performance, whereas verbalizing that involves metacognitive processing typically leads to improved performance. Thus, it is the kind of thinking one does, rather than the act of talking itself, that seems important.

A few studies have addressed the question of whether overt verbalization is required. For the disc-transfer problem, positive effects have been obtained by asking subjects to silently consider reasons for their moves (Wilder & Harvey, 1971) or to silently answer metacognitive questions (Berardi-Coletta et al., 1995). However, caution is in order when interpreting these results, as suggested by the findings of Zook and DiVesta (1989). In their study, college students worked on a series of mathematical problems requiring conversion of numbers between different base systems (e.g., Given 2331 [base 4], find the base 10 equivalent). Students were asked questions (e.g., What equation are you going to use? Why are you going to use it?) that they were required either to answer aloud or to think about. Overt verbalizers made fewer excess moves during acquisition and were more likely to adopt a more sophisticated strategy. There is not enough evidence to allow a comprehensive statement about the need for overt verbalization; at least in some circumstances it is not necessary.

EDUCATIONAL APPLICATIONS

There are several possible uses of verbalization techniques in educational settings. A teacher, when working with an individual student, could have the student think aloud while problem solving in order to provide the

teacher with a better understanding of the student's problem-solving approach and where difficulties might lie. As noted earlier, a teacher might be
well advised to ask probing questions when the student's verbalizations are
not clear regarding what the student is trying to do. The goal here would be
to maximize the teacher's understanding of the student's cognition. In
saying this, I would emphasize the difference between probing and prompting. To prompt a student to notice a particular problem feature, or to try this
or that approach, can be very tempting to one who knows the answer and
how to get it. But prompting can result in missing a critical feature of the
student's knowledge or strategy. Probing refers to asking for information
more specific than "Please talk aloud," while not suggesting any particular
direction to follow.

Let's consider some examples of probing. It is useful to have a broad
definition of "problem" so that a larger number of student tasks might be
considered. Math and science problems obviously qualify, as does any
situation requiring the student to deal correctly with a new example, but it
is worth remembering that a student's problem might be making sense of a
paragraph that is being read. The teacher can use cues from the student's
behavior to choose the kind of question to ask. If the student is trying some
procedure to solve a problem but the procedure is murky, the teacher might
ask, "What are you doing here?" If the procedural step is clear but the
purpose is not, one could ask, "Why did you do that?" If the student seems
to stop and be puzzled, one might ask, "What seems to be the difficulty?" In
other circumstances, students might be asked to explain the problem in their
own words, to describe any hypotheses they might have, or to describe any
solutions they have considered. Although such questioning is most easily
done in one-on-one situations, it is also possible to ask some questions to
be answered on paper, which allows questioning of groups of students.

It is clear that many of the questions described here suggest particular
kinds of thinking to the students and therefore might change their behavior.
Asking students if they have any hypotheses suggests that perhaps they
should have some; asking "why" clearly requests metacognitive processing.
Such effects pose no problems in an educational setting. Conversely, these
questions are broad or nondirective enough that asking them and allowing
any answer on the student's part, letting the student continue without help,
requires considerable patience on a teacher's part. Resisting the impulse to
give information, to suggest ways to proceed, is difficult. Becoming more
directive—prompting—might well get the current problem solved more
quickly, but one will learn less about the students' thinking. Also, prompting

raises questions about the longer term benefit to the student. Asking students to look for key words, or asking if the current problem reminds them of any problems they'd seen earlier, is to suggest particular strategies. At some point, for real success to occur, the students will need to think of doing such things without being prompted. Teachers must be concerned with efficient use of instructional time, a concern that promotes prompting or answer-giving rather than patient questioning. Perhaps teachers can take heart from the research findings that show that relatively nonspecific although metacognitive probing can produce positive results with reasonable speed.

The generally positive effects of eliciting metacognitive processing through questioning or requiring reasons imply that such techniques should be used to aid students' problem solving. Indeed, some of the cited research employed school content areas such as physics or mathematics. In addition, metacognitive techniques can be adapted to working with multiple students. In some studies, reasons were written on sheets of paper containing the problems to be solved. As seen earlier, there is the suggestion that asking problem solvers to engage silently in metacognitive processing can be beneficial (keep in mind that the robustness of this effect is unknown and might be limited). It would seem feasible to encourage metacognitive processing in a classroom situation.

In extending research findings to school settings, two cautions seem appropriate. First, in most research on reason giving and other metacognitive processing, it is safe to assume that people have sufficient problem-relevant knowledge. In contrast, students might lack adequate knowledge of what is being taught, which might affect the results. In research employing complex relations, Allwood (1990) found that requiring justification during statistical problem solving was not helpful and attributed the lack of effect to the students' inadequate knowledge of the domain. Therefore, as in the Berry and Broadbent (1984, 1987) studies, metacognitive processing might be effective only when preceded by a sufficient amount of initial instruction that explains effective problem-solving methods.

The second caution concerns the age or developmental level of the students. In the majority of research summarized here, the subjects have been young adults—college students. Metacognitive processing develops late, and the research findings suggest that even many college students do not engage in such processing unless prompted to do so. Younger students should be less likely to be able to usefully respond to requests for metacognitive processing. King (1991) studied pairs of fifth-graders working on computer-based problems in software packages commonly used in the fifth-grade curriculum. All students were encouraged to "think out loud" and were told that doing so could help them think more clearly. They were also told of the value of monitoring their solution attempts. The control group received no additional instruction; two other groups received instruction on the usefulness of using questioning during problem solving and observed a teacher modeling appropriate question-and-answer behavior. The unguided-questioning students were instructed to ask and answer questions when solving problems, whereas the guided-questioning students were given a set of metacognitive questions to choose from during problem solving. All pairs worked on the same sets of problems for multiple sessions before attempting to solve a difficult transfer problem (without provided questions) and individually taking a paper-and-pencil test on problem solving. The results showed that the guided-questioning students outperformed the other two groups on the transfer task and paper-and-pencil test; the unguided-questioning and control groups performed similarly. King (1991) refers to her earlier research indicating that less directive prompting was successful with high-school and college students. The implication is that one must carefully guide younger students to profitably engage in metacognitive processing.

CONCLUSIONS

Verbalizing during problem solving is a worthwhile procedure for researchers, teachers, and problem solvers themselves. Having people simply think aloud while working on a problem can provide useful information about problem-solving processes; task performance itself typically is not changed. Asking more specific questions (e.g., "What are you doing here?", "What seems to be the main obstacle?") can elicit additional information and might affect problem solving, presumably for the better. Asking people to focus on their own problem solving, to explain what they are trying to do, promotes metacognitive processing and leads to more effective problem solving, even when the questions are no longer asked. Metacognitive processing can be cultivated with a number of questioning procedures, and talking is not necessarily required. Having metacognitive probes answered in writing or just thought about has worked in some situations. Teachers are well advised to require and nourish metacognitive processing in their students; trying out different procedures to see which work best will probably be required. Patience, persistence, and flexibility in the initial stages could yield impressive outcomes.

ACKNOWLEDGMENTS

Thanks are due Bernadette Berardi-Colletta, Linda S. Buyer, Sharon Kristovich, and Pamela I. Ansbrug for their research and other contributions to my thinking about verbalization and problem solving.

REFERENCES

Ahlum-Heath, M. E., & Di Vesta, F. J. (1986). The effect of conscious controlled verbalization of a cognitive strategy on transfer in problem solving. Memory & Cognition, 14, 281–285.
Allwood, C. M. (1990). On the relation of justification of solution method and correctness of solution in statistical problem solving. Scandinavian Journal of Psychology, 31, 181–190.
Auden, W. H. (1962) The dyer's hand and other essays. NY: Random House.
Berardi-Coletta, B., Buyer, L. S., Dominowski, R. L., & Rellinger, E. A. (1995). Metacognition and problem solving: A process-oriented approach. Journal of Experimental Psychology: Learning, Memory, & Cognition, 21, 205–223
Berry, D. C. (1983). Metacognitive experience and transfer of logical reasoning. Quarterly Journal of Experimental Psychology, 35A, 39–49.
Berry, D. C., & Broadbent, D. E. (1984). On the relationship between task performance and associated verbalizable knowledge. Quarterly Journal of Experimental Psychology, 36A, 209–231.
Berry, D. C., & Broadbent, D. E. (1987). Explanation and verbalization in a computer-assisted search task. Quarterly Journal of Experimental Psychology, 39A, 585–609.
Bower, A. C., & King, W. L. (1967). The effect of number of stimulus dimensions, verbalization, and sex on learning bi-conditional classification rules. Psychonomic Science, 8, 453–454.
Byers, J. L., & Davidson, R. E. (1967). The role of hypothesizing in the facilitation of concept attainment. Journal of Verbal Learning and Verbal Behavior, 6, 595–600.
Chi, M. T. H., & Bassok, M. (1989). Learning from examples via self-explanation. In L. B. Resnick (Ed.), Knowing, learning & instruction: Essays in honor of Robert Glaser. Hillsdale, NJ: Lawrence Erlbaum Associates.
Dominowski, R. L. (1973). Required hypothesizing and the identification of unidimensional, conjunctive, and disjunctive concepts. Journal of Experimental Psychology, 100, 387–394.
Dominowski, R. L. (1974). How do people discover concepts? In R. L. Solso (Ed.), Theories in cognitive psychology: The Loyola Symposium (pp. 257–288). Potomac, MD: Lawrence Erlbaum Associates.
Dominowski, R. L. (1990). Problem solving and metacognition. In K. J. Gilhooly, M. T. G. Keane, R. H. Logie, & G. Erdos (Eds.), Lines of thinking: reflections on the psychology of thought (Vol. 2, pp. 313–328). Chichester, England: Wiley.
Dominowski, R. L., & Dallob, P. (1995). Insight and problem solving. In R. J. Sternberg & J. E. Davidson (Eds.), The nature of insight. (pp. 31–62). Cambridge, MA: MIT Press.
Dorner, D. (1978). Self reflection and problem solving. In F. Klix (Ed.), Human and artificial intelligence. Berlin: Deutscher Verlag der Wissenshaften.
Ericsson, K. A., & Simon, H. A. (1980). Verbal reports as data. Psychological Review, 87, 215–251.
Ericsson, K. A., & Simon, H. A. (1993). Protocol analysis. Cambridge, MA: MIT Press.
Evans, J. St. B. T., Barston, J., & Pollard, P. (1983). On the conflict between logic and belief in syllogistic reasoning. Memory & Cognition, 11, 295–306.

Flaherty, E. G. (1974). The thinking aloud technique and problem solving ability. *Journal of Educational Research, 68*, 223–225.

Gagne, R. M., & Smith, E. C., Jr. (1962). A study of the effects of verbalizations on problem solving. *Journal of Experimental Psychology, 63*, 12–18.

Gilhooly, K. J., & Gregory, D. J. (1989). Thinking aloud performance: Individual consistencies over tasks. *Current Psychology: Research and Reviews, 8*, 179–187.

Kaplan, C. A., & Simon, H. A. (1990). In search of insight. *Cognitive Psychology, 22*, 374–419.

Karpf, D. A. & Levine, M. (1971) Blank-trial probes and introtacts in human discrimination learning. *Journal of Experimental Psychology, 90*, 51–55.

Kellogg, R. T., & Holley, C. S. (1983). Interference of introspection with thinking in concept identification. *Perceptual and Motor Skills, 56*, 641–642.

King, A. (1991). Effects of training in strategic questioning on children's problem-solving performance. *Journal of Educational Psychology, 83*, 307–317.

McGeorge, P., & Burton, A. M. (1989). The effects of concurrent verbalization on performance in a dynamic systems task. *British Journal of Psychology, 80*, 455–465.

Norris, S. P. (1990). Effects of eliciting verbal reports of thinking on critical thinking test performance. *Journal of Educational Measurement, 27*, 41–58.

Schooler, J. W., Ohlsson, S., & Brooks, K. (1993). Thoughts beyond words: When language overshadows insight. *Journal of Experimental Psychology: General, 122*, 166–183.

Stinessen, L. (1985). The influence of verbalization on problem-solving. *Scandanavian Journal of Psychology, 26*, 342–347.

Vygotsky, L. S. (1962). *Thought and language*. Cambridge, MA: MIT Press.

Weisberg, R.W., & Suls, J. M. (1973). An information-processing model of Duncker's candle problem. *Cognitive Psychology, 4*, 255–276.

Wilder, L., & Harvey, D. J. (1971). Overt and covert verbalization in problem solving. *Speech Monographs, 38*, 171–176.

Zook, K. B., & DiVesta, F. J. (1989). Effects of overt controlled verbalization and goal-specific search on acquisition of procedural knowledge in problem solving. *Journal of Educational Psychology, 81*, 220–225.

3

Smart Problem Solving: How Metacognition Helps

Janet E. Davidson
Lewis & Clark College

Robert J. Sternberg
Yale University

Almost everything students do in school is a problem. For at least 12 years of their lives, children demonstrate their skills and knowledge by answering numerous questions and performing a wide range of problem-solving activities. Consider the following examples given to us by teachers:

> The minimum time required for a letter mailed in Chicago to arrive in Washington, DC, is as follows: straight first class, 22 hours and 45 minutes; airmail, 14 hours and 30 minutes; and special delivery airmail, 12 hours and six minutes. By using special delivery airmail, what percent of time is saved over first class mail?

> "George sure seems happy today," said David. "I think I'll strike while the iron is hot and ask him if I can borrow $5." What does it mean to strike while the iron is hot?

> Put a few drops of red food coloring into the bottom of a glass beaker filled with water. Slowly heat the water. What happens to the food coloring?

> Build a bridge out of toothpicks.

> What should be done if some members of our class do not follow the rules?

Obviously, these problems differ in the skills, mental processes, and domain-specific knowledge required to solve them. For example, the first three problems have only one correct answer, whereas the last two have several solutions. The first one requires mathematical knowledge and the third requires observational skills; either scientific or engineering knowledge can be applied to the fourth problem. However, these problems have two related commonalties. First, solving each one requires thinking that is directed toward achieving a goal. Second, solving each problem requires metacognition, which is awareness and management of one's mental processes, to guide this goal-directed thinking. The difference between being a good or a poor problem solver often lies in the ability to think about one's problem-solving activities (Gardner, 1991).

Reflecting on one's own problem-solving activities includes being aware of the different parts of a problem one is trying to solve. Every problem has three parts: givens, a goal, and obstacles (Anderson, 1985). The *givens* are the elements, their relations, and the conditions that compose the initial form of a problem. The *goal* is the desired outcome or solution. When students work on a problem, they actively try to transform the given state of a situation into a desired or goal state. *Obstacles* are the characteristics of both the problem and the student that make it difficult for the student to change the given state of the problem into the desired one or to recognize when the correct transformation has occurred.

Metacognition allows the solver to identify and work strategically with these three parts of a problem. Knowledge about problem solving, in general, and about their own mental processes, in particular, helps students become better problem solvers. More specifically, metacognitive skills help the student (a) strategically encode the nature of the problem and form a mental model or representation of its elements, (b) select appropriate plans and strategies for reaching the goal, and (c) identify and conquer obstacles that impede progress.

This chapter describes some of the metacognitive knowledge and processes that help individuals efficiently handle the givens, goals, and obstacles found in problem solving. There are five sections. The first three focus on the metacognitive knowledge and processes related to the three parts of a problem. In particular, the first section discusses the metacognitive knowledge that strategically enables the solver to encode and mentally represent the givens in a problem. The second part focuses on metacognitive processes used to select and revise strategies for accomplishing the goals. The third describes metacognitive processes for identifying and overcoming obstacles. The fourth section describes some of the general features of educational programs aimed at teaching these metacognitive skills. The final section summarizes the main points and discusses areas for future research and training.

METACOGNITIVE PROCESSING
OF THE GIVENS

Metacognition and Encoding

The first step in solving a problem is to encode the given elements (e.g., Newell & Simon, 1973). *Encoding* involves identifying the most informative features of a problem, storing these features in working memory and retrieving from long-term memory the information that is relevant to these features. This process helps the solver determine what is known, what is unknown, and what is being asked in the problem situation.

Unfortunately, incomplete or inaccurate metacognitive knowledge about problems often leads to incomplete or inaccurate encoding. For example, second graders, when questioned about their declarative (propositional) metacognitive knowledge of reading, were less likely than sixth graders to understand that the first and last sentences of a paragraph are particularly important ones that need careful encoding (Meyers & Paris, 1978). In contrast, elementary school students felt that the critical operations in math problems were located in the last sentence or question of the problem; therefore, the students believed there was no need to read the entire problem (Briars & Larkin, 1984). Some people who are told that they are about to receive a "trick" problem often read more carefully because they possess the metacognitive knowledge that this type of problem fosters inaccurate encoding of its elements. Consider the following "trick" problem:

> Tom's mother had three children. She named the first one Penny and the second one Nickel. What did she name her third child?

Individuals who are aware of the need to encode this problem carefully realize that they are given the names of all three children. Thus, they easily conclude that the third child is named Tom, rather than Dime (Davidson, 1995).

In addition to metacognitive knowledge about problems, metacognitive knowledge about procedures influences how information is encoded. For example, 7-and 8-year-old children often assume that skimming information involves saying as many words, including "a," "the," and "and," as quickly as possible. Older children have usually learned that skimming involves very shallow encoding of less meaningful words and deeper encoding of words that describe the content of the passage (Paris & Byrnes, 1989). Similarly, some individuals realize that they need to slow down and process deeply material that is unfamiliar or difficult. Familiar or loosely packed information does not require such careful encoding (Flavell, 1987).

As implied by some of the studies mentioned here, cognitive development and problem-solving experience influence children's metacognitive knowledge about how to encode a problem's critical features. For instance, Siegler (1978) found that a key source of improved performance on a balance-scale task in older children can be attributed to their awareness of the need thoroughly to encode the problem situation. Younger children are capable of encoding multiple dimensions but, unless they are instructed to do so, they tend to encode only one dimension.

In addition to metacognitive knowledge, the metacognitive process of *comprehension monitoring* helps promote effective encoding (Brown, Campione, & Day, 1981). Individuals need continually to assess how well they understand the material they are trying to encode. For example, older and more skilled readers are more aware of inconsistencies in material, and they spend more time reading and rereading sentences that conflict with previously encoded information in a passage (Baker & Anderson, 1982; Garner & Reis, 1981). Markman (1979) found that third graders did not possess comprehension monitoring skills; prompts to be on guard for nonsensical information did not improve their ability to detect confusing material. In contrast, sixth graders did not spontaneously monitor their comprehension but could perform this skill when prompted to do so. They possessed the ability to monitor their comprehension but did not know when to apply it.

Metacognition and Mental Representations

Encoding alone is not sufficient for successful problem solving. After a problem has been encoded, successful problem solvers use metacognition to create an internal representation or "mental map" of the givens, the relations among the givens, and the goals found in the problem. Information from the problem is mentally inserted, deleted, interpreted, and held in memory (Hayes, 1981). According to Newell and Simon (1972), there are four parts to a mental representation of a problem. The first part is a description of the problem's initial state. The second is a description of the problem's goal state. The third part is a set of operators that can be used to transform the initial state into the goal state. Finally, there is a set of constraints, such as a time limit, that impose further conditions on potential solution paths.

These four-part internal representations have important benefits for problem-solving performance (Ellis & Siegler, 1994; Kotovsky, Hayes, & Simon, 1985). One consequence is that good mental representations allow the solver to organize blocks of planned moves as a single "chunk" of memory. In other words, internal representations often reduce the memory demands found in many problems. Second, mental representations allow the solver to organize the conditions and rules of a problem and decide whether certain steps are legal and productive ones. Third, internal representations allow the solver to keep track of where he or she is in terms of reaching a solution and foresee potential obstacles that might impede progress. Finally, because they contain only critical structural features of a problem, good mental representations help generalization to new problems that might contain different surface features.

Unfortunately, students cannot be taught one single mental representation that will work for all problems. For some problems, such as geometric analogies, an attribute–value representation might be most efficient. For other problems, such as the linear syllogism "Peter is taller than Paul. Paul is taller than Mary. Who is the shortest?", a spatial representation is often best (Sternberg, 1986; Sternberg & Gardner, 1983). Hegarty, Mayer, and Monk (1995) found that successful problem solvers used an object-based representation for arithmetic word problems. These solvers tended to construct mental models of the situation depicted in a problem. In contrast, less successful problem solvers used a more impoverished propositional representation. They constructed a mental model based on the numbers and keywords found in a problem. In short, problem solvers who consider which type of representation works best for particular problems have an advantage over those individuals who do not make this assessment.

Specific cognitive abilities can also determine how a problem is best mentally represented. For example, MacLeod, Hunt, and Mathews (1978) presented people with a simple sentence followed by a simple picture and asked them to determine whether there was a match between the content of the sentence and the content of the picture. Individuals with high verbal ability tended to form verbal representations of both the sentence and the picture. Individuals who were high in spatial ability often formed a spatial representation of the sentence to compare with the picture. In other words, problem solvers who consider which type of representation works best for their abilities have an advantage over those individuals who do not make this assessment (MacLeod, Hunt, & Mathews, 1978; Sternberg & Weil, 1980).

Metacognition and Representational Change

Skilled problem solvers often use metacognitive processes to modify their mental representations during the course of problem solving (Hayes, 1981). Changes occur as individuals reflect on their own understanding of the givens, goals, and constraints in a problem. According to Davidson and Sternberg (1986; Davidson, Deuser, & Sternberg, 1994), new mental representations are often formed through three related mental processes: selective encoding, selective combination, and selective comparison.

Selective encoding involves seeing in a problem one or more relevant elements that previously have been nonobvious. Problems often present a solver with large amounts of information, yet only some of it is relevant to the solution. For example, teachers generally have the problem of too much material to cover in a short amount of time. They must select the information that is relevant for their pedagogical purposes and not focus on the less important material. Selective encoding contributes to problem solving by restructuring one's mental representation so that information that was originally viewed as being irrelevant is now seen as relevant to the problem's solution. Similarly, information that was originally seen as relevant may now be viewed as irrelevant and is, therefore, deleted from one's mental representation. For example, the first problem presented at the beginning of this chapter contains more information than is needed to answer the question. Through reflection, individuals who are trying to use the regular airmail time might realize that this information is irrelevant and delete it from their mental representations of the problem.

Selective combination involves putting together relevant elements of a problem situation in a way that previously has been nonobvious to the individual. This new way of combining the problem's elements results in a change in the solver's mental representation of the problem. Teachers may suddenly find a way to put together several seemingly disjointed facts in a way that tells a coherent story to students. Consider, too, the following example:

> Using six matches, make four equilateral triangles with one complete match making up the side of the triangle.

To solve this problem, individuals must combine steps in a nonobvious way to form a tetrahedron.

Selective comparison involves discovering a nonobvious relationship between new information and already acquired information. For example, analogies, metaphors, and models often help individuals solve problems. The solver realizes that new information is similar to old information in certain ways and then uses this information to form a mental representation based on the similarities. Teachers may discover how to relate new classroom material to information that students have already learned. Relating the new to the old can help the students learn the material more quickly and understand it more deeply. Similarly, seeing the bridges in Portland, Oregon may help some students form effective representations for the task mentioned earlier of building a bridge out of toothpicks.

When are selective encoding, selective combination, and selective comparison metacognitive processes that lead to representational change? According to Jackson and Butterfield (1986), these processes are metacognitive when they are used in regulating task analysis and in self-management of the problem-solving process. If individuals do not know an appropriate set of procedures for a problem, they often search through a space of alternative ways of approaching the problem (Newell & Simon, 1972). Successful problem solvers realize that they can guide this search by (a) looking for and recognizing previously overlooked relevant information in the problem (selective encoding), (b) looking for and recognizing previously overlooked ways of combining information (selective combination), and (c) looking for and recognizing previously overlooked connections between prior knowledge and the problem situation (selective comparison). Successful metacognitive search for, and selection of, this relevant information leads to a change in problem solvers' mental representations of the problem. In contrast, routine applications of encoding, combination, and comparison do not involve the self-management of a nonobvious search nor do they lead to a change in mental representations. For example, when "average" students were told what information to encode, how to combine information, and what information to compare, their problem-solving performance was similar to the performance of gifted students. However, unlike the gifted students, the average students did not spontaneously search for and select the information (Davidson & Sternberg, 1984).

Metacognition and Domain Specificity

Metacognition may to some extent be domain specific, and this contributes to varied quality of mental representations and uneven problem-solving performance across different types of content areas (Chi, 1981; Jackson &

Butterfield, 1986). For example, Wagner (1978) found that performance on memory problems administered to people in Morocco could make these individuals look either quite intelligent or quite stupid, depending on the familiarity of the content. When Oriental-rug dealers were given Western types of abstract content to recall, their performance was poor. When given Oriental-rug patterns to recall, their performance put Westerners to shame. The rug dealers could form effective mental representations of rug patterns, but not of the symbols used on standard Western memory tests.

In general, experts know how to create mental representations that are tied to abstract principles of the domain. In contrast, novices tend to categorize and mentally represent problems based on irrelevant, concrete features of the problems, such as whether pulleys are involved (Chi, Feltovitch, & Glaser, 1980; Chi, Glaser, & Rees, 1982; Larkin, McDermott, Simon, & Simon, 1980). In addition, novices spend less time than do experts in representing the problem, and they are less able to add new evidence to their representations than are experts (Lesgold, 1988; Lesgold, et al., 1988). In summary, problem solvers may be able to assess and update their mental representations in familiar domains but less able to use these metacognitive skills in unfamiliar ones.

METACOGNITIVE PLANNING FOR THE GOALS

After a problem has been encoded and a mental representation has been formed, an effective solver uses metacognition to decide how to go about solving the problem. Reviewing and selecting plans (a) allows the solver to anticipate the consequences of possible procedures, (b) can save the solver from making costly mistakes, and (c) provides information about what to expect from certain outcomes (Holyoak, 1995). Planning tends to be relatively abstract rather than concrete and complete. As people work through a problem, they need to update their plans based on metacognitive monitoring of how well the plans are working and on what opportunities for modifications are available (Pea, 1982; Pea & Hawkins, 1987).

Effective planning often involves a process of *problem decomposition* (Holyoak, 1995). Here a problem situation is divided into parts and a sequence of actions is developed for how to accomplish the goal of each part (Greeno, 1980; Hayes, 1981). Completing a series of "subgoals" often requires fewer steps, and results in fewer errors, than trying to devise and implement a global plan for reaching the overall goal for the entire problem (Holyoak, 1995). As children develop and make use of their problem-solving experiences, they become better able to decompose a problem into subgoals and better able to monitor increasingly large and complex subgoals (Siegler, 1991).

Effective planning also involves three metacomponents (Sternberg, 1977). First, the problem solver needs to select a set of lower order, strategic components to use on the problem. Selecting a nonoptimal set of processes can result in incorrect or inefficient problem-solving performance. Next, these lower order processes must be sequenced in a way that facilitates problem solving performance. In other words, an appropriate strategy for combining the lower order components needs to be selected. Finally, attentional resources need to be allocated. Good problem solvers tend to spend relatively more time on higher level planning (or metaplanning) and exercise more deliberate control over the planning process than do poor planners (Goldin & Hayes-Roth, 1980).

The type and amount of metacognitive planning in which people engage can be influenced by domain-specific knowledge. Individuals with less expertise in solving a particular type of problem seem to spend relatively less time in global, "upfront" planning, and relatively more time in attempting to implement a solution than do experts. This pattern of behavior has been found across age levels and across different levels of expertise within age levels (see, e.g., Chi, Glaser, & Rees, 1982; Larkin, McDermott, Simon, & Simon, 1980; Sternberg, 1981; Sternberg & Rifkin, 1979). Less skilled problem solvers do not have the available knowledge and processing resources that are required for extended global planning.

The Metacognitive Use of Heuristics

Problems that have clearly defined givens and goals often have steps to solution that can be easily identified by the problem solver. This type of problem generally requires several actions that change the initial state of the problem into the final state. The solution does not follow rapidly once one or two crucial steps have been made. Instead, finding a solution depends on selecting the correct sequence of steps. Consider the following "move" problem, so named because the goal state can only be reached by accomplishing a series of moves :

A woman, a fox, a duck, and some corn are on one side of a river with a boat. The goal is to transfer all of these entities to the other side of the river using the boat, which will carry the woman and one other entity. The fox and the duck cannot be left alone together, nor can the duck and the corn. What is the minimum number of times the boat must cross the river in order to get everything to the other side?

The solution to this problem is a sequence of seven correctly applied transformations. The problem's difficulty lies in deciding which transformations to make, holding these transformations in memory, and applying them correctly.

Problem solvers often rely on heuristics, or short-cuts, when they solve "move" problems and others like it (Greeno & Simon, 1988). These heuristics are applied in a problem space, which consists of all possible moves that can be applied to solve a problem. One obvious heuristic, working forward, involves starting at the initial state of a problem and working towards the goal state. The solver applies operators to the current state in order to transform it into the desired one. Problem solvers can also use the heuristic of working backward. This type of plan involves starting at the goal state and trying to find operators that can produce the initial state. One of the most useful forms of planning, means–ends analysis, uses a mixture of working forward and backward. This heuristic involves trying to decrease the distance between one's current position in the problem space and one's desired position in that space. An example of this heuristic applied to the "move" problem with the fox and duck would be to try to get as many entities on the far bank and as few entities on the near bank as possible.

Metacognitive awareness of what one already knows can help the problem solver select the appropriate heuristic for a problem. If the problem solver can restate the problem's goal in a new way based on his or her previous experience, then the working backward heuristic might be the most appropriate. If the individual can restate the givens in a new way that relates to his or her past experience, then the working forward heuristic might work best (Polya, 1957).

Transfer of Skills

Transfer of a correct strategy from one related problem to another is a hallmark of metacognitive ability because it is a sign that a problem solver not only knows how to use a strategy but also when to use it (Jackson & Butterfield, 1986). A teacher's task would be simplified if students generalized their correct strategies for solving one problem to other related problem situations. Unfortunately, it is often difficult to predict when transfer will be attained and when it will not be. However, there are several variables that seem relevant to whether metacognitive awareness of similar strategic requirements, and resulting transfer of strategies, will occur. One variable involves cognitive ability. More intellectually able subjects are more likely to show transfer from one situation to another (Sternberg, 1985). A second variable is similarity of the structure of two problems. More similar structures enhance the likelihood of two problems being recognized as isomorphic (Holyoak, 1995). A third variable is similarity of content. To the extent that the surface structures of two problems are similar, people are likely to see relations between them. Unfortunately, they may see relationships that are not useful: The surface structures of two problems may be close, despite differences in deep structures or solution procedures, that render the problems nonanalogous (Gentner, 1983). Finally, individuals are more likely to attain transfer when they have been exposed to several problems with the same solution procedure, rather than just one problem (Crisafi & Brown, 1986).

When individuals are unable to transfer strategic knowledge, other metacognitive and cognitive processes that individuals bring to bear on problem solving in one context are often not used in another context. For example, a study of Brazilian street children (Carraher, Carraher, & Schiemann, 1985) showed that these 9- to 15-year-olds could add, subtract, and multiply information quite well in their heads if the numbers were put in the context of items that they sold. The children were less good at manipulating numbers associated with items they did not sell. The lowest performance was found on problems where numbers were not associated with any concrete items. In short, the children in this study knew how to perform basic mathematical procedures. What they did not always know was when to perform these procedures.

Along similar lines, Siegler (1991) found that high-school students who knew how to use a pan balance scale often did not perform as well on comparable problems using an arm balance scale. Ceci and Brofenbrenner (1985) studied children's monitoring of time in home and laboratory settings. In particular, they looked at how children deal with time pressure in problem-solving tasks as a function of where they are doing the task. They found that the pattern of results was completely different in the two settings.

In other words, the situation in which problems are presented—whether through setting or content—can lead to vast differences in the conclusions one draws about individuals' metacognitive skills and problem-solving abilities. For example, Wagner and Sternberg (1986) found that business executives who may not score particularly well on standard tests of intelligence often do very well on tests of tacit knowledge—what one needs to know to succeed in an environment that generally one is not explicitly taught and that may not even be verbalized. These business executives, for example, may be excellent at planning and allocating their time and energy in a business situation, but not as good at allocating their time and energy in a standardized test situation.

METACOGNITIVE AWARENESS OF OBSTACLES

Stereotypy

There are at least three reasons why individuals may have difficulty in problem solving. One reason involves stereotypy (Kaplan & Davidson, 1988). In this case, the problem solver becomes fixated on one particular path to solution. "Poor students may have the requisite knowledge and skills, but fail to use them correctly or at the appropriate time. These students lack flexibility and may stick to one strategy even when it does not lead to successful solutions" (McAfee & Leong, 1994, p. 144).

Even when students realize that they are approaching a problem incorrectly, they often cannot break their fixation on this approach to develop a more worthwhile plan for solution. In other words, fixation keeps individuals from changing their problem-solving sets, even when they realize that old procedures are not relevant to the current situation. Studies conducted by Luchins (1942; Luchins & Luchins, 1950), Duncker (1945), and others (Adamson, 1952; Adamson & Taylor, 1954; Birch & Rabinowitz, 1951) illustrate how fixation on past procedures can interfere with the formation of new ones. Inadequate or inappropriate metacognitive processing can prevent problem solvers from reaching satisfactory solutions. Individuals are often unaware of set effects that are impeding their performance or they do not know how to free themselves from these effects. An incubation period often allows unproductive fixations to weaken and more useful associations to form. For example, Smith and Blankenship (1989, 1991) gave problem solvers misleading clues that caused them to fixate on inappropriate solutions. Breaks in problem solving weakened solvers' memories of the misleading clues and improved performance on the problems.

Reaching an Impasse

Another source of problem difficulty has to do with the inability to generate any plans or procedures for solving a problem (Kaplan & Davidson, 1988). If a problem is sufficiently novel or requires unavailable knowledge, the solver may simply not know how or where to begin. Consider the following problem:

How can you cut a hole big enough to put your head through in a three inch by five inch postcard?

If problem solvers do not consider cutting a spiral out of the card, they often are unable to generate any plans or strategies for solving the problem (Davidson, 1995).

Schooler and Melcher (1995) found that insight problems, such as the one just mentioned, were more likely than analytic problems to elicit metacognitive statements of impasse from problem solvers. When solving analytic problems, individuals had a better idea of the step-by-step strategies to use and they were less likely to make statements such as "I don't think I can solve it at all, no matter how much time I had" and "I am just wondering where to go from here" (p. 115). Taking a break when an impasse is reached on certain problems often helps people generate plans, especially if relevant information is encountered during the pause in problem solving (Seifert, Meyer, Davidson, Patalano, & Yaniv, 1995). When students reach points of impasse, instructional intervention offering problem-solving strategies and encouraging self-reflection has also been found to improve problem-solving performance (Delclos & Kulewicz, 1991).

Failure to Monitor and Evaluate

A final reason why some individuals have trouble correctly solving problems is that they do not monitor and evaluate their knowledge and solution procedures (Nickerson, Perkins, & Smith, 1985). Metacognitive shortfall occurs when solvers do not assess biases in their models, do not realize when a model can be extended, or do not reconsider a conclusion after receiving additional information (Perkins, 1989). Consider the following example from the National Assessment of Education secondary mathematics exam:

> An army bus holds 36 soldiers. If 1,128 soldiers are being bused to their training site, how many buses will be needed?

Twenty-nine percent of the students gave the answer "31 remainder 12" without evaluating whether this response made any sense (Schoenfield, 1987).

As individuals work on a problem, they need to keep track of what they have already done, what they are currently doing, and what still needs to be done (Flavell, 1981). Metacognitive solution monitoring and evaluation includes an individual's control over the internal representations he or she has formed and still needs to form for understanding and solving a problem. Often, new strategies need to be formulated as a person realizes that the old ones are not working.

Dallob and Dominowski (1992) found that when wrong answers were due to inadequate solution monitoring, simply informing problem solvers that they had made an error often led to the production of correct solutions. In other words, these individuals were able to solve certain problems after rechecking problem information and discovering they had made incorrect assumptions. Delclos and Harrington (1991) discovered that forcing fifth- and sixth-grade students to monitor their problem-solving strategies before, during, and after solving computer-based problems improved students' performance both in terms of increasing the complexity of the problems that could be solved and decreasing the time spent solving them. Similarly, King (1991) found that providing pairs of fifth-grade students with metacognitive questions about their planning, monitoring, and evaluation procedures improved their problem-solving performance. Transfer of the questioning strategy to an unprompted task also occurred. In short, individuals do not always apply metacognitive monitoring. When encouraged to do so, their problem-solving performance improves.

TRAINING METACOGNITION

Schools influence students' abilities to reflect on and verbalize their thought processes (Rogoff, 1981). Many schools even employ explicit training programs to develop metacognitive knowledge and processes in their students. This section describes some of the ways that metacognitive processes involving the givens, goals, and obstacles in problem solving are taught in educational settings. This is not an exhaustive review of all existing programs aimed at teaching metacognitive skills in problem solving. Instead specific aspects of certain programs are highlighted in order to emphasize the range of options and the emerging themes that appear in these options.

How to Work With the Givens

Whimbey and Lockhead (1981) used a procedure they called "pair problem-solving" to teach students to encode relevant facts, apply these facts, and to check sufficiently for accuracy. Students think aloud to a peer as they encode and solve well-structured problems. The peer serves as a listener-critic who monitors the adequacy of the encoding and thinking processes and points out misuse of information and premature conclusions. Through modeling, this approach teaches students metacognitive awareness of encoding and solution monitoring.

King (1989, 1990) developed a training program based on guided questions aimed at helping high school and college students learn lecture material. Students are trained to use a set of generic question stems, such as "How are _____ and _____ alike?" and "What would happen if?" to assist them in creating their own specific questions for the material to be learned. Students then pose and answer their questions while working in small groups. This guided cooperative questioning procedure helps students construct accurate and effective mental representations of the lecture material.

Davidson and Sternberg (1984) found that insightful problem solving could be trained on the basis of the three metacognitive processes promoting representational change discussed earlier: selective encoding, selective combination, and selective comparison. Their training program involved 14 hours of instruction, distributed over a 7-week period. A variety of procedures (e.g., group instruction, group problem solving, and individual problem solving) were used to train gifted and nongifted children in executing the three processes. After being given examples of highlighted relevant information in a problem, tables and charts for combining information, and explicit explanations of how old and new problems were related, students were encouraged to underline relevant information, develop methods for combining relevant information, and draw explicit relationships between new material and already acquired information. At the end of the program, the children were given a posttest that included mathematical and verbal insight problems (hypothesized to use the three insight processes) and deductive reasoning problems (hypothesized to require different processes). The nongifted children showed greater improvement on the insight problems than the gifted children. Most gifted children were already applying the three processes when they solved nonroutine problems. However, gifted and nongifted children who did not apply the processes spontaneously could be taught to do so in a variety of situations. Neither group showed improvement on the deductive reasoning problems, which involved processes that were unrelated to the training program (Davidson, 1991; Sternberg & Davidson, 1984).

How to Reach the Goals

Sternberg (1986), in his text *Intelligence Applied*, presents a thinking course that can be self-paced or integrated into a wide range of classrooms. The course is based on his triarchic view of intelligence and covers many aspects of adaptive problem solving. Of particular interest for metacognitive training is the section devoted to metacomponents. In this section, students are given instruction, examples, and extensive exercises on defining the nature of a problem, improving their selection of mental representations, lower order-components and strategies, allocating resources, and solution monitoring. The suggestions described for selection of task components involve choosing steps that are the right size for solving the problem, making the first step an easy one to get the task started, and considering alternate steps to solution before choosing any one set of steps. The specific steps described for strategy selection include considering the full problem, not assuming the obvious, and sequencing steps in a logical order for reaching the goal. The steps for allocating resources include devoting relatively large amounts of time to high-level planning, making full use of prior knowledge, and being flexible about changing plans and allocations of resources.

Paris and his colleagues (Paris & Byrnes, 1989; Paris, Cross, & Lipson, 1984; Paris & Jacobs, 1984) developed two programs, Informed Strategies for Learning and Reading and Thinking Strategies for students in Grades 3 through 8. One of the goals of the programs is to foster the use of declarative (propositional), procedural ("how to") and conditional ("knowing when and why") metacognitive knowledge so that students make better decisions about the strategies to use in different situations. In the 3- to 6-month programs, teacher instruction on what a strategy is and how, when, and why to use strategies is combined with peer interactions that encourage debate and conflict resolution about the effectiveness of the different reading strategies. The training programs also involve the immediate application of strategies to varied types of text and transfer is explicitly encouraged. Throughout the training, teachers provide guidance and urge students to read, write, and talk about the strategies.

To increase transfer of strategies across problems and situations, Resnick (1988) suggests that mathematics should be taught as an ill-structured discipline, rather than a well-structured one. She proposes that dialogues, debates, and small group work focus on mathematical ideas rather than formulas. Using everyday language to talk about a range of mathematical relationships and interpretations is proposed to result in more meaningful and generalizable problem solving.

How to Overcome Obstacles

Palincsar and Brown (1984) improved seventh graders' reading comprehension by focusing on the skills of summarizing what is read, clarifying what is not clear, questioning, and anticipating future questions. These researchers used the process of reciprocal learning, where the teacher models the appropriate skills and then each student takes a turn as a model. The skills were also taught in the same context in which they were to be used. At the end of the training, students showed dramatic improvement in their reading comprehension. Moreover, these results lasted over time and across domains.

Schoenfeld (1985) describes ways that students can be taught to monitor and evaluate their performance on math problems. For example, students are required to pause frequently during problem solving and ask themselves questions, such as "What am I doing right now?" Like Palincsar & Brown, Schoenfeld encourages reciprocal learning. In a cooperative group setting, the teacher guides the application of strategies and the evaluation of mathematical solutions and supports students' efforts to perform these processes on their own.

Obviously, a variety of programs is used to teach the metacognitive skills needed to work effectively with the givens, goals, and obstacles found in problem solving. Some of the programs cover a wide range of processes and some focus on only one or two. Several of the programs focus on multiple domains, while others are aimed at improving skills in a specific content area. However, there seems to be a trend away from isolated learning of these metacognitive skills and toward reciprocal learning. There appear to be several advantages to reciprocal learning (Brown & Palincsar, 1989; Ellis & Siegler, 1994): First, the social interactions are motivating and allow active participation even at the beginning of the learning process. Second, the guided questioning procedure encourages deep processing of the learning material. Finally, the technique allows metacognitive skills to be used in a wide range of domains, and this enables their general applicability to become apparent to students.

As illustrated in the programs already described, there also is a trend away from abstract learning of metacognitive skills and toward concrete learning in specific domains or "real" world contexts. Teaching metacognitive skills in conjunction with the domain-specific skills they are to control seems to be more effective than teaching each type of skill separately (Campione, 1987). In many of the training programs described here, metacognitive skills are practiced in one or more content areas and transfer to new areas is explicitly encouraged.

DIRECTIONS FOR THE FUTURE

The metacognitive knowledge and processes described in this chapter apply to a wide range of problems and to a wide range of problem solvers. In general, declarative and procedural metacognitive knowledge about problems help problem solvers strategically to encode and mentally represent the critical givens in a problem and their relation to the goals. Metacognitive planning and strategy selection help the solver determine where to begin and what outcomes to expect along the way. Effective problem solving can be hindered by obstacles, such as stereotypy, the inability to generate plans or procedures, and metacognitive shortfall. Metacognitive knowledge about breaks in problems solving, solution monitoring, and evaluation help the solver overcome these obstacles.

A great deal still needs to be discovered about the role of metacognition in problem solving. In particular, interactions between the metacognitive processes need to be explored. How do the processes work together on different types of problems? How can use of the processes, separately and together, be enhanced? How does metacognition influence affective aspects of problem solving?

In recent years, there has been a focus on teaching metacognitive processes through teacher mentoring and peer interaction. It would be useful for educators and researchers to understand more fully when reciprocal learning is most beneficial. In addition, causal links between cognition and metacognition still need further examination. We do not fully understand how metacognitive processes develop in relation to cognitive ones, and vice versa. Finally, more research needs to be conducted on the use and training of metacognition in natural contexts.

As illustrated in this chapter, several promising research programs have been developed to examine metacognitive skills used in problem solving and training programs have been designed to teach these metacognitive skills. However, many problems must still be solved before we can fully understand and enhance the role of metacognition in problem solving.

ACKNOWLEDGMENTS

The work reported herein was supported under the Javits Act program (Grant #R206R50001), as administered by the Office of Educational Research and Improvement, U.S. Department of Education. The findings and opinions expressed in this report do not reflect the positions or policies of the Office of Educational Research and Improvement or the U.S. Department of Education.

REFERENCES

Adamson, R. E. (1952). Functional fixedness as related to problem solving: A repetition of three experiments. *Journal of Experimental Psychology, 44*, 288–291.

Adamson, R. E., & Taylor, D. W. (1954). Functional fixedness as related to elapsed time and set. *Journal of Experimental Psychology, 47*, 122–216.

Anderson, J. R. (1985). *Cognitive psychology and its implications* (2nd ed.) New York: W. H. Freeman.

Baker, L., & Anderson, R. C. (1982). Effects of inconsistent information on text processing: Evidence for comprehension monitoring. *Reading Research Quarterly, 17*, 281–293.

Birch, H. G. & Rabinowitz, H. S. (1951). The negative effect of previous experience on productive thinking. *Journal of Experimental Psychology. 41*, 121–125.

Briars, D. J. & Larkin, J. M. (1984). An integrated model of skill in solving elementary word problems. *Cognition and Instruction, 1*, 245–296.

Brown, A. L., Campione, J. C., & Day, J. D. (1981). Learning to learn: On training students to learn from texts. *Educational Researcher, 10*, 14–21.

Brown, A. L, & Palincsar, A. M. (1989). Guided cooperative learning and individual knowledge acquisition. In L. B. Resnick (Ed.), *Knowing, learning, and instruction: Essays in honor of Robert Glaser*. Hillsdale, NJ: Lawrence Erlbaum Associates.

Campione, J. C. (1987). Metacognitive components of instructional research with problem learners. In F. E. Weinert, & R. H. Kluwe, (Eds.), *Metacognition, motivation, and understanding*. Hillsdale, NJ: Lawrence Erlbaum Associates.

Carraher, T. N., Carraher, D. W., & Schliemann, A. D. (1985). Mathematics in the streets and in schools. *British Journal of Developmental Psychology, 3*, 21–29.

Ceci, S. J., & Brofenbrenner, U. (1985). Don't forget to take the cupcakes out of the oven: Strategic time-monitoring, prospective memory and context. *Child Development, 56*, 175–190.

Chi, M. T. H. (1981). Knowledge structures and memory development. In R. S. Siegler (Ed.), *Children's thinking: What develops? Hillsdale*, NJ: Lawrence Erlbaum Associates.

Chi, M. T. H., Feltovich, P. J., & Glaser, R. (1980). Categorization and representation of physics problems by experts and novices. *Cognitive Science, 5*, 121–152.

Chi, M. T. H., Glaser, R., Rees, E. (1982). Expertise in problem solving. In R. J. Sternberg (Ed.), *Advances in the psychology of human intelligence* (Vol. 1). Hillsdale, NJ: Lawrence Erlbaum Associates.

Crisafi, M. A., & Brown, A. L. (1986). Analogical transfer in very young children: Combining two separately learned solutions to reach a goal. *Child Development, 57*, 953–968.

Dallob, P. I., & Dominowski, R. L. (1992, April). *Erroneous solutions to verbal insight problems: Fixation or insufficient monitoring?* Paper presented at the meeting of the Western Psychological Association, Portland, OR.

Davidson, J. E. (1991). Insights about giftedness: The role of problem solving abilities. In N. Colangelo, S. G. Assouline, & D. L. Ambroson (Eds.), *Talent development: Proceedings from the 1991 Henry B. and Jocelyn Wallace National Research Symposium on Talent Development*. Unionville, NY: Trillium Press.

Davidson, J. E. (1995). The suddenness of insight. In R. J. Sternberg & J. E. Davidson (Eds.), *The nature of insight*. Cambridge, MA: MIT Press.

Davidson, J. E., Deuser, R., & Sternberg, R. J. (1994). The role of metacognition in problem solving. In J. Metcalfe, & A. P. Shimamura, (Eds.), *Metacognition: Knowing about knowing.* Cambridge, MA: MIT Press.

Davidson, J. E., & Sternberg, R. J. (1984). The role of insight in intellectual giftedness. *Gifted Child Quarterly, 28,* 58–64.

Davidson, J. E., & Sternberg, R. J. (1986). What is insight? *Educational Horizons, 64,* 177–179.

Delclos, V. R., & Harrington, C. (1991). Effects of strategy monitoring and proactive instruction on children's problem-solving performance. *Journal of Educational Psychology, 83,* 35–42.

Duncker, K. (1945). On problem solving. *Psychological Monographs, 58:5,* Whole No. 270.

Ellis, S., & Siegler, R. S. (1994). Development of problem solving. In R. J. Sternberg (Ed.), *Thinking and problem solving.* San Diego, CA: Academic Press.

Flavell, J. H. (1981). Cognitive monitoring. In W. P. Dickson (Ed.), *Children's oral communication skills.* New York: Academic Press.

Flavell, J. H. (1987). Speculations about the nature and development of metacognition. In F. E. Weinert & R. H. Kluwe (Eds.), *Metacognition, motivation, and understanding.* Hillsdale, NJ: Lawrence Erlbaum Associates.

Gardner, H. (1991). *The unschooled mind.* New York: Harper & Row.

Garner, R., & Reis, R. (1981). Monitoring and resolving comprehension obstacles: An investigation of spontaneous text lookbacks among upper-grade good and poor comprehenders. *Reading Research Quarterly, 16,* 569–582.

Gentner, D. (1983). Structure-mapping: A theoretical framework for analogy. *Cognitive Science, 7,* 155–170.

Goldin, S. E., & Hayes-Roth, B. (1980, June). *Individual differences in planning processes.* (Rand Tech. Rep. No. N-1488-ONR).

Greeno, J. (1980). Trends in the theory of knowledge for problem solving. In D. T. Tuma & F. Reif (Eds.), *Problem solving and education: Issues in teaching and research.* Hillsdale, NJ: Lawrence Erlbaum Associates.

Greeno, J. G., & Simon, H. A. (1988). Problem solving and reasoning. In R. C. Atkinson, R. J. Hernstein, G. Lindzey, & R. D. Luce (Eds.) *Steven's handbook of experimental psychology* (Rev. Ed.). New York: Wiley.

Hayes, J. R. (1981). *The complete problem solver.* Hillsdale, NJ: Lawrence Erlbaum Associates.

Hegarty, M., Mayer, R. E., & Monk, C. A. (1995). Comprehension of arithmetic word problems: A comparison of successful and unsuccessful problem solvers. *Journal of Educational Psychology, 87,* 18–32.

Holyoak, K. J. (1995). Problem solving. In E. E. Smith & D. N. Osherson (Eds.), *Thinking.* Cambridge, MA: MIT Press.

Jackson, N. E., & Butterfield, E.C. (1986). A conception of giftedness to promote research. In R. J. Sternberg & J. E. Davidson (Eds.), *The nature of insight.* Cambridge, MA: MIT Press.

Kaplan, C. A., & Davidson, J. E. (1988). *Hatching a theory of incubation effects* (Tech. Rep. No. C.I.P. 472). Pittsburgh: Carnegie Mellon University, Department of Psychology.

King, A. (1989). Effects of self-questioning training on college students' comprehension of lectures. *Contemporary Educational Psychology, 14,* 1–16.

King, A. (1990). Enhancing peer interaction and learning in the classroom through reciprocal questioning. *American Educational Research Journal, 27,* 664–687.

King, A. (1991). Effects of training in strategic questioning on children's problem-solving performance. *Journal of Educational Psychology, 83,* 307–317.

Kotovsky, K., Hayes, J. R., & Simon, H. A. (1985). Why are some problems hard? Evidence from the tower of Hanoi. *Cognitive Psychology, 17,* 248–294.

Larkin, J. H., McDermott, J., Simon, D. P., & Simon, H. A. (1980). Expert and novice performance in solving physics problems. *Science, 208,* 1335–1342.

Lesgold, A. (1988). Problem solving. In R. J. Sternberg & E. E. Smith (Eds.), *The psychology of human thought* (pp. 188–213). New York: Cambridge University Press.

Lesgold, A., Rubinson, H., Feltovich, P., Glaser, R., Klopfer, D., & Wang, Y. (1988). Expertise in a complex skill: Diagnosing x-ray pictures. In M. T. H. Chi, R. Glaser, & M. Farr (Eds.), *The nature of expertise*. Hillsdale, NJ: Lawrence Erlbaum Associates.

Luchins, A. S. (1942). *The mentality of apes* (2nd ed.) New York: Harcourt Brace.

Luchins, A. S., & Luchins, E. S. (1950). New experimental attempts at preventing mechanization in problem solving. *Journal of General Psychology, 42,* 279–297.

MacLeod, C. M., Hunt, E. B., & Mathews, N. N. (1978). Individual differences in the verification of sentence–picture relationships. *Journal of Verbal Learning and Verbal Behavior, 17,* 493–507.

Markman, E. (1979). Realizing that you don't understand: Elementary school children's awareness of inconsistencies. *Child Development, 50,* 643–655.

Meyers, M., & Paris, S. G. (1978). Children's metacognitive knowledge about reading. *Journal of Educational Psychology, 70,* 680–690.

Newell, A., & Simon, H. A. (1972). *Human problem solving.* Englewood Cliffs, NJ: Prentice-Hall.

Nickerson, R. S., Perkins, D. N., & Smith, E. E. (1985). *The teaching of thinking.* Hillsdale, NJ: Lawrence Erlbaum Associates.

Palincsar, A. M., & Brown, A. L. (1984). Reciprocal teaching of comprehension-monitoring activities. *Cognition and Instruction, 1,* 117–175.

Paris, S. G., & Byrnes, J. P. (1989). The constructionist approach to self-regulation and learning in the classroom. In B. J. Zimmerman & D. H. Schunk (Eds.), *Self-regulated learning and academic achievement: Theory, research, and practice.* New York: Springer-Verlag.

Paris, S. G., Cross, D. R., & Lipson, M. Y. (1984). Informed strategies for learning: A program to improve children's reading awareness and comprehension. *Journal of Educational Psychology, 76,* 1239–1252.

Paris, S. G., & Jacobs, J. E. (1984). The benefits of informed instruction for children's reading awareness and comprehension skills. *Child Development, 55,* 2083–2093.

Pea, R. D. (1982). What is planning development the development of? In D. Forbes and M. T. Greenberg (Eds.), *New directions in child development: The development of planful behavior in children.* San Francisco: Jossey-Bass.

Pea, R. D., & Hawkins, J. (1987). Children's planning process in a chore-scheduling task. In S. L. Friedman, E. K. Scholnick, & R. R. Cocking (Eds.), *Blueprints for thinking: The role of planning in psychological development.* New York: Cambridge University Press.

Perkins, D. N. (1989). Reasoning as it is and could be: An empirical perspective. In D. M. Topping, D. C. Crowell, & V. N. Kobayashi (Eds.), *Thinking across cultures: The Third International Conference on Thinking.* Hillsdale, NJ: Lawrence Erlbaum Associates.

Polya, G. (1957). *How to solve it.* Garden City, NY: Doubleday/Anchor. (Originally published by Princeton University Press, 1945)

Resnick, L. B. (1988). Treating mathematics as an ill-structured discipline. In R. I. Charles & E. A. Silver (Eds.), *The teaching and assessing of mathematical problem solving* (pp. 32–60). Hillsdale, NJ: Lawrence Erlbaum Associates.

Rogoff, B. (1981). Schooling and the development of cognitive skills. In H. C. Triandis & A. Heron (Eds.), *Handbook of cross-cultural psychology* (Vol. 4). Boston: Allyn & Bacon.

Schoenfeld, A. H. (1985). *Mathematical problem solving.* New York: Academic Press.

Schoenfeld, A. H. (1987). What's all the fuss about metacognition? In A. H. Schoenfeld (Ed.), *Cognitive science and mathematics education* (pp. 189–215). Hillsdale, NJ: Lawrence Erlbaum Associates.

Schooler, J. W., & Melcher, J. (1995). The ineffability of insight. In S. S. Smith, T. B. Ward, & R. A. Finke (Eds.), *The creative cognition approach*. Cambridge, MA: MIT Press.

Seifert, C. M, Meyer, D. E., Davidson, N., Patalano, A. L., & Yaniv, I. (1995). Demystification of cognitive insight: Opportunistic assimilation and the prepared-mind perspective. In R. J. Sternberg & J. E. Davidson (Eds.), *The nature of insight*. Cambridge, MA: MIT Press.

Siegler, R. S. (1978). The origins of scientific reasoning. In R. S. Siegler (Ed.), *Children's thinking: What develops?* Hillsdale, NJ: Lawrence Erlbaum Associates.

Siegler, R. S. (1991). *Children's thinking*. Englewood Cliffs, NJ: Prentice Hall.

Smith, S. M., & Blankenship, S. E. (1989). Incubation effects. *Bulletin of the Psychonomic Society, 27*, 311–314.

Smith, S. M., & Blankenship, S. E. (1991). Incubation and the persistence of fixation in problem solving. *American Journal of Psychology, 104*, 61–87.

Sternberg, R. J. (1977). *Intelligence, information processing, and analogical reasoning: The componential analysis of human abilities*. Hillsdale, NJ: Lawrence Erlbaum Associates.

Sternberg, R. J. (1981). Intelligence and nonentrenchment. *Journal of Educational Psychology, 73*, 1–16.

Sternberg, R. J. (1985). *Beyond IQ: Toward a Triarchic Theory of intelligence*. New York: Cambridge University Press.

Sternberg, R. J. (1986). *Intelligence applied*. San Diego: Harcourt, Brace & Jovanovich.

Sternberg, R. J., & Davidson, J. E. (1983). Insight in the gifted. *Educational Psychologist, 18*, 51–57.

Sternberg, R. J., & Gardner, M. K. (1983). Unities in inductive reasoning. *Journal of Experimental Psychology: General, 112*, 80–116.

Sternberg, R. J., & Rifkin, B. (1979). The development of analogical reasoning processes. *Journal of Experimental Child Psychology, 27*, 195–232.

Sternberg, R. J., & Weil, E. M. (1980). An aptitude-strategy interaction in linear syllogistic reasoning. *Journal of Educational Psychology, 72*, 226–234.

Wagner, D. A. (1978). Memories of Morocco: The influence of age, schooling and environment on memory. *Cognitive Psychology, 10*, 1–28.

Wagner, R. K., & Sternberg, R. J. (1986). Tacit knowledge and intelligence in the everyday world. In R. J. Sternberg & R. K. Wagner (Eds.), *Practical intelligence* (pp. 51–83). New York: Cambridge University Press.

Whimbey, A., & Lockhead, J. (1981). *Problem solving and comprehension: A short course in analytical reasoning*. Philadelphia: The Franklin Institute Press.

4

Metacognition in Mathematics From a Constructivist Perspective

Martha Carr
Barry Biddlecomb
University of Georgia

Our goal is to discuss how the research on metacognition in mathematics can be interpreted from the perspective of constructivist theory. Much of what we present in this chapter is speculative in that very little theory or research has examined conscious reflection from a constructivist perspective. First, we discuss issues central to the development of metacognition and its relationship to problem solving. We then discuss the extant literature on metacognition in mathematics, specifically focusing on strategy knowledge and metacognitive awareness. We end with a discussion about how metacognition may be conceptualized from the perspective of radical constructivism and social constructivism, and focus on the potential implications of constructivist theory for the instruction of metacognition in mathematics.

Metacognition is multifaceted in that it includes knowledge about strategies, tasks, and the self as well as the skills to evaluate strategies (Flavell, 1978). Although we know that as children get older they gradually develop more metacognitive knowledge (Schneider & Pressley, 1989), we know little about how this knowledge is acquired. We know little as well about the relationships between developing higher level thinking skills and emerging domain-specific cognitive structures. This is primarily because metacognitive theory has not focused on how metacognitive processes develop with age.

Despite the neo-Piagetian framework used in much of the mathematics research today, research on metacognition within the domain of mathematics is based in an information-processing perspective. Two approaches that have included metacognition within the domain of mathematics have been advanced. Polya (1957) hypothesized that problem solving in mathematics is comprised of four processes: understanding the problem, planning the solution, carrying out the plan, and reviewing the procedure and outcome. Garofalo and Lester (1985) similarly hypothesized that problem solving in mathematics could be comprised of four stages: orientation, organization, execution, and verification. Whereas in Polya's model, metacognitive awareness was apparent only at the end of problem solving, Garofalo and Lester assumed that at each stage children will be using metacognitive knowledge about strategies and will be metacognitively monitoring those processes. For example, in the orientation stage, the children will consider the level of difficulty of a task, and in the organizational stage children will plan.

Neither Polya nor Garofalo and Lester, however, described how these metacognitive knowledge and processes develop in children. Neither model explains the role of metacognition in the development of conceptual knowledge of mathematics. Within the domain of mathematics, we do not know how children come to be aware of information that promotes the best strategic approaches to problem solving, how children come to realize that setting goals is helpful in problem solving, or how children understand that it is necessary to monitor and evaluate one's work. Metacognitive knowledge may be a product of developing schemes for mathematics or it may emerge as a result of social interaction with others.

Recent work by Kuhn, Garcia-Mila, Zohar, and Andersen (1995) suggests that a bidirectional relationship exists between developing conceptual knowledge and metacognitive knowledge. Kuhn and her colleagues examined the development of *metastrategic knowledge* (I. e., knowledge about when, where, and how to apply strategies and an understanding of the structure of the task) and *metacognitive competence* (I. e., an awareness of the need to reflect on the content of one's knowledge) in relation to children's and adults' emerging strategies in determining causality. They found that simply having well-understood strategies would not assure the correct use of the strategies. Instead, good strategy use required knowledge about when and when not to apply that strategy. In addition, individuals who best applied developing strategies were more likely to have an understanding of how the strategies fit together and fit to the tasks to which they would be applied. This metastrategic knowledge was not found to develop entirely before or after the development of a strategy, but seemed to emerge with the strategy. Children differed from adults primarily in that they were less likely to inhibit the use of invalid strategies because they lacked the metastrategic knowledge to do so. These findings suggest that metacognition emerges from knowledge, but that it also guides further learning. In looking at metacognition from a constructivist perspective, we must examine how children's developing domain-specific cognitive structures allow for and are promoted by metacognitive awareness.

Metacognitive knowledge also develops from children's interactions with peers and adults. Recent work by Pellegrini (Pellegrini, Galda, & Flor, 1996) indicates that when children learn with other children, literate language, including the ability to reflect on thought and language, develops as a function of conflict resolution during social interaction. Similarly, Kuhn and her colleagues hypothesize that the tendency of children to use theories as justification for decisions about causality may be lessened if children have to support their conclusions to others. Within the domain of mathematics, social constructivists hypothesize that children construct mathematical knowledge in collaboration with others. We believe that as a part of social interaction, individuals must reflect on their own thinking to accommodate new inconsistent information and to communicate thoughts. So, reflection is necessitated by children's communication needs and shared experiences. From a constructivist perspective, self-awareness and reflection on cognitive processes and states emerge through social interactions with others.

Considering that a primary problem in mathematics education is children's failure to plan and evaluate, research and theory on the role of higher level thinking in mathematics is critical. For many children, mathematics skills and knowledge appear to develop without the development of reflection. As a result, children are stymied in their attempts to transfer mathematical knowledge from the classroom to real-life activities. Similarly, children are less able to recognize the relationships among different types of mathematics taught in the classroom because they cannot see beyond the task. The following section presents research relevant to these ideas on metacognition in mathematics, emphasizing the roles of specific strategy knowledge and metacognitive awareness in children's ability to solve mathematics problems.

WHAT DO WE KNOW?

Research examining the relationship between metacognitive knowledge and achievement indicates that children who are aware of why, when, and how strategies should be used are more likely to be able to use those strategies successfully (Pressley, 1994). Cross-sectional studies have indicated that children develop this knowledge during the elementary school years and that the development of this knowledge benefits children's performance (Justice, 1986). The research on metacognitive awareness in mathematics indicates that children often develop specific strategy knowledge, but frequently do not develop monitoring skills.

Specific Strategy Knowledge

Specific strategy knowledge is metacognitive knowledge about oneself, a strategy, or a task that guides the use of strategies (Pressley, Borkowski, & Schneider, 1987). The bulk of research on specific strategy knowledge in mathematics is correlational. From this research, we know that children's understanding that mathematics is more than simply the application of algorithms and strategies is critical to their success as mathematicians (Garofalo & Lester, 1985). Even as early as the first grade, children who have specific strategy knowledge about when, where, and how to use different mathematics strategies are more able to use those strategies successfully than are students who do not have this knowledge (Carr & Jessup, 1997; Carr, Jessup, & Fuller, 1995).

Furthermore, metacognitive knowledge about strategies seems to be more important for strategies that children are just beginning to acquire. For instance, metacognitive knowledge predicted the correct use of strategies that include the manipulation of objects in the environment at the beginning of the first grade, but not at the end of the first grade or in the second grade (Carr, Alexander, & Folds-Bennett, 1994; Carr & Jessup, 1997). By the end of the first grade and throughout the second grade, the use of covert algorithmic strategies (e.g., decomposition strategies), but not the use of strategies using counters or fingers, was predicted by children's metacognitive knowledge about strategies (Carr et al., 1994; Carr & Jessup, 1995). Thus, an awareness of strategy characteristics, at least with young children, seems to be necessary for newly emerging strategies, but is less of a factor after children have had some experience with these strategies.

Metacognitive Awareness

Monitoring and evaluating one's work and actively processing new information are characteristics of successful learners. For example, older elementary school children who try to understand a mathematics lesson and use specific cognitive strategies (e.g., checking work, applying information, reworking problem, rereading directions and problems, relating new to old information) do better on a mathematics achievement test than children who do not report the use of cognitive strategies (Peterson, Swing, Braverman, & Buss, 1982; Peterson, Swing, Stark, & Waas, 1984). The research on children's metacognitive awareness, however, routinely finds that young and older children often fail to reflect on and evaluate their problem solving. Lester and Garofalo (1982) found that third- and fifth-grade children do little cognitive monitoring or evaluation of their work. Silver, Shapiro, and Deutsch (1993) found that sixth through eighth graders' success in division was compromised by students' failures to interpret the results of their computations. Also, children with learning disabilities, in contrast to younger average students, are less able to predict the number of problems they would solve correctly and are less accurate in the monitoring of problem solving when math skills were controlled (Slife, Weiss, & Bell, 1985). Lester and Garofalo (1982) believe that children do not perceive monitoring and evaluation skills to be necessary for good mathematics problem solving.

Children's failure to critically evaluate their work continues in middle and high school. Middle-school students frequently fail to interpret the numerical answers generated during division and, therefore, fail to produce a correct answer (Silver, Shapiro, & Deutsch, 1993). Silver, Shapiro, and Deutsch (1993) believed that students fail to evaluate because they do not use algorithms with the goal of solving real problems. Similarly, Schoenfeld (1987) found that many high-school-age children do not evaluate their answers or devise plans of action. Instead, problem solving in mathematics is often a system of taking one step at a time without any real understanding of the general principle of the problem. By contrast, Schoenfeld (1987) found that experts tend to plan, evaluate, and verify solutions repeatedly during problem solving.

Taken together, metacognitive research in mathematics is similar to metacognitive research in other domains: Children can benefit from both strategy-specific knowledge and from metacognitive awareness. Metacognitive research in mathematics, however, differs in showing that the use of cognitive monitoring and evaluation frequently do not appear to develop in children even in late childhood.

METACOGNITION FROM A CONSTRUCTIVIST PERSPECTIVE

Research on metacognition in mathematics has yet to provide insight into how metacognitive knowledge functions and develops within the evolving cognitive structures. We believe that by viewing the development of meta-cognition as a part of the construction of knowledge, both the role of metacognition in mathematics and on how metacognition and cognitive structures interact to improve children's mathematics skills and knowledge may be made clearer. The data on metacognition in mathematics, in turn, informs constructivists about aspects of cognitive development that need to be better explained in constructivism. Questions regarding the improvement of problem-solving abilities through reflective thinking, for example, are very interesting theoretically and have significant instructional application as well.

The constructivist interpretation of metacognition that we describe in this chapter does not take the subject matter of mathematics as a given apart from the learner. For constructivists, learning is an active experience in which what is to be learned depends on what faculties the learner brings to the situation. Specifically, students bring to learning prior knowledge, previous experiences, and cognitive and affective traits that may aid or hinder their ability to learn. Further, the constructivist interpretation of metacognition must explain how metacognitive knowledge emerges through children's experiences in learning, but must also explain why it may be difficult or impossible for some students to attain metacognitive knowledge.

The basis for our constructivist understanding of how metacognitive knowledge develops lies in scheme theory. Schemes of action and operation form the basis of conceptual knowledge and provide sites for the modification of this knowledge. Glasersfeld (1980) has interpreted Piaget's idea of a scheme as having three parts: an assimilatory structure, an activity, and an expected result. More recently, other researchers (Steffe, 1997) have incorporated the goal of a scheme into the structure of a scheme in such a way that the three parts interact with the goal.

The first part of the scheme, the assimilatory part, organizes sensory-motor signals to which a child is exposed into a situation of a scheme. These signals, in and of themselves, are not a stimulus for a particular scheme, in a behaviorist sense. They may, however, activate several schemes. What scheme is activated depends on many cues and also on what goal the child might have at any given moment. A child presented with a number of different-colored beads might assimilate the visual signals of those counters to several schemes. If a teacher has asked the child to count the beads and the child takes the teacher's request as a goal to be met, then the child might activate a counting scheme and assimilate those beads into that scheme. The child could also have considered those same beads as something to organize by color or shape, or the child might even have used them to make a picture, depending on the child's goal. Metacognition may come into play here in the goals children have when they encounter a problem. If the view of mathematics held by children is one of rote pencil-and-paper calculation, then when the teacher informs children that they will be doing mathematics, the children will approach any problems with the expectation that pencil-and-paper calculations will be involved. An awareness that mathematics is more than pencil-and paper calculations will increase the chances that children will apply their own creativity and schemes in their mathematics.

The second part of the scheme, the activity of the scheme, takes the situation as input. If children activate a counting scheme and the beads are available to count, the activity part of the scheme will be carried out without difficulty. It may be, however, that the activity of the scheme is blocked, as when a child who cannot yet count a hidden collection of beads is confronted by beads under a sheet of paper. At this juncture, the child may produce subgoals, such as peeking beneath the paper, and modify the activity of the scheme to try to achieve those subgoals, or the child may simply give up and say that the task is impossible. From the perspective of metacognitive theory, the ability to deal with these new and novel situations by altering existing schemes or setting new subgoals is indicative of an awareness of problems occurring when an activity is attempted.

The third part, the expected result of the scheme, is a template against which the actual result produced by the activity of the scheme is compared. The goal of the scheme can modify the expected result, but the goal and the expected result are not the same thing. The goal of a counting scheme might be to find how many beads are in the pile. It might also be to make the teacher happy. But the expected result of the counting scheme is probably a number. Sometimes children start to count a collection of objects, count them all, shake their heads, and recount the collection. Although the goal is to count a pile of beads, the result of their counting actions did not fit the expected result and so they reinitialized their counting scheme. In this case, an awareness that something has gone wrong may set off a reinitialization of the counting scheme or a reevaluation of the entire process. A perturbation was produced that resulted in the scheme being reinitialized.

The Role of Perturbation

Perturbation is a glitch in the smooth functioning of our cognitive processes, that must be neutralized somehow. For example, a perturbation occurs when a child is blocked from using a familiar way of solving a problem or solves a subtraction problem only to find a larger number rather than the expected smaller number. Children may respond to the perturbation in many ways. The perturbation may simply fade away of its own over time, such as when a child simply shrugs his or her shoulders and moves on to the next problem. The perturbation may result in children reevaluating their actions or the activation of a new and different scheme. The perturbation may also result in a modification of the scheme itself, called an *accommodation*, for example, when a child becomes able to count a hidden pile of beads.

Perturbation may be what Wellman (1983) refers to as cognitive feelings: a perception by the individual that something is wrong. For instance, students may feel as though a mathematics problem they have just read makes no sense. Perturbation may occur on an unconscious as well as on a conscious level. On an unconscious level, it can occasion a significant reorganization of one or more schemes onto a higher level. This reorganization can provide students metacognitive insights into commonalities among what had previously been unrelated situations. For example, this can occur when students develop fraction knowledge as a result of experiencing sharing, division, or measuring situations. The insight may be a sudden conscious one within the context of solving a problem, in which case it might provoke an "ah ha" reaction, or it may be unconscious, perhaps occurring while a student sleeps. Because mathematics is a highly generalized, highly abstract construction, this reorganization of schemes onto higher levels of generalization is desirable. The mechanism by which these reorganizations occur is the process of *abstraction*.

The Process of Abstraction

To reflect upon one's own thinking is a major facet of metacognition. The ability of a child to reflect on his or her own thinking can occur only when a scheme is sufficiently abstract so that the child can stand back from the scheme and hold it "at arm's length." A scheme at a low level of abstraction means that the child is completely within the activity of the scheme. This can be seen when children are first exposed to a new strategy that requires the production of a new scheme. They are focused upon the activity of the strategy. Initially, they would find it very difficult to imagine themselves performing the new strategy or what the outcome of the strategy might be. After performing the strategy several times, they might be able to activate the scheme using re-presented records of experience as a situation for the strategy. Later, they might be able to create situations for the scheme. This process of abstraction can occur in several ways.

Glasersfeld (1991) described four ways in which Piaget used the term *abstraction*. We discuss three of them: empirical, reflective, and reflected. *Empirical abstraction* is the process of producing abstractions based on sensory-motor material. It is this sort of abstraction that children are being asked to perform when they are shown many examples of triangles by their teacher. "Oh," they might think. "What do all these examples have in common?" They would be abstracting from sensory-motor material. Such empirical abstractions can form the basis for conceptual knowledge.

Empirical abstraction also occurs when students learn procedures for performing calculations, but have little or no meaning for the steps of the procedures. They learn procedures to solve particular types of mathematical problems. These procedures can be, and probably are, schemes. The students learn to perform the procedures on certain types of problems, but cannot transfer the procedures to other tasks. Certain calculations are performed: These form the activity of the scheme. A number is produced; this forms the expected result. Students can even learn to perform a procedure to check their answer by reversing the calculations. These actions based on empirical abstractions, however, do not necessarily indicate a metacognitive awareness of the appropriateness of the strategy for the problem or an awareness that the answer may be wrong and should be checked.

A second form of abstraction, *reflective abstraction*, acts at a higher level than empirical abstraction. Rather than making use of sensory-motor material as source material the way empirical abstraction does, reflective abstraction uses schemes and mental operations as source material. One form of reflective abstraction can occur when schemes are organized on a higher level without the awareness of the subject. It can involve a generalization in the assimilatory part or a generalization in the material on which the scheme can act. We see this when students move from merely being able to count actual physical items to being able to count cognitive representations of physical items (Steffe, Cobb, & Glasersfeld, 1988).

The second form of reflective abstraction, what Glasersfeld terms a reflected abstraction, involves the awareness of the student. It is this form of reflective abstraction that results in a reorganized scheme of which the student is aware. It is with the results of this form of reflective abstraction that children are able to reflect upon the process and results of reflection. They are able to re-present the operations of the abstracted scheme.

THE CONSTRUCTION OF SPECIFIC
STRATEGY KNOWLEDGE

With these ideas of scheme theory, perturbation, and abstraction, it becomes possible to see how metacognition might be interpreted in constructivist terms. Specific strategy knowledge regarding when, where, and how to use a strategy results from students re-presenting the experiential records related to the use of the strategy. But it is more than that. Whereas the records of experiences of specific strategy use may allow students to recall specific instances, empirical abstraction of those records results in more of a recognition template that can act as the assimilatory part of a scheme. This will allow a scheme to be called up when appropriate tasks are presented, but does not make it possible to treat the scheme as an object of thought. Rather, such empirical abstractions broaden the range of applicability of a scheme, making possible the activation of the scheme in novel situations. This specific strategy knowledge that develops out of empirical abstraction provides information about the appropriateness of a scheme, and the strategies that emerge from the scheme, for a given situation. This metacognitive knowledge may also guide children to alternative schemes and strategies when circumstances do not allow them to use a familiar and appropriate scheme.

When a scheme becomes abstracted, however, children become able to step back and look at the parts of a scheme. The scheme becomes an object of thought amenable to analysis by itself or by other schemes the child might possess. Thus, a child with an abstracted counting scheme will be able to reflect on that strategy and all of the information related to that strategy. At this point, metacognitive knowledge and awareness really begin to help guide scheme development. Not only will children be able to apply strategies to new situations, but they will also be able to reflect on the strategies and the situations to which the strategies may be applied. This will help evolve extant specific strategy knowledge.

Why is it that simply telling students why, when, and where they should use a strategy does not always allow students to use the strategy in new and appropriate settings? One reason is that children have not acquired the foundational mental operations and schemes that underlie the actions of strategies. If children have not acquired these operations and schemes, then providing information about when and how to use a strategy will be of little use to them. If children have acquired the operations and schemes, however, they will be able to take advantage of specific strategy instruction in that this information will become part of the assimilatory structure of schemes and develop as part of the scheme. Teachers should not look on specific strategic knowledge as distinct from the strategy, but rather as refinement and strengthening of the strategy.

A teacher attempting to encourage the development of metacognitive knowledge related to the use of a specific strategy cannot pour such knowledge into the mind of a student. Teachers instructing metacognitive knowledge may orient students so that they construct knowledge about the strategy that is compatible with that of the teacher. This can occur both by constraining the actions of the students and by orienting them to possibilities of the situation. For instance, knowing that the product of a multiplication of whole numbers should be a large number would make it less likely that a student would treat a small product as a correct answer.

Problems may occur when children do not have sufficient specific strategy knowledge to assimilate a problem to an appropriate scheme. For instance, Carr and Jessup (1997) frequently observed children using a counting-up strategy for the subtraction problem 22 − 3 even though it was not the best choice of a strategy. The children reported that their teacher had taught the strategy to them, telling them that it was "a good way to do math." The scheme that formed the basis for this strategy may have been selected because the counting-up strategy was the last strategy the teacher taught the students. Given their lack of specific strategy knowledge, this experience brought the scheme to a state of activation. In this case, the children could carry out the activity of the scheme procedurally. However, the assimilatory part of the scheme was not sufficiently developed to discriminate between appropriate and inappropriate situations. The children could not reflect on their understanding of the activity and draw conclusions about when the strategy should be appropriately applied. Another factor resulting in this outcome is that these children may be approaching the activity with the goal of doing the task in the way supported by the teacher.

Another outcome of poor specific strategy knowledge and poorly developed schemes is the misdirected use of exploration as an approach to problem solving. Schoenfeld (1992) found this to be particularly problematic in older children. According to Schoenfeld, children fall back on the trial and error "discovery" technique that frequently leads nowhere, primarily because the children had no idea where they need to go. This may happen when no particular scheme resonates to a problem or possibly when many schemes resonate to the problem bringing about a "paralysis of analysis" in which the students seem to be unable to decide which of several schemes might work. This latter case might occur in instances where the teacher

intended the problem to have several possible solutions. This is an unin-
tended side effect of what normally would be considered as good constructivist instruction. However, it can also result when the assimilatory
structures of several schemes lack sufficient discrimination and overlap
inappropriately; that is, the students lack specific strategy knowledge.

THE CONSTRUCTION OF METACOGNITIVE AWARENESS

Research has frequently indicated that children rarely consciously compare
a scheme's actual outcome to the expected outcome (e.g., Schoenfeld,
1987). It is not clear whether children do not evaluate because their
expected outcome is so vague that any outcome is acceptable or whether
they simply do not evaluate any outcome. Metacognitive awareness such as
monitoring arises naturally from comparing the actual result of the activity
of a scheme to the expected result contained within the scheme. If a child
successfully applies her counting scheme to a pile of counters in front of her,
she will obtain the numerosity of the pile. All of the counters before her
have been counted and she uttered a number word as she ran out of
counters. The number word reflects the number of counting acts that she
has performed and is taken as the numerosity of the pile of counters. Suppose
her counting were wildly off, say that she counted by twos instead of
counting by ones. It is crucial that the child monitor her activity while in
the process of counting or realize that the number word she spoke at the
end is far too high to describe the pile.

I (Biddlecomb) documented the development of this monitoring in the
context of counting discrete items called toys within a computer mi-
croworld. The two third-grade students, Jerry and Melissa, had completed
a task in which they counted how many toys were hidden beneath a cover.
They found there were 40 toys hidden. Jerry was asked to place two sets of
linked toys, called strings, underneath a cover, hiding them. He and his
partner Melissa were asked to find out how many individual toys were
beneath the cover.

Protocol 1

Teacher: Jerry, can you put two more fours under there?

Jerry: (Copies two more fours under the large cover for a total of 12
            fours)

T: Okay, now we have two more fours under there. How many toys do we have now?

Melissa: We added two more fours?

T: Yes.

M: I know the answer.

J: (Stares off into the distance and moves his fingers slightly. He moves his lips, but we can't tell what he's saying. He finally speaks.) 58?

T: Good. (To Melissa) What did you get?

M: 48.

T: Now that's different, isn't it? How do you think ...? Now you talk it over and see who's right. (To Jerry) Can you show Melissa how you did yours and maybe she can tell?

J: (Holds up a finger for each pair as he counts by twos) Forty, 42, ...

M: You added 2 more to 40.

J: (Looks over at Melissa as she makes her comment, then continues counting) ... 44, 46, 48 (has four fingers up, pauses and lowers the fingers, then raises them again as he continues to count), 50, 52, 54, 56 (has another four fingers up).

T: Oh, you counted by twos. I see what you're doing. So how many fours did you put under there?

J: Two.

T: Two more fours. How many toys did you have under there?

J: Forty.

T: Forty. And how many did you put with it?

J: Two.

T: Two what?

J: Two fours.

T: Two fours. And how many toys is two fours?

J: (Pauses) Eight.

T: Eight! You counted 42, 44, like that, eight times, didn't you?

J: (Nods)

T: You're supposed to do that for how many more toys? How would
      you do that now? You've got two, four, eight more toys.

J: (Stares off into the distance and silently raises fingers) 56.

T: 56! (Jerry looks sheepish) That's okay! That's okay!

We can see from Protocol 1 that Jerry had difficulty monitoring the
activity of his scheme. Jerry had no difficulty in counting on, by the way.
Jerry realized that he needed to make eight counting acts beyond 40 to
obtain the total number of toys under the cover, but in spite of that
realization, his number word sequence for twos was used in an inappropriate
way. Even with the best efforts of the teacher in Protocol 1 and in subsequent
tasks, Jerry continued to count by twos inappropriately. One hypothesis as
to why Jerry counted in this way is because he had been counting by twos
in tasks prior to Protocol 1, so his number word sequence for twos was
already in a state of activation. Jerry persisted in his counting by twos despite
the teacher prompting Jerry to think about the two sets of four items he put
under the cover. In addition, the expected result of Jerry's counting scheme
was a number word, but he had no way of determining whether or not that
expected result was reasonable without uncovering the toys and counting
the visible toys by one.

To monitor the activity of a scheme while in the activity requires a certain
interiorization of the scheme. In Protocol 1, Jerry would have needed to
listen to the number words he was saying even as he said them to realize
that he was counting by twos. In a teaching episode with Jerry and Melissa
a week later, we were able to see Jerry exhibit the monitoring lacking in
Protocol 1. Again, the students were counting strings of four as they did in
Protocol 1. They had just placed six strings of four under a cover, for a total
of 24 toys.

Protocol 2

Teacher: That's a big cover. How many toys were under there?

Melissa: 24.

T: Right, 24 toys. What I'd like to do is.... Melissa, can you make three more copies of that string (a string of four) and put them under the cover?

M: I know how many will be there.

T: With three more copies?

M: Thirty-six.

T: Wow. (To Jerry) How many do you think will be under there?

Jerry: Thirty-six.

T: How do you know?

J: I already had 24, so I'd have 26, 20- ... , no wait. (Puts up a finger in synchrony with saying the number word) 24, 25, 26, 27, 28; (folds down his fingers) 29, 30, 31, 32; (folds down his fingers) 33, 34, 35, 36.

It is not clear exactly why Jerry monitored in this situation. Jerry may have taken advantage of Melissa's answer of 36 to help him in the use of his counting scheme. In this instance, Jerry probably counted the toys on his own, but used Melissa's answer as a way of checking his own answer before he said it. This helped Jerry refine the expected result of his counting scheme. Jerry began to count on by twos from 24 but stopped himself and reorganized the task as a situation for counting by ones when he realized that he would not be able to meet the expected result of 36 by counting in three sets of two. It may also be that Jerry reached the answer of 36 independently of Melissa and that the monitoring that occurred when Jerry justified his results took place because Jerry became aware that he was not repeating the same counting sequence as before.

Protocols 1 and 2 provide examples of our suggestions for encouraging reflective thinking in mathematics. For purposes of encouraging reflective activity, heterogeneous grouping seemed to have been helpful in this instance and may be helpful in others. Melissa's answer provided Jerry with confidence in his own answer. This has to be balanced against the person-alities of the students involved and the fact that if the schemes possessed by the students of the group are at different levels, then the explanations of the students with more powerful schemes may not be understood by others.

Verbalizing their reasoning was also helpful in this case. By actually counting aloud in this case, Jerry was able to hear himself counting, which provided the occasion to reorganize the task as a situation for counting by ones. By asking students for explanations or encouraging students to explain their results to their group partners, teachers can provide students with opportunities to hear their own explanations and monitor their own reasoning.

Research has indicated that children rarely evaluate for an expected outcome (e.g., Schoenfeld, 1987). The failure of children to check for an expected result decreases the chances that perturbation will occur. For example, in the case of the students in Schoenfeld's study, an appropriate expected result to the problem of dividing students up among buses would be a whole number. Schoenfeld found that 29% of the students simply calculated the long division and reported the answer of 32.12 without realizing that there is no such thing as .12 of a bus. Only 23% of the students appeared to evaluate the logic of the resulting answer and correctly rounded the answer down to 32. Schoenfeld's work indicates that most students never evaluate whether their calculated answers to problems make sense in the real world. When children fail to evaluate an expected result they will not reevaluate the appropriateness of the activated scheme; nor will they search out more appropriate schemes or make accommodations in the scheme they used. In this case, asking children to verbalize their reasoning may have elicited a recomparison of the actual result with the expected result of the scheme and bring about perturbation and the realization that in some cases fractional results are impossible: Individual students cannot be split up among buses.

The fact that children appear to be checking their work does not mean that they are metacognitively aware. Nor does it indicate that children have a well-developed understanding of what it means to justify an answer. Checking procedures are a specific instance of the more general idea of justification. If an answer is called into question, the understanding of the student would be revealed more by the justifications he or she gives than by the mere fact that the answer was correct. Answers may be justified by merely reversing the calculations, which may be a rote procedure or a product of the understanding of the relationship between addition and subtraction. There is more to checking an answer, however, than repeating or reversing the calculations. Students also need to justify their answers based on the reasoning they used to determine which calculations would be performed. It is the ability to check their answer using abstract reasoning for their choice of strategy that indicates that children truly understand what they are doing.

SOCIAL CONSTRUCTIVISM: HIGHER LEVEL THINKING IN MATHEMATICS

At one point, Vygotsky wrote, "Any higher mental function necessarily goes through an external stage in its development because it is initially a social function" (as cited in Wertsch, 1985, p. 62). Therefore, mathematical schemes and related metacognitive knowledge are constructed through social interaction. As shown in Protocols 1 and 2, social interactions with others can provide a site for monitoring. Students can experience monitoring through others' critiques of their own reasoning and through hearing others voice the same reasoning. Social interaction can also promote the construction of specific strategy knowledge in that when children discuss their approaches to problem solving they will likely think about and report information about how, why, and when a strategy should be used and how the strategies are tied to the underlying schemes.

Social interaction can either hinder or facilitate the development of reflective thought and children's construction of mathematical knowledge. If the teacher believes that mathematics is the rote application of algorithms, then he or she will teach simple procedural algorithms without concern for the development of schemes to guide the activities of the procedure or strategy. In contrast, when a teacher views the instruction of mathematics as the development of schemes for mathematics, then he or she will present mathematics as a series of problems to be solved through reflection on the problem and the potential ways in which the problem can be solved.

We believe that a developmental theory of metacognition in mathematics should include explanations of how social interaction facilitates or stymies the development of metacognitive knowledge. The research, in particular, needs to focus on the interactions among children and between children and adults. With the exception of work by Brown (1997) on the collaboration of adults and students in the development of reflection, there is a dearth of this type of research. The studies discussed here have examined these interactions, and fewer studies have examined them from a constructivist perspective.

Peers

With regard to the role of peers in the development of metacognitive knowledge, a growing body of literature suggests that children can prompt each other to reflect on their thinking and that this improves mathematics performance. Steffe and his colleagues (Steffe, 1994) have observed children working in pairs to solve mathematics problems. In these situations, the students would each answer teacher's questions, sometimes using each other's responses as perturbations prompting a reexamination of their own solutions. Other times, there was a competitiveness so that the students would hurry to get an answer for a task. Upon stating each of their solutions, the students would sometimes challenge each other's solutions, causing a reflection on their own solutions.

A study by Artzt and Armour-Thomas (1992) examined the role of metacognition in group problem solving. They found that when solving problems in a group setting, children monitored expected outcomes for each other and informed the group when an outcome was incorrect (e.g., "That doesn't work"). Just being in a group, however, did not guarantee that cognitive monitoring and reflection occurred (Artzt, & Armour-Thomas, 1992). Artzt and Armour-Thomas found that the personalities and attitudes of the participants rather than their ability levels predicted whether children would share metacognitive insights. Participants in groups that worked well together were more likely to be metacognitive in that they attempted to understand, analyze, plan, and verify the problem. Children in groups that did not function as well tended to be high on cognitive activities in that they read the problem and explored, but the exploration tended to be trial and error. Thus, having children work together does not guarantee a better quality of interaction including improved metacognitive awareness. Teachers need to be aware of personality and attitude differences that may help or hinder group interactions.

Why is it that peer groups can foster reflective thinking? It may be that children are better able to reflect on other children's work than on their own. This may happen because the activity part of the scheme may suppress or overwhelm children's abilities to reflect on their own work. It may also be that children become aware of the need to communicate and defend their actions. As children challenge the logic of other children and point out alternative views of a problem, perturbation may result. It is this socially induced cognitive conflict and subsequent perturbation that is believed to cause children to think about what they are doing and to bring to consciousness their understanding of what they are doing. For instance, when children must come up with a plan for solving a mathematics problem in a group they must create a rationale for that plan in order to convince the other children to use the plan. A plan that may seem entirely appropriate to a child on the surface may not stand up to deeper examination by the child and his or her peers. The realization that a once acceptable, logical plan does not hold water may make children realize that a belief they hold about problem solving is not valid.

Teachers

The majority of research has focused on how teachers affect higher level reasoning in mathematics. Unfortunately, the bulk of the research indicates that mathematics classrooms tend to focus on lower order learning instead of higher level, abstract learning (Peterson, 1988). This is particularly true in the early elementary years when classroom instruction in mathematics has traditionally focused on rote memorization of basic facts and the rote application of algorithms. Teachers also rarely instruct children to monitor their work (Moely et al., 1989).

Children's mathematics schemes may be hindered by classroom practices that reinforce mathematics activities but do not provide children with experiences that encourage assimilation or evaluation. Teachers may teach strategies, but there is no guarantee that children will abstract sufficient information about a mathematics strategy or problem to allow them to assimilate new problems into that strategy or to evaluate outcomes. Peterson's (1988) research suggests that teachers need to actively model and instruct cognitive and metacognitive strategies and use small-group cooperative learning to promote children's acquisition of mathematics schemes. By teaching ways to understand problems, activate appropriate schemes, recognize different ways to solve problems, and evaluate expected outcomes, children have been taught to improve their mathematics skills (Cardelle-Elawar, 1992).

CONCLUSIONS

Metacognitive instruction has traditionally been taught by providing children with facts to be learned along with a strategy. Constructivist theory suggests that children must truly understand how this metacognitive information is related to the strategy and to their underlying conceptual knowledge before they can actively and independently reflect on themselves as learners and their mathematical experiences. Metacognition is reconceptualized as an aspect of children's experiences and knowledge as opposed to add-on information. It is through the development of a strong conceptual knowledge base and the strategies and metacognition that emerge from this knowledge that children will become self-regulated learners.

Constructivist theory suggests that teachers need to help students interpret their mathematical experiences. In doing so, teachers can encourage empirical abstraction to take place, allowing the assimilatory part of schemes to become more developed. As children become better able to assimilate their experiences, they will activate the appropriate schemes for the situations. For example, teachers should question students about the commonalities and differences among strategies to elicit specific strategy knowledge. Teachers may also elicit monitoring by having children explain how they got their answers and why their logic is correct. As students abstract the situations, they are able to improve the generality of the assimilatory parts of their schemes and become less dependent on the teacher for this information. For example, when children become aware of the problem type that underlies a given problem, they will be able to activate an appropriate scheme even though they have never worked such a problem in the past.

Furthermore, instruction of metacognitive knowledge and skills may be particularly helpful to students whose schemes are in a transition state. Discussion of where and how a strategy might be applied can help students interiorize the schemes involved with the use of that strategy. Care must be taken, however, because a discussion of a particular strategy may be meaningless to students who are not developing a scheme for the strategy. Thus, teachers need to keep in mind not only the strategy and metacognitive knowledge that is being taught, but also the developing underlying cognitive structures.

Finally, as a cautionary note, there have been instances in which students have developed specific strategy knowledge and metacognitive awareness independent of teacher instruction. This metacognitive knowledge was very idiosyncratic and inconsistent with an adult view of mathematics. One such instance, involving a student named Benny was described by Erlwanger (1973). The focus of Benny's instruction was obtaining the correct answer to problems generated through individualized programmed instruction. Erlwanger interviewed Benny to learn his conception of mathematical concepts. Rather than developing the generalized concepts that most adults would consider as mathematics, Benny had developed a large number of specific rules to solve the problems he was given. Benny showed metacognitive knowledge and awareness in that he could talk about these rules and reflected on why he got incorrect answers. The problem was that the rules were not tied together by any underlying cognitive structure. Benny would therefore modify and change his rules without regard for consistency. He conceptualized mathematics as being nothing but a set of independent rules. Benny's example indicates that an emphasis on procedures and results does not guarantee the development of powerful cognitive structures, even though children may display metacognitive knowledge. We suggest that teachers consider and evaluate children's developing cognitive structures in their instruction.

REFERENCES

Artzt, A. F., & Armour-Thomas, E. (1992). Development of a cognitive–metacognitive framework for protocol analysis of mathematical problem solving in small groups. *Cognition and Instruction, 9*, 137–175.

Brown, A. L. (1997). Transforming schools into communities of thinking and learning about serious matters. *American Psychologist, 52*, 399–413.

Cadelle-Elawar, M. (1992). Effects of teaching metacognitive skills to students with low mathematics ability. *Teaching & Teacher Education, 8*, 109–121.

Carr, M., Alexander, J., & Folds-Bennett, T. (1994). Metacognition and mathematics strategy use. *Applied Cognitive Psychology, 8*, 583–595.

Carr, M., & Jessup, D. (1995). Cognitive and metacognitive predictors of mathematics strategy use. *Learning and Individual Differences, 7*, 235–247.

Carr, M., & Jessup, D. (1997). Gender differences in first grade mathematics strategy use: Social, metacognitive, and attributional influences. *Journal of Educational Psychology, 89*, 318–328.

Carr, M., Jessup, D. L., & Fuller, D. (1995, April). *Gender differences in first grade mathematics strategy use: Parent and teacher influences.* Paper presented at the Annual Meeting of the American Educational Research Association, San Francisco.

Erlwanger, S. H. (1973). Benny's conception of rules and answers in IPI Mathematics. *Journal of Children's Mathematical Behavior, 1*(2), 7–25.

Flavell, J. H. (1978). Metacognitive development. In J. M. Scandura & C. J. Brainerd (Eds.), *Structural/process models of complex human behavior* (pp. 213–246). Alphen a.d. Rijn, Netherlands: Sijthoff & Noordhoff.

Garofalo, J., & Lester, F. K. (1985). Metacognition, cognitive monitoring, and mathematical performance. *Journal of Research in Mathematics Education, 16*, 163–176.

Glasersfeld, E. V. (1980). The concept of equilibration in a constructivist theory of knowledge. In F. Benseler, P. M. Hejl, & W. K. Koeck (Eds.), *Autopoiesis, communication, and society: The theory of autopoietic systems in the social sciences* (pp. 75–85). Frankfurt: Campus Verlag.

Glasersfeld, E. V. (1991). Abstraction, re-presentation, and reflection: An interpretation of experience and Piaget's approach. In L. P. Steffe (Ed.), *Epistemological foundations of mathematical knowledge.* New York: Springer-Verlag.

Justice, E. M. (1986). Developmental changes in judgments of relative strategy effectiveness. *British Journal of Developmental Psychology, 4,* 75–81.

Kuhn, D., Garcia-Mila, M., Zohar, A., & Anderson, C. (1995). *Strategies of knowledge acquisition.* Monographs of the Society for Research in Child Development, 60(4245).

Lester, F. K., & Garofalo, J. (1982, March). *Metacognitive aspects of elementary school children's performance on arithmetic tasks.* Paper presented at the Annual Meeting of the American Educational Research Association, New York.

Moely, B. E., Leal, L., Hart, S. S., Santulli, K. A., Zhou, Z:, McLain, E., & Kogut, D. (1989, March). *A developmental perspective on teachers' cognitions about memory strategies and metacognition in classroom teaching.* Paper presented at the Annual Meeting of the American Educational Research Association, San Francisco.

Pellegrini, A. D., Galda, L., & Flor, D. (1996). *Relationships, individual differences, and children's use of literate language.* Unpublished manuscript.

Peterson, P. L. (1988). Teaching for higher order thinking in mathematics: The challenge of the next decade. In D. A. Grouws & T. J. Cooney (Eds.), *Perspectives on research on effective mathematics teaching* (pp. 2–26). Reston, VA: National Council of Teachers of Mathematics.

Peterson, P. L., Swing, S. R., Braverman, M. T., & Buss, R. (1982). Student aptitudes and their reports of cognitive processes during direct instruction. *Journal of Educational Psychology, 74,* 535–574.

Peterson, P. L., Swing, S. R., Stark, K. D., & Waas, G. A. (1984). Students' cognitions and time on task during mathematics instruction. *American Educational Research Journal, 21,* 487–515.

Polya, G. (1957). *How to solve it.* Princeton, NJ: Princeton University Press.

Pressley, M. (1994). Embracing the complexity of individual differences in cognition: Studying good information processing and how it might develop. *Learning and Individual Differences, 6,* 259–284.

Pressley, M., Borkowski, J. G., & Schneider, W. (1987). Cognitive strategies: Good strategy users coordinate metacognition and knowledge. In R. Vasta (Eds.), *Annals of child development* (pp. 80–129). Greenwich, CT: JAI.

Schneider, W., & Pressley, M. (1989). *Memory development between 2 and 20.* New York: Springer-Verlag.

Schoenfeld, A. H. (1987). What's all the fuss about metacognition? In A. H. Schoenfeld (Ed.), *Cognitive science and mathematics education* (pp. 189–215). Hillsdale, N.J.: Lawrence Erlbaum Associates.

Schoenfeld, A. H. (1992). Learning to think mathematically: Problem solving, metacognition, and sense making in mathematics. In D. A. Grouws (Ed.), *Handbook of research on mathematics teaching and learning* (pp. 334–370). New York: MacMillan.

Silver, E. A., Shapiro, L. J., & Deutsch, A. (1993). Sense making and the solution of division problems involving remainders: An examination of middle school students' solution processes and their interpretations of solutions. *Journal of Research in Mathematics Education, 24,* 117–135.

Slife, B. R., Weiss, J., & Bell, T. (1985). Separability of metacognition and cognition: Problem solving in learning disabled and regular students. *Journal of Educational Psychology, 77,* 437–445.

Steffe, L. P. (1994). Introduction to this special issue: Mathematical learning in computer microworlds. *Journal of Research in Mathematics Education, 8,* 85–86.

Steffe, L. P. (1997). *A framework for establishing a mathematics of children.* Manuscript in preparation.

Steffe, L. P., Cobb, P., & Glasersfeld, E. V. (1988). *Construction of arithmetical meanings and strategies.* New York: Springer–Verlag.

Wellman, H. M. (1983). Metamemory revisited. In M. T. Chi (Ed.), *Trends in memory development research* (pp. 31–51). Basel, Switzerland: Karger.
Wertsch, J. W. (1985). *Vygotsky and the social formation of mind.* Cambridge, MA: Harvard University Press.

5

Knowing How to Write: Metacognition and Writing Instruction

Barbara M. Sitko
Washington State University

Metacognition in writing has stimulated much research and teaching interest in the past decade. The 1980s saw a shift of attention from product to process, marked by the publication of the Flower and Hayes cognitive process model of writing (Hayes & Flower, 1980) and Bereiter and Scardamalia's (1987) comprehensive research program. Both research initiatives emphasized the differences between the composing processes of experts, or more experienced writers, and novices, or their less experienced counterparts.

From this research were derived both specific objectives for instruction and principles for designing instructional methods. Programs of research have followed traditional lines of cognitive psychology, beginning with the identification of processes of more skilled writers, construction of a tentative model, testing of the model, design of instructional applications based on the models and theories, and, finally, testing of these applications.

This chapter outlines these developments, describes the models and their components in some detail, and provides examples of how these findings have been disseminated in instructional programs. My intent is to present educational psychologists, teacher educators, and teachers with detailed descriptions and relevant information about work on metacognition and writing, so that a clear direction for instructional methodology emerges.

WHAT DO WE KNOW FROM RESEARCH?

Research centers that have supported the majority of the explorations into metacognition and writing are the Center for the Study of Writing and

93

Literacy at Berkeley and Carnegie Mellon University (Flower, 1994; Flower & Hayes, 1981; Flower, Hayes, Carey, Schriver, & Stratman, 1986; Flower, Wallace, Norris, & Burnett, 1993; Higgins, Flower, & Petraglia, 1992; Peck, Flower, & Higgins, 1995; Penrose & Sitko, 1993), the Ontario Institute for Studies in Education (OISE; Bereiter & Scardamalia, 1982; 1987; Bracewell, 1983), and Michigan State University Center for the Institute for Research on Teaching (Englert, Raphael, Anderson, Anthony, & Stevens, 1991). Most of the work reported in this chapter was developed in these centers. In the United States, instructional principles and methods have been developed primarily in The National Writing Project, headquartered in the University of California at Berkeley, a long-term effort presently comprising about 120 national programs. Both primary research and instructional applications were addressed by OISE, where work is currently being conducted on a Computer Supported Intentional Learning Environment (CSILE), described later in this chapter. The Michigan State Center supported Cognitive Strategy Instruction in Writing (CSIW), a 1-year project with an emphasis on cognitive instruction and metacognitive learning.

Researchers in writing have generally followed the definitions of metacognition initiated by Flavell and Wellman (1977) and elaborated by Brown (1987). These definitions include knowledge of the task and one's own cognitive resources, and monitoring, or the ability to control and regulate one's own thinking. In addition, two content areas of knowledge are discriminated: (a) *process knowledge*, such as setting goals, evaluating goal progress, and making necessary adjustments; and (b) *product knowledge*, such as awareness of text types, structures, and organization. Process research makes distinctions between declarative or factual knowledge and procedural or strategic knowledge. Process cognitions include beliefs about competence, motivation, affect, and strategies. Product knowledge includes not only knowledge of models, paragraph development, and sentence development, but, increasingly, the function and purpose of a text in a defined social context, written for a specific purpose and particular audience.

Conceptually, writing is closely linked to reading, and some research in writing instruction resembles work on metacognition and reading. The two activities obviously inform each other. Writers read their texts and often construct texts from sources that they have read. While reading their own texts during composing, they exhibit the same moves as when reading the texts of others, such as backtracking to aid comprehension and building a representation in memory. This granted, the primary focus of writing research has been on the production of texts rather than on their comprehension. The one area where the two activities interface most notably is in revision, particularly revision involving peer review or editing. This research is reviewed later in the chapter.

Reading research and writing research blend to inform some instructional applications. For example, Bereiter and Scardamalia's (1987) procedural facilitation (described later in this chapter) is designed to reduce the load on short-term memory, as is Flower's (1994) collaborative planning. Both methods resemble reciprocal teaching of reading (Palincsar & Brown, 1984), in which demands on short-term memory are reduced through the use of verbal cues and/or partners to assume the function of monitoring text planning and organizing. In such ways, reading and writing are closely related in research and instructional design, just as they are in construct, mental activity, and school curricula.

Models of the Writing Process

The most frequently cited model of composing processes results from the Flower and Hayes (1981) research into the writing of experts and novices. From think-aloud protocols, Hayes and Flower (1980) discriminated three major processes, which they call planning, translating, and reviewing (see Fig. 5.1). This empirical description closely resembles earlier theoretical work into the "stages" of writing classified as prewriting, writing, and rewriting (Rohman, 1965). However, the Flower and Hayes model modifies and specifies the crucial processes in two important ways. First, interactivity is emphasized. Symbolized by the arrows in the visual representation of the model, interactivity shows that writing is a recursive rather than a linear process, a finding that had been suggested by early process research (Emig, 1971).

The second important way in which the Flower and Hayes model specifies the writing process is its explicit identification of subprocesses. The planning process includes three subprocesses: *goal setting, generating,* and *organizing.* The three subprocesses are also highly interactive and may come into play at any time during composing. Goal setting includes both establishing a purpose and short-term goals, such as providing an example. Generating describes development of ideas and content, whereas organizing refers to how writers arrange their content into a coherent structure. *Translating* is the Flower and Hayes term for transforming ideas into written text. Working memory is consumed by this process, but with practice, translating can become more automated.

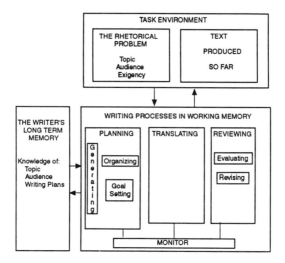

FIG. 5. 1. The Hayes and Flower model of the writing process. From *Cognitive Processes in Writing* edited by L. W. Gregg and E. R. Steinberg, 1980, Hillsdale, NJ: Lawrence Erlbaum Associates. Copyright © 1980 by Lawrence Erlbaum Associates. Reprinted with permission.

Reviewing is the process in which writers reexamine what has been written and compare it to their internal representation of intended text. The two subprocesses identified here are evaluating (comparing the text to criteria) and revising (the rewriting and restructuring of text). The identification of a monitor to manage these processes is crucial to metacognitive research, because the monitor represents the conscious control and regulation of processes exercised by the writer. Because processes are recursive, planning may be invoked during editing, or reviewing may serve to help organize. The monitor represents metacognitive awareness of how and when to invoke strategies appropriately.

In their exploration into the composing processes of both young and older children, Bereiter and Scardamalia (1987) distinguish two modes that discriminate between experts and novices: *knowledge-telling* and *knowledge-transforming*. Distinguishing a "psychology of the natural," from a "psychology of the problematic" (p. 5), the two modes attempt to account for the texts habitually produced by younger and older children.

Knowledge-telling results in a plan and a text that is primarily a list. Calling on linguistic resources derived from the ordinary social experience of conversation, knowledge-telling is an easily acquired writing strategy used by novice writers who simply recite what they know about a topic in a relatively free associationist manner. The process talk of such a writer is marked with verbalizations, such as "What else can I say?" The model can be accurately used to describe developmental changes, with 10-year-olds consistently conforming to the knowledge-telling model and 12-year-olds beginning to show signs of conceptual planning.

Knowledge-transforming enables the writer to "accomplish alone what is normally accomplished only through social interaction—namely the reprocessing of knowledge" (Bereiter & Scardamalia, 1987, p. 5). Knowledge-transforming is a strategy demanding mental effort, engaging the writer in metacognitively guided planning, audience considerations, problem solving, and diagnosing. What distinguishes these more mature patterns is that they involve conscious control over parts of the process that are ignored by the less mature writer. This distinction provides an important principle for analyzing patterns of development and in designing instruction.

Furthermore, Bereiter and Scardamalia (1987) use the term *procedural facilitation* to describe "routines and external aids designed to reduce the processing burden involved in bringing additional self-regulatory mechanisms into use" (p. 253). These simplified routines are introduced as external supports, usually in the form of cards with statements prompting children to reconsider their text (e.g., "People won't see why this is important" or "I'd better say more"). Designed as methods that will help children acquire rules through their own activity, the prompts need to be gradually incorporated into the students' own processes.

Expert–Novice Differences

Whereas little discrimination between skilled and unskilled writers can be made on the basis of intelligence, academic achievement, or motivation, distinction can be identified in a number of process areas and in knowledge of text structure (Benton, Glover, Kraft, & Plake, 1984). For example, skilled and unskilled writers at the same grade level differ in the amount of writing they have been required to produce in academic settings, with more skilled writers required to write more (Mazzie, 1987).

While planning, experienced writers appear to be able to translate high-level goals into subgoals and to develop strategies for handling the overload on working memory by embedding solutions (B. Hayes-Roth & F. Hayes-Roth, 1979). The generation of subgoals appears to be dynamic rather than pre-established (Matsuhashi & Gordon, 1985), so that the end product is more likely to be surprising to an experienced writer than to a novice. The planning episodes of more experienced writers consider larger rhetorical elements such as overarching purpose, audience needs, and genre conventions (Bereiter & Scardamalia, 1987; Flower & Hayes, 1981).

Revising, likewise, appears to differ between more and less experienced writers. Experienced writers are better at both detecting and diagnosing problems in texts written by others (Flower et al., 1986) and in texts of their own making (Sitko, 1992). Less experienced writers define revision as word and sentence-level change (Matsuhashi & Gordon, 1985; Nold, 1981; Sommers, 1980), and although they can be taught to look for other text difficulties, less experienced writers often decide to leave potential problems in their texts (Fitzgerald & Markham, 1987; Sitko, 1992).

Editing, which was the emphasis of many school writing curricula prior to the influence of cognitive psychology, is often represented in the form of sentence correction exercises. Young writers commonly report seeking adult help while editing, most often from older family members (Raphael, Englser, & Kirschner, 1989) rather than from instructors. Their exaggerated attentiveness to this step may be a natural adaptation to the school context, particularly the feedback they receive and the instructional emphasis on assessment (Applebee, 1984). Older writers and writers in nonschool contexts, in comparison, establish a variety of personal purposes for writing, take into account the needs of different readers, and take advantage of conventions of the genre they have selected.

In summary, inexperienced writers fail to search their memories or their environments for help in generating content; they organize what they write primarily into lists; they do not identify audience as a crucial rhetorical influence on their purpose and goal, nor do they review globally or consider reader needs as criteria for rewriting. They appear to lack awareness that memory search, organization guided by purpose, and attention to the readers are required for effective writing. Heightening awareness of these specific areas has guided instructional strategy design and research.

Methodologies and Their Impact

Writing research methodologies have followed the patterns established in cognitive science and in educational psychology. Most notable are the introspective methods of think-aloud protocols and interviews, which were developed first as research methodologies and have now become part of instructional design. Instructional design researchers have taken into account the cautions about introspective methods but have found these methods to be the most practical techniques, both for identifying primary processes and for studying the effectiveness of instructional applications. Researchers often note the positive effect on instruction of thinking aloud as a form of self-talk. All of the studies reported here use introspection, online thinking aloud protocols, retrospective interviews, or questionnaires.

Researchers are appropriately cautious about their conclusions, noting that measures of reflective talk can be misleading. Reflective talk is likely to occur under difficult or unfamiliar task conditions. When all is going smoothly, heightened awareness helps us to keep track of goals and progress, and we may not need verbal reflection (Flower, 1994). But as researchers incorporate reflective talk in the design of instructional strategies, they note that, in general, students do what they say (Raphael et al., 1989; Sitko, 1992).

Thus, methods of cognitive research, verbal protocols, and retrospective interviews have become significant tools in the design of instruction. The following section on instructional strategies shows that the most common method for describing writing process strategies is verbal thinking aloud, either modeled by a teacher or monitored by a trained conversation partner. Modeling is used to demonstrate how to plan, invoke a wide range of search strategies, mentally rehearse ideas and images, talk with others to gain information, and use planning methods such as brainstorming or freewriting to generate content.

HOW DOES STRATEGY INSTRUCTION WORK
IN THE CLASSROOM?

In the previous section, I discussed findings from research into the processes of less experienced (novice) and more experienced (expert) writers. Comparison of the two kinds of writers, using the Flower and Hayes model, yields several points at which strategic instruction can be designed. Experienced writers have a repertoire of strategies, a large "tool box," from which to draw appropriate actions. Younger and less experienced writers have not yet developed this repertoire, and may even have mistaken notions of how writers work. Thus, the principles underlying strategy training for less experienced writers include reducing the load on the writer's short-term or working memory, redefining tasks, and aid in setting goals and subgoals. Educational interventions and writing curricula must be designed to cue appropriate strategy use related to planning, drafting, revising, and editing.

The assumptions that underlie strategy training in writing are restatements of the Flower and Hayes model applied to instruction. First, writing is a complex process that must be regulated by writers themselves. The high level of interactivity among the subprocesses argues for considerable "artfulness" in managing them. Second, planning involves self-questioning strategies designed to identify an audience, determine purpose, activate background knowledge, and organize brainstorming ideas. Third, drafting involves gathering ideas generated in planning, translating them according to audience and purpose, including and expanding relevant ideas, and discarding irrelevant ones. And last, revising involves reading from the point of view of the intended audience and purpose, making and executing plans to add, delete, substitute, and modify text. All of these activities receive the attention of experienced writers, and all are apt targets for instruction. In addition to needing practice in the activities, students need writing curricula that cue these activities appropriately for their age and for their work in progress.

It should be evident that writers themselves must develop metacognitive knowledge and strategies for planning, organizing, drafting, revising, and editing. Strategy instruction is considered metacognitive only when it actively engages students in understanding their own learning (Bereiter & Scardamalia, 1987; Brown, 1987; Flower, 1994). Instruction in metacognitive awareness and control of writing has focused on cognitive processes, specifically, planning and revising, on text structure knowledge, and on the social context.

Where Should Strategy Instruction Begin?

Before looking at actual interventions, it may be instructive to pause a moment to consider what beliefs and practices students may need to "unlearn." Research into school writing practices has unearthed some discouraging findings, indicating that students have much to unlearn and that schools provide little incentive to develop writing expertise. Applebee's (1984) extensive study of writing in American schools echoes the findings of a similar earlier study in the United Kingdom (Britton, Burgess, Martin, McLeod, & Rosen, 1975). Most of the writing done by students is designed to convince the teacher that they have learned content that has been presented. The form of this writing is often a short-answer response on a test. Writing of even paragraph length is rarely demanded, and when it is, it is usually produced in one class period, first and final drafts included. Summary is called for, not analysis. Assessment practices appear to penalize students who make unsuccessful attempts at more difficult analytic tasks as opposed to practicing the easier and more familiar patterns. Although students successfully learn popular school formats such as the book report and lab report, they appear to learn a formula for producing writing for different classes and write for an audience of one, the teacher.

Applebee's study does not present a wholly bleak picture; it also provides some positive indicators of student learning ability, many of which reflect research on metacognitive learning. Students appear to be efficient language learners, able to vary their processes to meet the demands of different contexts and different teachers. For example, revisions become more frequent as writing becomes more demanding, and more experienced writers build arguments around a small number of points where the less experienced provide a single long list. Younger students master the narrative form early and successfully embed it in assignments that call for analysis. Students ask for feedback and help, notably from family members. To some extent, then, students naturally control and regulate how and when they use strategies. Instruction in new or unfamiliar strategies can be enhanced by helping them imagine the conditions under which they would use the strategy and helping them reflect on how they might evaluate its usefulness and incorporate what works for them.

Two Extended Examples of Metacognitive Instruction

Applebee's (1984) list of needed skills coupled with the extensive list of unproductive habits may be daunting, but several lines of instructional research are addressing aspects of these problems. Two extended examples, one from elementary education and one from secondary, will serve to illustrate the complexity of writing instruction based on metacognitive learning. The two studies are similar in joining knowledge of text structure to knowledge and practice of writing processes.

Cognitive Strategy Instruction in Writing (Englert et al., 1991) emphasizes cognitive instruction and metacognitive learning through combinations of strategies. Principles that underlie the development of instruction are an emphasis on the role of dialogue in writing development (Vygotsky, 1978; Wertsch, 1980), scaffolded instruction (Tharp & Gallimore, 1988), graduated questions, and procedural facilitation (Bereiter & Scardamalia, 1987), and transforming solitary writing into a collaborative activity (Nystrand, 1989). The program employs direct explanation of writing strategies and modeling of their use, daily writing with topics usually selected by students, use of procedural facilitation in the form of think-sheets, peer review and feedback, frequent writing conferences, and publication of student papers.

Englert et al. (1991) evaluated the effectiveness of these instructional features coupled with the development of students' knowledge of the writing process and the role of expository text structures. The study involved 183 students in Grades 4 and 5 at 12 schools. Students were drawn both from regular programs and from learning disabled programs and were randomly assigned to control or strategy instruction groups. A posttest required students to write an explanation, a comparison–contrast, and a third paper on a self-selected topic exhibiting their own expertise. Results indicated that the papers of the cognitive strategy group were superior to the control group when judged holistically and by primary trait (a method in which characteristics of the particular genre are assessed). Readers found that the cognitive strategy writers were also more sensitive to audience needs, wrote better expertise papers, and could describe their planning, writing, and revision processes more explicitly.

In a study that compared the effectiveness of analyzing models versus procedural instruction, Smagorinsky (1991) instructed high school students on how to write definitions and also provided either general writing strategies or task-specific procedural knowledge. The study was based on two premises. First, writing requires knowledge of and control of many kinds of tasks, text structures, and procedures. Second, traditional writing instruction often emphasizes the study of models, well-written exemplars of a particular genre or paragraph structure, such as comparison–contrast or explanation.

Thus, Smagorinsky set out to compare the effectiveness of declarative knowledge of form alone with declarative knowledge of form plus either general procedural knowledge or task-specific procedural knowledge. All groups were taught the elements of a definition (criteria, examples, and contrasting examples) through study of an essay. The models group studied, labeled, and evaluated additional models of definition essays, were provided criteria and exemplars, and evaluated a series of definitions. The general procedures group was taught freewriting and brainstorming to generate the elements of a definition, plus strategies for revision and peer feedback. The task-specific procedures group was taught specific procedures of studying problematic examples to generate the elements of a definition, plus strategies for revision and peer feedback.

Qualitative and quantitative analysis of think-aloud protocols generated during the posttest showed that the group taught task-specific procedures scored significantly higher on two measures: purposeful composing and critical thinking. That is, writers in this group were better able to integrate their ideas purposefully and to anticipate readers' needs than writers in the other two groups. General procedures of brainstorming and freewriting also were more effective than the study of models alone. Smagorinsky (1991) notes that, although the study of models is a common educational practice, students have trouble teaching themselves how to write in the fashion of the exemplars. Students neither learned the structure of a definition nor thought clearly about the ideas they generated. Clearly, although more class time is required, teaching students general prewriting strategies produces better learning than study of examples alone.

Writing Process Interventions

Planning With Procedural Facilitation.   The development of planning abilities appears to be aided by procedural facilitation, which Bereiter and Scardamalia (1987) describe as explicit guides designed to reduce the strain on working memory and encourage a range of activities such as goal setting and problem identification. Although these guides are designed to pull students beyond thinking about what to write, younger children (below age 12) will tend to circumvent their intent and turn the cues into opportunities to generate more text content. Older children and adults, however, respond to facilitations in the form of cards, verbal cues or computer-generated prompts. The Englert (Englert et al., 1991) study cited earlier employed several types of procedural facilitations. Procedural facilitation used in either personal or computerized tutoring has been shown to improve writing (Beach & Eaton, 1984; Burns & Culp, 1980; Daiute & Kruindenier, 1985; Florio-Ruane & Dunn, 1987; Scardamalia, Bereiter, McLean, Swallow, & Woodruff, 1989; Zellermayer, Salomon, Globerson, & Givon, 1991).

Collaborative Planning.   Although most educational interventions that involve collaborative planning have a duration of a few weeks or several papers, some longer projects have been initiated. Flower (1994) reports on a course, Cognition and Rhetoric, built on readings about cognition and students' self-observations of how they learned and reflected on a variety of process techniques.

The primary strategy used in this course was the Planner's Blackboard (see Fig. 5.2). Drawn from the Hayes and Flower (1980) research, the planner uses the metaphor of postings on a chalkboard to draw students' attention to elements typically lacking in learners' representations of the writing process. In addition to content generation, specific elements addressed are audience, genre, conventions, and key point or purpose. Students worked alone at first and later with a partner who functions as a monitor of the planning conversation, eliciting verbal responses and guiding consideration of all rhetorical concerns.

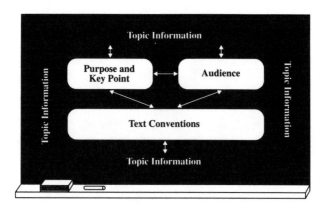

FIG. 5.2. Planner's Blackboard for developing rhetorical plans. Figure from *Problem-Solving Strategies for Writing, 4th Edition*, by Linda Flower, copyright © 1993 by Harcourt Brace & Comany. Reproduced by permission of the publisher.

Results show that writers' reflective statements can be clustered into three areas: affect (including attitude, motivation, emotion, and self-image); context (including history, assumptions, and rhetorical situation); and cognition (including goals, strategies, and metacognitive awareness). Affect, context, and cognition interrelate in different ways at different times in the reflections of the students. For example, students might focus on the cognitive dimension of the map (goals, strategies, intentions, and decisions) while building representations that include affect (being "discouraged and frustrated" at their inability to assign causes to their writing problems) and using social context (their partners' collaboration or conversations with friends) to gain insights.

However, an important caution about reflection is raised in a related study. Reflection, although an important metacognitive outcome, cannot be assumed even when collaborative planning conversation is emphasized and when peers provide a challenging communicative context. Writers' awareness may be raised by working through an intellectual problem with partners, but writers must also evaluate and make decisions about their own thinking (Higgins, Flower, & Petraglia, 1992). Writers might learn to take critical positions on their own ideas by explaining and defending them in the presence of a responsive audience, but Higgins, Flower, and Petraglia's research raises questions about the surety of this outcome.

Looking for how students critically reflected on their own ideas, and whether critical reflection resulted in better writing plans, the authors examined the collaborative planning of 22 college freshmen for explicit evaluation of plans, consideration of alternatives, or justification of suggestions. After coding the transcripts for reflective comments and having them rated holistically for quality, the researchers found a significant correlation between amount of reflective conversation and the quality of writing plans: Students used reflection in metacognitively defensible ways to identify problems, to search for and evaluate alternative plans, and to elaborate and justify ideas. But, they also found that collaboration did not guarantee reflection. Some sessions contained no reflective comments, and some students used collaboration in a way that undermined reflective thinking. The authors concluded that some students' mental representations of collaboration and of the writing assignment may resist influence by instruction.

Revising. Revising practices differentiate clearly between less experienced and more experienced writers (Flower, Hayes, Carey, Schriver, & Stratman, 1986; Matsuhashi & Gordon, 1985), and thus, revising has been targeted by several kinds of strategy instruction. Fitzgerald and Markham (1987) provided direct instruction in revision, explicit practice in detecting where readers might have difficulty, and decisions about where to add or delete text. Writers were two groups of sixth graders, one receiving four 3-day instructions in revision, the other reading good literature. The experimental group was taught how to detect where a reader might have difficulty, as well as how to add and delete information. Reviewing in order to detect differences between intended and instantiated texts intensifies control over the meaning of the text and provides an important metacognitive awareness. Making decisions about whether to elaborate or delete information likewise locates control in the author. Thus students' awareness of how they might improve texts through the revising process was heightened. Revised drafts of this experimental group were judged higher in quality than those of the control.

Revising with procedural facilitation simplifies the processes of reviewing by reducing them to three actions: compare, diagnose, and operate. In one reported experiment (Bereiter & Scardamalia, 1987), 90 children ages 10, 12, and 14 used cards with statements representing phrases that specified the three processes needed for revising text: compare, diagnose, and operate. The procedure of writing a sentence, then stopping to evaluate using one of the phrases, was modeled to show how goal-directed planning is guided by a mental representation of text and audience. Results indicate that children revised more than they had previous to instruction and that they claimed to find writing easier. Evaluations of the text quality were less conclusive, with changes for the better outnumbering changes for the worse, but overall quality showing no difference.

College freshmen are more likely to think of sentence and word-level changes than global meaning changes when asked to revise. An example of a well-focused instructional intervention is the Wallace and Hayes (1991) work on teaching global revision. In this study, one group received 8 minutes of instruction on global revision and another was simply asked to revise a passage. The texts written by students who received the instruction were judged both to be of significantly better quality and to have included significantly more global revision. Wallace and Hayes had discriminated several sources of possible difficulty in younger students, inappropriate task definition, the lack of essential revision skills, as well as the lack of executive or monitoring procedures. Their results appear to confirm their hunch that inappropriate task definition was the culprit.

A related approach to revising and editing a text globally is provided by Schriver (1993), who demonstrates varying ways in which students can learn both to redefine revision as global, whole text, rhetorical, organizational change and to review texts considering the needs of readers. Students assigned the task of revising a nature conservancy brochure on bird-watching quickly discovered, through think-aloud protocols by both experienced and inexperienced bird-watchers, that readers had different needs, were looking at different parts of the text, and were more affected by global features than students had anticipated. Schriver designed a list of prompts to focus students' attention sequentially on whole-text, sections, paragraphs and transitions, sentences, and words. Metacognitively, the method functions to help students discriminate among a variety of possible text problems and attend to them appropriately. By first considering a text globally and rhetorically, from the point of view of the readers' needs, and by later looking at the details of local revision, students can reduce the demands on cognitive resources and carry out multiple revision tasks more efficiently.

Revising With Feedback. Interpreting feedback in order to make decisions about revising is a striking example of metacognition. Writers have to attend to and arbitrate significant and sometimes conflicting voices. The task requires that they construct, out of their own previous understanding of what they wrote and out of their readers' understanding, yet another version of their task and their text. How can teaching help them heighten conscious awareness of the metacognitive task of interpreting the feedback?

Sitko (1993) designed an educational intervention to help students perceive their own texts in new ways and revise appropriately. The intervention used peer collaborative partners, a method called interpretive reading to provide writers with an "online" hearing of readers' constructive processes, and instruction in how to make conscious decisions about revising. Interpretive feedback requires readers to work through a text aloud, stopping periodically to summarize the point and make a prediction about what is likely to come next. This reading provides the writer with a firsthand observation of how readers build a mental representation of a text, as well as how they use textual signals to guide understanding. Thus, writers can test whether their written texts are understood by readers in the same ways as they are represented in the writers' minds. A second instructional element important to the study is designed to show that using feedback to make productive decisions is not an automatic process, but one that embeds a series of smaller decisions, from understanding the feedback to setting a goal. A decision tree abstracted from think-aloud protocols acts as a metacognitive aid in helping writers consider appropriate alternatives (see Fig. 5.3).

Results of several studies (Sitko, 1992) suggest that, given peer feedback in the form of interpretive reading and the metacognitive support of a decision tree as they revise, writers made more "expert" decisions about texts (i.e., revising globally, reorganizing information, and adding appropriate information for readers). Further, both protocols and the interviews suggest that writers learned to consciously represent a broader range of options, test their observations by experimenting with alternative texts, and report the results of their experiments as conscious learning.

When feedback takes the form of a conference with a teacher or tutor, the social context becomes more complex, implicating the relationships of the participants, their respective representations of the task, their goals, and their differing strategies. Social balance must be maintained in this context if teachers are to support and not usurp students' authority over their goals and texts (Bowen, 1993). Conferences provide unique opportunities for reflecting on students' metacognitive awareness of the decisions that underlie writing, with questions such as "How did you decide to start the piece in this way?" and "What other relationship could you establish with your readers?"

The results of these studies of revision with feedback suggest that age-appropriate interventions can be sequenced in instruction to help students develop skills effectively. Young children can be taught how to elicit feedback that educates them about their readers' understanding. Older students can learn to focus attention on the information contained in feedback as an aid to informed decisions. Cumulatively and over time, curricula that help students to understand how readers interact with text can further their revision skill.

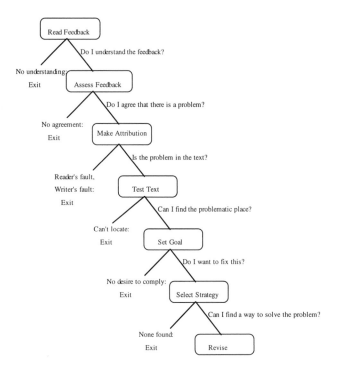

FIG. 5.3. Decision tree of revising after feedback. From *Hearing Ourselves Think*, edited by
Ann Penrose and Barbara Sitko, copyright © 1993 by Ann Penrose and Barbara Sitko. Used
by permission of Oxford University Press, Inc.

Computer-Assisted Writing.   A computer-assisted writing partner
is a special kind of procedural facilitation built to reduce memory overload and guide writing processes. Computer-assisted writing is designed
specifically for the writer who may lack the necessary memory capacity
to mentally represent and may also lack effective metacognitive strategies for memory search to support higher order planning.

Zellermayer et al. (1991) tested the general hypothesis that ongoing
computerized procedural facilitation with strategies and writing-related
metacognitions during writing would improve learners' writing. Planning
prompts consisted of audience and planning questions (e.g., "Do you
want your composition to persuade or to describe?" and "Are you writing
for a reader who's an expert on this topic, or for someone that may need
some basic facts?"). Drafting prompts asked the writers to add more,
explain, or move ideas; and revision prompts requested that writers
reread looking for supporting information. One group of high school

students wrote five essays with unsolicited guides presented by a computer tool (the Writing Partner); a second group received the same guidance but only when invoked by the writer; and the third group received no guidance and wrote with only a word processor. The group that was provided with automatic prompts wrote better essays and could describe their processes more explicitly than could the other two groups. The authors suggest that the unsolicited prompts focused the attention of the writers more specifically and engaged them more closely in the metacognitive activities of goal-directed planning, diagnosis of gaps between the writers' mental representation of the text and the text produced so far, and evaluation of ways to close the gap.

Instructional Costs and Benefits

Teachers who have instructed metacognitive strategies note that they typically require more class time than other types of instruction. Smagorinsky's (1991) intervention for example, required 12 days of instruction. Scardamalia and Bereiter's (1983) procedural facilitations, executed during class time, required not only the writing time but also the time needed to process the questions and prompts. Collaborative planning requires conversational space and time. Moreover, results are not always immediately apparent, with little demonstrable difference in a single paper. Thus, educators find themselves having to make a considerable commitment of time to insure the needed practice before they see improvement.

Metacognitive instruction does demand more of teachers. Instructional planning time is needed for teacher analysis of tasks, both in terms of the knowledge needed and procedures required. However, there is help available. Bereiter and Scardamalia's (1987) suggested steps for task analysis and designing a procedural facilitation follow a cognitive processing approach that both simplifies the task and reduces the information processing load. The method requires, first, identifying a self-regulatory function missing from novice process, such as whole text revision (Nold, 1981) or planning (Flower & Hayes, 1981). Second, the function is described as explicitly as possible in terms of mental operations. For example, revision can be described as comparing, diagnosing, choosing a revision tactic, and generating alternatives. The third step is to design a method of cueing the beginning and end of the process with minimal demands on mental resources. The fourth step is to design external supports such as cards or teachable routines for reducing the information-processing burden of the mental operations.

Also, as the corpus of methods emerges from research on metacognitive instruction and becomes available to educators, individual teacher planning time commitments are reduced. These methods will increasingly become available as they enter the mainstream of textbook curricula. Further, students can be assured that their cumulative repertoire of appropriate strategies will continue to build with each year of instruction. Thus, consistent and careful attention to metacognitive learning will, in the long run, save instructional time. The success of the National Writing Project in creating realistic contexts for writing in the classroom, from purposeful communication to publication for one's peers and wider audiences, bodes well for the future of metacognitive instruction.

HOW DOES STRATEGY INSTRUCTION WORK IN OTHER CONTEXTS?

Making Thinking Visible

The restrictions of the school context, noted by Applebee (1984), can militate against students' experiencing real writing and accumulating the repertoire of strategies needed for life situations. One project that expanded classroom walls, provided for community-based cooperation, and resulted in powerful theory building on the part of participants is the Making Thinking Visible Project (Flower et al., 1993). This experiment in metacognition embedded collaborative planning in an educational cooperative of 32 educators: teachers in Pittsburgh middle and high schools, faculty in community colleges and universities, and community literacy leaders. The cooperative shared ongoing education in writing, collaborative planning, and classroom inquiry; developed writing across the curriculum; became authors and audience for ongoing discovery memos; and cooperated in extensive classroom research.

One of the metacognitively rich sources of information in this study was the discovery memo. These reflective papers captured students' awareness of their own learning, particularly how they connected collaborative planning with their ongoing growth in composing. Students report learning how to use planning decisions, selecting information to support their points, applying their personal purpose as an organizational principle, considering alternatives and making conscious choices, and elaborating ideas with specific detail and examples. Teachers, who also wrote discovery memos to share with each other and the researchers, reported witnessing growth in important verbal skills, such as listening, questioning, answering rather than ignoring the questions of others, and connecting the major planning areas of purpose, audience, and text conventions (Flower et al., 1993, p. 176).

Observation-Based Learning

Research applied explicitly and consistently to the design of classroom instruction across the range of processes from goal-setting to publication is contained in studies from the Research-for-Teaching Seminar Series at Carnegie Mellon University (Penrose & Sitko, 1993). This comprehensive collection of studies of metacognition in the college classroom is based on students' observations of ways in which they can reflect on, monitor, and control their own cognitive processes in writing. The assumption of the collection is that students can "listen in" on their own processes, discuss their observations with peers and teachers, and design for themselves more effective strategies for the classroom and workplace. Learning through self-reflection is an explicit aim of these applications of cognitive strategy research applicable to a variety of learning contexts.

A common workplace writing phenomenon that students may not experience in school is co-authoring. This special type of collaborative writing requires writers to integrate their own representations of the task, their goals, and their strategies with those of other writers. Burnett (1993) provides examples of co-authoring as collaborative decision making and argues that students can become more reflective learners and more effective collaborators if they study examples different from the immediate agreement they might seek. Self-observation provides students with alternative patterns of interaction, such as elaborating a single point, or substantive conflict generating a thorough consideration of alternatives. Reflection on the range of possibilities partners might generate can have a positive influence on the quality of decisions they make, their satisfaction with those decisions, and the quality of the documents they write.

Community Literacy Building

Theories of the social context of writing posit an interaction of readers and writers in a literacy community (Dyson & Freedman, 1991; Nystrand, 1989). Increasing attention is being given to instruction that emphasizes collaboration as a central element in the production of text. Two ongoing undertakings are Toronto's Computer Supported Intentional Learning Environment (CSILE) and Pittsburgh's Community Literacy Center.

Writing, although not the primary objective of CSILE, becomes an important element in this development of young children's learning. The creation of Scardamalia, Bereiter, and colleagues at Ontario Institute for Studies in Education, CSILE is a tool for knowledge transforming (Bruer, 1993; Scardamalia, Bereiter, McLean, Swallow, & Woodruff, 1989). It consists of an information management environment: a student-created database consisting of student work relevant to each topic being studied, electronic linking of students contributions, and a desktop publisher. Using CSILE, students are prompted to activate prior knowledge, use inquiry-based questions, and key search words to retrieve more information from the database. Students create their own links, collaborate in knowledge building, evaluate the associative links, and use language throughout to communicate with each other and with wider audiences. Measures of students' writing skills are beginning to show positive results, with essays demonstrating the knowledge transformation CSILE was constructed to encourage.

A Community Literacy Center on Pittsburgh's north side is the site of a program that explicitly applies metacognitive principles to engage both intercity youth and university students in self-reflective, strategic learning. For 9 weeks, this nonacademic context for writing hosts teenage writers, adult literacy leaders, and college writing mentors (Peck et al., 1995). The program emphasizes collaborative planning methods (Flower et al., 1993) as teens develop a 12-page document on dealing with street life. Four specific strategies are taught: collaborative planning, generating rival hypotheses, decision making by exploring options and outcomes, and revising. A literacy leader presents a 15-minute introduction to each strategy; writers and mentors try it out in pairs and groups, and reflect on its use, effectiveness, and value. Collaboration is intercultural, and, as the teens, mentors, and literacy leaders work together, their strategies for collaboration and problem solving expand to include intercultural issues, language issues, questions of authority, issues of rhetorical power (Flower, 1996). This program is an example of strategic approaches being embedded in the larger purpose of a community literacy agenda designed to support inquiry-based learning, intercultural conversation, and social change.

DOES METACOGNITION BELONG IN WRITING INSTRUCTION?

Writing is a complex activity. Learning how to write is even more complex. Skilled writers have become knowledgeable about planning, drafting, revising, and editing and are practiced in monitoring these processes, invoking them as needed throughout composing. Skilled writers have become proficient in the use of text structures as tools for generating, organizing, and revising texts. Skilled writers are aware of how their texts will function in a particular social context, and they are sensitive to the needs of their readers.

Student writers are not well practiced in controlling the complex interaction of skills required for successful composing. As they mature, and as more complex writing is required, students need regular strategy instruction in the processes of planning, drafting, revising, and editing. They need instruction in how to use appropriate text conventions and how to consider the needs of different readers. More importantly, however, as these more complex strategies are being introduced and practiced, students need regular metacognitive instruction to help them understand their own learning. Metacognitive instruction in how to monitor and control their learning will help them evaluate and integrate strategies into their own repertoire so that they can control the complex cognitive and social processes involved in producing text. Student writers who become knowledgeable about their own cognitions will be able to employ them for a variety of contextual and rhetorical purposes.

It is evident that metacognitive instruction is a natural environment for active learning in writing. It holds great promise for future research and development.

REFERENCES

Applebee, A. N. (1984). *Contexts for learning to write: Studies of secondary school instruction.* Norwood, NJ: Ablex.

Beach, R., & Eaton, S. (1984). Factors influencing the self-assessing and revising by college freshmen. In R. Beach & L. Bridwell (Eds.), *New directions in composition research* (pp. 149–170). New York: Guilford Press.

Benton, S. L., Glover, J. A., Kraft, R. G., & Plake, B. S. (1984). Cognitive capacity differences among writers. *Journal of Educational Psychology, 75,* 727–742.

Bereiter, C., & Scardamalia, M. (1982). From conversation to composition: The role of instruction in a developmental process. In R. Glaser (Ed.), *Advances in instructional psychology,* (Vol. 2, pp. 1–64). Hillsdale, NJ: Lawrence Erlbaum Associates.

Bereiter, C., & Scardamalia, M. (1987). *The psychology of written composition.* Hillsdale, NJ: Lawrence Erlbaum Associates.

Bowen, B. A. (1993). Using conferences to support the writing process. In A. M. Penrose & B. M. Sitko (Eds.), *Hearing ourselves think: Cognitive research in the college writing classroom* (pp. 188–200). New York: Oxford University Press.

Bracewell, R. (1983). Investigating the control of writing skills. In P. Mosenthal, L. Tamor, & S. A. Walmsley (Eds.), *Research on writing: Principles and methods* (pp. 177–203). New York: Longman.

Britton, J., Burgess, T., Martin, N., McLeod, A., & Rosen, H. (1975). *The development of writing abilities*. London: Macmillan.

Brown, A. (1987). Metacognition, executive control, self-regulation, and other more mysterious mechanisms. In F. Weinert & R. Kluwe (Eds.), *Metacognition, motivation, and understanding* (pp. 65–116). Hillsdale, NJ: Lawrence Erlbaum Associates.

Bruer, J. T. (1993). *Schools for thought: A science of learning in the classroom*. Cambridge, MA: MIT Press.

Burnett, R. (1993). Decision-making during the collaborative planning of coauthors. In A. M. Penrose & B. M. Sitko (Eds.), *Hearing ourselves think: Cognitive research in the college writing classroom* (pp. 125–146). New York: Oxford University Press.

Burns, H. L., & Culp, G. H. (1980). Stimulating invention in English composition through computer-assisted instruction. *Educational Technology, 20,* 5–10.

Daiute, C., & Kruindenier, J. (1985). A self-questioning strategy to increase young writers' revision processes. *Applied Psycholinguistics, 6,* 307–318.

Dyson, A. H., & Freedman, S. W. (1991). Writing. In J. Flood, J. Jensen, D. Lapp, & J. R. Squire (Eds.), *Handbook of research on teaching the English language arts*. New York: Macmillan.

Emig, J. (1971). *The composing processes of twelfth graders* (Research Report No. 13). Urbana, IL: National Council of Teachers of English.

Englert, C. S., Raphael, T. E., Anderson, L. M., Anthony, H. M., & Stevens, D. D. (1991). Making strategies and self-talk visible: Writing instruction in regular and special education classrooms. *American Educational Research Journal, 28,* 337–372.

Fitzgerald, J., & Markham, L. (1987). Teaching children about revision in writing. *Cognition and Instruction, 4,* 3–24.

Flavell, J. H., & Wellman, H. M. (1977). Metamemory. In J. R. V. Kail & W. Hagan (Eds.), *Perspectives on the development of memory and cognition,* (pp. 3–33). Hillsdale, NJ: Lawrence Erlbaum Associates.

Florio-Ruane, S., & Dunn, S. (1987). Teaching writing: Some perennial questions and some possible answers. In V. Richardson-Koehler (Ed.), *Educator's handbook: A research perspective* (pp. 13–27). New York: Longman.

Flower, L. (1993). *Problem solving strategies for writing* (4th ed.). New York: Harcourt Brace.

Flower, L. (1994). *The construction of negotiated meaning: A social cognitive theory of writing*. Carbondale: Southern Illinois University Press.

Flower, L. (1996). Negotiating the meaning of difference. *Written Communication, 13*(1), 44–92.

Flower, L., & Hayes, J. R. (1981). A cognitive process theory of writing. *College Composition and Communication, 32,* 365–387.

Flower, L., Hayes, J. R., Carey, L., Schriver, K. A., & Stratman, J. (1986). Detection, diagnosis and the strategies of revision. *College Composition and Communication, 37,* 16–55.

Flower, L., Wallace, D. L., Norris, L., & Burnett, R. E. (1993). *Making thinking visible: Writing, collaborative planning, and classroom inquiry*. Urbana, IL: National Council of Teachers of English.

Hayes, J. R., & Flower, L. (1980). Identifying the organization of writing processes. In L. W. Gregg & E. R. Steinberg (Eds.), *Cognitive processes in writing*. Hillsdale, NJ: Lawrence Erlbaum Associates.

Hayes-Roth, B., & Hayes-Roth, F. (1979). A cognitive model of planning. *Cognitive Science, 3,* 275–310.

Higgins, L., Flower, L., & Petraglia, J. (1992). Planning text together? The role of critical reflection in student collaboration. *Written Communication, 9*(1), 48–84.

Matsuhashi, A., & Gordon, E. (1985). Revision, addition, and the power of the unseen text. In S. W. Freedman (Ed.), *The acquisition of written language: Response and revision* (pp. 126–249). Norwood, NJ: Ablex.

Mazzie, C. A. (1987). An experimental investigation of the determinants of implicitness in spoken and written discourse. *Discourse Processes, 10*, 31–42.

Nold, E. (1981). Revising. In C. H. Frederiksen & J. F. Dominic (Eds.), *Writing: The nature, development and teaching of written communication* (pp. 67–79). Hillsdale, NJ: Lawrence Erlbaum Associates.

Nystrand, M. (1989). A social-interactive model of writing. *Written Communication, 6*, 66–85.

Palincsar, A., & Brown, A. L. (1984). Reciprocal teaching of comprehension-fostering and comprehension-monitoring activities. *Cognition and Instruction ,I*, 117–175.

Peck, W. C., Flower, L., & Higgins, L. (1995). Community literacy. *College Composition and Communication, 46*(2), 199–222.

Penrose, A. M., & Sitko, B. M. (Eds.). (1993). *Hearing ourselves think: Cognitive research in the college writing classroom.* New York: Oxford University Press.

Raphael, T. E., Englser, C. S., & Kirschner, B. W. (1989). Students' metacognitive knowledge about writing. *Research in the Teaching of English, 23*(4), 343–379.

Rohman, D. G. (1965). Pre-writing: The stage of discovery in the writing process. *College Composition and Communication, 16*, 106–112.

Scardamalia, M., & Bereiter, C. (1983). The development of evaluative, diagnostic, and remedial capabilities in children's composing. In M. Martlew (Ed.), *The psychology of written language: Developmental and educational perspectives*, (pp. 67–95). New York: Wiley.

Scardamalia, M., Bereiter, C., McLean, R., Swallow, J., & Woodruff, E. (1989). Computer supported intentional learning environments. *Journal of Educational Computing Research, 5*, 51–68.

Schriver, K.. (1993). Revising for readers: Audience awareness in the writing classroom. In A. M. Penrose & B. M. Sitko (Eds.), *Hearing ourselves think: Cognitive research in the college writing classroom* (pp. 147–169). New York: Oxford University Press.

Sitko, B. M. (1992). Writers meet their readers in the classroom: Revising after feedback. In M. Secor & D. Charney (Eds.), *Constructing rhetorical education* (pp. 278–294). Carbondale: Southern Illinois University Press.

Sitko, B. (1993). Exploring feedback: Writers meet readers. In A. M. Penrose & B. M. Sitko (Eds.), *Hearing ourselves think: Cognitive research in the college writing classroom* (pp. 170–187). New York: Oxford University Press.

Smagorinsky, P. (1991). The writer's knowledge and the writing process: A protocol analysis. *Research in the Teaching of English, 25*(3), 339–364.

Sommers, N. (1980). Revision strategies of student writers and experienced adult writers. *College Composition and Communication, 31*, 78–88.

Tharp, R. G., & Gallimore, R. (1988). *Rousing minds to life: Teaching, learning, and schooling in social context.* New York: Cambridge University Press.

Vygotsky, L. (1978). *Mind in society: The development of higher psychological processes* (M. Cole, V. John-Steiner, S. Scribner, & E. Souberman, Trans.). Cambridge, MA: Harvard University Press.

Wallace, D. L., & Hayes, J. R. (1991). Redefining revision for freshmen. *Research in the Teaching of English, 25*(1), 54–66.

Wertsch, J. V. (1980). The significance of dialogue in Vygotskky's account of social, egocentric, and inner speech. *Contemporary Educational Psychology, 5*, 150–162.

Zellermayer, M., Salomon, G., Globerson, T., & Givon, H. (1991). Enhancing writing-related metacognitions through a computerized writing partner. *American Educational Research Journal, 28*(2), 373–391.

6

Test Predictions Over Text Material

Ruth H. Maki
Texas Tech University

An important aspect of learning in educational settings is deciding when studied material is known. Students must constantly make decisions about their learning of material to decide whether to continue to study the material, to return later to study, or to cease studying because the material is known adequately. I refer to the process of monitoring learning from text as *metacomprehension* (Maki & Berry, 1984). Although metacomprehension is an integral part of education, research on the ability to do this type of monitoring has been fairly recent and sparse. Some of the earliest research on this ability was conducted with children using a comprehension monitoring paradigm (e.g., Markman, 1977) in which children heard text that was missing information, and the investigators noted whether or not the children indicated that they did not understand. Generally, the research showed that children often did not spontaneously report inadequacies in the text, but when direct questions were asked, they showed some understanding that texts were internally inconsistent or inconsistent with general knowledge (see Anderson & Beal, 1995, for a recent report). Although it may be thought that the failure to report inconsistencies in text is confined to immature readers, adult readers are also quite poor at detecting inconsistencies in text (e.g., Glenberg, Wilkinson, & Epstein, 1982).

The error detection paradigm has been useful in showing that people are poor at comprehension monitoring, but it may not be relevant to learning from normal text that is relatively error-free. Thus, this chapter focuses on methods of studying metacomprehension that are closer to what actually occurs in education. After reading error-free text, students need to make judgments about how well they have learned material and how well they will do on a test. Research using paradigms involving such predictions by older students who are presumably mature readers is the domain of this chapter. Unless otherwise noted, the participants in the studies to be reported in this chapter were college students, so the theoretical domain concerns metacomprehension of relatively advanced readers.

CAN STUDENTS MAKE ACCURATE PREDICTIONS

The earliest reports concerning the accuracy of predictions by college students yielded mixed conclusions. Maki and Berry (1984) reported that college students had some ability to predict future test performance over text material, but Glenberg and Epstein (1985) reported that college students' predictions were no better than chance.

Maki and Berry (1984) had students read paragraphs from chapters in introductory psychology texts. After reading each paragraph, students made a prediction rating about how well they would do on a multiple-choice question related to the paragraph. This rating was made in response to the question "How well will you do on a multiple-choice test on the material that you just read?" The scale ranged from 1 (very poorly) to 6 (very well). For students who scored above the median on tests, mean ratings of material related to correct questions were higher than ratings of material related to incorrect questions. Students who scored below the test median did not give differential ratings to material related to correct and incorrect answers. Maki and Berry concluded that better students could make predictions that were more accurate than expected by chance.

At about the same time, Glenberg and Epstein (1985) asked college students to read short paragraphs of text on different topics. After reading each paragraph, they were asked to rate how well they would be able to use what they learned in the text to draw an inference about the central theme of the text. For each participant, Glenberg and Epstein calculated point-biserial correlations between the rating given each text and the performance on that text. They found that the correlations between ratings and accuracy on the inferences were not greater than 0 regardless of whether the students made ratings immediately after reading or following a delay, or whether or not they were familiarized with the types of inference questions. The only judgments that were more accurate than chance were students' postdictions made after they had responded to the inference items.

Although Maki and Berry (1984) reported some accuracy in predictions, the effects were small and limited to the better students. Glenberg and Epstein (1985) reported that predictions were not accurate; only postdictions showed any accuracy. Later, Glenberg, Sanocki, Epstein, and Morris (1987) reported a series of eight experiments in which prediction accuracy was generally not better than chance. One problem with this early research, however, was that generally only one test question per prediction rating was used. In a condition in which Glenberg et al. (1987) used the recognition of four items as the criterion test for each prediction, they did find greater than chance accuracy. The importance of using more than one test item per rating was demonstrated by Weaver (1990). He showed that prediction accuracy was close to 0 with only one test item per prediction, but that it was quite high with four test items per rating. Most research on test prediction accuracy conducted after 1990 has used multiple test items per prediction, and generally, greater than chance accuracy has been observed (e. g., Gillström & Rönnberg, 1995; Magliano, Little, & Graesser, 1993; Maki, 1995; Maki & Serra, 1992a, 1992b; Weaver & Bryant, 1995).

WHAT PROCESSES ARE INVOLVED IN PREDICTIONS?

Making a prediction about performance on a future test after reading text is a complex process that may involve three different types of judgments. First, a student must judge how well he or she has understood the text and how much learning has occurred; however, these judgments may also be based on familiarity with the topic domain. Second, the student must predict forgetting that might result both from the retention interval and from learning other material. Third, the accuracy of predictions will depend on correct knowledge about the nature of the test, including the types of questions and their level of difficulty. Given the complexity of these processes, it is not surprising that prediction accuracy is often low. Accuracy can be limited because of inappropriate use of topic familiarity, incorrect judgments about level of learning, incorrect predictions about the amount of forgetting, or incomplete knowledge about the nature of the test.

Judging Domain Familiarity

It is possible that students do not judge how much they have learned from a text when they predict future performance. They may use their general familiarity with the topic of the text, or what I call *domain familiarity* (Glenberg et al., 1987). If so, then students are not assessing their comprehension or learning of the text. Therefore, whether students have read the texts or not, their predictions of future test performance should be identical.

Prior Research on Domain Familiarity

Glenberg et al. (1987) tested the hypothesis that predictions are based on familiarity with the texts and not on the amount learned from the texts. They tested three groups of students: One group read texts and was asked to rate the familiarity of the central idea from each text, a second group was asked to recall the central point of the text as close to verbatim as possible, and a third group was asked to predict future performance on inferences. When dependent measures were averaged across students and correlations were computed across texts, prediction ratings correlated with familiarity judgments but not with recall. Neither recall nor familiarity judgments correlated with performance on the inference items. Thus, Glenberg et al. concluded that prediction ratings are based on familiarity. However, because familiarity with the central points of the texts was judged after the text had been read, this experiment did not allow a distinction between domain familiarity and familiarity with the text.

In another experiment, Glenberg et al. (1987) manipulated familiarity with the central points of the texts by presenting either verbatim copies or paraphrases of text sentences in advance of reading. Although this affected familiarity with the texts (with higher familiarity in the verbatim condition), it did not affect predictions about future test performance. This suggests that students used domain familiarity and not familiarity with the texts to make predictions.

Glenberg and Epstein (1987) found further evidence for the use of domain familiarity by varying students' expertise. Music majors gave higher prediction ratings to music texts than to physics texts, and physics majors showed just the opposite pattern. Of course, music majors performed better on music passages, and physics majors performed better on physics passages. Therefore, predictions were accurate across domains. However, music students did not accurately predict differential performance across music texts, and physics students did not accurately predict differential performance across physics texts. Thus, Glenberg and Epstein concluded that predictions could be accurate when domain familiarity predicts performance, but they were not accurate when differences in domain familiarity did not predict performance.

Although Glenberg et al. (1987) produced evidence that students use domain familiarity in their predictions, they found that students could not predict performance at greater than chance levels. Thus, from their studies, we do not know whether students rely mainly on domain familiarity under conditions in which predictions are more accurate than chance. Maki and Serra (1992a), who found predictions that were more accurate than expected by chance, also investigated the role of domain familiarity in test predictions. They asked students to make prereading judgments concerning their familiarity with text topics. The prereading familiarity judgments were related to postreading predictions but not to future test performance. However, explicit predictions of performance made after reading were related to test performance. Thus, the students must have been using something more than domain familiarity in making their predictions of performance. In addition, students who read the texts predicted their performance better than students who predicted solely on the basis of the titles and descriptions.

New Experiments on the Use of Domain Familiarity

Ratings of domain familiarity are related to prediction ratings both when familiarity leads to accurate predictions as in the case of differential expertise (Glenberg & Epstein, 1987) and when familiarity is not a valid cue for accurate predictions (Glenberg et al., 1987; Maki & Serra, 1992a). The Glenberg and Epstein finding suggests that the use of variations in domain familiarity may improve students' abilities to predict test performance if domain familiarity is a valid cue for later performance. However, they used a strong manipulation of domain familiarity by using groups having different academic majors.

I conducted two experiments to investigate the use of domain familiarity in text predictions when the domain familiarity manipulation is not so extreme. In the first experiment, I investigated whether reading texts from different domains results in greater prediction accuracy than reading a single text with all parts from the same domain. Students cannot use variations in domain familiarity when they predict future performance on different sections of a single text. However, they can use domain variation in predicting performance over a series of different texts. In the second experiment, I manipulated the utility of domain familiarity as a predictor of future test performance. One group of students read texts having topics that differed in prereading familiarity and the texts resulted in corresponding differences in performance (i.e., domain familiarity was correlated with test performance). A second group read texts having prereading familiarities that were uncorrelated with test performance. If students use prereading familiarity in making predictions after reading, then correlated texts should produce more accurate predictions than uncorrelated texts. If, however, students base their predictions on what they have learned from reading, the correlation between domain familiarity and actual performance may not matter.

Predictions for Multiple Topics Versus a Single Topic. In the first domain familiarity experiment, half of the students predicted their performance over paragraphs from a long single text, and the other half predicted their performance over four shorter texts. In addition, the four text topics produced differential ratings of prereading familiarity, and that familiarity predicted test performance. The main question was whether students would take advantage of the differential prereading familiarity when they made predictions for texts on the different topics. If so, then those students who read texts on different topics should be able to predict their performance better than students who read a single text on one topic.

Four texts on different science-related topics were selected from *Science News.* Each text was divided into four sections of approximately 400 words and each of those sections was further divided into four paragraphs. Four four-alternative multiple-choice questions were written for each of the 16 paragraphs of text. Because these texts contained many details, the majority of the multiple-choice questions tested memory for details.

First, all students rated their familiarity with each of the four text topics. Then, all students read about 1,600 words of text at their own pace. The 24 students who were assigned to the multiple topics condition read the first section (approximately 400 words) of each of the four texts. After each 100-word paragraph, they predicted their performance over the paragraph. Next, they responded to 16 multiple-choice questions from the text, four questions for each of the four paragraphs. The second, third, and fourth texts were then presented and rated in the same way. The order in which the four texts was presented was randomized for each student. In the single topic condition, the procedures were identical except that the 24 students who were assigned to this condition read sixteen 100-word paragraphs from only one of the four texts.

Contingency tables were created to correlate each type of rating with performance for each student. The nonparametric gamma correlation (Goodman & Kruskal, 1954) was used to determine the degree of relationship between the ratings and performance. Nelson (1984) has shown that gamma is the best measure for determining relationships with noninterval data such as ratings. In the multiple topics condition, the prereading familiarity ratings for each text was correlated with test performance for each student. The mean gamma correlation was .418 (SEM = .138), which was significantly greater than 0. Thus, prereading domain familiarity correlated with performance on the four texts.

Predictions were made following each paragraph in both the single and multiple topics conditions. In the multiple topics condition, the predictions for each text were correlated with the prereading familiarity ratings for each student. The mean gamma correlation was .152 (SEM = .156), which was not significantly different from 0. In addition, each prediction rating was correlated with the number of test questions correct for each paragraph. In the multiple topics condition, the mean gamma was .275 (SEM = .092), which was significantly greater than 0. In the single topic condition, the mean gamma was .138 (SEM = .072), which was not significantly greater than 0. Although the relationship between predictions and performance appears to be higher in the multiple topics condition than in the single topic condition, the gammas for these two groups did not differ significantly.

If students use prereading familiarity with texts to predict their performance over those texts, then those students who show the highest relationship between prereading familiarity ratings and test performance should also be the best predictors. Students in the multiple topics condition were split at the median gamma (G = .22) relating prereading familiarity and test performance. The gamma relating predictions and test performance for the high group was .189 (SEM = .098) and the mean for the low group was .361 (SEM = .157). This nonsignificant difference is in the wrong direction to support the idea that prereading familiarity is helpful in predicting performance after reading text. The students whose prereading familiarity better predicted performance did not show more accurate predictions than those students whose prereading familiarity matched their performance more poorly.

These results do not support the hypothesis that students use prereading domain familiarity to predict performance accurately across texts having different levels of familiarity. The topics of the present texts varied in familiarity and topic familiarity was predictive of final performance. This is in contrast to the findings of Maki and Serra (1992a) in which the use of prereading familiarity would not have been beneficial to students because variations in topic familiarity did not predict future performance. Yet, students in the multiple topics condition who could have taken advantage of topic variation did not predict their performance significantly better than students in the single topic condition who could not take advantage of topic variation (although the trend was in the correct direction and the correlation between predictions and performance was significant in the multiple topics but not in the single topic condition). In addition, the correlation between predictions and ratings of domain familiarity was low. Finally, students who should have been better predictors given the relationship between their familiarity ratings and their performance did not predict better than those students who should have predicted more poorly based on their prereading familiarity–performance relationships. Overall, then, there was little evidence that students used variations in their prereading familiarities with text topics to aid them in making accurate predictions.

Manipulating the Relationship Between Familiarity and Performnce.
To investigate further the role of prereading topic familiarity in accurate test predictions, texts were varied in the degree of relationship between topic familiarity and performance: A correlated set of texts produced mean topic familiarity ratings that correlated with actual test performance; an uncorrelated set of texts produced mean topic familiarity ratings that were uncorrelated with actual test performance. If accurate predictions are partially based on domain familiarity, then existence of a correlation between familiarity and performance should increase students' abilities to predict performance.

Twelve 400-word texts from a timed reading series (Spargo, 1989) were used. The topics of the texts were range plants preferred by grazing animals, the design of kitchens, the history of the Virgin Islands, natural and synthetic drugs, controlling insect pests, functions and types of food preservatives, home wine-making, bird migration, the Confederate prison Andersonville, employee evaluation, history and properties of chocolate, and problems with recycling. Each text was divided into two paragraphs containing about 200 words each. Five multiple-choice questions were taken from the reading series, although the three-alternative format was modified by providing four alternatives for each question instead of only three.

First, a pilot study was conducted to create the correlated and uncorrelated sets of texts. Students made prereading familiarity ratings based on short sentences describing the topics of each. Students then read the texts and answered the multiple-choice questions for each text. The mean ratings and proportions correct were determined for each of the 12 texts. On the basis of these mean familiarity ratings and performance, the texts were divided into groups of six correlated and six uncorrelated texts. A Pearson

r correlation was computed between the average performance and the average familiarity rating for the six texts. The correlation of these mean values for the correlated set was +.96, and the Pearson r for the uncorrelated set was -.41. Thus, these two sets of texts are different in terms of the relationship between their prereading familiarity and their difficulty as measured by the multiple-choice test.

Thirty-two volunteer students were randomly assigned to either the correlated texts condition or the uncorrelated texts condition. Before reading the texts, each student made a familiarity rating of the text topic based on short descriptive sentences. Students then read each text and made a prediction concerning their future test performance. Finally, the five multiple-choice questions were presented and answered for each text with the order of texts and the order of questions from a text randomized for each student.

A gamma correlation between the prereading familiarity ratings and performance for each text was calculated for each student. The means of these gammas were .284 (SEM = .092) in the correlated condition and -.211 (SEM = .171) in the uncorrelated condition.[1] These two correlations differed, showing that the relationship between prereading familiarity and performance was successfully manipulated with these two text sets. The mean gamma for prereading familiarity and predictions was .218 (SEM = .154) in the correlated condition and .191 (SEM = .181) in the uncorrelated condition. Neither of these correlations differed from 0, and they did not differ from each other. Thus, postreading predictions were based on something other than prereading familiarity.

The relationship between predictions and test performance was gamma = .379 (SEM = .068) in the correlated condition and gamma = .369 (SEM = .126) in the uncorrelated condition. Although both of these gammas were significantly greater than 0, the difference between them was not significant. Students predicted their test performance equally well whether prereading familiarity was positively correlated with test performance or not.

If students based their test predictions on prereading familiarity with text topics, they should have been more successful in predicting their test performance with the correlated set of texts than with the uncorrelated set. The correlated set of texts did show a positive relationship between familiarity and performance whereas the uncorrelated set did not, yet, there was no difference in the relationship between predictions and performance for

[1]These correlations are lower than those from the pilot study because these correlations were calculated for each student and the earlier ones were calculated from mean ratings and mean test performance on each text.

these two sets of texts. Further, the correlations between prereading familiarity and postreading predictions were not significant in either condition.

Conclusions About the Use of Domain Familiarity

Research both by Glenberg et al. (1987) and by Maki and Serra (1992a) shows that students use domain familiarity in making prediction ratings. However, the experiments already presented show that the ability to make use of domain familiarity and the utility of using domain familiarity did not affect the accuracy of predictions. There was a slight hint that predicting performance on multiple texts on different topics led to more accurate predictions than predicting performance on a single text in that the correlation between predictions and performance was significantly greater than 0 with multiple texts but not with one text. Still, the difference between these correlations was not significant. Moreover, manipulating the correlation between topic familiarity and performance did not affect prediction accuracy. In the two studies just presented, ratings of prereading domain familiarity were not related to test predictions. Thus, the bulk of the evidence suggests that students use more than topic familiarity in making accurate test predictions. Accurate predictions must be based on some aspect of learning from the text.

Judging Level of Learning

Instead of basing their predictions solely on topic familiarity, students may also base their predictions on factors related to their level of learning. One such factor is the ease of comprehension, or an assessment of the processes of learning from the text. Another such factor is the retrievability of ideas from the text, or an assessment of the products of learning. Research related to each of these potential bases for prediction ratings is discussed next.

Ease of Comprehension

Researchers have varied the questions they have used when asking students to assess their learning from text. Weaver (1990) and Glenberg and Epstein (1985, 1987; Glenberg et al., 1987) asked students to assess their confidence in using what they learned to answer an inference question correctly. In my laboratory, we have asked students to predict future performance explicitly (Maki, 1995; Maki & Berry, 1984; Maki & Serra, 1992b;). Other investigators (e.g., Magliano et al., 1993; Walczyk & Hall, 1989; Weaver & Bryant, 1995) asked students to judge their comprehension of texts. Also, Gillström and Rönnberg (1995) first asked students to rate their comprehension of texts and then to predict the amount they could recall from the same texts.

Asking students to predict future performance and asking about comprehension may be different. Ease of comprehension may be one factor considered by students when they predict future performance, but there may be other factors as well. In two series of studies, we investigated the similarity of ease of comprehension judgments and explicit predictions by asking one group of students to predict future performance explicitly and another group to rate how easy texts were to comprehend.

Maki, Foley, Kajer, Thompson, and Willert (1990) varied the judgments that students made after they had read intact text or text with some letters deleted. It was expected that the text with deleted letters would be perceived as more difficult to understand but that it would not lead to poorer test performance. In one experiment, half of the text paragraphs contained deleted letters and half were intact. After reading each paragraph, one group of students made a prediction rating about future performance and the other group judged ease of comprehension. All students later responded to a cued recall test for specific text information.

As expected, paragraphs with deleted letters were given lower comprehension ratings than intact paragraphs, but predictions of future test performance did not differ for the two types of paragraphs. How well the ratings related to actual performance was tested by correlating the comprehension ratings and performance and the prediction ratings and performance. Correlations between ratings and performance were significantly greater than 0 in all conditions. The relationship between comprehension ratings and performance did not differ for intact and deleted-letter text, but performance on deleted-letter text was predicted more accurately than was performance on intact text. The different patterns of the comprehension and prediction ratings across the two types of text suggest that the students used something more than ease of comprehension when they predicted future performance.

Maki and Serra (1992a) also compared ease of comprehension ratings and prediction ratings. In those experiments, we presented texts in sets of four. Students read the four texts and then rank ordered them in terms of either how easy they were to understand or how well they thought they would perform on a future test over the text. Students then took a four-item multiple-choice test for each text. In three experiments, the relationship between the prediction ranks and test performance was higher than the relationship between comprehension ease ranks and test performance. The stronger relationship between actual performance and ranks based on predicted performance than between performance and ranks based on ease of comprehension suggests that students who were predicting future performance were using something in addition to ease of comprehension.

Gillström and Rönnberg (1995) also found differences between the accuracy of comprehension judgments and explicit predictions. They had the same students rate their comprehension and predict recall. The accuracy of comprehension judgments was assessed by relating comprehension ratings to answers on a multiple-choice test, and recall prediction accuracy was assessed by relating predicted and actual recall. They found that both types of predictions were accurate but that verbal skill differences were evident in the accuracy of recall predictions but not in the accuracy of comprehension predictions. However, because different types of tests were used for the two types of judgments, it is unclear whether the different types of judgments or the different types of tests were critical in producing the different patterns. Still, they observed different patterns for ratings of comprehension and explicit predictions.

Each of these studies in which students made either ease of comprehension judgments or explicit predictions showed some differences between the two types of judgments. Thus, it is unlikely that predictions are made solely on perceived comprehension; instead they must be based on something more. That something may well be retrievability of information learned from the texts.

Text Retrievability

Effective learners should make judgments about how much they have learned from texts when they predict future test performance. Yet, Glenberg et al. (1987) concluded that students did not base judgments on knowledge retrieved from text because recall of the important parts of texts did not correlate with prediction ratings. However, Morris (1990) argued that prediction ratings may not correlate with retrieval because prediction judgments are made in about 10 seconds, whereas self-paced retrieval from text takes much longer. Thus, to equalize prediction and retrieval times, he asked students to give speeded recalls after reading short texts. He found that predictions correlated both with retrieval latency and with retrieval rate, suggesting that students assessed momentary accessibility of text material when they predicted future test performance.

Level of Processing.   If text accessibility is important in predictions, then variables that increase accessibility should increase the level of predictions. The results are mixed on this. As described earlier, Maki et al. (1990) manipulated the amount of processing that students did while reading by using text with deleted letters and intact text. Filling in the letters while reading should make the text representation stronger in memory and make it more retrievable. Experiment 1 used a within-subjects design with half of the paragraphs having deleted letters and half not. Students did better on a cued recall test for the deleted-letter paragraphs, but they did not predict a higher level of future performance. Thus, although the text was differentially retrievable, there was no evidence for a higher level of predictions for the more accessible text. In Experiment 2, in which the deleted letters were manipulated between subjects, neither cued recall performance nor the level of predictions differed for text with deleted letters and intact text. In both experiments, the mean prediction ratings were higher for intact text, but the differences in rating levels were not significant. Thus, these studies do not support the idea that increasing the level of processing increases accessibility and, hence, prediction ratings.

There is evidence, however, that deeper processing influences the accuracy of predictions with more elaborative processing producing greater correlations between predictions and performance. In both of the experiments described earlier, we (Maki et al., 1990) found larger correlations between predictions and performance for text with deleted letters than for intact text. More processing while reading text may allow students to better assess their degree of learning of parts of texts.

Schommer and Surber (1986) also manipulated the level of processing. College students were instructed to read easy or difficult texts with either the goal of deciding whether the passage could be understood by an average student (i.e., a shallow level of processing) or the goal of preparing a summary of the passage for presentation to another student (i.e., a deeper level of processing). Students rated comprehension of the passage and answered multiple-choice comprehension questions. Schommer and Surber did not report mean ratings in the two conditions, so whether higher ratings were given for the more deeply processed texts can not be determined. However, they did find a difference in the accuracy of ratings. They defined illusions of knowing as cases in which two of the three multiple-choice questions were answered incorrectly along with a high rating of comprehension. Illusions of knowing were greatest with difficult passages and a shallow level of processing. Thus, deeper processing led students to a more accurate understanding of what was actually learned from passages.

Magliano et al. (1993) had students use either (a) deep comprehension strategies including forming questions, summarizing, using the context, and identifying trouble spots; or (b) superficial strategies, such as analyzing the letters in words, grouping words correctly, sounding the syllables, and motivating oneself to excel. They found no differences in the levels of the ratings for the two processing groups, but they found some evidence for better prediction with the deep instructions.

Gillström and Rönnberg (1995) also showed a dissociation between performance and metacomprehension ratings. They manipulated instructions given to students before reading texts. In one condition, students were instructed simply to read to understand. In a second condition, students were given five words from the text and instructed to use them while reading the text and as cues during predictions and later recall. In a third condition, students were instructed to select five words that they could use as cues. Multiple-choice performance did not differ as a function of instructions, but students gave lower comprehension ratings in the condition in which they selected their own cue words. Furthermore, the cue manipulation affected the accuracy of comprehension ratings with lower accuracy in the read only and the cue selection conditions than in the condition in which the cues were given. Gillström and Rönnberg also asked students to make explicit recall predictions and measured how accurately these affected recall. Processing instructions did not influence recall, the level of predictions, or prediction accuracy.

The studies in which level of processing was manipulated show that mean ratings do not vary in any systematic way with processing depth. However, in many of the studies, performance did not vary with type of processing either, so the hypothesis that ratings are based on accessibility has not had a very strong test. Interestingly, the accuracy of metacomprehension ratings often varies with level of processing. Generally, deeper processing leads to more accurate assessments of future memory performance.

Text Characteristics.   The manipulations previously described had the potential to influence text retrievability either by varying the effort needed to read text (by deleting letters) or by giving students different processing instructions. The retrievability of text can also be manipulated with text characteristics. More difficult texts reduce comprehension, and predictions should vary with text difficulty if students are making judgments of comprehension difficulty. Weaver and Bryant (1995) had students read either expository or narrative texts. Test performance and comprehension ratings were higher for narrative texts. However, the accuracy of predictions tended to be greater for expository texts, but type of text interacted with type of test question. For narrative texts, thematic test questions produced more accuracy than detailed test questions; and for expository texts, the reverse was true. Weaver and Bryant also manipulated text difficulty. In two experiments, they found that texts of medium difficulty (recognition scores of about 50%) produced more accurate predictions than texts that were easy (recognition of about 60%) or more difficult (recognition scores of 47%). However, 50% correct on multiple-choice questions is quite low, lower than that found in other studies (e.g., Maki & Serra, 1992a). It might be that the specific texts used by Weaver and Bryant produced the high prediction accuracy, or it might be that moderately difficult texts are predicted best.

Walczyk and Hall (1989) used expository texts and varied the number of specific examples embedded in the texts. Assessments of comprehension were higher with texts that contained examples, and there was a trend for higher scores on multiple-choice questions when texts contained examples. In addition, the correlation between comprehension assessments and test performance was higher in the examples than in the no examples conditions.

Conclusions About Level of Learning

Students apparently judge the ease of comprehension when making predictions about text, but they also do more than this: They make explicit test predictions. There is evidence that immediate retrievability of text is related to the level of predictions (Morris, 1990). In addition, performance on text that is processed more elaboratively is often predicted more accurately than performance on text that is more shallowly processed (Magliano et al., 1993; Maki et al., 1990; Schommer & Surber, 1986). The accuracy of predictions varies with specific texts although the characteristics of texts that support accurate predictions are not clear: Texts with examples are predicted better than texts without specific examples, and texts of moderate difficulty may produce more accuracy than easier or very difficult texts.

Predicting Forgetting

To predict future test performance accurately, students need to project how much they will forget from the time of the prediction to the time of the test. One of the largest effects in the metacognition literature is the delayed-judgment-of-learning effect first demonstrated by Nelson and Dunlosky (1991). They found that the correlations between judgments of learning for word pairs and memory for those word pairs were very high (gammas about .80) if the judgments were delayed and the test of the word pairs was also delayed.

This condition was contrasted to one in which the judgments of learning were made immediately after learning, a condition that produced lower correlations (gammas about .30). One explanation for this is that the immediate judgments are made while the word pair is still in an active memory store and can easily be retrieved. Students may not be able to judge how retrievable an active response will be later when it is retrieved from an inactive store. Many of the studies on metacomprehension have used procedures similar to the Nelson and Dunlosky (1991) immediate judgment of learning paradigm (e.g., Maki & Berry, 1984; Maki & Serra, 1992b; Weaver, 1990; Weaver & Bryant, 1995). However, procedures that are more similar to delayed judgments of learning may improve students' abilities to predict future performance.

Glenberg and Epstein (1985) manipulated the interval between reading a text and making the prediction while keeping constant the interval between reading and the test. When the predictions were made immediately after reading, students needed to predict forgetting; when the predictions were made after a delay and immediately before the test, forgetting had already occurred so there was no need to predict it. Glenberg and Epstein (1985) found that predictions were no more accurate than chance in either condition.

Glenberg et al. (1987) held the interval between predictions and the test constant but varied the interval between reading and the predictions. In the immediate condition, reading, prediction, and test for each text occurred with minimal intervening time delays. In the delayed condition, there was a delay between reading and the predictions that immediately preceded each test. Correlations between predictions and performance were not significantly greater than chance in either the immediate or delayed conditions when the test consisted of single inference or single verbatim recognition items. However, when each text was tested with four idea recognition items, students did show a significant correlation between predictions and performance in the immediate but not in the delayed condition.

I have recently found some evidence to corroborate the trends in Glenberg et al.'s (1987) data in experiments in which the delays between reading and predictions, reading and test, and predictions and the test were varied (Maki, in press). Predictions were the most accurate when they were made immediately following learning and when the test also followed immediately. Predictions made immediately with a delayed test produced the least accuracy. Delaying both predictions and the test produced prediction accuracy that was intermediate to the other two conditions. This finding also fits with Morris' (1990) momentary accessibility hypothesis in that text material that is accessible immediately after reading is most likely to also be accessible on an immediate test.

The situation with respect to the spacing of learning, predictions, and the test appear to be different for word pairs and for text material. With word pairs, delayed predictions and delayed tests produce the highest prediction accuracy. With text, immediate predictions and an immediate test appear to produce the greatest accuracy. This is not good news from an educational standpoint. Immediate predictions and immediate tests are not what normally occurs in the real world. Instead, tests are delayed. Ideally, delayed predictions about text should be as accurate as delayed predictions with word pairs, but this appears not to be the case.

Predicting the Test

Postdictions

Many studies have shown that postdictions following the test are more accurate than predictions preceding a test (Glenberg & Epstein, 1985; Glenberg et al., 1987; Maki et al., 1990; Maki & Serra, 1992a). Averaging across about 25 studies conducted in our laboratory, the mean gamma correlation for predictions was .27 and the mean gamma for postdictions was .48. When postdictions are made, students potentially have access to much information that is unavailable for predictions, including the difficulty of the text, the amount they learned from the text, the amount of forgetting that occurred during the retention interval, and the nature of the test. The large increase in gamma correlations for postdictions from all of the previously discussed prediction conditions suggests that knowledge of the test questions is critical in producing the high level of postdiction accuracy.

Practice Tests

If postdictions are accurate because students know about the test questions, then predictions may be made more accurate with partial knowledge about the test. Pressley, Snyder, Levin, Murray, and Ghatala (1987) interspersed adjunct questions in expository text and instructed students to answer the questions in their heads. After reading an entire text, students were to make a global prediction about how well they would do overall on a test. The students who had interspersed questions were more accurate in predictions than students who did not have interspersed questions. Also, Walczyk and Hall (1989) embedded a question after each paragraph in an expository text, but students were not asked to respond to each question. These embedded questions produced no effects on rated comprehension or on later test performance; however, some evidence suggested that the embedded questions improved students' accuracy at assessing their comprehension. In both the Pressley et al. (1987) and Walczyk and Hall (1989) studies, improved predictions occurred when the test questions were interspersed in the text and global predictions were made after reading.

Glenberg et al. (1987) tested a modified feedback hypothesis that postulated that students can use feedback from a pretest to predict posttest performance provided that the pretest questions are similar to the posttest questions. Students were shown a recognition item as a pretest, they made a prediction rating, and then they were shown three recognition items as a posttest. One item was the same as the pretest, one was related, and one was unrelated. Predictions were accurate for the repeated pretest and posttest items, but not for the related and unrelated posttest items. The correlation between performance on the same and related posttest items was very low, suggesting that different aspects of memory were being tapped by these "related" test items.

Maki and Serra (1992b) presented practice tests before students predicted performance on final tests. In the identical condition, the three questions on the practice test made up the final test; in the similar condition, the three practice test questions were randomly drawn from a pool of six possible questions and the remaining three questions made up the final test; and in the control condition, students did not answer practice test questions before predicting final test performance. Predictions were most accurate when the same test questions were answered before and after the predictions, and they were least accurate when practice test questions were randomly drawn from the same pool as the actual test questions. One reason for the low accuracy was that the correlation of scores between the three practice test questions and the final three test questions was quite low. Another problem may have been the same as in the case of immediate predictions and delayed testing: What students knew immediately did not predict what they remembered after a delay. Thus, these findings place a caveat on the use of practice tests to guide students in knowing how well they know text material. The practice tests should be answered following some delay after reading, and they should be extensive enough to produce positive correlations with the final tests.

Type of Test Question

Format of Test Questions.   Pressley, Ghatala, Woloshyn, and Pirie (1990) asked whether the type of test question embedded into expository text would affect students' abilities to regulate their learning. After reading a text passage once, students answered either a short-answer essay question or a multiple-choice question. They were told to go on and read the next passage if they thought their answer was correct, but to reread the passage if they thought their answer was incorrect. More appropriate decisions were made with the short-answer than with the multiple-choice tests. This may be because the short-answer format forced students to retrieve information from memory, but the multiple-choice format allowed them to bypass the active retrieval process.

True–false inference questions of the type used by Glenberg et al. (1987) may produce particularly poor metacomprehension accuracy. Morris (1995), using four inference questions per text (as prescribed by Weaver, 1990) rather than the one used by Glenberg et al. (1987), found only chance-level prediction accuracy. Although Morris (1995) concluded that his results show that students cannot predict their performance on texts, my interpretation is that these inference questions may be particularly difficult for students to predict.

We have some evidence to support this interpretation. Maki, Mikkelsen, and Gerlach (1988) compared three types of test questions based on the texts used by Glenberg et al. (1987). Students predicted performance on true–false inference questions of the type used by Glenberg et al. (1987) and by Morris (1995), on two-alternative inference questions that included a correct and an incorrect inference, and on two-alternative multiple-choice questions. We found that students could predict performance on the multiple-choice questions with greater than chance accuracy, but they could not predict performance on the true–false inference questions. The accuracy of predictions on two-alternative forced-choice inference questions was between the two other types. Students are probably not used to true–false inference questions, and factors other than their understanding of the text may play a larger role in these types of questions than in multiple-choice questions.

The interpretation that true–false inference questions pose a unique difficulty is also supported by findings of greater than chance levels of prediction accuracy when other types of questions have been used. Accurate predictions have been observed with multiple-choice questions (Maki & Serra, 1992a, 1992b; Magliano et al., 1993; Weaver, 1990; Weaver & Bryant, 1995), with cued recall (Maki et al., 1990; Magliano et al., 1993), and with free recall (Gillström & Rönnberg, 1995; Maki & Swett, 1987).

Content of Test Questions.   Weaver and Bryant (1995) manipulated both the type of text (narrative vs. expository) and the type of test question. Multiple choice questions tapped either detailed information or thematic information. In one of their experiments, performance on thematic questions was predicted more accurately for narrative texts but performance on detailed questions was predicted better for expository texts. However, in two other studies in which text difficulty was controlled, the interaction between text type and question type disappeared. Thus, it is difficult to draw conclusions from this study about metacomprehension accuracy and the type of information tapped by test questions.

Although the earlier work by Morris (1995) and by Maki et al. (1988) suggested that inference questions result in particularly poor prediction accuracy, I recently found good accuracy with multiple-choice questions that required inferences (Maki, 1995). Test questions could be answered directly from the most important text sentences, from the least important text sentences, or from generalizations and inferences that could not be found directly in the text. Results showed that predictions were most accurate for the generalizations and inferences. Thus, students may make a global assessment of understanding of the texts which may best match these higher level questions. The apparent conflict of this conclusion with the results of Glenberg et al. (1987) and Morris (1995) may be resolved by looking at the type of true–false inference questions they used. In many of their questions, the true and false versions were practically verbatim from the text with very few words changed to create the false versions (e.g., from "to eat" to "to stop eating"). Students may have difficulty with discriminations this fine, even if they have some idea about how well they have understood the text.

Difficulty of Test Questions.   Although there are no text prediction studies in which the difficulty of test questions was manipulated, Schraw and Roedel (1994) examined the accuracy of posttest confidence judgments for questions of varying difficulty. Students read passages of expository texts and answered multiple-choice questions that varied in difficulty. Predictions were made on a confidence scale varying from 0% to 100%. The difference between actual performance and predicted performance was the measure of prediction accuracy. Schraw and Roedel found that students showed more overconfidence for difficult than for medium test items, and they showed some underconfidence on easy items. Overall, the smallest difference between confidence judgments and performance was for the easy test items. This may have occurred because students tended to estimate performance at about 75% correct with both easy and moderately difficult questions. That value was closer to actual performance for easy than for moderately difficult test items.

Summary of Test-Related Factors

Postdictions are more accurate than predictions, but practice test questions given immediately before predictions do not increase prediction accuracy. For practice tests to improve prediction accuracy, performance on them must correlate with actual test performance, and practice questions may be most effective if answered following a delay after study. Some types of test questions, including short-answer questions and multiple-choice questions covering broad text concepts, produce higher prediction accuracy than other types of questions, such as true–false inference questions. Finally, easy test questions may produce more metacomprehension accuracy than difficult test questions.

INDIVIDUAL DIFFERENCES AND METACOMPREHENSION ACCURACY

Prediction Ability and Verbal Abilities

Although there are some suggestions in the literature that students with higher verbal abilities are more accurate in predictions over text, the bulk of the evidence suggests that these abilities are not related. In our initial experiment on metacomprehension (Maki & Berry, 1984), we found some evidence that better students were able to make more accurate metacomprehension judgments. Some research is consistent with this conclusion. Glover (1989) asked college students to make a global prediction about how they would do on a test after reading expository text. Good readers predicted scores that were closer to actual test scores than did poor readers who tended to give predictions that were considerably higher than their actual performance.

However, other studies have shown no relationship between verbal abilities and metacomprehension accuracy. One type of measure is the correlation between performance on the text itself and prediction accuracy. Lovelace (1984) found that the recall of sentences did not relate to the ability to predict recall. Glenberg and Epstein (1985) found that the ability to answer inference questions did not correlate with the accuracy of predictions on those questions. Maki and Swett (1987) found no relationship between prediction accuracy and performance on recall tests over narrative text.

A better way to measure ability than performance on the text itself is an independent assessment using a standardized verbal or reading ability test. Pressley et al. (1987) used the reading comprehension passages from the Scholastic Aptitude Test and the Graduate Record Examination as their measures of reading ability. They found no relationship between these measures and the accuracy of overall test performance predictions. Given the similarity of Pressley et al.'s procedures to those of Glover (1989), it is not clear why Glover found higher prediction accuracy for better comprehenders while Pressley et al. did not. Maki, Jonas, and Kallod (1994) assessed comprehension ability both with the Nelson-Denny Reading Test and the Multi-Media Comprehension Battery developed by Gernsbacher and Varner (1988). The later presents auditory, written, and pictorial narratives and measures comprehension ability with a cued recall test. Maki et al. found very little relationship between the various measures of comprehension ability and prediction accuracy, although the overall accuracy of predictions in that study was fairly low.

Gillström & Rönnberg (1995) have recently reported a negative relationship between prediction accuracy and verbal ability. When students predicted recall of expository texts, those who were lower in reading ability predicted recall the best. However, the relationship between comprehension ratings and multiple-choice test answers did not relate to verbal ability in any consistent way. Gillström & Rönnberg suggested that reading is more automatic for skilled readers, and therefore, they are less aware of the processes involved in understanding.

Postdiction Ability and Verbal Abilities

The accuracy of posttest confidence judgments for test performance showed a positive relationship with the types of comprehension ability studied by Maki et al. (1994). However, this finding is inconsistent with findings of Pressley and colleagues (Pressley et al., 1990; Pressley & Ghatala, 1988) who did not find relationships between verbal abilities and posttest confidence judgment accuracy. In their studies, the correlations between verbal abilities and posttest confidence judgment accuracy were often in the .30 to .35 range, which is similar to the magnitude of correlations found by Maki et al. The discrepancy between the two conclusions may be explained by differences in statistical power. Maki et al. used a larger sample size than Pressley et al. and Pressley and Ghatala.

Further evidence for a relationship between posttest confidence accuracy and abilities comes from two studies in which students taking actual classroom tests rated their confidence in test answers. Shaughnessy (1979) and Sinkavich (1995) found that students who did better on exams in psychology courses were better able to indicate the correctness of answers on multiple-choice tests than students who did more poorly on the tests. Thus, the best conclusion from the studies of posttest confidence judgment accuracy and verbal ability is that there is a positive relationship with better students better able to assess how well they have done on tests.

Reliability of Metacomprehension Ability

The lack of a relationship between verbal ability and prediction ability may occur because we do not have a reliable way of measuring prediction ability. In the Maki et al. (1994) study in which comprehension ability correlated with posttest confidence accuracy but not with prediction accuracy, the gamma correlation between predictions and test performance was only .114, but the correlation between posttest confidence judgments and test performance was .551. If individuals' prediction accuracy correlations are invalid estimates of their ability to predict, then one would not expect this to relate to individual differences in comprehension. Thompson and Mason (1996) recently found a lack of stability in measures of metacognitive accuracy when using split-half reliability. However, Maki et al. calculated 12 gammas for each individual student by using random halves of the ratings and their associated test questions. The Cronbach's alpha on these repeated measures of prediction and confidence judgment accuracy were quite high. This suggests that there is good internal validity when the ratings and tests are split in many different ways to determine internal reliability.

Schraw, Dunkle, Bendixen, and Roedel (1995) have also presented some evidence that there are stable individual differences in posttest confidence judgment accuracy across tasks. They had students answer questions from many domains, including naming U.S. Presidents, estimating distances, and answering vocabulary questions. Students gave confidence judgments about the correctness of their answers. When the absolute level of performance was equated across domains, Schraw et al. found evidence for a general monitoring skill in that the accuracy of confidence judgments was correlated across domains. This suggests that there are stable individual differences in posttest confidence judgments. However, there is no evidence as yet for a similar stable skill in pretest predictions.

Other evidence that individual differences in metamemory are stable comes from a longitudinal study using metamemory questionnaires. McDonald-Miszczak, Hertzog, and Hultsch (1995) had younger and older adults fill out questionnaires about their perceptions of their memory abilities across either 2-year or 6-year periods. Perceptions of memory ability remained fairly stable across time, as did actual memory ability. However, these investigators examined only the reliability in subjective perceptions of memory and did not examine stability in the accuracy of predictions. Thus, it may be that we still do not have a measurement tool that allows us to examine prediction ability in a relatively noise-free paradigm. If the small correlations between predictions and performance that are normally observed are contaminated by a great degree of error, then it is not surprising that these do not correlate with other individual differences.

Conclusions About Individual Differences

The data concerning the ability to predict performance and individual differences in verbal and comprehension abilities is mixed. Only two studies (Glover, 1989; Maki & Berry, 1984) have found evidence that individuals who do better on comprehension tests make more accurate predictions. A number of studies have found no relationship (Glenberg & Epstein, 1985; Lovelace, 1984; Maki & Swett, 1987; Maki et al., 1994; Pressley et al., 1987), and one study found that better readers predicted more poorly than poorer readers (Gillström & Rönnberg, 1995). The reason for these mixed results may be that our measures of prediction accuracy contain a great deal of noise, so relationships with more stable individual differences are difficult to detect. Other types of metamemory, however, appear to be stable, and there is consistent evidence that postdiction accuracy correlates with individual differences in verbal abilities (Maki et al., 1994; Shaughnessy, 1979; Sinkavich, 1995).

CONCLUSIONS

The bulk of the literature argues for a greater than chance ability to predict performance over text material (Gillström & Rönnberg, 1995; Magliano et al., 1993; Maki, 1995; Maki et al., 1990; Maki & Serra, 1992a, 1992b; Weaver, 1990; Weaver & Bryant, 1995). The early work of Glenberg and Epstein (1985; Glenberg et al., 1987) probably produced chance-level prediction accuracy because of the use of true–false inference questions and because performance on single test items is an unreliable measure of knowledge gained from a text. We also know that students rely to some extent on their familiarity with the text topics when performance over multiple texts is predicted, but this use of domain familiarity is not the source of accurate predictions. The fact that the interval between the time of reading the text and the time of the test influences prediction accuracy also argues against the simple use of domain familiarity. Accurate predictions are based on aspects of learning from the text, including ease of comprehension, perceived level of learning, and perceived amount of forgetting. Variables that influence level of learning and amount of effort expended in reading influence the accuracy of predictions. Finally, the type of test is important in determining test prediction accuracy with true–false inference tests related to particularly inaccurate predictions. Although better comprehenders are better at judging the accuracy of their test answers, once the answers have been given, there is no solid evidence that they are also better predictors. Finally, we need measures of prediction accuracy that are more stable and less noisy to answer many of the remaining questions about individual differences and the specific factors that might improve the accuracy of predictions.

IMPLICATIONS FOR EDUCATION

The ability to judge what one has learned from reading text material is an important skill to acquire if individuals are going to be efficient learners. Continuing to study what is already known to an adequate degree is a waste of time; ceasing study of material that is not known adequately will lead to poor performance on criterion tasks. If education is to prepare students for life-long learning, an important goal should be to teach students to know when they need to learn more. The studies discussed in this chapter suggest that students can predict future performance with some accuracy, but the correlations are typically quite small. Thus, we might ask whether such metacomprehension can be taught.

There have been few studies on the teaching of metacomprehension with increases in predictive accuracy as the goal. However, training to improve the accuracy of confidence judgments for answers to general knowledge questions has been only moderately successful. Zechmeister, Rusch, and Markell (1986) trained students to make confidence judgments by giving personal feedback and teaching them to weigh evidence. Training reduced overconfidence, especially in lower ability students, but it did so mainly by reducing the students' use of the high end of the confidence scale. Arkes,

Christensen, Lai, and Blumer (1987) found that experience with items that appeared easy but that were actually difficult also reduced overconfidence. These training procedures have shown some success with posttest confidence judgments on general knowledge questions, but whether they would be successful with metacomprehension is unclear because posttest confidence judgments are more accurate than text predictions.

The low accuracy of text predictions may mean that students cannot predict performance well, and that prediction is not a teachable skill. Alternatively, low predictive accuracy may indicate that our measurement of metacomprehension accuracy is too unreliable for us to detect changes. A more positive view is that there is much room for improvement in prediction accuracy so that successful training is possible. Although the latter alternative is the most promising from an educational standpoint, the lack of a good way to measure metacomprehension accuracy is probably closer to the truth. I remain optimistic that students can accurately predict future performance, and they could learn to do it better, but we just need better paradigms in which to study the ability to predict future test performance over text.

ACKNOWLEDGMENT

Portions of this chapter were presented at the meetings of the Midwestern Psychological Association, Chicago, 1996, as the Presidential Address "Knowing What You Know."

REFERENCES

Anderson, G., & Beal, C. R. (1995). Children's recognition of inconsistencies in science texts: Multiple measures of comprehension monitoring. *Applied Cognitive Psychology, 9,* 261–272.

Arkes, H. R., Christensen, C., Lai, C., & Blumer, C. (1987). Two methods of reducing overconfidence. *Organizational behavior and human decision processes, 39,* 133–144.

Gernsbacher, M. A., & Varner, K. R. (1988). *The multi-media comprehension battery* (Tech. Rep. No. 88-07). Eugene, OR: Institute of Cognitive and Decision Sciences.

Gillström, Å., & Rönnberg, J. (1995). Comprehension calibration and recall prediction accuracy of texts: Reading skill, reading strategies, and effort. *Journal of Educational Psychology, 87,* 545–558.

Glenberg, A. M., & Epstein, W. (1985). Calibration of comprehension. *Journal of Experimental Psychology: Learning, Memory, and Cognition, 11,* 702–718.

Glenberg, A. M., & Epstein, W. (1987). Inexpert calibration of comprehension. *Memory and Cognition, 15,* 84–93.

Glenberg, A. M., Sanocki, T., Epstein, W., & Morris, C. (1987). Enhancing calibration of comprehension. *Journal of Experimental Psychology: General, 116,* 119–136.

Glenberg, A. M., Wilkinson, A., & Epstein, W. (1982). The illusion of knowing: Failure in the self-assessment of comprehension. *Memory and Cognition, 10,* 597–602.
Glover, J. A. (1989). Reading ability and the calibrator of comprehension. *Educational Research Quarterly, 13,* 7–11.
Goodman, L. A., & Kruskal, W. H. (1954). Measures of association for cross classification. *Journal of the American Statistical Association, 49,* 732–764.
Lovelace, E. A. (1984). Metamemory: Monitoring future recallability during study. *Journal of Experimental Psychology: Learning, Memory, and Cognition, 10,* 756–766.
Magliano, J. P., Little, L. D., & Graesser, A. C. (1993). The impact of comprehension instruction on the calibration of comprehension. *Reading Research and Instruction, 32,* 49–63.
Maki, R. H. (1995). Accuracy of metacomprehension judgments for questions of varying importance levels. *American Journal of Psychology, 108,* 327–344.
Maki, R. H. (in press). Predicting performance on text material: Delayed versus immediate predictions and test. *Memory and Cognition.*
Maki, R. H., & Berry, S. (1984). Metacomprehension of text material. *Journal of Experimental Psychology: Learning, Memory, and Cognition, 10,* 663–679.
Maki, R. H., Foley, J. M., Kajer, W. K., Thompson, R. C., & Willert, M. G. (1990). *Journal of Experimental Psychology: Learning, Memory, and Cognition, 16,* 609–616.
Maki, R. H., Jonas, D., & Kallod, M. (1994). The relationship between comprehension and metacomprehension ability. *Psychonomic Bulletin and Review, 1,* 126–129.
Maki, R. H., Mikkelsen, B. H., & Gerlach, T. L. (1988, November). *Metacomprehension of text: A comparison of measures of accuracy and types of test.* Paper presented at the meeting of the Psychonomics Society, Chicago.
Maki, R. H., & Serra, M. (1992a). The basis of test predictions for text material. *Journal of Experimental Psychology: Learning, Memory, and Cognition, 18,* 116–126.
Maki, R. H., & Serra, M. (1992b). Role of practice tests in the accuracy of test predictions on text material. *Journal of Educational Psychology, 84,* 200–210.
Maki, R. H., & Swett, S. (1987). Metamemory for narrative text. *Memory and Cognition, 15,* 72–83.
Markman, E. M. (1977). Realizing that you don't understand: A preliminary investigation. *Child Development, 48,* 986–992.
McDonald-Miszczak, L., Hertzog, C., & Hultsch, D. F. (1995). Stability and accuracy of metamemory in adulthood and aging: A longitudinal analysis. *Psychology and Aging, 10,* 553–564.
Morris, C. C. (1990). Retrieval processes underlying confidence in comprehension judgments. *Journal of Experimental Psychology: Learning, Memory, and Cognition, 16,* 223–232.
Morris, C. C. (1995). Poor discourse comprehension monitoring is no methodological artifact. *The Psychological Record, 45,* 655–668.
Nelson, T. O. (1984). A comparison of current measures of the accuracy of feeling-of-knowing predictions. *Psychological Bulletin, 95,* 109–133.
Nelson, T. O., & Dunlosky, J. (1991). When people's judgments of learning (JOLs) are extremely accurate at predicting subsequent recall: The "delayed JOL effect." *Psychological Science, 2,* 267–270.
Pressley, M., & Ghatala, E. S. (1988). Delusions about performance on multiple-choice comprehension tests. *Reading Research Quarterly, 23,* 454–464.
Pressley, M., Ghatala, E. S., Woloshyn, V., & Pirie, J. (1990). Sometimes adults miss the main ideas and do not realize it: Confidence in responses to short-answer and multiple-choice comprehension questions. *Reading Research Quarterly, 25,* 232–249.

Pressley, M., Snyder, B. L., Levin, J. R., Murray, H. G., & Ghatala, E. S. (1987). Perceived readiness for examination performance (PREP) produced by initial reading of text and text containing adjunct questions. *Reading Research Quarterly, 22,* 219–236.

Schommer, M., & Surber, J. R. (1986). Comprehension-monitoring failure in skilled adult readers. *Journal of Educational Psychology, 78,* 353–357.

Schraw, G., Dunkle, M. E., Bendixen, L. D., & Roedel, T. D. (1995). Does a general monitoring skill exist? *Journal of Educational Psychology, 87,* 433–444.

Schraw, G., & Roedel, T. D. (1994). Test difficulty and judgment bias. *Memory and Cognition, 22,* 63–69.

Shaughnessy, J. J. (1979). Confidence-judgment accuracy as a predictor of test performance. *Journal of Research in Personality, 13,* 505–514.

Sinkavich, F. J. (1995). Performance and metamemory: Do students know what they don't know? *Journal of Instructional Psychology, 22,* 77–87.

Spargo, E. (1989). *Timed readings* (3rd Ed., Vols. 5, 7 and 10). Providence, RI: Jamestown Publishers.

Thompson, W. B., & Mason, S. E. (1996). Instability of individual differences in the association between confidence judgments and memory performance. *Memory and Cognition, 24,* 226–234.

Walczyk, J. J., & Hall, V. C. (1989). Effects of examples and embedded questions on the accuracy of comprehension self-assessments. *Journal of Educational Psychology, 81,* 435–437.

Weaver, C. A. III (1990). Constraining factors in calibration of comprehension. *Journal of Experimental Psychology: Learning, Memory, and Cognition, 16,* 214–222.

Weaver, C. A. III, & Bryant, D. S. (1995). Monitoring of comprehension: The role of text difficulty in metamemory for narrative and expository text. *Memory and Cognition, 23,* 12–22.

Zechmeister, E. B., Rusch, K. M., Markell, K. A. (1986). Training college students to assess accurately what they know and don't know. *Human Learning, 5,* 3–19.

7

Influence of Knowledge Activation and Context on Comprehension Monitoring of Science Texts

José Otero
Universidad de Alcalá, Madrid, Spain

Comprehension monitoring has been conceptualized in several ways. One line of inquiry is based on what Winograd and Johnston (1982) called the "error detection paradigm" (p. 61). It was started in the late 1970s by Ellen Markman's (1977, 1979) research on children's awareness of inconsistencies. Subjects are provided with inconsistent information, typically textual contradictions or information that contradicts subjects' knowledge, and comprehension monitoring is assessed by subjects' ability to identify and react to these inconsistencies. Work on *calibration of comprehension*, which started in the 1980s, represents another kind of research on comprehension monitoring. It consists in measuring the relation between readers' predictions of understanding text and their actual performance as measured by questions on main points of the text (Glenberg & Epstein, 1985, 1987). Related to this work is research on predictions of memory for text or *metamemory* and predictions of comprehension or *metacomprehension* (Maki & Berry, 1984; Maki & Swett, 1987).

Two components have been distinguished in comprehension monitoring: evaluation and regulation of comprehension (Baker, 1985; Otero, 1996; Zabrucky & Ratner, 1986, 1989, 1992). *Evaluation* refers to the identification of a comprehension problem; *regulation* refers to the remedial strategies used to solve these problems, for example inferencing or rereading portions of a text. The difference is illustrated in studies using the error detection paradigm.

A failure to detect an inconsistency indicates an evaluation problem. Inconsistency detection has been measured through verbal report responses following reading (Zabrucky, Moore, & Schultz, 1987), by asking subjects to underline any problem found in the text (Otero & Campanario, 1990), through online measures like lookbacks (Anderson & Beal 1995; Garner & Reis, 1981), or reading times of problematic sentences (Anderson & Beal, 1995; Baker & Anderson, 1982; Zabrucky & Ratner, 1989, 1992). Many of these studies indicate that both young subjects and adults have difficulty detecting clear inconsistencies when reading.

Not noticing an inconsistency in a text may be due to inadequate reading strategies. For example, secondary school students may overlook an inconsistency like a circular argumentation in a science "proof." In a pilot study, Otero (1992) provided students in the last year of secondary education with an incorrect "Proof of Newton's Second Law," involving a circular argumentation. The students were asked to read the text and to request an explanation if they did not understand it. They also had to recall the text in writing. Some of these students did not notice any problem in the proof, and further, when asked to recall the text, they restated the information that they had read including the circular argument. This points to a problem with comprehension evaluation that could be caused by inadequate reading strategies. In this case, a failure occurs for the *structure strategy* (Meyer, Brandt, & Bluth, 1980), which means looking for the most general relations in the text. These students pay attention to the microstructure of the text without identifying the top level structure of the false proof, as previous research has shown (Brincones & Otero, 1994; Cook & Mayer, 1988). Consequently, comprehension evaluation also fails.

The problem with comprehension evaluation just described results from a violation of one of the comprehension-monitoring standards summarized by Baker (1985): structural cohesiveness. This standard refers to the integration of individual propositions within the main theme of the text. Other failures in comprehension evaluation may also result from not applying other comprehension-monitoring standards: lexical (understanding of individual words), syntactic (grammaticality of words or groups of words), propositional cohesiveness (integration of adjacent propositions in the text), external consistency (congruence between text information and what is already known), internal consistency (congruence between pieces of information within the text), and information completeness (clarity and completeness of information, especially regarding instructions to carry out a task).

Readers who notice a comprehension problem (e.g., a contradiction in a text) engage in a variety of "fix-up" or regulation procedures to solve the problem (Alessi, Anderson, & Goetz, 1979; Baker, 1979; Markman, 1979; Otero & Campanario, 1990). Inadequate regulation of comprehension is a common problem that appears in many domains in addition to text comprehension. Consider the explanation of one of the students interviewed by Hammer (1994) in a study on epistemological beliefs in introductory physics. In trying to solve a problem, the student had calculated different accelerations for two blocks connected by a cord, when in fact these accelerations should be the same:

> ...Oh geez, how could one be accelerating faster than the other? ... That would mean the velocities would have to be different. ... Yeah, I guess so.... Well I don't know; I'd check and see if I got the right answer. I'm 90% sure.

In this case the student notices a discrepancy between his results and his knowledge of kinematics, but inadequately solves the failure to comprehend by "[choosing] to reject his notion of plausibility rather than his solution" (Hammer, 1994, p. 166). This is an instance of bad regulation. A low coherence of the resulting interpretation of the problem situation is tolerated, instead of either reworking the problem so that the inconsistency disappears or tagging the problem as unsolved.

This chapter analyzes comprehension monitoring when reading science texts. I consider some of the interactions existing among the factors influencing comprehension evaluation and regulation. The chapter includes, first, a brief review of the variables influencing text comprehension monitoring. Then, the effect of one of these variables on the detection of internal inconsistencies in science texts is examined: activating portions of inconsistent knowledge. An explanatory mechanism based on the effect of activation was proposed by Otero & Kintsch (1992) to account for failures in detecting contradictions in a text. One consequence of this explanatory hypothesis is presented here: the interaction of knowledge activation and subjects' academic ability when detecting contradictions in a text. Next, two contextual factors influencing comprehension monitoring of science texts are examined: subject matter setting and the epistemic authority of the source. Again, an interaction between this last variable and a subject variable, gender, is considered. Finally, some educational consequences of the previous findings are synthesized.

VARIABLES INFLUENCING TEXT COMPRE-
HENSION MONITORING

Three types of variables have been proposed as influential in comprehension monitoring: learner characteristics, text, and task (Brown, Armbruster, & Baker, 1986). These should be complemented with a fourth kind of variable whose importance in strategy use, and specifically in science text processing, also has been noted: characteristics of context or situation (Alexander, in press; Alexander & Kulikowich, 1994; Garner, 1990).

Learner characteristics have been found to influence text comprehension monitoring: for example, learning conception (Van Rossum & Schenk, 1984), self-perception of ability (Schunk, 1985), motivational orientation (Kroll & Ford, 1992; Nolen, 1988), and verbal skill and ability to generate inferences (Glenberg & Epstein, 1985, 1987; Walczyk, 1990). Also, text variables influence comprehension monitoring. For example, explicit contradictions in texts are more easily detected than implicit contradictions (Markman & Gorin, 1981); contradictions involving main points are detected better than those involving details (Baker & Anderson, 1982; Yussen & Smith, 1990); and contradictions that are near each other in the text are found in some studies to be better detected than those that are located far apart (Baker, 1979; Garner & Kraus, 1981–1982; Glenberg, Wilkinson & Epstein, 1982), although other studies have not found this difference (Walczyk & Hall, 1989). Regarding science texts, local coherence in physics paragraphs is found to be more easily monitored by secondary school students than global coherence (Brincones & Otero, 1994; Dee-Lucas & Larkin, 1991). Local coherence involves the connection of a proposition to others corresponding to immediately preceding information still in short-term memory. These connections could be established, for example, through argument overlap or through causal links. Global coherence involves linking the currently processed proposition to relevant information that is no longer in short-term memory but that occurred earlier in the text (Albrecht & O'Brien, 1993), or establishing a relation to the theme or topic of discourse (Van Dijk & Kintsch, 1983).

Task characteristics have also influenced comprehension monitoring. For example, error detection in texts has improved when subjects are advised to look for specific problems in the information to be processed, instead of just reading for comprehension (Baker, 1979, 1985; Markman, 1979; Markman & Gorin, 1981).

Three of the variables having an effect on comprehension monitoring of science texts will be considered in more detail here: a learner characteristic variable, activated knowledge, and two context variables—subject matter or domain setting and epistemic authority of the source.

INFLUENCE OF ACTIVATED KNOWLEDGE

The relation between learners' knowledge and new scientific information has been a topic of interest in science education research since the late 1970s. This relation plays an essential role in approaches to science education that have been based on the work of Ausubel (Ausubel, Novak, & Hanesian, 1978; Novak, 1977). Research, however, has shown that students' knowledge of natural phenomena is frequently at variance with scientific knowledge (Clement, 1982; Confrey, 1990; Gilbert & Watts, 1983; McCloskey, 1983; Pfund & Duit, 1994; Viennot, 1979). Attention has been paid to the interaction of these "misconceptions" or "alternative conceptions" with scientific knowledge that students find at school.

Conceptual change refers to the progression from students' inadequate conceptions to established scientific knowledge, and to the strategies that are useful to achieve this change. One of these strategies is the creation of *cognitive conflict* (Posner, Strike, Hewson, & Gertzog, 1982), or presenting information that is inconsistent with subjects' knowledge. For example, experimental evidence may be presented that contradicts predictions made by a student on the physical behavior of an object. Although the effectiveness of cognitive conflict in leading to subjects' conceptual change is corroborated both in the literature on science education and reading education (Guzzetti, Snyder, Glass, & Gamas, 1993), its effect is not automatic.

The effectiveness of cognitive conflict depends on the way comprehension is monitored. It depends, first, on the individual noticing the inconsistency and, second, on the way it is resolved. For example, Gunstone & White (1981) presented first-year university students with an experimental arrangement consisting of a pulley with a cord that connected a bucket of sand and a block of wood of the same mass. The participants were asked to predict what would happen when a large scoop of sand was added to the bucket. Thirty percent of the participants predicted that there would be only a small change of the system shifting to a new equilibrium position. The inconsistency in the prediction was apparent when students observed the accelerated downward motion of the bucket. However, none of these subjects attempted to regulate their comprehension by reconciling their knowledge with external evidence. Consequently, no learning resulted in this case from cognitive conflict. Thus, it is important to analyze the comprehension monitoring involved in the interaction between students' knowledge and incompatible scientific information.

Activated Knowledge and Conceptual Change

The interaction between students' activated knowledge and incompatible scientific information provided through texts has received attention from researchers interested in conceptual change in science education. The results from many of these studies are conflicting. Subject's extant or activated knowledge has been found in some studies to hinder the acquisition of information inconsistent with this knowledge. Lipson (1982) studied the effects of knowledge and reading ability on third-grade students' understanding of natural sciences and social sciences texts. Students were evaluated with the same test before and after reading the text. The study showed that a posttest item had a higher probability of being answered correctly when the student had indicated ignorance of the same item in the pretest than when a wrong answer was given. Consequently, in this study, inadequate or incorrect knowledge appears more detrimental in the acquisition of new information than the absence of knowledge.

Smith, Readence, & Alvermann (1984) examined the effect of activating relevant knowledge to understand a passage taken from a sixth-grade science textbook. Two versions of the passage were used, compatible and incompatible. The incompatible form resulted from manipulating the passage so that it contained information contrary to general knowledge. Part of the subjects activated their background knowledge by writing about the topic of the passage prior to the reading task. No differences in recall were found between students who had background knowledge activated and those who had not. However, nonactivators gave more correct answers than activators in a multiple choice test both for items tapping congruous information and incongruous information. It was concluded that activating prior knowledge does not facilitate learning information that is incompatible with reader's knowledge. In another study, Alvermann, Smith, & Readence (1985) provided sixth-grade students with a science paragraph containing text that was inconsistent with subjects' knowledge. Some of the subjects had relevant information activated using a similar procedure as in the previous experiment, before reading the text. The researchers found an interference effect of activated prior knowledge on recall and recognition of new information that was incompatible with this knowledge.

Alvermann & Hague (1989) studied the effect of activating prior knowledge on the comprehension of a counterintuitive text about Newtonian mechanics. The subjects of the study were students entering college with less-than-average high-school grades or SAT scores. Three levels were created for activation: (a) activation (corresponding to activation of students' knowledge), (b) augmented activation (corresponding to activation plus a warning to be alert for information incompatible with currently held beliefs), and (c) control (no activation). The augmented level of activation was more effective than activation alone in learning new information, according both to short-answer and multiple-choice posttests. Warning of possible inconsistencies facilitated the comprehension of text that was incongruent with subjects' beliefs, thereby apparently overriding the negative effect of activation found in other studies.

In this last study, activation alone was less effective than no activation. However, in another study where the same variables were manipulated, Alvermann and Hynd (1989) found opposite results. Activation facilitated learning (as measured by short-answer and true–false tests) from a text that presented Newtonian principles inconsistent with college students' misconceptions about the principles of motion. Finally, in still another study, Hynd and Alvermann (1989) found that college students performed equally well in the activation and augmented activation conditions. Also, the activated group performed better than the nonactivated group on the short-answer test but not on the true–false posttest.

Guzzetti (1990) also studied the influence of augmented activation. She examined comprehension and application of Boyle's law by 11th- and 12th-grade chemistry students who held misconceptions on the relation between pressure and volume. Augmented activation, in this case, consisted of a teacher's demonstration of the conflicting phenomenon followed by a discussion of students' reactions of surprise. No differences were found between groups who received or did not receive augmented activation on measures of comprehension and application of the new information.

Finally, one of the first studies where activating prior knowledge was found to facilitate processing of new ideas that are inconsistent with this knowledge was conducted by Peeck, van den Bosch, & Kreupeling (1982). Eleven-year-old students either did or did not activate knowledge about the appearance and way of life of foxes before reading a text that presented information on a fictional fox that was incompatible with students' ideas. It was found that activators recalled more incompatible information than did nonactivators. However, no differences were found due to activation of information consistent with students' knowledge.

Given these and other conflicting results, "researchers have cited the need for and begun to take a more qualitative look" (Guzzetti, 1990, p. 50). The comprehension of how cognitive conflict operates is still limited. Guzzetti, Snyder, and Glass (1992) synthesized recommendations for conceptual change based on the kind of research reported earlier. These strategies included using augmented activation activities, refutation text, or a type of structured discussion, the Discussion Web (Alvermann, 1991). The authors identify a commonality in these strategies: "Each strategy found effective as a single intervention in some way created in students' minds a degree of discomfort with their prior beliefs" (Guzzetti, Snyder, & Glass, 1992 , p. 648). However, the operation of cognitive conflict and the creation of this discomfort involves processes that should be more closely examined.

Activated Knowledge and Detection of Internal Inconsistencies

Identification of the component processes of comprehension monitoring will be helpful in explaining the previous disparate results on the effect of activation. Processing of internal inconsistencies in the text provides a way to examine the interaction between pieces of inconsistent information. Failures of subjects of various ages to detect internal inconsistencies in narratives (Vosniadou, Pearson, & Rogers, 1988), expository texts (Baker, 1985; Glenberg, Wilkinson, & Epstein, 1982; Markman, 1979) and, specifically, science texts (Otero & Campanario, 1990) are well documented. However, most of these studies have been descriptive.

To detect an internal inconsistency, both incompatible text propositions should be active in working memory at the same time. A resonance process has been proposed as an explanation for the reinstatement of information in working memory when readers encounter local or global coherence breaks (O'Brien, 1995). For example, when a reader finds an anaphoric phrase, potential antecedents in the text resonate. That which resonates most is reinstated in working memory, and the connection is established. This resonance process might be expected to happen when a reader finds the second inconsistent proposition of a textual contradiction. However, several factors influencing the resonance process could cause a failure in reinstating the antecedent proposition, for example, the distance between elements of related information in a text (O'Brien, 1987). In the case that the first inconsistent proposition is not brought to working memory, a contradiction may go unnoticed.

The Suppression Hypothesis

Another mechanism that could explain nondetection of explicit contradictions in a text was proposed by Otero and Kintsch (1992). It is based on the inhibitory effect caused by an excessive activation of an inconsistent proposition within a network. The explanation is framed within the Construction–Integration (CI) model of text comprehension (Kintsch, 1988).

The CI model inherits some of the characteristics of the previous Kintsch and Van Dijk's model (1978). Texts are processed in cycles, due to limitations of short-term memory, and their representation in memory is propositional. Two stages are distinguished in the operation of the model. First, there is a construction phase in which propositions derived from the text are joined in a network together with propositions retrieved from memory. These knowledge propositions are retrieved from memory without regard for their contextual adequacy. Both text and knowledge propositions are interconnected using argument overlap as a default criterion. Connection strengths are assigned to these links creating a connectivity matrix. Negative links may exist, for example, between contradictory propositions or between alternative meanings of a homonym.

The second stage consists of an integration process carried out in the connectionist manner. Activation spreads between propositions depending on the existing links. Pieces of the network that hang together reinforce each other, whereas those nodes that are isolated or connected through negative links are deactivated. The integration process gives as a result the final activation of propositions. In this way, the model achieves with weak rules (i.e., those allowing for the initial aggregation of inadequate, redundant, or inconsistent propositions to the network) what has been usually been done by means of smart, but less flexible procedures like schemata, frames, or scripts. Inappropriate propositions are filtered out in the integration phase, and activation is only accumulated in the contextually relevant nodes.

The CI model naturally provides an explanatory mechanism for failures in detecting internal inconsistencies in texts. This mechanism is based on the effect of activation: An excessive activation of one of the contradictory text propositions leads in the integration phase to the inhibition of the other and its consequent disappearance from the final representation of the text in long-term memory. Increased activation of a proposition may be caused by the connection patterns in the propositional network. Some subjects may emphasize certain connections between text information and portions of their knowledge that they have overlearned or learned more recently. For example, a 12th-grade student who read one of the contradictory texts in the Otero and Campanario (1990) experiment, where superconductivity was defined as "the disappearance of resistance to the flow of electric current," recalled after about 15 minutes, that, "Superconductivity appears in surfaces which do not have friction." A post hoc explanation is provided by the CI model if connections to the student's knowledge related to friction are weighted too heavily. The intrusion may be simulated in terms of the CI model by the disproportionate activation that the term *resistance* caused on the *friction* portion of her physics knowledge. (Both concepts can be linked as friction implies resistance to motion; Otero, 1990, p. 16).

According to this interpretation, suppression of inconsistent information will take place when one of the contradictory propositions is excessively activated. If this is not so, the contradiction may be detected and the reader may attempt to solve the inconsistency by generating inferences that could explain away the contradiction. This elaboration activity results in enhanced memory that has been found for inconsistent or unexpected information. O'Brien and Myers (1985), for example, found better recognition memory for lexical items in a nonpredictive context compared to the same items in a predictive context. Also, reading times for sentences including an unpredictable item were longer than those for sentences where the unpredictable item was substituted by one that was predictable. Longer reading times are interpreted as due to the need to integrate the unexpected item into the text representation. This is supported by the finding of improved memory for the text preceding the unpredictable word as compared to text preceding a predictable word.

Interaction Between Activated Knowledge and Ability

The previous inhibitory mechanism provides an explanation of failures to detect an inconsistency in terms of the excessive activation of one of the inconsistent propositions. Indeed, unequal weighting of propositions when reading a text should always be expected. For example, macropropositions, (i.e., propositions that synthesize the semantic information of discourse as a whole), have a special status in discourse processing (Van Dijk & Kintsch, 1983, chap. 10) and more saliency in memory of text (Guindon & Kintsch, 1984). In a network model of text comprehension, like the CI model, this would be simulated by assigning them more weight. However, unequal weighting of propositions in normal reading may be exaggerated by some readers. This would be the case for readers believing too strongly in their initial interpretation of a text, or for readers holding strong prior beliefs that are inconsistent with text information. Consequently, an interaction would be expected between external manipulations of activation, like those used in the previous studies, and readers' characteristics. The suppression effect due to external activation is hypothesized to affect differently above-average students and below-average students: Exaggerated activation of propositions would be more frequent for the latter.

Cuerva and Otero (1996) examined this hypothesis in an experiment that also involved other factors, in addition to knowledge activation. A set of six science paragraphs was given to 10th-grade students with instructions to evaluate their understandability and to point out any difficulty that they may find. The target paragraph, taken from a previous study (Otero & Campanario, 1990), was the following:

> Neutrinos are particles with nearly zero mass. Their detection is very difficult because they do not react to magnetic or nuclear forces. In order to detect them, a great amount of water is necessary, placed in a deep place underground, where it could be free from other radiations. A great amount of water is necessary because neutrinos seldom interact with matter. Several countries have set up neutrino detectors which will be useful in the future. The great facility with which neutrinos are detected makes them very suitable, for example, for the study of cosmic phenomena.

This paragraph occupied the fourth place in a series of six paragraphs. The activation of one of the contradictory propositions in this target paragraph—DIFFICULT (DETECT (NEUTRINOS))was accomplished by including three preceding paragraphs with main ideas synthesized by propositions having the same predicate as the proposition to be activated. For example, the proposition corresponding to the main idea for one of these activating paragraphs was DIFFICULT (SCIENTIFIC (RESEARCH)).

The results regarding the effect of activation were consistent with the suppression hypothesis. No main effect was found for activation on the detection of the contradiction, but the expected interaction appeared: Below-average students (i.e., those whose grade point average was below the median for the grade level) detected fewer contradictions in the activation condition compared to the nonactivation condition. An opposite effect was found for above-average students: More contradictions were detected in the activation condition compared to the nonactivation condition. Activation apparently facilitated the resonance process in advantaged students, causing the first contradictory proposition to be reinstated in working memory when the second was found. Thus, activating subject's knowledge had different effects on the detection of inconsistent information, and consequently on creating cognitive conflict, depending on subjects' ability.

The interaction of external activation with subjects' characteristics evidenced in this result illustrates the complexity of the influences on comprehension evaluation of science texts. The following section focuses on another of these influences.

INFLUENCE OF CONTEXT

The previous interaction is an example of the possible interactions existing among learner, text, and task variables that could be used to explain the disparate results found on the relation between prior knowledge and new information incompatible with it. Context variables also should be expected to participate in these interactions.

Few studies have been done on the influence of context variables on comprehension monitoring, although the influence of context or situation variables in learning (Brown, Collins, & Duguid, 1989) and specifically on conceptual change (Pintrich, Marx, & Boyle, 1993) has been already acknowledged. Walczyk and Hall (1989) found no differences on the effect of a reading setting versus an arithmetic setting on comprehension monitoring by third- and fifth-grade students. However, the lack of significant results was considered due to a weak manipulation of the variable: Setting was operationalized solely by telling the students that the material they were reading would be used by a math teacher or, alternatively, by a reading teacher.

Mosenthal (1979) examined the influence of social context on strategy preferences for restructuring contradictory story information, that is, for regulating comprehension. The results for sixth graders showed that the more formal the context, the less likely incompatible information was restructured: Reading inconsistent stories as a part of a recall experiment (i.e., a more formal context) resulted in less restructuring than reading these stories for the purpose of explaining them to first graders (i.e., a less formal context).

Influence of Subject-Matter Setting

In an attempt to study the effects of context in the domain of science, García-Arista, Campanario, and Otero (1996) examined the influence of class setting and subject-matter setting on evaluation and regulation of comprehension of science texts. Twelfth-grade students were led to believe that they were reading science passages either from a science textbook as part of a university research project related to their science class, or from a newspaper as part of a university research project related to their language class. Some of the passages—the same in both conditions—included explicit contradictions. As in previous studies, students were instructed to evaluate the texts for comprehensibility and to point out any problems that they may find. Evaluation of comprehension was ascertained in terms of the detection of the contradictions in the paragraphs. Regulation of comprehension was measured in terms of the actions taken by subjects once the contradiction was noticed: Subjects may ignore the contradiction, fix it up by inadequate inferencing, or explicitly point out the problem (Otero & Campanario, 1990).

The results showed a significant improvement of evaluation and regulation of comprehension in the science setting as compared to the language setting. Students detected more contradictions when they thought that they were reading science paragraphs as part of a science class than as part of a language class, and they regulated their comprehension in the science setting better by explicitly pointing out contradictions. In part, this was an unexpected finding. According to some science education research results, students often think of scientific research as producing incontrovertible truth (Meichtry, 1993; Rubba & Anderson, 1978). The "inviolability of text" (Garner, 1987, p. 86), pointed out as a reason for failures in error-detection performance, should be expected to be more severe in the scientific domain. This could lead students to suspend their critical ability when processing information from a scientific source. However, the effect of a scientific context showed the opposite. Of course, the external validity of these results is limited in that only texts with scientific content were used, although they were intended to be accessible to the nonspecialist. But these results provide an example of the dependency of metacognitive strategies on the situation where learning takes place.

Thus, subject matter and class setting appear to be contextual factors that influence the translation into action of procedural knowledge of comprehension monitoring strategies. Readers are sensitive to these contextual demands and seem to adjust comprehension monitoring according to academic domain.

Influence of Epistemic Authority

Converging evidence supporting the effects of subject matter and class setting was provided by findings on the effect of epistemic authority on comprehension monitoring. Epistemic authority refers to subjective beliefs about the knowledgeability or expertise of a source in a certain domain (Bar-Tal, Raviv, Raviv, & Brosh, 1991; Ellis & Kruglanski, 1992). In the study reported earlier on the effect of activation on contradiction detection, Cuerva and Otero (1996) also manipulated the epistemic authority of the source. The same contradictory paragraphs were presented to part of the sample of 10th-grade students as taken from introductory college textbooks (i.e., high epistemic authority), and to other students they were presented as taken from primary level textbooks (i.e., relatively low epistemic authority). The dependent variable of interest was the detection of contradictions. Although no main effect was found for epistemic authority, an interaction between this variable and gender appeared: Significantly more contradictions were detected by boys in the high epistemic authority condition than in the low epistemic authority condition, whereas an opposite trend was found for girls. Thus, an effect of a contextual variable was again found, mediated this time by learners' characteristics. These different effects of epistemic authority on the detection of contradictions may be related to different views of self-efficacy in boys and girls. Lower self-concepts of ability in science-related subjects have been found for girls than for boys (Fennema & Sherman, 1978). This implies that girls may be using less deep learning strategies and engaging in less comprehension monitoring when reading scientific texts (Paris & Oka, 1986).

In conclusion, I argue that knowledge activation, learners' characteristics, and context interact to provide a complex picture of the factors influencing comprehension monitoring of science texts. These interactions should be taken into account in efforts to improve comprehension monitoring in educational situations. I turn next to these educational implications.

EDUCATIONAL AND RESEARCH IMPLICATIONS

Some of the factors influencing comprehension monitoring of science texts and their interactions have been examined in this chapter. Teachers and educational researchers should pay attention to these factors in their attempts to improve students' comprehension monitoring. Adequate comprehension monitoring is frequently the key for the appropriate use of other learning strategies (Garner, 1990). For example, creating cognitive conflict by activating students' knowledge that is inconsistent with scientific information is a strategy designed to promote conceptual change in science learning. But this activation has been shown to have different effects depending on the way that students faced with an inconsistency evaluate and regulate comprehension. Evaluation and regulation of comprehension, in its turn, depend on personal factors. Above-average students notice the inconsistency and take profit from cognitive conflict. However, a prerequisite for the strategy to be effective with below average students is to improve their defective comprehension monitoring ability.

Failures in comprehension monitoring are shown not to be necessarily linked to individuals but also to the situation. Garner's (1990) warning about the context dependency of strategy use applies to comprehension monitoring strategies: Students may have declarative and procedural knowledge of these strategies, but may not use them because of influences of the situation. Examining these influences in particular domains, like science or language in schools, appears as an interesting problem for educational and psychological research. For example, identifying factors responsible for the improvement in comprehension monitoring in a science setting compared to a language setting, as shown previously, could throw light on ways to improve comprehension monitoring in unfavorable settings.

Use of comprehension monitoring strategies when reading texts is also dependent on evaluation practices. Students' perceptions about the demands of evaluation will influence students' use of skills and strategies (Crooks, 1988; Entwistle & Ramsden, 1983; Ramsden, 1985). Consequently, the importance given to comprehension monitoring should influence students' use of this strategy. However, comprehension monitoring has a limited weight in the evaluation practices of some educational systems.

Otero, Campanario, and Hopkins (1992) studied the relationship between school grades, as a measure of academic achievement, and comprehension-monitoring ability of Spanish secondary-school students. Comprehension-monitoring ability was operationalized through the use of comprehension evaluation and regulation strategies when reading contradictory texts in a school science setting. Modest correlations between academic achievement and comprehension monitoring ability were obtained for Grades 9 through 12: None of the correlations was higher than .53. In addition, there was a decreasing trend from the lower to the upper grade levels.

The results were basically replicated in a new study involving Spanish and Portuguese students from eighth grade to the university level (Campanario, García-Arista, Otero, Caldeira, Prata-Pina, Patricio, Costa, & Hopkins, 1997). This suggests a limited role of comprehension-monitoring ability as an explanation of individual differences in academic achievement, as measured by traditional evaluation instruments. Moreover, this role seems to be less important as grade level increases. Consequently, devising evaluation practices that place a greater weight on this ability should have a beneficial effect on its development.

Research by Acredolo and Connor (1991) suggests some steps that could be taken to improve the sensitivity of school evaluation to comprehension monitoring. Acredolo and O'Connor termed "choice procedure" those diverse methods in cognitive assessment that "imply to subjects that every problem has one deducible solution and that they will be evaluated based *only* on whether or not they can identify that solution" (p. 206). They suggest that this may cause the observed appearance of confidence of subjects whose judgments in cognitive assessment tasks are however inaccurate. Given that much of standard school science evaluation relies on the choice procedure, it may also prevent assessing students' awareness of uncertainty. Evaluating in such a way that students were allowed to reveal their uncertainties would probably improve the assessment of students' comprehension monitoring (see Rowell, 1995, for an example of implementation of this evaluation approach within a science teachers' training course). This implies testing for knowledge, valuing the extent to which students possess it, but also testing for ignorance, valuing the extent to which students are aware of it.

ACKNOWLEDGMENTS

The research presented in this chapter was supported by DGICYT of the Ministry of Education, Spain, through Grant PB93-0478.

REFERENCES

Acredolo, C., & O'Connor, J. (1991). On the difficulty of detecting cognitive uncertainty. *Human Development, 34,* 204–223.

Albrecht, J. E., O'Brien, E. J. (1993). Updating a mental model: maintaining both local and global coherence. *Journal of Experimental Psychology: Learning, Memory and Cognition, 19,* 1061–1070.

Alessi, S. M., Anderson, T. H., & Goetz, E. T. (1979). An investigation of lookbacks during studying. *Discourse Processes, 2,* 197–212.

Alexander, P. A. (in press). The interplay between domain and general strategy knowledge: Exploring the influence of motivation and situation. In A. Pace (Ed.), *Beyond prior knowledge: Issues in text processing and conceptual change.* Norwood, NJ: Ablex.

Alexander, P. A., & Kulikowich, J. M. (1994). Learning from physics text: A synthesis of recent research. *Journal of Research in Science Teaching, 31,* 895–911.

Alvermann, D. E. (1991). The discussion web: A graphic aid for learning across the curriculum. *The Reading Teacher, 45,* 92–99.

Alvermann, D. E., Smith, L. C., & Readence, J. E. (1985). Prior knowledge activation and the comprehension of compatible and incompatible text. *Reading Research Quarterly, 20*, 420–436.

Alvermann, D. E., & Hague, S. (1989). Comprehension of counterintuitive science text: Effects of prior knowledge and text structure. *Journal of Educational Research, 82*, 197–202.

Alvermann, D. E., & Hynd, C. R. (1989). Effects of prior knowledge activation modes and text structure on nonscience majors' comprehension of physics. *Journal of Educational Research, 83*, 97–102.

Anderson, G., & Beal, C. R. (1995). Children's recognition of inconsistencies in science texts: Multiple measures of comprehension monitoring. *Applied Cognitive Psychology, 9*, 261—272.

Ausubel, D. P., Novak, J. D., & Hanesian, H. (1978). *Educational psychology: A cognitive view.* New York: Holt Rinehart & Winston.

Baker, L. (1979). Comprehension monitoring: Identifying and coping with text confusions. *Journal of Reading Behavior, 11*, 363–374.

Baker, L. (1985). Differences in the standards used by college students to evaluate their comprehension of expository prose. *Reading Research Quarterly, 22*, 297–313.

Baker, L., & Anderson, R. I. (1982). Effects of inconsistent information on text processing: Evidence for comprehension monitoring. *Reading Research Quarterly, 17*, 281–294.

Bar–Tal, D., Raviv, A., Raviv, A., & Brosh, M. (1991). Perception of epistemic authority and attribution for its choice as a function of knowledge area and age. *European Journal of Social Psychology, 21*, 477–492.

Brincones, I., & Otero, J. (1994). Students' conceptions of the top-level structure of physics texts. *Science Education, 78*, 171–183.

Brown, A., Armbruster, B., & Baker, L. (1986). The role of metacognition in reading and studying. In J. Orasanu (Ed.), *Reading comprehension: From research to practice.* Hillsdale, NJ: Lawrence Erlbaum Associates.

Brown, J. L., Collins, A., & Duguid, P. (1989). Situated cognition and the culture of learning. *Educational Researcher, 18*, 32–41.

Campanario, J. M., García-Arista, E., Otero, J., Caldeira, M. H., Prata-Pina, E. M., Patricio, A., Costa, E., & Hopkins, K. (1997). *Comprehension monitoring and academic achievement from primary to tertiary education in two educational systems.* Manuscript submitted for publication.

Clement. J. (1982). Students' preconceptions in introductory mechanics. *American Journal of Physics, 50*, 66–70.

Confrey, J. (1990). A review of the research on student conceptions in mathematics, science and programming. In C. Cazden (Ed.), *Review of research in education* (Vol. 16, pp. 3–56). Washington, DC: American Educational Research Association.

Cook, L., & Mayer, R. E. (1988). Teaching readers about the structure of scientific text. *Journal of Educational Psychology, 80*, 448–456.

Crooks, T. J. (1988). The impact of classroom evaluation practices on students. *Review of Educational Research, 58*, 438–481.

Cuerva, J., & Otero, J. (1996, September). *Influence of epistemic authority and knowledge activation on the detection of inconsistencies in science texts.* Paper presented at the International Seminar Using Complex Information Systems, UCIS'96, Poitiers, France.

Dee-Lucas, D., & Larkin, J. H. (1991). Equations in scientific proofs: Effects on comprehension. *American Educational Research Journal, 28*, 661–682.

Ellis, S., & Kruglanski, A. W. (1992). Self as an epistemic authority: effects on experiential and instructional learning. *Social Cognition, 10*, 357–375.

Entwistle, N. J., & Ramsden, P.(1983) *Understanding student learning.* London: Croom Helm.

Fennema, E., & Sherman, J. (1978). Sex-related differences in mathematics achievement and related factors: A further study. *Journal for Research in Mathematics Education, 9,* 189–203.

García-Arista, E., Campanario, J. M., & Otero, J. (1996). Influence of subject matter setting on comprehension monitoring. *European Journal of Psychology of Education, 21,* 427–441.

Garner, R. (1987). *Metacognition and reading comprehension.* Norwood, NJ: Ablex.

Garner, R. (1990). When children and adults do not use learning strategies: Toward a theory of settings. *Review of Educational Research, 60,* 517– 529.

Garner, R., & Kraus, C. (1981–1982). Good and poor comprehenders' differences in knowing and regulating reading behaviors. *Educational Research Quarterly, 6,* 5–12.

Garner, R., & Reis, R. (1981). Monitoring and resolving comprehension obstacles: An investigation of spontaneous text lookbacks among upper grade good and poor comprehenders. *Reading Research Quarterly, 16,* 569–582.

Gilbert, J. K., & Watts, D. M. (1983). Concepts, misconceptions and alternative conceptions: Changing perspectives in science education. *Studies in Science Education, 10,* 61–98.

Glenberg, A. M., & Epstein, W. (1985). Calibration of comprehension. *Journal of Experimental Psychology: Learning, Memory, and Cognition, 11,* 702–718.

Glenberg, A. M., & Epstein, W. (1987). Inexpert calibration of comprehension. *Memory and Cognition, 15,* 84–93.

Glenberg A. M., Wilkinson A. C., & Epstein, W. (1982). The illusion of knowing: Failure in the self-assessment of comprehension. *Memory and Cognition, 10,* 597–602.

Guindon, R., & Kintsch, W. (1984). Priming macropropositions: Evidence for the primacy of macropropositions in the memory for text. *Journal of Verbal Learning and Verbal Behavior, 23,* 508–518.

Gunstone, R. F., & White, R. T. (1981). Understanding of gravity. *Science Education, 65,* 291–299.

Guzzetti, B. J. (1990). Effects of textual and instructional manipulations on concept acquisition. *Reading Psychology: An International Quarterly, 11,* 49–62.

Guzzetti, B. J., Snyder, T. E., & Glass, G. V. (1992). Promoting conceptual change in science: Can texts be used effectively? *Journal of Reading, 35,* 642–649.

Guzzetti, B. J., Snyder, T. E., Glass, G. V., & Gamas, W. S. (1993). Promoting conceptual change in science: A comparative meta-analysis of instructional interventions from reading and science education. *Reading Research Quarterly, 28,* 117–159.

Hammer, D. (1994). Epistemological beliefs in introductory physics. *Cognition and Instruction, 12,* 151–183.

Hynd, C. R., & Alverman, D. E. (1989). Overcoming misconceptions in science: An on-line study of prior knowledge activation. *Reading Research and Instruction, 28,* 12–26.

Kintsch, W. (1988) The Construction–Integration model of text comprehension. *Psychological Review, 95,* 163–182.

Kintsch, W., & van Dijk, T. A. (1978). Toward a model of text comprehension and production. *Psychological Review, 85,* 363–394.

Kroll, M. D., & Ford, M. L. (1992). The illusion of knowing, error detection and motivational orientations. *Contemporary Educational Psychology, 17,* 371–378.

Lipson, M. Y. (1982). Learning new information from text: The role of prior knowledge and reading ability. *Journal of Reading Behavior, 14,* 243–261.

Maki, R. H., & Berry, S. L. (1984). Metacomprehension of text material. *Journal of Experimental Psychology: Learning, Memory and Cognition, 10,* 663–679.

Maki, R.H., & Swett, M. (1987). Metamemory for narrative texts. *Memory and Cognition, 15,* 72–83.

Markman, E. M. (1977). Realizing that you don't understand: A preliminary investigation. *Child Development, 46,* 986–992.

Markman, E. M. (1979). Realizing that you don't understand: Elementary school children's awareness of inconsistencies. *Child Development, 50,* 643–655.

Markman, E. M., & Gorin, L. (1981). Children's ability to adjust their standards for evaluating comprehension. *Journal of Educational Psychology, 73,* 320–325.

McCloskey, M. (1983). Naive theories of motion. In D. Gentner & A. Stevens (Eds.), *Mental models* (pp. 299–324). Hillsdale, N.J.: Lawrence Erlbaum Associates.

Meichtry, Y. J. (1993). The impact of science curricula on student views about the nature of science. *Journal of Research in Science Teaching, 30,* 429–443.

Meyer, B., Brandt, D., & Bluth, G. (1980). Use of top-level structure in text: Key for reading comprehension of ninth-grade students. *Reading Research Quarterly. 16,* 72–103.

Mosenthal, P. (1979). Children's strategy preferences for resolving contradictory story information under two social conditions. *Journal of Experimental Child Psychology, 28,* 323–343.

Nolen, S. B. (1988). Reasons for studying: Motivational orientations and study strategies. *Cognition and Instruction, 5,* 269–287.

Novak, J. D. (1977). *A theory of education.* Ithaca, NY: Cornell University Press.

O'Brien, E. J. (1987). Antecedent search processes and the structure of text. *Journal of Experimental Psychology: Learning, Memory and Cognition, 13,* 278–290.

O'Brien, E. J. (1995). Automatic components of discourse comprehension. In R. F. Lorch & E. J. O'Brien (Eds.), *Sources of Coherence in Reading.* Mahwah, NJ: Lawrence Erlbaum Associates.

O'Brien, E., & Myers, J. L. (1985). When comprehension difficulty improves memory for text. *Journal of Experimental Psychology: Learning, Memory and Cognition 11,* 12–21.

Otero, J. (1990). *Failures in monitoring text comprehension: An explanation in terms of the Construction–Integration model* (ICS Tech. Rep. No. 90-17). Boulder: University of Colorado.

Otero, J. (1992). El aprendizaje receptivo de las ciencias: preconcepciones, estrategias cognitivas y estrategias metacognitivas [Meaningful reception learning of science: preconceptions, cognitive strategies and metacognitive strategies]. *Tarbiya, 1,* 57–66.

Otero, J. (1996). Components of comprehension monitoring in the acquisition of knowledge from science texts. In K. M. Fisher & M. R. Kibby (Eds.), *Knowledge acquisition organization and use in biology.* Berlin: NATO-Springer Verlag.

Otero, J., & Campanario, J. M. (1990). Comprehension evaluation and regulation in learning from science texts. *Journal of Research in Science Teaching, 27,* 447–460.

Otero, J., Campanario, J. M., & Hopkins, K. D. (1992). The relationship between academic achievement and metacognitive comprehension monitoring ability of Spanish secondary school students. *Educational and Psychological Measurement, 52,* 419–430.

Otero, J., & Kintsch, W. (1992). Failures to detect contradictions in a text: What readers believe vs. what they read. *Psychological Science, 3,* 229–235.

Paris, S. G., & Oka, E. R. (1986). Children's reading strategies, metacognition and motivation. *Developmental Review, 6,* 25–26.

Peeck, J., van den Bosch, A. B., & Kreupeling, W. J. (1982). Effect of mobilizing prior knowledge on learning from text. *Journal of Educational Psychology, 74,* 771–777.

Pfundt, H. & Duit, R. (1994). *Bibliography: Students' alternative frameworks and science education* (4th ed.). Kiel: IPN, University of Kiel.

Pintrich, P. R., Marx, R. W., & Boyle, R. A. (1993). Beyond cold conceptual change: The role of motivational beliefs and classroom contextual factors in the process of conceptual change. *Review of Educational Research, 63,* 167–199.

Posner, G. J., Strike, K. A., Hewson, P. W., & Gertzog, W. A. (1982). Accommodation of a scientific conception: Toward a theory of conceptual change. *Science Education, 66,* 211–227.

Ramsdem, P. (1985). Student learning research: Retrospect and prospect. *Higher Education Research and Development, 4,* 51–69.

Rowell, J. A. (1995). Raising Awareness of Uncertainty: A useful addendum to courses in the history and philosophy of science for science teachers? *Science & Education, 4,* 87–97.

Rubba, P., & Anderson, H. (1978). Development of an instrument to assess secondary students' understanding of the nature of scientific knowledge. *Science Education, 62,* 449–458.

Schunk, D. (1985). Self-efficacy and school learning. *Psychology in the Schools, 22,* 208–223.

Smith, L. C., Readence, J. E., & Alvermann, D. E. (1984). Effects of activating background knowledge on comprehension of expository prose. In J. A. Niles & L. A. Larris (Eds.), *Thirty-Third Yearbook of the National Reading Conference* (pp. 188–192). Rochester, NY: National Reading Conference.

Van Dijk, T., & Kintsch, W. (1983). *Strategies of discourse comprehension.* New York: Academic Press.

Van Rossum, E., & Schenk, S. (1984). The relationship between learning conception, study strategy and learning outcome. *British Journal of Educational Psychology, 54,* 73–83.

Viennot, L. (1979). *Le raisonnement spontané en dynamique elementaire.* [Spontaneous reasoning in elementary dynamics]. Paris: Hermann.

Vosniadou, S., Pearson, P. D., & Rogers, T. (1988). What causes children's failures to detect inconsistencies in text? Representation versus comparison difficulties. *Journal of Educational Psychology, 80,* 27–39.

Walczyk, J. J. (1990). Relation among error detection, sentence verification and low-level reading skills of fourth graders. *Journal of Educational Psychology, 82,* 491–497.

Walczyk, J. J., & Hall, V. C. (1989). The effects of setting, thematic familiarity, and type of contradiction on comprehension monitoring. *Contemporary Educational Psychology, 14,* 145–152.

Winograd, P., & Johnston, P. (1982). Comprehension monitoring and the error detection paradigm. *Journal of Reading Behavior, 14,* 61–76.

Yussen, S. R., & Smith, M. C. (1990). Detecting general and specific errors in expository texts. *Contemporary Educational Psychology, 15,* 224–240.

Zabrucky, K., Moore, D., & Schultz, N. (1987). Evaluation of comprehension in young and old adults. *Developmental Psychology, 23,* 39–43.

Zabrucky, K., & Ratner, H. (1986). Children's comprehension monitoring and recall of inconsistent stories. *Child Development, 57,* 1401–1418.

Zabrucky, K., & Ratner, H. H. (1989). Effects of reading ability on children's comprehension evaluation and regulation. *Journal of Reading Behavior, 21,* 69–83.

Zabrucky, K., & Ratner, H. H. (1992). Effects of passage type on comprehension monitoring and recall in good and poor readers. *Journal of Reading Behavior, 24,* 373–391.

8

Self-Regulated Comprehension During Normal Reading

Douglas J. Hacker
The University of Memphis

Cognitive psychologists and educational psychologists have not always agreed on the kinds of cognitive processes that should be included under the rubric of comprehension monitoring, nor have they always agreed on a common usage of the term *comprehension monitoring*. In general, cognitive psychologists have used the terminology *metamemory for text*, *calibration of comprehension*, or *metacomprehension* and have restricted the kinds of processes to those that concern prediction of whether text has been or will be understood (e.g., Glenberg & Epstein, 1985; Glenberg, Wilkinson, & Epstein, 1982; Maki & Serra, 1992; Weaver, 1990). The concept underlying these terms often has been operationalized by relating readers' predictions of comprehension with their actual performance on comprehension-type questions. Readers whose predictions and performance are highly correlated are judged to have good calibration of comprehension, whereas readers whose predictions and performance are minimally correlated are judged to have poor metacomprehension.

By contrast, educational psychologists have tended to favor the term *comprehension monitoring* and typically have conceptualized it as a multidimensional process that includes evaluation and regulation (e.g., Baker, 1985; Brown, 1980; Hacker, Plumb, Butterfield, Quathamer, & Heineken, 1994; Palincsar & Brown, 1984; Zabrucky & Ratner, 1992). Evaluation involves monitoring of one's understanding of text material, and regulation involves control of one's reading to resolve problems and increase comprehension. Often, comprehension monitoring has been operationalized

165

through the use of the error-detection paradigm in which readers detect and resolve various kinds of textual errors that have been deliberately planted in texts. Good comprehension monitoring is demonstrated by those readers who detect and resolve all or most of the errors; poor comprehension monitoring is demonstrated by those who fail to detect the errors or who detect the errors but fail to resolve them.

However, there is growing agreement among researchers to view this process called metamemory for text, calibration of comprehension, meta-comprehension, comprehension monitoring, or whatever term is favored, as processing that involves both evaluation and regulation of reading comprehension (e.g., Baker, 1989; Markman, 1985; Otero & Campanario, 1990; Weaver, 1995; Zabrucky & Moore, 1989). Perhaps this growing agreement has been encouraged by an increasingly shared interest among cognitive psychologists and educational psychologists to examine reading processes during normal reading conditions.

In contrast to reading for the purposes of detecting errors or predicting comprehension, the purpose of normal reading is to construct meaningful interpretations from text that is assumed to be considerate (i.e., consistent, coherent, and written at a level commensurate with the reader's abilities and knowledge). As long as readers are able to construct meaning that is compatible with developing interpretations, reading is likely to proceed uninterrupted. In this case, ongoing evaluation of comprehension provides information to the reader that understanding is occurring and reading can proceed. However, when readers fail to establish consistency or coherence during normal reading, or when constructed meaning fails to fit with their developing interpretations of the text, ongoing evaluation alerts readers to comprehension failures.

Because of the assumption of text considerateness held by most readers during normal reading, readers are likely to look first to themselves as the source of comprehension failure. Is the failure due to gaps in their linguistic or topic knowledge? Is the failure due to lack of perceived coherency, or to an inability to generate an interpretation of the text that is compatible with their own expectations for the text or with their understanding of the author's intended meaning? During or after this search, readers may get a sense that the failure is due not to them but to the text itself, at which point the focus of the search is directed to textual inadequacies.

Whatever the source of the failure, once it is evaluated, readers must resolve it, and further, as reading continues, they must periodically reevaluate whether their resolution continues to establish consistency, coherence, and compatibility with the ongoing interpretation of the text. Thus, when comprehension failures are monitored during normal reading, comprehension monitoring is more than a metacognitive judgment that a failure has occurred. Comprehension monitoring becomes a goal-directed metacognitive process through which the processes of evaluation *and* regulation interplay for the purposes of reestablishing the construction of a text's meaning and developing its interpretation.

One purpose of this chapter is first to propose a standardization in the terminology that has been used to describe evaluation and regulation of reading comprehension. Because of the growing agreement among researchers concerning the kinds of processes that are involved in reading, there is a growing need to standardize the terminology used to describe those processes. Developing a common language that strives for precision in its meaning is essential for the communication of scientific knowledge. Therefore, rather than favoring "comprehension monitoring," which is something of a misnomer in that only part of the overall process appears to be implicated, or any of the other terms that have been used (e.g., metamemory for text, calibration of comprehension), which lack precision, I propose the use of the term self-regulated comprehension. This term not only connotes both monitoring and control of reading processes, it brings the concept closer to the growing corpus of research that has focused on self-regulated learning.

A second purpose of the chapter is to describe a cognitive-metacognitive model of self-regulated comprehension. This model conceptualizes self-regulated comprehension as monitoring and control of cognitive processes by related metacognitive processes. Using this cognitive-metacognitive model, self-regulated comprehension during normal reading will be examined. Finally, although much research has shown that comprehension can be facilitated by encouraging readers to monitor and control their reading, there may be limits to how much readers can monitor and control their own construction of meaning. The notion of one level of thought monitoring and controlling another level is problematic in that it represents a closed system that can act on itself only to the extent to which its own subjective standards are applied. In other words, it is possible that readers may judge their understanding of text as complete, consistent, and compatible with their prior knowledge even though the text may be inaccurate or inconsistent with standards external to them. To overcome this limitation, readers must monitor and control their reading of text using not only their own internal standards but standards external to them. In an educational context, this can be accomplished by engaging readers in a dialogue about the text.

A COGNITIVE-METACOGNITIVE MODEL OF
SELF-REGULATED COMPREHENSION

Flavell's (1979) model of cognitive monitoring has been a useful theoretical foundation for researchers interested in the metacognitive aspects of human thinking. According to his model, cognitive monitoring occurs through the actions and interactions among four classes of phenomena: metacognitive knowledge, metacognitive experiences, goals, and strategies. Metacognitive knowledge consists of a person's stored world knowledge that has to do with people, their cognitive tasks, goals and strategies for achieving them, actions, and experiences. Metacognitive experiences are concerned with one's awareness of his or her cognitive or affective processes and whether progress is being made toward the goal of a current process. Metacognitive experiences can add to, delete from, or revise one's metacognitive knowledge. They can cause one to abandon goals and establish new ones, or they can lead to the activation of cognitive or metacognitive strategies. Furthermore, Flavell's model has both declarative and procedural aspects: The former concern understanding strategic demands of tasks and one's limits and strengths as a problem solver; the latter concern monitoring and regulation of ongoing cognition.

Many theorists have amended Flavell's conceptualization of metacognition. Noteworthy among them have been Nelson and Narens (1990). Their model of metacognition integrates the declarative aspects of Flavell's model, called metacognitive understanding, with the procedural aspects, called monitoring and control. Underlying the Nelson and Narens' model are three principles: (a) Mental processes are split into two or more specifically interrelated levels, a cognitive level and a metacognitive level; (b) the metacognitive level contains a dynamic model of the cognitive level; and (c) there are two dominance relations called control and monitoring, which are defined in terms of the direction of flow of information between the metacognitive and cognitive levels. A distinction that can be made between cognition and metacognition is that the former involves knowledge of the world and strategies for using that knowledge to solve problems, whereas the latter concerns monitoring, controlling, and understanding one's knowledge and strategies (Butterfield, Albertson, & Johnston, in press).

Thus, metacognition can be viewed as monitoring and controlling of a lower level thought process by a higher level thought process (Broadbent, 1977). This relationship can be characterized as a dynamic interplay between monitoring, in which information regarding the status of knowledge or strategies at a cognitive level is provided to a corresponding metacognitive level, and control, in which understanding at a metacognitive level is used to influence thought at a corresponding cognitive level. Through the interplay of information, a metacognitive level controls or modifies thought at a cognitive level by treating it as the object of thought, and thought at a metacognitive level can in turn be modified by the kinds of information monitored at a cognitive level or by being treated as the object of thought by yet higher levels of thought.

When considering the relation between metacognitive and cognitive processes, it is important to consider that neither one occurs in isolation. The cognitive-level process being controlled must first be monitored, and secondly, must be contained as a model within the metacognitive level (i.e., there must be a representation of the cognitive-level process for it to be understood and modified; Conant & Ashby, 1970). Thus, control depends on the processes being monitored and how those processes are represented at a metacognitive level, and monitoring depends on the processes that are being controlled or potentially controlled (Butterfield, Albertson, & Johnston, in press). Therefore, the Nelson and Narens' model of metacognition must be considered as a system of interacting thought processes and not as a collection of independent parts.

The Components of Self-Regulated Comprehension

Butterfield, Albertson, & Johnston (in press) argue that many task-specific models of cognition can be conceptualized using this cognitive-metacognitive framework. Thus, as another kind of task-specific cognition, self-regulated comprehension can be conceptualized as the interaction between two levels of thought, a metacognitive level that monitors and controls a cognitive level (see Fig. 8.1). At the metacognitive level is understanding of both world knowledge and strategies. Understanding at a metacognitive level is made possible through dynamic mental models of the person's cognitive system (Johnson-Laird, 1983; Nelson & Narens, 1990). At the cognitive level are comprehension processes, strategies, standards of text evaluation (e.g., lexical, syntactic, and semantic), and world knowledge. World knowledge, strategies, and standards of evaluation affect comprehension, and in turn, can be affected by comprehension, and hence, the relationships among them and comprehension are represented by double-headed arrows. Furthermore, a reader's strategies for increasing comprehension may include using standards of evaluation; therefore, the relation between strategies and standards of evaluation is represented by an arrow directed from the former to the latter.

Theoretical mechanism of comprehension monitoring.

Comprehension is the process through which understanding is derived through the construction of an internal representation of a text. It is a process that occurs in parallel at several levels, with a special kind of text representation being associated with each level and with the outputs of each level interacting in important ways (Adams & Collins, 1979; Carpenter & Just, 1989; Graesser, Singer, & Trabasso, 1994; Just & Carpenter, 1992; Kintsch, 1988; Rumelhart & McClelland, 1981). First, there is a verbal representation consisting of words and syntactical units such as phrases, sentences, and paragraphs. Second, the verbal representation is parsed into semantic units called text propositions. Propositions are stored in memory as interrelated chunks of text information forming a representation of the text that can form

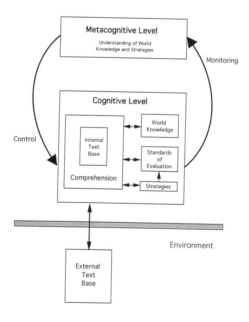

FIG. 8.1. Theoretical mechanisms of comprehensive monitoring.

or modify the reader's world knowledge. The reader's modified world knowledge is another level of representation that in turn can be used to modify his or her representation of the text. Finally, there is a representation of the overall gist of the text, which can be used to modify all previously constructed levels or influence those levels yet to be constructed.

Either before or during reading, people set certain goals for their reading. Most often, readers focus their goals on higher semantic levels of text representation (e.g., to identify the main idea of a paragraph); however, in the event readers fail to meet their goals, they must be prepared to evaluate the monitored failure at all levels of text representation. Is the failure due to a mistakenly identified word? Is it due to the use of poor syntax? Is it due to a lack of topic knowledge? Evaluation at each level of text representation occurs by applying a standard of evaluation specific to that level (Baker, 1985). Readers can consciously select standards to evaluate comprehension failures, or, as Just and Carpenter (1992) suggest, standards may be selected according to implicit allocation policies that readers rely on in the event of excessive demands on comprehension.

Strategies are "composed of cognitive operations over and above the processes that are a natural consequence of carrying out the task, ranging from one such operation to a sequence of interdependent operations. Strategies achieve cognitive purposes (e.g., comprehending, memorizing) and are potentially conscious and controllable activities" (Pressley, Forrest-Pressley, Elliot-Faust, & Miller, 1985, p. 4). Strategies provide ways to lessen demands on working memory and therefore facilitate information processing. In the present context, strategies serve to facilitate comprehension. They include both monitoring strategies (e.g., rereading a difficult passage, looking back to prior text, predicting upcoming information, comparing two or more propositions) and control strategies (e.g., summarizing text information, clarifying text information by using reference sources external to the text, correcting incomplete or inaccurate text information).

The remaining element of the model is the external text base, which is any written representation of linguistic input (e.g., a word, sentence, book, one's own writing). The external text base is represented internally within the comprehension process through constructive processing of the external text (e.g., August, Flavell, & Clift, 1984; Bransford & Franks, 1971; Kintsch, 1988; Markman, 1985). The relation between the external text base and the internal processing of the text is represented by a double-headed arrow to denote that the external text base serves as linguistic input to comprehension, and as a result of these processes, the reader (or writer) can in turn modify the external text base.

In addition to placing self-regulated comprehension within a general theory of cognition, the proposed cognitive-metacognitive model offers a coherent interpretation of the existing literature and provides a useful taxonomy for sources of comprehension failure. At a general level, failures to comprehend written discourse can be attributed either to a failure to monitor comprehension or a failure to control comprehension. Each of these general sources can be divided into more specific ones. Table 8.1 provides a description of each specific source along with examples of research that have investigated it. With the exception of motivation, which can affect the model at all of its components, each source of failure can be identified with a specific component of the proposed model.

Self-Regulated Comprehension in Operation

The cognitive-metacognitive model of self-regulated comprehension indicates that people's understanding of their world knowledge is distributed among mental models at metacognitive levels of their cognitive systems. In the context of reading, metacognitive models include readers' understanding of their prior knowledge and their goals for reading and comprehending, understanding of an author's intent, understanding of text propositions, and understanding of the ways in which knowledge from the text is integrated with their own knowledge (cf. Kintsch's, 1988, situation model of the text). As a person reads a text and constructs an internal representation of it at a cognitive level, any part of that representation can be compared to a model at a related metacognitive level. The basis on which the comparison is made at the metacognitive level is determined by the reader's implicit or explicit application of a standard or standards of evaluation.

Thus, evaluation of comprehension occurs when readers monitor similarities and differences between their cognitive representation of a text and their metacognitive models by applying standards of evaluation. Similarities monitored between the representation at the cognitive level and the models at the metacognitive level serve as indicators that comprehension is occurring and reading can proceed. Differences monitored are taken as signs that comprehension has failed or textual problems have been encountered. If, however, readers are unaware of either similarities or differences, comprehension at the cognitive level may be occurring, but monitoring has not occurred.

TABLE 8.1

Failures to Comprehend Written Discourse Due to Failures to Monitor Comprehension or Failures to Control Comprehension

Failures to Monitor Comprehension

Source	Part of Model	Citations
1. Readers lack linguistic or topic knowledge necessary to monitor sources of dissonance.	World knowledge	Hacker et al. (1994) Pressley, El-Dinary, & Brown (1992); Weaver (1995)
2. Readers possess necessary linguistic or topic knowledge but lack monitoring strategies.	Strategies	Armbruster, Anderson, & Ostertag (1987); August, Flavell, & Clift (1984); Baker (1989); Garner and Anderson (1982); Hacker (1996); Hacker et al. (1994); Zabrucky & Ratner (1986)
3. Readers possess strategies but lack metacognitive understanding about where and when to apply them.	Metcognitive understanding	Hansen & Pearson (1983); Palincsar & Brown (1984); Pressley, El-Dinary, & Brown (1992); Pressley et al. (1987); Reder (1987)
4. The standard of standards of evaluation used by readers are inappropriate for the levels of text representation that need to be monitored.	Standards of evaluation	Baker (1985); Garner & Anderson (1982); Glenberg, Wilkinson, & Epstein (1982); Markman (1979); Winograd & Johnston (1982); Zabrucky & Moore (1989)
5. Sources of dissonance are resolved by the inferences readers make during the comprehension process.	Comprehension	August, Flavell, & Clift (1984); Baker (1979); Beal (1990); Vosniadou, Pearson, & Rogers (1988)
6. Comprehension and/or monitoring are too demanding of the reader's resources thereby hindering his or her ability to monitor reading.	Interaction of cognitive with metacognitive level	Baker (1984); Brown et al. (1977); Hacker (1986); Just & Carpenter (1992); Oakhill (1993); Plumb et al. (1994); Vosniadou & Brewer (1987); Vosniadou, Pearson, & Rogers (1988)
7. Although not specifically noted in the model but implicit in all controlled cognitive processes, readers lack motivation to monitor their reading		

Failures to Control Comprehension

Source	Part of Model	Citations
1. Readers lack linguistic or topic knowledge necessary to control the problems they monitor.	World knowledge	Hacker (1994); Pressley, El-Dinary, & Brown (1992)
2. Readers possess necessary linguistic and topic knowledge but lack strategies to apply their knowledge.	Strategies	Hacker (1994); Otero & Campanario (1990); Vosniadou, Pearson, & Roger (1988); Zabrucky & Moore (1989); Zabrucky & Ratner (1986)
3. Readers possess strategies but lack metacognitive understanding about where and when to apply them.	Metacognitive understanding	Palincsar & Brown (1984); Pressley, El-Dinary, & Brown (1992); Pressley et al. (1987); Reder (1987)
4. Comprehension and/or control are too demanding of the reader's resources thereby hindering his or her ability to control reading.	Interaction of cognitive with Metacognitive level	Baker (1984); Brown et al. (1977); Hacker (1986); Just & Carpenter (1992); Oakhill (1993); Plumb et al. (1994); Vosniadou & Brewer (1987); Vosniadou, Pearson, & Rogers (1988)
5. Although not specifically noted in the model but implicit in all controlled cognitive processes, readers lack motivation to control their reading.		

173

Differences monitored during the constructive processing of a text, regardless of whether their source is comprehension failure or problematic text, can produce a sense of dissonance in the reader, dissonance that has been described on intuitive bases as a sense of confusion, uncertainty, or some similar feeling of not understanding (Flower, Hayes, Carey, Schriver, & Stratman, 1986; Markman, 1979). Such feelings may occur spontaneously, as when an unfamiliar jargon word is encountered (Markman, 1979), or they may result from explicitly questioning underlying assumptions or stating hypotheses and implications clearly and unambiguously (Palincsar & Brown, 1984).

When dissonance is sensed, readers can exert control over subsequent reading to identify and correct the source of dissonance and reestablish a coherent representation of the text. To this end, the reader has linguistic knowledge, topic knowledge, and strategies represented at a metacognitive level (Butterfield, Hacker, & Plumb, 1994) that can be invoked to facilitate further monitoring of the dissonance and ultimate correction of the problem. What knowledge or strategy will be invoked depends on the reader's metacognitive understanding of the source of the dissonance and the possible actions that could be taken to resolve it. If the reader can specify precisely how to change a text so that it is consistent with his or her model of a content domain, the monitored source of dissonance can be attributed to the text (correctly if one's model is correct). However, if the reader cannot specify how to make a text consistent with his or her model of a content domain, the monitored source of dissonance is attributed to one's inability to comprehend (correctly if the text is correct). Whatever the source of dissonance, once it is identified and resolved, the reader must further evaluate whether the resolution of the problem remains compatible with his or her evolving constructions of subsequent text information. If not, the monitored source of failure may need to be revisited.

SELF-REGULATION OF MEANING MAKING

In this section, self-regulated comprehension during normal reading is described within the framework of the proposed cognitive-metacognitive model. First is a brief discussion of normal reading and normal reading problems. A discussion follows on the relation between meaning and interpretation during normal reading and how self-regulated comprehension can facilitate that relation. Finally, this section ends with suggestions for future research on self-regulated comprehension during normal reading.

Normal Reading and Normal Reading Problems

Because the majority of comprehension monitoring research has been conducted using texts with planted errors or ambiguities, our knowledge of self-regulated comprehension may be restricted primarily to atypical reading and may have little transfer to normal reading. In fact, because an abundance of research has shown that readers' purposes for reading and the kinds of problems that are encountered during reading strongly affect the kinds of reading in which readers engage (e.g., Baker & Zimlin, 1989; Beal, 1990; Beal, Bonitatibus, & Garrod, 1990; Hacker, in press; Hacker et al., 1994; Markman, 1985), it is quite possible that much of what is known about self-regulated comprehension during atypical reading does not generalize to the kinds of reading typically encountered in educational contexts. Thus, it is necessary to revisit research on self-regulated comprehension from the standpoint of normal reading.

Before discussing self-regulated comprehension during normal reading, however, a brief look at factors influencing how readers' construct textual representations during normal reading and the kinds of problems they may encounter during this construction is necessary to understand whether and how those problems can be regulated. Most theories of reading involve the notion of internal representation of meaning. Reading is a process during which "a mental representation is constructed of the discourse in memory, using both external and internal types of information, with the goal of interpreting (understanding) the discourse" (van Dijk & Kintsch, 1983, p. 6; also see Bransford & Franks, 1971; Perfetti & McCutchen, 1987). Much research has focused on just how this mental representation is constructed (e.g., Adams & Collins, 1979; Kintsch, 1988; Rumelhart & McClelland, 1981), but for present purposes we need accept only the notion that reading is the generation of an internal representation of the external text base. In the case of normal reading, the internal text representation usually is used by the reader to derive a coherent interpretation of the author's intended meaning. As this interpretation evolves, it also can affect further construction of the reader's mental representation of the text (Otero & Kintsch, 1992).

Each reader's internal representation of a text is likely to be constructed somewhat differently, even for very simple texts. People differ in the kinds and amounts of knowledge they have concerning the topic being read; they differ in the ways they reason about what has been read and in the kinds of inferences they may draw from their reasoning. They also may differ in the goals they have for reading a particular text. Even the meaning ascribed to the same words may differ from one reader to the next. In fact, with all of these potential differences among readers, any agreement on what a text "says" seems remarkable! And yet, even with these differences, careful readers are able to agree on at least the major features of their constructed representations of text (Otero & Kintsch, 1992). Perfetti and McCutchen (1987) argue that any given text will have a range of possible representations, and as long as the reader's constructed representation overlaps in some way with the possible representations, the reader is said to have comprehended the text. Therefore, any number of readers will each construct a given text differently, but as long as those individually constructed text representations share some commonality, the readers will share some common understanding of the text.

Agreement among readers on what a text "says" is in no small part due to the ability of the author to constrain the number of potential representations a text can assume. This can be done by precisely defining words within the text or providing a glossary, organizing chapters around logically sequenced themes, dividing each chapter into headings and subheadings, or illustrating key concepts with graphics. Also, authors can constrain the range of potential text representations by writing for a specific audience. Many studies have shown that attending to audience contributes significantly to writing quality and clarity (e.g., Beal, 1996; Roen & Willey, 1988; Traxler & Gernsbacher, 1993; Wong, Butler, Ficzere, & Kuperis, 1994).

But perhaps more important, readers themselves constrain the construction of text representations. As part of their construction-integration model of reading, van Dijk and Kintsch (1983) propose that during normal reading, readers often use key propositions within a text as organizing principles around which other text information is interpreted. For example, in expository texts, these key propositions, or "macropropositions" (van Dijk & Kintsch, 1983), are often contained within the topic sentence of each paragraph. Identifying the macropropositions that are central to the author's intended meaning and using them as organizing principles can constrain the construction of the text in a way that facilitates comprehension. The use of macropropositions as organizers has been identified as a strategic process typical of what good comprehenders do (Pressley, El-Dinary, & Brown, 1992).

However, if readers believe too strongly in a macroproposition, or if they hold too strongly to prior beliefs or knowledge, "an imbalance between what readers believe and what they actually read" can result that may hinder comprehension (Otero & Kintsch, 1992, p. 229). An exaggerated emphasis on a macroproposition, one's prior beliefs, or one's prior knowledge can cause the reader to ignore or resolve textual information that amends, contradicts, or is inconsistent with the macroproposition, beliefs, or knowledge (Otero & Kintsch, 1992; Vosniadou, Pearson, & Rogers, 1988). Otero and Kintsch propose that many of the failures to detect textual contradictions reported in the comprehension monitoring literature can be explained as a result of this imbalance between what readers believe and what they actually read.

Also, constraints are placed on the construction of internal text representations because readers are occasionally unable to manage excessive demands imposed by reading. Just and Carpenter (1992) have compiled considerable support for their thesis that comprehension is constrained by working memory capacity. Their review of the literature and their own research has led them to conclude that "constraints on every person's capacity limit the open-ended facets of comprehension, so that a reader or listener cannot generate every possible forward inference, represent every interpretation of every ambiguity, or take into consideration every potentially relevant cue to an interpretation" (p. 135). Furthermore, these constraints on comprehension are greater for readers with small working memory capacity versus large working memory capacity, which is often a difference between poor comprehenders and good comprehenders, respectively. Thus, during normal reading, readers constrain their representations of text not only as a normal consequence of reading, but as a result of constraints on working memory that may prohibit simultaneous construction or consideration of alternative text representations.

No doubt, constraints that are placed on the construction of a text, both by the author and reader of the text, help to narrow its possible representations so that author and reader can share common meaning. However, even with the narrowing of possible representations, there remains a great deal of uncertainty whether the text representation constructed by the reader overlaps in an appreciable way with the constructions of other readers or with the construction intended by the author. Readers can agree on the major features of texts, but what agreement can be reached on the more subtle or complex aspects? And with words themselves carrying a range of meaning rather than fixed meanings (Rosch, 1973; Wittgenstein, 1958), how much overlap can be achieved between reader's constructed text and author's actual text? "Our understanding of written tradition per se is not such that we can simply presuppose that the meaning we discover in it agrees with what its author intended" (Gadamer, 1993, p. 372). Literary theory, semiotics, and cognitive theory have all moved away from the notion that the actual text has an entirely objective meaning that can be extracted (Hartman, 1994). Meaning "resides either in the reader, in the cultural systems in which the reader resides, or in the transaction of reading" (p. 617). And, as long as meaning resides "outside the text," agreement on what is "in the text" will be in question.

Understanding that a text can have multiple interpretations likely is not developed until later in the elementary school years (Ackerman, 1988; Castell, 1993). Even after this understanding has developed, readers have little reason to consider alternative interpretations during normal reading as long as the interpretation they are generating is consistent and meaningful, and their goals for reading are being satisfied. With the additional demands on working memory, some readers may not have the resources necessary to construct and consider alternative interpretations, and those who do would need to be convinced that additional expenditures of time and effort will pay off. Moreover, for those readers who are convinced, it may be difficult for them to construct alternative interpretations if they have already invested in an interpretation that conforms with their prior knowledge and purposes for reading. Put differently, readers may not question their reading unless some triggering event calls their attention to a comprehension failure (Brown, 1980). The old adage, "If it's not broken, don't fix it," in general seems to apply to most reading: If you don't believe comprehension is broken, don't fix it. Unfortunately, though, comprehension is often broken, and it is often broken without the reader's awareness that it is.

Comprehension of a text can become "broken" during normal reading in a variety of ways without the reader's awareness. Normal comprehension problems include failing to amend current understanding of a text in light of newly encountered information, glossing over unfamiliar words, drawing incorrect inferences, failing to compare information with prior knowledge, failing to encode key information, forgetting key information, failing to identify main propositions, failing to understand information but continuing to read with the expectation that sooner or later understanding will be achieved. Some or all of these failures may occur, and yet readers can come away from reading believing they have comprehended the text; that is, readers are left with "illusions of knowing" (Glenberg, Wilkinson, & Epstein, 1982).

Using the proposed cognitive–metacognitive model of self-regulated comprehension, "illusions of knowing" can be explained in one of two ways. First, readers simply may fail to monitor or control comprehension. In this case, triggering events alerting readers to comprehension failures never occur, and readers come away from the text believing they have comprehended even though one or more comprehension failures may have occurred.

Alternatively, "illusions of knowing" can occur even when readers monitor and control comprehension. Recall that self-regulated comprehension involves monitoring similarities and differences between the cognitive representation of a text and the reader's metacognitive models, which consist of readers' understanding of their prior knowledge, text propositions, goals for reading, and author's intent. When similarities are monitored between what is represented in the text and what is represented in their metacognitive models, readers will believe that comprehension has occurred; when differences are monitored and readers are able to control them in satisfactory ways, they again will believe that comprehension has been achieved. And yet, if the metacognitive models that readers relied on to monitor similarities and differences have no bases in the actual text, readers will have failed to comprehend. In other words, as readers conform their constructions of text to fit their metacognitive models, deviations between what readers believe to be in a text versus what is actually in the text can and often do occur (Bransford & Franks, 1971; Paris, 1975; Paris & Lindhauer, 1976; Paris & Mahoney, 1974). Otero (1998) argues that deviations between a reader's understanding of text and the actual text can occur when excessive activation of certain propositions leads to the suppression of other propositions. Excessive activation can occur as a result of the reader's emphasis of specific connections between text information and knowledge recently learned or overlearned. Moreover, Mannes and Kintsch (1987) have shown that readers' memory for text is often more reflective of what readers know about the topic than what is in the text itself.

Thus, in either of these two ways an "illusion of knowing" can occur, but the reasons for each differ. In the first, the "illusion of knowing" occurs because self-regulated comprehension is never engaged. In the second, the "illusion of knowing" occurs not because self-regulation of comprehension fails, but because readers construct a text that conforms with their metacognitive models of the text (i.e., their understanding of what is believed to be in the text) rather than the actual text.

The second explanation of "illusions of knowing" also explains the role that self-regulated comprehension can play when comprehension has not failed and yet differences in meaning making keep readers apart in their interpretations. In the course of normal reading, a reader can activate relevant knowledge, understand all words and concepts, appropriately represent all text propositions in memory, and make relevant comparisons of related textual information, in other words, comprehend the text, and yet still encounter a comprehension problem if his or her interpretation of

the text differs from the author's intentions or from other readers' constructions (Beal, 1996). Problems of interpretation are not at all uncommon and
have long been the focus of hermeneutic inquiry. Awareness of the range of
possible interpretations a text may have can bring readers together in what
a text "says." Therefore, understanding the role that self-regulated comprehension can play in facilitating that awareness is essential to knowing how
meaning making can be shared during normal reading.

Encouraging Self-Regulated Comprehension at the Nexus Between Meaning Making and Interpretation

Reading comprehension is the nexus between meaning and interpretation
(Perfetti & McCutchen, 1987): Readers affix meaning to the words and
propositions of a text, build on that meaning within the context of the text,
and bring understanding to the contextualized meaning, that is, interpret
the text, by melding it with what one already knows. As long as readers
affix similar meanings to the words and propositions of a text and share a
similar knowledge base, they likely will find agreement in what a text says.
By contrast, because of ambiguities in word meaning and differences in
knowledge, readers may comprehend a text, but differences in comprehension will arise.

Rarely is a word defined by precise and invariant characteristics. Rather,
words are represented by spectrums of meaning (Wittgenstein, 1958).
Where within a spectrum a word is temporarily affixed depends on cultural,
social, and historical conventions, the writer's intent, the reader's understanding, and the context in which the word is embedded. Despite this
ambiguity of meaning, the conveyance of understanding through words is
made possible because there are at least some constraints on words. For
example, the word *dog* carries with it a spectrum of meaning, and where it
is affixed within that spectrum will vary depending on conventions, intent,
understanding, and context. But, the word is constrained to that particular
spectrum, and it does not carry a meaning that could be confused with the
words *horse*, *building*, or *flying*.

Readers build on word meaning within the context of the text by
combining word meanings to form propositions, combining propositions to
form sentences, and combining sentences to form paragraphs. The resulting
mental representation does not carry just any meaning. Rather, as described
earlier, the text is constrained by the meaning of the words and propositions
and the syntax that governs the ways in which the words and propositions
are combined (Perfetti & McCutchen, 1987). Similarly, because interpretation depends on word meaning, not just any interpretation can be given to

that mental representation. Just as a word represents a spectrum of meaning, the text represents a spectrum of interpretation, but the spectrum is constrained by the meanings ascribed to the words and propositions of the text (Perfetti & McCutchen).

For example, the meaning of the sentence, *The dog ran home*, is constrained by the meaning of each word and the syntax of the proposition in which those words appear. Depending on the extent of the reader's knowledge of dogs, running, and home, there will be ambiguity in meaning regarding just what kind of dog, how it was running, and what kind of home or to whose home it was running. Despite this ambiguity, the meaning of the sentence is constrained in that a dog is involved, not a cat, moose, or whale; that the dog was running, not skipping, hopping, or jumping; and that the dog's running was taking it home, not to school, work, or the grocery store. In this case, as with many ordinary texts, interpretation of sentence meaning (i.e., understanding of the contextualized meaning) and knowledge of word meaning are highly overlapping (Perfetti & McCutchen, 1987).

In contrast, consider the sentence, "The Vietnam War, in the final analysis, was a contest between the U.S. with its abundantly subsidized, protected surrogate, and a Revolutionary movement whose class roots and ideological foundations gave it enormous resiliency and power" (Kolko, 1985, p. 553). This sentence demonstrates how interpretation, although constrained by meaning of words and propositions, varies greatly depending on the reader's knowledge. Knowledge of Vietnam and its history, knowledge of the United States, its history and its politics during the 1950s through 1970s, knowledge of the author and his political position, knowledge of China, the U.S.S.R., and France, all affect the interpretation of the text's meaning, and depending on differences in knowledge, differences in interpretation are likely to arise. In this case, interpretation of sentence meaning and knowledge of word meaning are not highly overlapping. It is apparent that the interpretation of text depends on meaning and how meaning is built within the context of the text, but interpretation is also strongly influenced by the reader's knowledge. Moreover, the text itself contains information that will likely alter or amend the reader's knowledge. Altered or amended knowledge then provides feedback into further construction of the text representation. Reading, therefore, is a doubly interactive process (Hesse, 1991): The text modifies the reader's knowledge, which then modifies the meaning affixed to the text and the interpretations of the text, which further modify the reader's knowledge.

By encouraging monitoring and control of comprehension at the nexus between meaning making and interpretation, readers can open up alternative possibilities of text understanding. Increasing awareness of ambiguities in word meaning and differences in knowledge can help readers consider ranges of textual meaning. Greater awareness of what has been learned from the text can serve as self-feedback in the further construction of text. And, self-regulation of reading can help readers gain awareness of the differences in textual construction that arise when interpretation of sentence meaning and knowledge of word meaning are not highly overlapping.

One way of encouraging self-regulation of meaning making and interpretation is through questioning. "Questioning opens up possibilities of meaning, and thus what is meaningful passes into one's own thinking on the subject" (Gadamer, 1993, p. 375). Questioning provides a means for readers to test their constructions of text against their metacognitive models (i.e., their understandings of text propositions, prior knowledge, goals, and the author's intent). The information generated from these tests is essential for readers to know whether their understanding of the text is actually founded in the text.

Also, understanding of text can be questioned by encouraging readers to monitor and control the inferences and assumptions they make as they read. When inferences and assumptions are not identified, monitoring and controlling discrepancies between a reader's interpretations of a text and the actual text are more difficult (Beal, 1990), as is the reinterpretation of the text when new information is encountered (Ackerman, 1988). By focusing readers' attention on the making of meaning at the inference level, a broader spectrum of interpretation can be encouraged. Consider the following illustration of the role of inference:

> As the fading light of a dying day filtered through the window blinds, Roger stood over his victim with a smoking .45, surprised at the serenity that filled him after pumping six slugs into the bloodless tyrant that had mocked him day after day, and then he shuffled out of the office with one last look back at the shattered computer terminal lying there like a silicon armadillo left to rot on the information highway. (Brill, 1995)

Granted, even though this is not a typical kind of text, it does illustrate very well how inferences can lead the reader to some quite surprising results. Often, an incorrect interpretation of text is constructed because authors are insufficiently explicit (in this case, intentionally) to constrain the possible interpretations (Olson, 1994). Awareness of meaning derived through inference and assumption, therefore, plays a critical role in the interpretation and reinterpretation of text.

These are just a few of the ways that readers can question their understanding of text (i.e., their metacognitive models), and more will be described in the following section. The point here is that in the quest to create coherent meaning from the written word, readers may hold too strongly to their prior beliefs or knowledge and construct an interpretation of the text that differs from the literal or intended meaning (Otero & Kintsch, 1992). If readers are to become aware of interpretive differences, they must learn to question their metacognitive models. By evaluating the answers to their questions and controlling reading and comprehension in light of their answers, readers are better able to set one interpretation aside so that another can be considered.

Directions for Research

Hartman (1994) provides an excellent example of the role that self-regulated comprehension can play in the interpretation of text. The purpose of this study was to highlight the on-line intertextual links that readers make among multiple passages. Hartman argues that "much of what good readers do while reading is connect and relate ideas to their previous reading experiences over time. The net effect of these connected and accumulated readings is that the reader's understanding transcends that of any single passage" (p. 616). Readers "transpose texts into other texts, absorb one text into another, and build a mosaic of intersecting text.... Adopting this intertextual view of reading, then, readers are conceived of as generators of interconnections or 'links' between texts, resulting in a web of meaning — an evolving mental web" (p. 617). Furthermore, readers use their interpretations of a currently read text to revise their interpretations of previously read texts, and their revised interpretations feedback to affect the interpretation of the current text. Thus, the interpretations that readers give to a text depend on the kinds of interpretations they have constructed from other texts and how they have linked those interpretations to the current text.

In Hartman's study, eight high school students, all capable readers, were asked to read a five-passage tableau designed to present a variety of perspectives and rhetorical styles. Students were asked to silently read the passages, to report aloud their thoughts while reading, and to mark the text with a pen whenever they stopped reading and thought aloud. Following reading, students were asked 9 prompting questions designed to encourage insights into the passages and to form links among them, and 14 debriefing questions designed to gather self-descriptive data on what students had done while reading the text and answering the prompting questions.

Analysis of the think-aloud protocols and answers provided abundant evidence of readers metacognitively monitoring and controlling their intertextual linking of texts. Monitoring was demonstrated in many ways. Students consciously and deliberately identified ideas, characters, and settings that served as links not only among the five texts but to previously read texts. They evaluated whether they understood a passage and recognized that understanding of one text "spills over" to the understanding of another. They were aware that their own interest or lack of interest in a passage could affect how they interpreted it. They were aware of the task complexities and of the demands placed on them. They considered the indeterminacy and openness of interpretation, and after generating alternative interpretations and weighing each, they reevaluated the texts according to each. They also linked their own affective feelings to each text by developing a discourse stance and then used the discourse stance as a measure of the texts' content. Finally, they not only sought to clarify the author's intent by evaluating a text from the author's perspective, but they also sought to bring greater breadth of meaning to the texts by evaluating them from multiple perspectives.

Information generated through their monitoring enabled students to exert various kinds of cognitive control over their comprehension. In response to their self-generated questions, readers either continued reading or reread passages flipping back and forth among them to elaborate and revise the meaning and interpretations they had given to them. Acknowledging their lack of interest in a specific passage, readers either consciously directed more attention to the task or they glossed over the passage and directed greater attention to those passages that did interest them. Readers tested alternative interpretations against previously and currently read material. They summarized passages and compared and contrasted summaries to one another and to prior knowledge. Evaluations of the passages from the perspective of the author or another reader often led readers to revise the meaning they had given to earlier passages, which in turn revised the meaning they were giving to those currently read. Finally, to bring greater meaning to the passages and to aid in their interpretation, readers occasionally created metaphors in which their prior knowledge was linked with their current understanding of the passages.

Hartman's research suggests a rich program for research of self-regulated comprehension during normal reading. This paradigm could be used to guide descriptive as well as experimental studies. Descriptive studies could include examinations of intertextual linking in other domains (e.g., science, math, or history), or in similar domains but using less capable or younger readers versus more capable or older readers. Experimental studies could include examinations of monitoring and control using texts that differ thematically versus texts that are thematically linked, texts that contain information known to the readers versus novel information, or texts that contain compatible versus incompatible information. I am currently exploring some of these research possibilities. Certainly, how we derive meaning and interpretations from the written word and how knowledge of meaning and interpretation further affect reading are fundamental questions of literacy. The study of self-regulated comprehension can do much to provide answers.

OVERCOMING THE CONSTRAINTS ON SELF-REGULATED COMPREHENSION THROUGH DIALOGUE

Much research has shown that the more actively readers monitor and control comprehension during reading, the more likely they are to understand the text and to know that they understand (e.g., Baker, 1984; Brown, 1980; Markman, 1985; Palincsar & Brown, 1984; Pressley, El-Dinary, & Brown, 1992; Raphael, Kirschner, & Englert, 1986). However, apart from obvious constraints such as working memory capacity, insufficient knowledge, reading ability, and ambiguous goals, there may be limits to the extent to which readers can monitor and control their making of meaning from a text. In other words, even capable readers who read for clearly specified goals in content domains familiar to them may encounter still other constraints that prohibit their monitoring and controlling comprehension to the extent they need.

As readers construct an internal representation of text, they integrate the knowledge contained in the text with their prior knowledge. Monitoring this construction and judging that comprehension has failed indicates to readers that they need to control their reading to reestablish comprehension. Monitoring and judging that comprehension is complete, internally consistent, and compatible with prior knowledge indicates that reading can continue. In both cases, self-regulated comprehension has succeeded. However, as was argued earlier, readers can actively monitor and control their comprehension but still fail to comprehend the text if the metacognitive models on which they relied have no bases in the actual text. In this case, even though readers believe they understand, they need to question whether their understanding is actually supported by the text. Questioning during normal reading fosters text comprehension by focusing readers on the ambiguities of word meaning, the role of inference, and differences in interpretation.

There are limits, however, to how much readers can monitor and control their own construction of meaning. The notion of one level of thought monitoring and controlling another level of thought is problematic in that it represents a closed system that can act on itself only to the extent to which its own subjective standards are applied. Readers can question their meta-cognitive models in an attempt to test their understanding of a text against what is actually in the text, but because what is actually in the text is known only by their mental constructions of it, they ultimately end up testing one kind of mental representation against another kind of mental representation. If compatibility between the mental representations has been achieved, finding further discrepancies in one on the basis of the other is simply attempting to box with one's own shadow (Gadamer, 1993). This does not mean that a more complete understanding of a text cannot be gained through questioning. What it does mean is that because readers cannot "know" the text but through their own knowing, there are necessarily constraints on the quantity and quality of understandings they can bring to the text through their own subjective standards.

To overcome these other constraints on understanding, readers should be encouraged to monitor and control their comprehension using not only their own subjective standards of evaluation but objective standards as well. Readers can access objective standards in at least two ways. They can go beyond the primary reading source and consult secondary sources. Once a text has been read, readers can read secondary sources in which alternative interpretations of the primary source are provided. By questioning one's understanding of a text against the understanding of others, a deeper comprehension can be gained.

Readers also can engage in a dialogue with other readers. The educational significance of dialogue cannot be overstated (Hacker & Graesser, in press). Among other things, dialogue encourages (a) active construction of knowledge through culturally meaningful activities, (b) generation of questions to guide comprehension, and (c) reflection on the progress of learning throughout the learning event (Daiute & Dalton, 1993). Through question and answer, give and take, talking at cross purposes, and assuming other perspectives, readers actively construct knowledge together and expand on their individual understandings of the text by merging their understandings with others. Meaning and interpretation are no longer constrained by one's knowledge, but rather are negotiated by the group (Pearson & Raphael, 1990). In addition, readers who have difficulty with word meaning and interpretation can receive help from others in the group. No longer constrained by their own constructions of the text, readers can test their understanding of the text against other's understanding of it. Eventual internalization of this dialogue into one's cognitive system can provide additional bases on which to direct future self-regulated comprehension (cf. Vygotsky, 1978)

Thus, it is not only desirable to encourage dialogue in the classroom as a way to facilitate instruction, it is imperative to encourage dialogue as a way for students to expand their understanding of text beyond themselves. The role of dialogue has been identified in many areas of learning as key to development (Goodwin & Heritage, 1990; Roschelle, 1992; Suchman, 1987; Vygotsky, 1978). Certainly, the role it plays in the development of reading can be included among these.

CONCLUSION

The purpose of this chapter was first to propose a standardization in the terminology that has been used to describe evaluation and regulation of reading comprehension. Because of the growing agreement among researchers concerning the kinds of processes that are involved in reading and the growing need to standardize the terminology used to describe those processes, the term self-regulated comprehension was proposed. Next, a cognitive–metacognitive model of self-regulated comprehension was described, and a conceptualization of self-regulated comprehension during normal reading was given. Using this model, the relation between meaning and interpretation during normal reading was described and ways in which self-regulated comprehension could facilitate that relation were provided. Suggestions for future research on self-regulated comprehension during normal reading also were given. Finally, ways in which potential limitations of one level of thought monitoring and controlling another level of thought were discussed. The proposed model of self-regulated comprehension suggests that these limitations can be overcome by encouraging readers to apply standards of evaluation that are external to their own cognitive system. This can be done by asking readers to go beyond the primary reading source and consult secondary sources, or by engaging readers in a dialogue with other readers. Both ways have significance for education.

Very little research of self-regulated comprehension has focused on the role that comprehension monitoring plays when comprehension has not failed but differences in meaning making keep readers apart in their interpretations of text. Believing that one has comprehended a text when in fact one's understanding is not supported by the actual text, or not knowing that one's understanding differs from that of the author or other readers are fundamental problems that can occur during normal reading. Encouraging readers to monitor and control their comprehension at the nexus between meaning making and interpretation can help readers overcome these problems by focusing them on the ambiguities of word meaning, the role of inference, and differences in interpretation.

Research that attempts to examine the role of self-regulated comprehension during normal reading is more difficult to conduct than research that has relied on texts with planted errors or ambiguities. It is easier to test for comprehension failures than comprehension successes. However, the difficulties of the task should not dissuade researchers from undertaking it. Current research on how readers monitor and control their making of meaning during normal reading has provided insightful views into the ways meaning is constructed; however, much more needs to be done. As a meaning-making process, reading has particular significance to our cultural, historical, social, and psychological understanding of ourselves. It is important, therefore, to know how readers of all ages and abilities engage in it. It is equally important to know how readers of all ages and abilities can consciously and deliberately regulate meaning making to further increase its usefulness.

REFERENCES

Ackerman, B. P. (1988). Reason inferences in the story of comprehension of children and adults. *Child Development, 59,* 1426–1442.

Adams, M. J., & Collins, A. (1979). A schema-theoretic view of reading. In R. O. Freedle (Ed.), *Discourse processing: Multidisciplinary perspectives* (pp. 486–502). Norwood, NJ: Ablex.

August, D. L., Flavell, J. H., & Clift, R. (1984). Comparison of comprehension monitoring of skilled and less skilled readers. *Reading Research Quarterly, 20,* 39–53.

Baker, L. (1984). Children's effective use of multiple standards for evaluating their comprehension. *Journal of Educational Psychology, 76,* 588–597.

Baker, L. (1985). How do we know when we don't understand? Standards for evaluating text comprehension. In D. L. Forrest-Pressley, G. E. MacKinnon, & T. G. Waller (Eds.), *Metacognition, cognition, and human performance* (pp. 155–205). New York: Academic.

Baker, L. (1989). Metacognition, comprehension monitoring, and the adult reader. *Educational Psychology Review, 1,* 3–38.

Baker, L., & Zimlin, L. (1989). Instructional effects on Children's use of two levels of standards for evaluating their comprehension. *Journal of Educational Psychology, 81*, 340–346.

Beal, C. R. (1990). The development of text evaluation and revision skills. *Child Development, 61*, 247–258.

Beal, C. R. (1996). The role of comprehension monitoring in children's revision. *Educational Psychology Review, 8*, 219–238.

Beal, C. R., Bonitatibus, G. J., & Garrod, A. C. (1990). Fostering children's revision skills through training in comprehension monitoring. *Journal of Educational Psychology, 82*, 275–280.

Bransford, J. D., & Franks, J. J. (1971). The abstraction of linguistic ideas. *Cognitive Psychology, 2*, 331–350.

Brill, L. (1995). Winner of the Bulwer-Lytton contest, San Jose Mercury News.

Broadbent, D. E. (1977). Levels, hierarchies, and the locus of control. *Quarterly Journal of Experimental Psychology, 29*, 181–201.

Brown, A. L. (1980). Metacognitive development and reading. In R. J. Spiro, B. C. Bruce, & W. F. Brewer (Eds.), *Theoretical issues in reading comprehension* (pp. 453–481). Hillsdale, NJ: Lawrence Erlbaum Associates.

Butterfield, E. C., Albertson, L. R., & Johnston, J. (in press). On making cognitive theory more general and developmentally pertinent. In F. Weinert & W. Schneider (Eds.), *Memory performance and competencies: Issues in growth and development*. Hillsdale, NJ: Lawrence Erlbaum Associates.

Butterfield, E. C., Hacker, D. J., & Plumb, C. (1994). Topic knowledge, linguistic knowledge, and revision skill as determinants of text revision. In E. C. Butterfield (Ed.), *Children's writing: Toward a process theory of the development of skilled writing*. Greenwich, CT: JAI.

Carpenter, P. A., & Just, M. A. (1989). The role of working memory in language comprehension. In D. Klahr & K. Kotovsky (Eds.), *Complex information processing: The impact of Herbert A. Simon* (pp. 31–68). Hillsdale, NJ: Lawrence Erlbaum Associates.

Castell, M. A. (1993). Effects of inference necessity and reading goal on children's inferential generation. *Developmental Psychology, 29*, 346–357.

Conant, R. C., & Ashby, W. R. (1970). Every good regulator of a system must be a model of that system. *International Journal of Systems Science, 1*, 89–97.

Daiute, C., & Dalton, B. (1993). Collaboration between children learning to write: Can novices be masters? *Cognition and Instruction, 10*, 281–333.

Flavell, J. H. (1979). Metacognition and cognitive monitoring: A new area of cognitive-developmental inquiry. *American Psychologist, 34*, 906–911.

Flower, L., Hayes, J. R., Carey, L., Schriver, K., & Stratman, J. (1986). Detection, diagnosis, and the strategies of revision. *College Composition and Communication, 37*, 16–55.

Gadamer, H. G. (1993). *Truth and method* (2nd ed.), New York: Continuum.

Glenberg, A. M., & Epstein, W. (1985). Calibration of comprehension. *Journal of Experimental Psychology: Learning, Memory, & Cognition, 11*, 702–718.

Glenberg, A. M., Wilkinson, A. C., & Epstein, W. (1982). The illusion of knowing: Failure in the self-assessment of comprehension. *Memory & Cognition, 10*, 597–602.

Goodwin, C., & Heritage, J. (1990). Conversational analysis. *Annual Review of Anthropology, 19*, 283–307.

Graesser, A. C., Singer, M., & Trabasso, T. (1994). Constructing inferences during narrative text comprehension. *Psychological Review, 101*, 371–395.

Hacker, D. J. (in press). Comprehension monitoring across early-to-middle adolescence. *Reading and Writing: An Interdisciplinary Journal*.

Hacker, D. J., & Graesser, A. C. (in press). The role of dialogue in reciprocal teaching and naturalistic tutoring. *Journal of Reading*.

Hacker, D. J., Plumb, C., Butterfield, E. C., Quathamer, D., & Heineken, E. (1994). Text revision: Detection and correction of errors. *Journal of Educational Psychology, 86,* 65–78.

Hartman, D. K. (1994). The intertextual links of readers using multiple passages: A postmodern/semiotic/cognitive view of meaning making. In R. B. Ruddell, M. R. Ruddell, & H. Singer (Eds.), *Theoretical models and processes of reading* (pp. 616–636). Newark, DE: International Reading Association.

Hesse, D. (1991, November). *Strange attractors: Chaos theory and composition studies* (Report No. CS 213 191). Paper presented at the Annual Meeting of the National Council of Teachers of English. (ERIC Document Reproduction Service No. ED 342 010)

Johnson-Laird, P. N. (1983). A computational analysis of consciousness. *Cognition and Brain Theory, 6,* 499–508.

Just, M. A., & Carpenter, P. A. (1992). A capacity theory of comprehension: Individual differences in working memory. *Psychological Review, 99,* 122–149.

Kintsch, W. (1988). The role of knowledge in discourse comprehension: A construction–integration model. *Psychological Review, 95,* 163–182.

Kolko, G. (1985). *Anatomy of a war: Vietnam, the United States, and the modern historical experience.* New York: Pantheon Books.

Maki, R. H., & Serra, M. (1992). The basis of test predictions for text material. *Journal of Experimental Psychology: Learning, Memory, & Cognition, 18,* 116–126.

Mannes, S. M., & Kintsch, W. (1987). Knowledge organization and text organization. *Cognition and Instruction, 4,* 91–115.

Markman, E. M. (1979). Realizing that you don't understand: Elementary school children's awareness. *Child Development, 50,* 643–655.

Markman, E. M. (1985). Comprehension monitoring: Developmental and educational issues. In S. F. Chipman, J. W. Segal, & R. Glaser (Eds.), *Thinking and learning skills: Vol. 2 Research and open questions* (pp. 275–291). Hillsdale, NJ: Lawrence Erlbaum Associates.

Nelson, T. O., & Narens, L. (1990). Metamemory: A theoretical framework and new findings. *The Psychology of Learning and Motivation, 26,* 125–141.

Olson, D. R. (1994). *The world on paper: The conceptual and cognitive implications of writing and reading.* Cambridge: Cambridge University Press.

Otero, J. C. (1998). Influence of knowledge activation and context on comprehension monitoring of science texts. In D. J. Hacker, J. Dunlosky, & A. C. Graesser (Eds.), *Metacognition in educational theory and practice.* Hillsdale, NJ: Lawrence Erlbaum Associates.

Otero, J. C., & Campanario, J. M. (1990). Comprehension evaluation and regulation in learning from science texts. *Journal of Research in Science Teaching, 27,* 447–460.

Otero, J. C., & Kintsch, W. (1992). Failures to detect contradictions in a text: What readers believe versus what they read. *Psychological Science, 3,* 229–235.

Palincsar, A. S., & Brown, A. L. (1984). Reciprocal teaching of comprehension-fostering and comprehension-monitoring activities. *Cognition & Instruction, 1,* 117–175.

Paris, S. G. (1975). Integration and inference in children's comprehension and memory. In F. Rustle, R. Shiffrin, J. Castellan, H. Lindman, & D. Pisoni (Eds.), *Cognitive theory* (Vol. 1). Hillsdale, NJ: Lawrence Erlbaum Associates.

Paris, S. G., & Lindhauer, B. K. (1976). Constructive processes in children's comprehension and memory. In R. V. Kail & J. W. Hagen (Eds.), *Memory in cognitive development.* Hillsdale, NJ: Lawrence Erlbaum Associates.

Paris, S. G., & Mahoney, G. J. (1974). Cognitive integration in children's memory for sentences and pictures. *Child Development, 45,* 633–642.

Pearson, P. D., & Raphael, T. E. (1990). Reading comprehension as a dimension of thinking. In B. F. Jones & L. Idol (Eds.), *Dimensions of thinking and cognitive instruction.* Hillsdale, NJ: Lawrence Erlbaum Associates.

Perfetti, C. A., & McCutchen, D. (1987). Schooled language competence: Linguistic abilities in reading and writing. In S. Rosenberg (Ed.), *Advances in applied psycholinguistics: Vol. 2, Reading, writing, and language learning* (pp. 105–141). New York: Cambridge University.

Pressley, M., El-Dinary, P. B., & Brown, R. (1992). Skilled and not-so-skilled reading: Good information processing and not-so-good information processing. In M. Pressley, K. R. Harris, & J. T. Guthrie (Eds.), *Promoting academic competence and literacy in school* (pp. 91–127). San Diego: Academic.

Pressley, M., Forrest-Pressley, D. L., Elliot-Faust, D. J., & Miller, G. E. (1985). Children's use of cognitive strategies, how to teach strategies, and what to do if they can't be taught. In M. Pressley & C. J. Brainerd (Eds.), *Cognitive learning and memory in children* (pp. 1–47). New York: Springer-Verlag.

Raphael, T. E., Kirschner, B. W., & Englert, C. S. (1986). *Students' metacognitive knowledge about writing* (Research Series No. 176). East Lansing: Michigan State University, Institute for Research on Teaching.

Roen, D. H., & Willey, R. J. (1988). The effect of audience awareness on drafting and revising. *Research in the Teaching of English, 22,* 75–88.

Rosch, E. (1973). On the internal structure of perceptual and semantic categories. In T. E. Moore (Ed.), *Cognitive development and the acquisition of language* (pp. 111–144). New York: Academic.

Roschelle, J. (1992). Learning by collaboration: Convergent conceptual change. *Journal of the Learning Sciences, 2,* 235–276.

Rumelhart, D. E., & McClelland, J. L. (1981). Interactive processing through spreading activation. In A. M. Lesgold & C. A. Perfetti (Eds.), *Interactive processes in reading* (pp. 37–60). Hillsdale, NJ: Lawrence Erlbaum Associates.

Suchman, L. A. (1987). *Plans and situated actions: The problem of human–machine communication.* Cambridge, MA: Cambridge University Press.

Traxler, M. J., & Gernsbacher, M. A. (1993). Improving written communication through perspective taking. *Language and Cognitive Processes, 8,* 311–334.

van Dijk, T. A., & Kintsch, W. (1983). *Strategies of discourse comprehension.* New York: Academic.

Vosniadou, S., Pearson, P. D., & Rogers, T. (1988). What causes children's failure to detect inconsistencies in text? Representation versus comparison difficulties. *Journal of Educational Psychology, 80,* 27–39.

Vygotsky, L. S. (1978). *Mind in society.* Cambridge, MA: Harvard University Press.

Weaver, C., III. (1990). Constraining factors in calibration of comprehension. *Journal of Experimental Psychology: Learning, Memory, & Cognition, 16,* 214–222.

Weaver, C. A., III. (1995). Monitoring of comprehension: The role of text difficulty in metamemory for narrative and expository text. *Memory & Cognition, 23,* 12–22.

Wittgenstein, L. (1958). *Philosophical investigations* (2nd ed.). Oxford, England: Blackwell.

Wong, B. Y. L., Butler, D. L., Ficzere, S. A., & Kuperis, S. (1994). Teaching problem learners revision skills and sensitivity to audience through two instructional modes: Student–teacher vs. student–student interactive dialogues. *Learning Disabilities Research and Practice, 9,* 78–90.

Zabrucky, K., & Moore, D. (1989). Children's ability to use three standards to evaluate their comprehension of text. *Reading Research Quarterly, 24,* 336–352.

Zabrucky, K., & Ratner, H. H. (1992). Effects of passage type on comprehension monitoring and recall in good and poor readers. *Journal of Reading Behavior, 24,* 373–391.

9

Metacognition, Childhood Bilingualism, and Reading

Georgia Earnest García and Robert T. Jiménez
University of Illinois at Urbana-Champaign
P. David Pearson
Michigan State University

In and of itself, the topic of bilingualism—individuals' knowledge and use of two languages—has provoked considerable controversy in the political, psychological, and educational arenas. Prior to the 1960s, bilingualism was commonly viewed in a negative light (see Crawford, 1993; Hakuta, 1986). Politicians, such as Teddy Roosevelt, educators, and even researchers (Smith, 1931) reported that bilingualism could cause delays, interference, and confusion in children's language acquisition or learning. In stark contrast to these earlier views, more recent scholarship suggests that certain types of bilingualism can result in enhanced cognitive development (for reviews, see Bialystok, 1991; Hakuta, 1986). A major focus of this more positive portrayal of bilingualism has been the metalinguistic awareness (ability to define and control language processes) that bilinguals develop. In studying childhood bilingualism, many researchers focus on "whether or not bilingualism affects the way in which children process language and the insights which they subsequently derive about the structure of language" (Bialystok, 1991, p. 7).

Although our collective work is informed by this research (see García & Nagy, 1993; Jiménez, García, & Pearson, 1995, 1996; Nagy, García, Durgunoglu, & Hancin-Bhatt, 1993), our emphasis and approach are somewhat different. We are interested in understanding the relationship between bilingual children's metacognitive and metalinguistic development and their biliteracy—their ability to read and write in two languages. In our work, we have attempted to document how bilingual (really biliterate) children use knowledge and strategies gained in reading one language to address (and facilitate) reading in a second language. Our work spans methodological traditions. Some of it is quantitative; most of it is qualitative. Through the use of think-aloud protocols, interviews, and retellings, we document Latina/o bilingual children's use of metacognitive strategies while they are in the process of reading and comprehending text.

In this chapter, we briefly review historical attitudes toward bilingualism in the United States and the different types of research conducted on bilingual children's metacognition and metalinguistic awareness. We review this body of literature both for its contribution to current conceptual frameworks and to our own work in this area. Next, we present research findings on bilingual children's use of metalinguistic strategies in their English and Spanish reading. Then, we turn to our collective research on Latina/o bilingual children's use of metacognitive reading strategies. We conclude the chapter by presenting the assessment and instructional implications of our newer work, which has moved from a characterization of the role of metacognitive knowledge in accounting for the success of bilingual readers to an investigation of strategies that might help Spanish–English bilingual children improve their literacy performance (García, 1996; Jiménez, 1997; Jiménez & Gámez, 1996).

EARLY VIEWS ON BILINGUALISM

Although in Western society the study of classical languages—such as Hebrew, Greek and Latin—was regarded more positively, in the United States bilingualism generally was viewed negatively. As early as the 1750s, Benjamin Franklin accused German-speaking Americans of immorality, lack of patriotism, and ignorance (Crawford, 1993; Heath, 1981). Crawford argued that much of the early criticism was due to the immigrant status of bilinguals. Hakuta (1986) noted that early studies of bilinguals focused more on immigrants' intelligence than on bilingualism per se. In the early 1900s, psychologists, enamored with intelligence testing, compared the English test performance of recently arrived immigrant groups from Southern and Eastern Europe with assimilated immigrant groups from Northern Europe. Not surprisingly, the "new" immigrants, who were learning English as a second language, did far worse on the intelligence tests than did the "old" immigrants, who either came from English-speaking countries or who already were fluent in English. As Hakuta explained, almost all of the psychologists accepted the finding that the "new" immigrants demonstrated low levels of intelligence. Where the psychologists differed was in their attribution of this finding to genetic or environmental origins.

Based on the intelligence test findings, many psychologists in the 1930s–1950s conducted research that questioned the wisdom of raising children bilingually (see Hakuta, 1986). The general conclusion of this line of work was that childhood bilingualism resulted in mental retardation (Thompson, 1952). Although Sánchez (1934) warned that bilingual children should not be tested in English without first ascertaining their knowledge of English, the general belief was that bilingual immigrants' low performance on intelligence tests in English reflected their inability to learn English due to their low intelligence (see Hakuta, 1986).

Time and perspective have unmasked such research as ethnocentric. Beginning in the 1960s, scholars (e.g., Hakuta, 1986; McLaughlin, 1978; Peal & Lambert, 1962) criticized these studies on a number of grounds: subject selection, use of inappropriate tests, comparison between monolinguals and bilinguals, bilingual subjects' varied English proficiency and degree of bilingualism, and failure to control for subjects' socioeconomic status, age, and sex. In spite of these defects, conclusions from early studies of bilingualism, and the prejudices that spawned them, remain a part of today's discourse on the merits of bilingualism in American society.

In contrast to the early negative views of bilingualism, the seminal work of three scholars (Leopold, 1949; Peal & Lambert, 1962; Vygotsky, 1962, 1980) provided theoretical and empirical evidence that bilingualism might be beneficial. For example, earlier this century the Soviet psychologist Vygotsky proposed that the experience of learning two languages could provide children with opportunities to reflect on language in a manner that was difficult or impossible for the monolingual child. He described learning a foreign language as "conscious and deliberate from the start" (1962, p. 109). His theoretical proposal grew out of his knowledge of different populations learning Russian as a second language in school settings. Vygotsky (1980) was aware, however, that under some circumstances bilingualism was associated with low levels of academic and cognitive achievement.

Leopold's (1949) detailed descriptive study of his daughter's German–English bilingualism (as described in Hakuta, 1986) was one of the first studies to document specific, favorable effects of bilingualism on cognition. He postulated that bilingualism provided his daughter with two means for naming and expressing ideas, allowing her to focus more of her attention on the deeper meanings associated with words and phrases rather than solely on their phonological representations. For example, she would insert meaningful substitutions for words in nursery rhymes that destroyed the rhyme and meter but that preserved the meaning. Leopold viewed this behavior as an indication that she possessed a heightened awareness of both meaning and thought: In his words, "bilingualism may well be a gain, because it induces concentration on the subject matter instead of the words" (p. 35).

Although the work of Leopold was largely ignored until recent times, that of Peal and Lambert (1962) galvanized research interest in bilingualism. These researchers examined the relationship of bilingualism to intelligence in the Canadian context by comparing the IQ performance of 10-year-old, highly proficient French–English bilingual children with French monolingual peers, all from middle-class backgrounds. They concluded that the bilingual children were "profiting from a language asset" rather than "suffering from a language handicap" (p. 15). According to their findings, the children's bilingualism resulted in enhanced mental flexibility as compared to the monolingual children. Peal and Lambert provided corroborating evidence for the theoretical constructs and previous research of Vygotsky and Leopold.

MORE RECENT WORK

Monolinguals Versus Bilinguals

Work in the 1970s and 1980s tended to compare the performance of monolingual and bilingual children from similar backgrounds on metalinguistic (Ben-Zeev, 1977; Feldman & Shen, 1971; Ianco-Worrall, 1972) and metacognitive tasks (Bain & Yu, 1980). A major aim of this work was to explore the relationship between bilingualism and intelligence. Many of the researchers (Ben-Zeev, 1977; Feldman & Shen, 1971; Ianco-Worrall, 1972) focused on subjects' performance on Piagetian substitution tasks, such as, "If we called the sun the moon, would it still shine during the day?" In general, the bilingual children outperformed their monolingual counterparts up to the age of 6. Also, Ianco-Worrall found that when the children were asked to identify which word was more like "cap," "can" or "hat?", the bilingual children answered "hat" significantly more often than the monolingual children. She concluded that the bilingual children were paying more attention to the semantic dimensions of words than to their phonetic qualities. After the age of 6, such differences in performance seemed to disappear.

Bain and Yu (1980) compared the longitudinal performance (22–24 months of age vs. 46–48 months of age) of Chinese–English bilinguals in Hong Kong, French–German bilinguals in Alsace, and French-English bilinguals in Canada with their monolingual peers on a series of metacognitive tasks designed by Luria (1976) to evaluate children's cognitive development. Bain and Yu actually were interested in testing the effectiveness of raising bilingual children in a household where one parent spoke one language to the children, and the other parent spoke a different language. They found no significant differences in the young bilingual and monolingual children's (22–24 months) cognitive performance, where the delay between parental information (e.g., "The marble is under the cup") and instructions (e.g., "Find the marble") was manipulated (p. 308). However, when the children were older (46–48 months), there were significant differences in their "voluntary control of processes" (p. 311). Across three tasks, the children were told to respond to an increasingly complex series of instructions by squeezing or not squeezing a rubber ball according to which eye on a stationary clown face was lit. In the first task, the children merely had to listen to the researcher's instructions and respond accordingly ("When the red eye goes on, squeeze the ball. When the green eye goes on, don't squeeze the ball", p. 310). In the second task they were told to repeat orally what the researcher said before they performed the task, and in the third task they were told to repeat silently what the researcher said before they performed the task. The bilingual children significantly outperformed the monolingual children on the last two tasks. Bain and Yu concluded that the children's bilingualism appeared to give them a developmental cognitive advantage that surfaced at the approximate age of 4.

Cognitive Variation Within Bilinguals

The preceding genre of research stimulated more careful study on the part of other researchers. For example, instead of comparing bilingual children with monolingual children, two research studies (Hakuta, 1987; Jarvis, Danks, & Merriman, 1995) examined the cognitive abilities displayed by ethnically and linguistically homogenous groups of children. That is, they examined the relationship of the children's cognitive abilities to their overall levels of bilingual proficiency. Neither study included a monolingual control group. The rationale for these studies was that if bilingualism is associated with higher levels of cognitive functioning, one would expect to find that those children with higher levels of second language proficiency perform at higher cognitive levels than their linguistically less-gifted companions. The findings for these studies were mixed. Hakuta reported confirmation of the hypothesis, whereas Jarvis et al. found no differences. Jarvis et al., however, examined the performance of Mexican students in Grades 3 and 4 in private Mexican schools. These students were older than the Puerto Rican students in New Jersey included in Hakuta's study.

Accordingly, one possible resolution of the contradictory results focuses on stages of development. It might be that bilingualism accelerates cognitive development before and during the initial stages of schooling, but that by the time children have received typical first grade literacy instruction, these effects are no longer in evidence. A second possibility is that while monolingual children almost always receive instruction that by default or design enhances both their cognitive and metalinguistic abilities and knowledge, there are few programs explicitly designed to build upon, enhance, and promote the cognitive and metalinguistic advantage of bilingual children. As a result, bilingual children quickly lose any potential advantages except in programs that strive to maintain their two languages.

BILINGUAL CHILDREN'S METACOGNITIVE KNOWLEDGE AND READING

Much of the research related to young bilingual children's reading has tended to compare their performance with that of monolingual children on isolated metalinguistic tasks related to reading (such as phonological awareness, word awareness, word recognition, and syntactic awareness). For example, Bruck and Genesee (1995) found that middle-class kindergarten children in bilingual French-English immersion schools demonstrated superior performance on tests of onset-rime awareness (the child recognizes that the word *bat* is composed of an initial *b* sound that is followed by *at*) when compared to monolingual children. Göncz and Kodzopeljic (1991) found that bilingual preschool and kindergarten children in the former Yugoslavia were better able than monolingual children to explain how and why words like *mosquito* and *ox* differ in terms of their length and their referents. In a study by Galambos and Goldin-Meadows (1990), young Spanish–English bilingual children in El Salvador outperformed their Spanish monolingual counterparts in detecting, correcting, and explaining their corrections of ungrammatical sentences. They performed as well as a sample of English monolinguals in New Haven, who possessed higher levels of English language proficiency.

Another line of research has focused on testing Cummins' interdependence and threshold hypothesis theory (for discussions of the theory, see Cummins, 1979, 1980). Cummins argued that a major reason why many Latina/o bilingual students in the United States do not do well in school is that they have not had the opportunity to first develop a sound conceptual and proficient base in one language, which, if developed, would enable them to transfer knowledge and strategies to learning in their second language. Instead, he argued, they have been prematurely placed in second-language settings based on their apparent oral proficiency in English. A number of researchers have attempted to test the universality of Cummins' theory and argument by examining the extent to which bilingual students' reading performance in their second language is predicted by their second-language oral proficiency or their first-language reading performance (among others, see Tregar & Wong, 1984; Langer, Bartolomé, Vásquez, & Lucas, 1990; Verhoeven, 1990). In a review of this research (García, Pearson, & Jiménez, 1994), we pointed out that "the contradictory nature of the findings suggests that the results are influenced by the age of the students, the type of instruction they have received in their two languages, and the types of measures used to determine reading and oral proficiency" (p. 16). In a qualitative study comparing how Latina/o bilingual students of different language proficiencies constructed meaning in their reading, Langer et al. (1990) reported that the dimension that distinguished the proficient from the less proficient biliterates was their capacity to use good meaning-making strategies in the two languages. This capacity was more important than their proficiency in either of the two languages.

Researchers in the field are just beginning to identify and investigate the specific types of knowledge and strategies that bilingual readers transfer across two languages. In a series of quantitative (García & Nagy, 1993; Nagy et al., 1993) and qualitative studies (García, 1996; Jiménez, 1992; Jiménez et al., 1995, 1996), we investigated the extent to which Spanish–English bilingual students in the United States transfer vocabulary knowledge in one language to reading in another language through the use of cognate strategies. Cognates are words in two languages with common linguistic roots, which are closely related both in form and in meaning across the two languages. If bilingual students—especially those whose first language is Spanish—recognize the possibility of a cognate relationship, and know the

Spanish cognate, then they should be able to use their Spanish knowledge to help access the meaning of the unknown English cognate.

In a study focusing on fourth-, fifth-, and sixth-grade Latina/o students' recognition and use of cognates while reading (Nagy et al., 1993), we measured students' knowledge of specific cognates and vocabulary in English and Spanish, administered a reading test on passages in which we had embedded cognates, presented students with a brief definition of cognates, and then asked them to circle all the cognates they could identify in the passages they had just read. After controlling for English vocabulary knowledge, we found that the students' English reading comprehension performance was significantly related to their Spanish vocabulary knowledge and post-hoc ability to recognize cognates, indicating that the students were making use of cognate relationships in their English reading. On the other hand, careful examination of the cognate recognition data (García & Nagy, 1993) indicated that the majority of the students identified less than half of the cognates that they previously had reported knowing separately in both Spanish and English, suggesting that they were underutilizing this strategy. We concluded that the students had an "emerging" concept of cognate. To use cognate strategies in their reading effectively required considerable metalinguistic awareness and flexibility, which many of the students did not yet appear to possess.

A limited amount of work has focused on documenting the types of metacognitive strategies bilingual middle-school and high-school students use while reading in their two languages. Most of this research is informed by research on monolingual students' use of reading strategies and involves asking bilingual students to indicate on reading strategy surveys the reading strategies they use in their two languages. For example, Pritchard (1990) found that bilingual Latina/o high-school students used the same reading strategies across languages. Padrón, Knight, and Waxman (1986) and Calero-Breckheimer and Göetz (1993) reported that intermediate grade Spanish–English bilingual children also used the same reading strategies when reading in their two languages. Calero-Breckheimer and Göetz documented a relationship between the number of student-reported strategies and overall levels of reading comprehension. Unfortunately, the survey data do not indicate whether bilingual students use strategies not documented in the monolingual research, or if their use of strategies varies dependent on their proficiencies in the two languages, the type of text, or the context of the task. The work that serves as the core of this chapter is informed by the preceding efforts, but focuses more specifically on understanding how Latina/o bilingual children approach reading in their two languages.

OPPORTUNITIES AND OBSTACLES IN BILINGUAL READING: A STUDY OF METACOGNITIVE STRATEGIES

The major objective of our research (Jiménez et al., 1995, 1996) was to explore the question of how bilingualism and biliteracy affect metacognition. We focused on understanding what eight bilingual Latina/o sixth-and seventh-grade students in the United States knew about their reading and use of reading strategies across two languages, how they used certain strategies, and when they used them. We selected bilingual students who were considered to be successful English readers, based on their reading test scores and ranking by educational personnel (teachers, principals, and bilingual directors). For comparative purposes, we included two smaller samples of three monolingual Anglo students considered to be successful English readers and three bilingual Latina/o students considered to be marginally successful English readers. Because we wanted to understand the actual ways in which the students used metacognitive strategies while reading, we chose to conduct an intensive qualitative study that included unprompted and prompted think alouds, interviews, a measure of prior knowledge, and passage recalls. The think-aloud procedure was the major source of our data, and we chose it for its potential to provide inferences about cognitive procedures (see Ericsson & Simon, 1984). All of the students read an English narrative text and two English expository passages. The bilingual students also read two narrative texts and two expository passages in Spanish (for details of the research design and methodology, see Jiménez, 1992).

We have organized our discussion of the findings first to focus on the strategic adaptations made by successful bilingual readers to the task of biliteracy. Then, we briefly compare the types of strategies that both successful bilingual readers and successful monolingual readers used in their English reading. Next, we discuss the responses of the less-successful bilingual readers to the task of biliteracy. Here we reflect on the different performances of the bilingual successful and marginally successful readers in terms of what this type of variation might indicate about the relationship between bilingualism and metacognition.

The Strategic Adaptations of Successful Bilingual Readers

Although literacy in any language makes a common list of demands on those who would master it, biliteracy requires something more. Biliteracy requires a minimum of dual language proficiencies, an understanding of the features shared by the written systems of the two languages, and a sense of how the systems diverge, vary, and distinguish themselves as separate entities.

The successful bilingual readers in our study had developed their biliteracy in less than promising conditions: Only one of them had received recent instruction in the two languages; three of the eight never had received formal instruction in Spanish; the other four had participated in bilingual education, but had been exited into all-English classrooms by the beginning of second or third grade. In spite of their limited exposure to Spanish literacy instruction, these students were biliterate. In the next section, we focus on some of the ways that high-achieving bilingual readers successfully managed, negotiated, and conceptualized biliteracy. What seemed to underlie their success was a set of dispositions toward and strategies for negotiating meanings from texts.

View of Reading.   The successful bilingual readers tended to have a unitary view of reading; that is, they recognized the many similarities between reading in Spanish and English. As can be seen in some of their comments, they emphasized the similarities. Similar to young bilingual children who frequently are able to separate form from function in spoken language (Ben-Zeev, 1977; Feldman & Shen, 1971; Ianco-Worrall, 1972), five of the eight successful bilingual readers indicated that the form of written language was arbitrary. Marcos', Lisa's, and Alberto's explanations of how they viewed reading in two languages illustrate this point:

Marcos: When I learned to read in English I just needed to know the pronunciation and the spelling of the words. Because I could read in Spanish and English. [I] Just needed to know how to say the words.

Lisa: [E]verything's the same what you have to know (to read in English and Spanish).

Alberto: There aren't really any differences (between reading in English and Spanish), I mean they're both based on the same thing, how you understand it, how you read it, how you take it and how you evaluate it and all that.

It is interesting to speculate about whether monoliterate students would discover the arbitrary character of orthography as readily as biliterate students. Although our data do not permit us to evaluate the claim (not enough data from monoliterate readers), it is noteworthy that this insight emerged, without specific prompting, from five of the eight biliterate readers.

Knowledge and Use of Bilingual Strategies. All eight of the successful bilingual readers indicated their awareness and use of strategies unique to their bilingual status, such as searching for cognates, code-mixing, and translating. The use of cognates was one tool these readers could use to deal with the difficult task of encountering large numbers of unknown words in reading English or Spanish (Twadell, 1973). Gilda demonstrated that she knew the value of English–Spanish cognate relationships:

Gilda: *Yo sé que hay unas palabras que se parecen pero no sé que quiere decir. Proportional, hmm. Estoy buscando que quiere decir, no sé.*

(I know that there are some words that look alike but I don't know what it means. Proportional, hmm. I'm looking for what it means, I don't know.)

Although all eight of the successful bilingual readers mentioned their understanding of the strategy to search for cognates, their actual use of the strategy was quite limited. Their high degree of awareness, combined with their limited verbalization of the strategy during their think alouds, suggests that the students either underutilized the strategy or reserved its use for special occasions, paralleling the García and Nagy (1993) findings.

Two students said that they substituted words from their other language when they encountered unknown vocabulary. In other words, these students used code-mixing to help them to comprehend the passages. In a Spanish passage, Pamela did not understand what a key word *cerillas* (matches) meant. Through the use of code-mixing she was able to reflect on what she thought the word might mean (underlining indicates the code-mixing):

Pamela: *Yo creo que son esas cositas que hacen <u>sparks</u> así...es algo que se encienda....*

(I think that they are the little things that make sparks like that...it's something that is lit....)

Four successful bilingual readers described translating as a strategic activity. One student mentioned that he could better recall information if he translated English text into Spanish. Gilda said she translated when reading in her weaker language. She felt that translating could be costly in terms of time and effort, and should be used cautiously so as not to interfere with comprehension. She discussed the difficulty that translating caused her when trying to remember material during a passage recall:

Gilda: I get confused (translating for a sentence or paragraph).

Investigator: So you just do it (translate) for a word?

Gilda: Yea, just a word. When I was little, when I just came here, I would try to translate and…I would always translate to see if I understood it, and then I would know what the words meant.

The use of searching for cognates, code-mixing, and translating as beneficial reading strategies have not been widely discussed in the second-language reading literature. Our work suggests that these strategies ought to be given attention in future work.

Transfer of Metacognitive Knowledge and Strategies.   Other researchers have invoked the notion of strategy transfer to explain why bilingual students who are good readers of their native languages are often good readers of English (Miramontes & Commins, 1989; Saville-Troike, 1984). Our successful bilingual readers knew that information and strategies learned or acquired in one language could be used to comprehend text written in another language. Their awareness of the transference of knowledge across languages was inferred from comments such as that made by Lisa, "It's familiar to me porque en inglés nos enseñan todo esto" (It's familiar to me because in English they teach us all of this). Marcos demonstrated his declarative knowledge of strategy transfer during an interview, and he suggested that this knowledge was easier to learn in one's dominant language:

Marcos: Because, let's say there are rules to be a good reader, like you have to read carefully if it's something difficult to read and read however you want if it's easy. And in Spanish…you could learn those rules easier cuz you know more Spanish than English if you are Latin American, but if you are an American…it should be easier in English than in Spanish.

He later demonstrated that when approaching a topic in one language, he thought about what he had read in the other language:

Marcos: *Las novas me recuerdan con los libros que leo en inglés, las estrellas. A mi me interesa mucho este artículo.*

(The novas remind me of the books that I read in English, the stars. I'm very interested in this article.)

Several of the successful bilingual readers mentioned specific metacognitive strategies that could be transferred from one language to another. Strategies they named were questioning, rereading, evaluating, and the notion that reading must make sense regardless of the language of the text, in other words, monitoring.

Similarities and Differences Between Successful Bilingual and Monolingual Readers

Several reading strategies used by the successful bilingual readers appear to be indicators of a well-functioning approach to interacting with text irrespective of bilingual status. Exemplary in this respect are the strategies of integrating prior knowledge into ongoing meaning construction, the making of inferences, asking and answering questions, monitoring comprehension, and determining the meanings of unknown words. By and large, these strategies characterized the monolingual readers as well.

Where the successful bilingual and monolingual readers substantially differed was that the monolingual readers did not identify as many comprehension problems as the bilingual readers. Accordingly their protocols revealed fewer instances of less comprehension monitoring and repair. In addition, the monolingual readers did not identify as many unknown English words as did the bilingual readers.

Connecting Prior Knowledge With Text. Integrating prior knowledge with textual information is crucial for comprehending text (Anderson & Pearson, 1984). Both groups of readers demonstrated that they were able to relate what they were reading with their background knowledge. Both groups of readers also showed how important this strategy was by making explicit their prior knowledge of relevant topics. For example, while reading a Spanish expository text, which discussed uses of solar energy, Lisa, one of the successful bilingual readers, exemplified successful integration of relevant prior knowledge with textual information:

Lisa: *Y en Chicago me acordé que ví en las noticias que hay un laundrymat, una lavandería, donde ellos no meten dinero, la energía lo obtienen del sol....*

(And in Chicago I remember that I saw on the news that there is a
laundrymat, where they don't insert money. They get the energy from the
sun....)

Another bilingual reader, Betty, accessed relevant prior knowledge when
she read the "Octopus" passage, describing how the octopus can regenerate
missing tentacles:

> Betty: I learned in fifth grade something [about]...worms. I don't
>   remember if they cut off their head if they would grow two
>   heads....

Then when Betty read about the siphon of the octopus, she made an analogy
to something she thought was similar: "[S]iphon, it's a funnel shaped
opening under the head, maybe it's like a whale how it squirts out water."
    Michelle, one of the successful monolingual readers, talked about how
she used prior knowledge when she interacted with text:

> Michelle: I relate it [the text] to something I've seen before or what-
>   ever...like if I already knew from the movie "20,000 Leagues
>   Under the Sea" that an octopus lives in the sea, you remember
>   that...the things about the octopus because it was in the movie.

The successful English monolingual readers easily integrated prior knowledge with textual information by drawing upon a rich knowledge base and
by demonstrating a sensitivity to textual information. For example, Bruce,
one of the successful monolingual readers, provided an example of how
well-developed vocabulary knowledge interacts with prior knowledge when
he referred to the biologist in the story "The King of the Beasts" as a
professor. Tricia did the same thing when she referred to him as an archae-
ologist. Their behavior indicated that they possessed a sophisticated semantic knowledge base that was not demonstrated by the successful bilingual
readers. It was this level of detail that differentiated the successful English
monolingual readers from the successful Spanish–English bilingual readers.

Effective Inferencing.   Both groups of students demonstrated that
they were able to make accurate inferences across sentences and text. They
also checked their inferences with the textual information to make sure that
they were not making incorrect inferences. Although there were qualitative
differences between the two groups of successful readers in terms of the types
and sophistication of inferencing made, both groups used this checking
strategy in their English reading with approximately the same frequency.

The successful bilingual readers also made large numbers of inferences while reading Spanish text. In addition, they often qualified their inferences with "maybe" or "probably" signifying a willingness to revise their thoughts, which they later explicitly confirmed or disconfirmed. When making inferences, they tended to focus their attention on higher-level elements of the text. Alberto, for example, inferred an important outcome of the story "The King of the Beasts" but indicated that he was willing to wait until the end of the story to confirm his prediction:

> Alberto: [T]here might be a chance that I finish the story and...all human beings might be extinct for all the pollution and stuff.

Gilda inferred important information for understanding the humor in the Spanish narrative, "*Como Estos Hay Pocos*":

> Gilda: Oh! *¡Ya sé que va a hacer él! Que el abrigo no es de él, es del señor.*
>
> (Oh! Now I know what he's going to do! So the coat is not his: it belongs to the man.)

Where the succcessful bilingual and monolingual readers differed was in the successful monolingual readers' careful attention to textual detail. For example, during a think aloud, Bruce, one of the monolingual readers, reported that the characters in the English narrative text were in a tank, but then revised his understanding by stating that they were near a tank. The prepositions *in* and *near* can change the meaning of a text. It was this level of detail that distinguished the successful monolingual Anglo readers as superior to the successful Latina/o bilingual readers.

Asking and Answering Questions. The successful bilingual readers exploited the strategy of questioning to aid comprehension only occasionally; in fact, they used this strategy less frequently than the successful monolingual readers. Even so, on the few occasions when they did use it, their questions were quite pertinent. The following series of questions, asked by Gilda as she read "The King of the Beasts," focused on a key element of the story:

> Gilda: Well, why are they making a man, aren't they people? They're biologists aren't they? Why would they be scared if it was a man?

In fact, Gilda's questions allowed her to determine that "they" were not human beings. The main characters in this story were extraterrestrials, but this information was not explicitly stated.

Kathy also attempted to determine the identity of the unknown creature featured in the English narrative text by asking a question:

> Kathy: [F]irst the biologist says, "Poor little thing, it's so alone but I'll give it love," and then the visitor asks, "Is it dangerous?" But what are they talking about? I don't know what they're talking about.

While reading the Spanish narrative text, Marcos asked a question that helped him understand the problem faced by the protagonist:

> Marcos: *Él está trabajando mientras que todos están con abrigos, y dice que va a buscar una tienda, un abrigo. ¿Pero cómo lo va a hacer así con el frío que había, sin abrigo él?*
>
> (He is working while everyone else has on coats, and it says that he is going to look for a store, a coat. But how is he going to do it when it is so cold outside without a coat?)

Monitoring Comprehension.   The successful bilingual readers demonstrated more monitoring of their comprehension than did the successful monolingual readers. In and of itself, the lack of visible monitoring by the monolingual readers might be construed as a sign that they were not comprehending as fully as they could. Careful examination, however, suggests that their lower level of monitoring was more a function of their perception that the texts were fairly easy for them to comprehend. And, in fact, their passage recalls demonstrated that they comprehended much of what they read. The few times that the monolingual readers noted difficulties, they quickly resolved them by making inferences and invoking prior knowledge.

The successful bilingual readers carefully monitored their comprehension by identifying comprehension obstacles. Alberto, for example, indicated he was monitoring his comprehension after he read the sentence, "These, almost ready to be taken from the tank, are tiger cubs." He commented, "[T]his sentence doesn't make sense." He reread the sentence aloud and then added the following comment, which also reflected the use of the rereading strategies and demonstrated awareness:

> Alberto: Oh! OK... I sometimes read the sentence outloud, then it makes more sense than when I read it to myself.

Samuel demonstrated how important comprehension monitoring can be to a reader trying to capture the gist of a story:

> Samuel: So maybe I was wrong. I finished but I really didn't get what was happening. ...I'm checking something I said wrong.

It was Samuel's monitoring that triggered further action, and his willingness to rethink his assumptions facilitated his drawing of the following inference:

> Samuel: *Ya tiene más sentido este cuento. A lo mejor estos extraterrestres es el biólogo que...hace más gente y todo eso....*
>
> (This story makes more sense now. Maybe these aliens is [are] the biologist that...makes more people and all of that....)

The question of whether biliteracy, particularly successful biliteracy, nurtures a disposition toward more careful monitoring of comprehension remains open. The interplay between bilingualism and high levels of biliteracy still needs to be more fully explored. Nonetheless, the remarkable consistency of our successful biliterate students in their elaborate comprehension monitoring suggests that biliteracy may dispose students to actively monitor their reading.

Resolving Unknown Vocabulary. The successful bilingual readers focused considerably more attention on unknown vocabulary than did the successful monolingual readers. Focusing on vocabulary, however, did not radically interfere with the bilingual readers' overall comprehension (as indicated by the passage recalls). Their determination to resolve problems often resulted in accurate identifications of unknown vocabulary.

The successful bilingual readers used a variety of techniques to construct working definitions of unknown vocabulary, such as using context, invoking relevant prior knowledge, questioning, inferencing, searching for cognates, and translating. For example, to construct an interpretation of the word *wantonly* while reading the English narrative text, Gilda first monitored her reading, then used context and inferencing strategies to arrive at an interpretation. "Want, wan–tan–ly. What is that?" Her comment, "Well, I don't know the meaning of a word," demonstrated her interest in this vocabulary item. Her determination led her to specify the item's grammatical function: "[T]hey're talking about a kind of way they were killed." Gilda resolved the situation to her satisfaction by reading ahead:

Gilda: [B]ecause the next sentence, it says that, … I'm trying as it were
to make, oh! OK, so he wants to do this because people, he
thinks people were like really mean and stupid and everything,
now I know.

Pamela relied on her prior knowledge about extinct animals to help her
define the term *extinct*:

Pamela: [E]xtinct *no quiere decir* (doesn't that mean) like when they're
almost gone? Like the African elephant, I think there aren't any
more.

The strategy "focusing on vocabulary" was conspicuously absent in the
think-aloud protocols of the successful monolingual readers. A case can be
made that the successful monolingual readers did not need this strategy as
much as the successful bilingual readers. Whereas the successful bilingual
readers may be more sensitive to the need to define and comprehend
unknown vocabulary, it is probably also true that successful monolingual
readers simply know more English vocabulary.

The Response of the Less-Successful Bilingual Readers to the Demands of Biliteracy

The differences between successful and less-successful bilingual readers may
be, in some ways, more informative than the differences we have identified
between successful bilingual and successful monolingual readers. Careful
understanding of the less-successful bilingual readers' struggles might provide useful information for the improvement of literacy instruction for
bilingual students. Two of these students had participated in a bilingual
education program for 5 years (Grades K–4); the third student had participated in a bilingual education program for 2 years (Grades 2–3). Similar to
their more successful counterparts, they were stronger readers in English
than they were in Spanish.

View of Reading in Two Languages.   The less successful bilingual
readers were more apt to see bilingualism as damaging than were the
successful bilingual readers. Michael, for instance, said that children learning English as a second language were much more likely to be in the lower
reading group than native-English speakers. Two of the three indicated that
their knowledge of another language caused them confusion when reading.
For example, Celina said that native speakers of English had an advantage
over native Spanish speakers and remarked, "I get mixed up because I talk
Spanish and English." Catalina mentioned that the vowel sounds in Spanish

and English were not the same and that knowing the two writing systems was confusing:

Catalina: I think what confuses you is the … the letters cuz like *e,e* in English is like the *e* and then in Spanish you say, wait, in Spanish it's *i* in English, so people get mixed up.

Limited Use of Bilingual Strategies. The less successful bilingual readers believed that the two languages were more different than similar and that knowledge of one was not useful for reading the other. This belief may have been one of the reasons why the less successful readers did not make appreciable use of the bilingual strategies. Because they saw the two languages as distinct, they failed to make connections. They did not search for cognates, code-mix, or actively transfer knowledge and strategies. They very occasionally translated Spanish to English when they read in Spanish.

Metacognitive Knowledge and Use of Metacognitive Strategies. On the few occasions that the less successful bilingual readers invoked prior knowledge, they were as likely to bring irrelevant prior knowledge to bear on their interpretation of the text as they were to bring relevant prior knowledge. Michael, for example, when reading the "Flea" stated, "I don't know why I got the picture (in my mind) of a wrestling ring." It is impossible to know why he visualized this because no mention of wrestling or a ring occurred in the passage.

The less successful bilingual readers tended to adopt one interpretation of a text, or part of it, even when presented with contradictory information. Unlike the successful bilingual readers who were tentative in their inferences and drawing of conclusions, the less successful bilingual readers often tried to force subsequent text information to fit earlier interpretations. For example, Celina inferred that the unidentified creature in the story "The King of the Beasts" was an animal. She did not revise her comprehension even when faced with explicit textual information to the contrary:

Celina: Well, it said it's a man and I don't think it was a man cuz a man couldn't be more dangerous than an elephant or a tiger or a bear.

Despite receiving the same instructions as the other readers, the less successful bilingual readers seemed to view finishing the task as more important than comprehending the text. The less successful bilingual readers could identify problems (monitor) but did not often resolve them. Two of the three less successful bilingual readers, Celina and Catalina, consistently exclaimed, "I'm done" after reading the last word of a text. In contrast, the successful bilingual readers continued to question their comprehension or to mull over their understanding after their first pass through a text.

The less successful bilingual readers most closely resembled the successful bilingual readers in their relatively frequent identification of unknown vocabulary items. For example, Celina indicated that she did not recognize the word *wantonly* when reading "The King of the Beasts." Her only concern, though, seemed to be to approximate the pronunciation of the word. After doing so, she abandoned interest in the item:

Celina: Is this "want only?"

Investigator: What do you think?

Celina: Yea.

Consistent with their goal of finishing rather than comprehending, the less successful bilingual readers tended toward similar profiles of strategy use across text types and languages. Golinkoff (1975–1976), in a seminal study of cognitive reading strategies, believed that poor readers approach all texts in essentially the same way. The less successful bilingual readers tended to approach Spanish and English text in essentially the same manner. We can understand why the less-successful bilingual readers viewed their bilingualism negatively; unlike their more successful counterparts, they did not know how to take advantage of knowledge learned in one language when reading in the other. What was regarded as a strength for successful biliterates was viewed as a weakness for those who were less successful.

ASSESSMENT AND INSTRUCTIONAL IMPLICATIONS

Most of the research included in the introductory section of this chapter compared the performance of bilingual children on measures of general intelligence and metalinguistic knowledge with that of comparable monolingual children, or the researchers sought to establish a correlation between children's level of bilingual proficiency with their performance on various measures. The research is informative in terms of how bilingualism affects cognitive abilities. It also is useful for allaying the fears of parents who would like to raise their children bilingually or who would like to place their children in language immersion programs. Although the research has included children from language minority communities in the United States and elsewhere, it has not provided specific guidance on how to most effectively promote the literacy learning of students who are bilingual.

Our findings suggest that heightened metacognitive awareness as applied to reading is not an automatic outcome of children's bilingualism or bilingual education. Not all bilingual children know how to transfer knowledge and strategies across the two languages. These findings would have been difficult to obtain if we had simply relied on bilingual students' performance on pen and pencil measures or on reading tests (see García, 1991, 1994). What helped us to discover these findings was our use of the think-aloud procedure, clinical type interviews, and retellings. The assessment reform movement, with its emphasis on performance-based assessment and classroom authentic assessment (see García & Pearson, 1994), should help teachers to better understand the reading performance of bilingual students, as long as tasks are included that allow them to document bilingual students' knowledge and strategy use across two languages (García, 1994). Extrapolating from the rich data we were able to obtain in our research, we are confident that think-aloud protocols, clinical interviews, and retellings can provide teachers with very useful information about the competence and potential of bilingual readers.

In terms of instruction, we are currently engaged in a series of studies designed to improve the reading competence of bilingual students by providing them with instruction that focuses on metacognitive awareness and strategic reading. This work is informed by the preceding findings and those of other researchers interested in second-language children's literacy instruction. In one line of work (García, 1996), instructional scaffolding was used to heighten 13 Mexican-American fourth-graders' knowledge and use of transfer strategies in their English and Spanish reading, with a specific focus on cognate recognition strategies. In another line of work (Jiménez, 1997; Jiménez & Gámez, 1996), strategic reading instruction, characterized by the use of culturally relevant and familiar text, a comprehension focus, and opportunities to build reading fluency, was presented to five low-literacy Latina/o middle-school students who were experiencing great difficulty with literacy (three were in a self-contained special education classroom, and the other two had been identified as "at-risk" for referral to special education).

In both lines of research, explicit focus on strategies, modeling, teacher–student interaction, and teacher scaffolding through the use of a modified think-aloud approach has resulted in positive improvements. For example, Jiménez (1997; Jiménez & Gámez, 1996) found that after spending about 2 weeks teaching three specific strategies to the five students, the students made statements about their reading that reflected increased metacognitive knowledge about themselves as readers and the use of strategies for increasing their text comprehension. They described and used the reading strategies of asking questions, determining the meanings of unknown words, and making inferences similar to the more successful bilingual readers previously discussed. We continue to pursue these lines of research, although we must confess to some frustration with the limited instructional opportunities offered to students in the United States who desire to become bilingual and biliterate (García et al., 1994).

CONCLUSION

Ever since Peal and Lambert's (1962) cogent critique of earlier research on the cognitive effects of bilingualism, there has been a tendency within the field of second-language research to include only students from additive bilingual contexts. Additive bilingualism occurs when an individual is provided with an opportunity to learn a second language to a high degree of proficiency but without any loss or deterioration of that individual's first language. Although such a shift in research interest allowed for much deeper insight into the cognitive effects of bilingualism than had ever been possible previously, such a shift has been responsible for a bias toward the best case scenario. In other words, much of the research on the effects of bilingualism tells us what occurs under supportive conditions. Sadly, the majority of children from culturally and linguistically diverse backgrounds have not yet been able to benefit from such conditions.

Paradoxically, most educational research has focused on the worst case scenario, what has been called *subtractive bilingualism* (where students lose one language in the process of acquiring another), and has portrayed these students as bundles of deficiencies (see García et al., 1994). These two fundamentally conflicting paradigms—additive versus subtractive research—have not been reconciled. As a result, students from language minority communities have received instructional programs that make odd and contradictory assumptions about the students. On the one hand, native-language instruction is provided with the assumption that such instruction will provide a higher degree of cost–benefit return than will instruction solely in English. In other words, it is expected that these students will benefit from native-language instruction in much the same way that students from the majority culture benefit from instruction in their native language, and that they will transfer this learning to English-language contexts. On the other hand, instruction for language minority students often is predicated upon quite low expectations with respect to academic achievement. As a result, these students seldom receive a content-rich curriculum, one that will provide them with the necessary information and experiences for success in later grade levels. Exacerbating these problems, bilingual students' Spanish language literacy is almost never supported or recognized beyond the bilingual classroom.

We believe that an adequate rationale exists for providing bilingual students with native-language instruction. That rationale includes research support (Ramirez, 1992; Thomas & Collier, 1996; Willig, 1985), as well as a critical theoretical basis (Freire & Macedo, 1987; Macedo, 1994), and affective and moral claims (Nieto, 1992). Despite this firm scholarly foundation, it would appear that something has gone awry. Language minority students, by and large, are not benefiting from native-language instruction (de la Rosa, Maw, & Yzaguirre, 1990; Waggoner, 1991): Something is missing from their educational programs. We would like to suggest that what is missing is the rich array of information, knowledge, and strategies demonstrated by the successful bilingual readers whom we have examined in such detail.

Although exceptional, these readers provide a glimpse of the possibilities we might achieve if we were to provide all bilingual students with consistently high-quality reading instruction in their two languages. The successful bilingual readers' understanding and use of a sophisticated set of reading strategies demonstrate one possible model that appears to be successful for balancing their dual identities and bilingual language proficiencies. These readers embraced their identities and attained success in English-language literacy in adverse conditions by learning how to manage, negotiate, and even flourish while dealing with two literacy systems. Cummins (1986) and Nieto (1992) and other multicultural theorists have concluded that students from culturally and linguistically diverse backgrounds must not be expected to abandon their cultures, ethnicities, or linguistic backgrounds in pursuit of mainstream sanctioned success. We think that the experiences of the successful bilingual readers, and our new instructional findings, point the way for improvements in how we teach and assess bilingual students.

More than anything, however, the research we have reviewed, and most particularly the work in which we have been involved personally, suggests a number of fruitful areas of scholarship for bilingual researchers. In addition to the more transparent opportunities for new instructional research (helping students acquire and use the strategies we have found so successful), there is still much to learn about the basic processes in which successful bilingual readers engage while reading. For example, the theoretically and practically important question of whether biliteracy inherently disposes students to more consistent and serious comprehension monitoring remains unresolved in our work. The extent to which bilingual students automatically transfer knowledge and strategies across their two languages is also an area that needs further research, as is the possibility that students' knowledge of bilingual strategies, such as cognate recognition, could enhance their ability to recognize that several words share a family resemblance (e.g., *inspect, respect, retrospect, prospect*) within English and/or Spanish. Also unresolved is the ultimate source and role of cognate awareness: Where does it come from, and does its salutary effect work within as well as across languages?

These examples point to a broader theoretical question that we have assumed but left largely unexamined in our work: If bilingualism and biliteracy bring added value to students' metacognitive repertoires, what is the broader theoretical linguistic or cognitive mechanism that accounts for that advantage? One speculation, and it is only a speculation at this point, is that a second language and a second literacy provide students with something very much akin to what Gee (1990) has identified as the advantage that accrues to monolingual students when they acquire a second discourse (where a discourse refers to the linguistic, pragmatic, and paralinguistic patterns of a particular community of language users). Gee argues that secondary discourses provide language users with a perspective, a tool, that can be used to examine one's primary discourse (or other secondary discourse) with a critical eye. In other words, we cannot examine, analyze, and reflect on one discourse from within its boundaries, but secondary discourses provide us with the distance and the linguistic tools for doing so. Perhaps second languages provide something similar for bilingual students—a language and a perspective for thinking critically and reflectively, and hence metacognitively, about how things work in the other language. It is a provocative thought, one that will occupy our, and we hope your, interest for the next several years.

REFERENCES

Anderson, R. C., & Pearson, P. D. (1984). A schema-theoretic view of basic processes in reading. In P. D. Pearson, R. Barr, M. L. Kamil, & P. Mosenthal (Eds.), *Handbook of reading research* (pp. 255–292). New York: Longman.
Bain, B., & Yu, A. (1980). Cognitive consequences of raising children bilingually: "One parent, one language". *Canadian Journal of Psychology, 34*(4), 304–313.

Ben-Zeev, S. (1977). The influence of bilingualism on cognitive strategy and cognitive development. *Child Development, 48,* 1009–1018.

Bialystok, E. (1991). Metalinguistic dimensions of bilingual language proficiency. In E. Bialystok (Ed.), *Language processing in bilingual children* (pp. 113–140). Cambridge, England: Cambridge University Press.

Bruck, M., & Genesee, F. (1995). Phonological awareness in young second language learners. *Journal of Child Language, 22*(2), 307–324.

Calero-Breckheimer, A., & Göetz, E. T. (1993). Reading strategies of biliterate children for English and Spanish texts. *Reading Psychology, 14*(3), 177–204.

Crawford, J. (1993). *Bilingual education: History, politics, theory and practice.* Los Angeles: Bilingual Educational Services.

Cummins, J. (1979). Linguistic interdependence and the educational development of bilingual children. *Review of Educational Research, 49*(2), 222–251.

Cummins, J. (1980). The cross–lingual dimensions of language proficiency: Implications for bilingual education and the optimal age issue. *TESOL Quarterly, 14*(2), 175–187.

Cummins, J. (1986). Empowering minority students: A framework for intervention. *Harvard Educational Review, 56*(1), 18–36.

de la Rosa, D., Maw, C. E., & Yzaguirre, R. (1990). *Hispanic education: A statistical portrait 1990.* Washington, DC: Policy Analysis Center, Office of Research, Advocacy, and Legislation, National Council of La Raza.

Ericsson, K. A., & Simon, H. A. (1984). *Protocol analysis: Verbal reports as data.* Cambridge, MA: MIT Press.

Feldman, C., & Shen, M. (1971). Some language-related cognitive advantages of bilingual 5-year olds. *The Journal of Genetic Psychology, 118,* 235–244.

Freire, P., & Macedo, D. (1987). *Literacy: Reading the word and the world.* Westport, CT: Bergin & Garvey.

Galambos, S. J., & Goldin-Meadow, S. (1990). The effects of learning two languages on levels of metalinguistic awareness. *Cognition, 34,* 1–56.

García, G. E. (1991). Factors influencing the English reading test performance of Spanish-speaking Hispanic children. *Reading Research Quarterly, 26*(4), 371–392.

García, G. E. (1994). The literacy assessment of second-language learners: A focus on authentic assessment. In K. Spangenberg-Urbschat & R. Pritchard (Eds.), *Kids come in all languages: Reading instruction for second-language learners* (pp. 183–208). Newark, DE: International Reading Association.

García, G. E. (1996, December). *Improving the English reading of Mexican-American bilingual students through the use of cognate recognition strategies.* Paper presented at the National Reading Conference, Charleston, SC.

García, G. E., & Nagy, W. E. (1993). Latino students' concepts of cognates. In D. J. Leu & C. K. Kinzer (Eds.), *Forty-second yearbook of the National Reading Conference: Examining central issues in literacy research, theory, and practice* (pp. 367–373). Chicago: The National Reading Conference.

García, G. E., & Pearson, P. D. (1994). Assessment and diversity. *Review of Research in Education, 20,* 337–391.

García, G. E., Pearson, P. D., & Jiménez, R. T. (1994). *The at-risk situation: A synthesis of reading research* (Special Report). Champaign, IL: Center for the Study of Reading, University of Illinois.

Gee, J. P. (1990). *Social linguistics and literacies. Ideology in discourses.* Bristol, PA: Taylor & Francis.

Golinkoff, R. M. (1975–1976). A comparison of reading comprehension processes in good and poor comprehenders. *Reading Research Quarterly, 11*(4), 623–659.

Göncz, L., & Kodzopeljic, J. (1991) Exposure to two languages in the preschool period: Metalinguistic development and the acquisition of reading. *Journal of Multilingual and Multicultural Development, 12*(3), 137–163.

Hakuta, K. (1986). *Mirror of language.* New York: Basic Books.

Hakuta, K. (1987). Degree of bilingualism and cognitive ability in mainland Puerto Rican children. *Child Development, 58,* 1372–1388.

Heath, S. B. (1981). English in our language heritage. In C. A. Ferguson & S. B. Heath (Eds.), *Language in the USA* (pp. 6–20). Cambridge, England: Cambridge University Press.

Ianco-Worrall, A. D. (1972). Bilingualism and cognitive development. *Child Development, 43,* 1390–1400.

Jarvis, L. H., Danks, J. H., & Merriman, W. E. (1995). The effect of bilingualism on cognitive ability: A test of the level of bilingualism hypothesis. *Applied Psycholinguistics, 16,* 293–308.

Jiménez, R. T. (1992) *Opportunities and obstacles in bilingual reading.* Unpublished doctoral dissertation, University of Illinois at Urbana–Champaign.

Jiménez, R. T. (1997). The strategic reading abilities and potential of five low-literacy Latina/o readers in middle school. *Reading Research Quarterly, 32*(3), 224–243.

Jiménez, R. T., & Gámez, A. (1996). Literature-based cognitive strategy instruction for middle school Latina/o students. *Journal of Adolescent and Adult Literacy, 40*(2), 84–91.

Jiménez, R. T., García, G. E., & Pearson, P. D. (1995). Three children, two languages, and strategic reading: Case studies in bilingual/monolingual reading. *American Educational Research Journal, 32*(1), 31–61.

Jiménez, R. T., García, G. E., & Pearson, P. D. (1996). The reading strategies of Latina/o students who are successful English readers: Opportunities and obstacles. *Reading Research Quarterly, 31*(1), 90–112.

Langer, J. A., Bartolomé, L., Vásquez, O., & Lucas, T. (1990). Meaning construction in school literacy tasks: A study of bilingual students. *American Educational Research Journal, 27*(3), 427–471.

Leopold, W. F. (1949). *Speech development of a bilingual child: A linguist's record: Vol. 4. Diary from age 2.* Evanston, IL: Northwestern University.

Luria, A. R. (1976). *Cognitive development: Its cultural and social foundations.* Cambridge, MA: Harvard University Press.

Macedo, D. (1994). *Literacies of power: What Americans are not allowed to know.* Boulder, CO: Westview Press.

McLaughlin, B. (1978). *Second-language acquisition in childhood* (1st ed.). Hillsdale, NJ: Lawrence Erlbaum Associates.

Miramontes, O., & Commins, N. L. (1989, April). *A study of oral and reading proficiency of mixed-dominant Hispanic bilingual students.* Paper presented at the Annual Convention of the American Educational Research Association, New Orleans.

Nagy, W. E., García, G. E., Durgunoglu, A. Y., & Hancin-Bhatt, B. (1993). Spanish–English bilingual students' use of cognates in English reading. *Journal of Reading Behavior, 24*(3), 241–259.

Nieto, S. (1992). *Affirming diversity.* New York: Longman.

Padrón, Y. N., Knight, S. L., & Waxman, H. C. (1986). Analyzing bilingual and monolingual students' perceptions of their reading strategies. *The Reading Teacher, 39*(5), 430–433.

Peal, E., & Lambert, W. E. (1962). The relation of bilingualism to intelligence. *Psychological Monographs, 76,* 1–23.

Pritchard, R. (1990, December). *Reading in Spanish and English: A comparative study of processing strategies.* Paper presented at the National Reading Conference, Miami, FL.

Ramirez, J. D. (1992). Executive summary. *Bilingual Research Quarterly, 16*(1 & 2), 1–62.

Sánchez, G. I. (1934). Bilingualism and mental measure: A word of caution. *Journal of Applied Psychology, 18,* 765–771.

Saville–Troike, M. (1984). What really matters in second language learning for academic achievement. *TESOL Quarterly, 18*(2), 199–219.
Smith, M. E. (1931). A study of five bilingual children from the same family. *Child Development, 2,* 184–187.
Thomas, W. P., & Collier, V. (1996). Language–minority student achievement and program effectiveness. *NABE News,* 33–35.
Thompson, G. G. (1952). *Child psychology.* Boston, MA: Houghton Mifflin.
Tregar, B., & Wong, B. F. (1984). The relationship between native and second language reading comprehension and second language oral ability. In C. Rivera (Eds.), *Placement procedures in bilingual education: Education and policy issues* (pp. 152–164). Clevedon, Avon, England: Multilingual Matters.
Twadell, F. (1973). Vocabulary expansion in the TESOL classroom. *TESOL Quarterly, 7*(1), 61–78.
Verhoeven, L. T. (1990). Acquisition of reading in a second language. *Reading Research Quarterly, 25*(2), 90–114.
Vygotsky, L. S. (1962). *Thought and language.* Cambridge, MA: MIT Press.
Vygotsky, L. S. (1980). Multilingualism in children. *Polyglot, 2*(2).
Waggoner, D. (1991). *Undereducation in America: The demography of high school dropouts.* New York: Auburn House.
Willig, A. C. (1985). A meta–analysis of selected studies on the effectiveness of bilingual education. *Review of Educational Research, 55*(3), 269–317.

10

Impaired Awareness of Deficits in a Psychiatric Context: Implications for Rehabilitation

Susan M. McGlynn
McLean Hospital, Belmont, MA
Community Rehab Care, Inc., Newton, MA

Neurological insult or disease can produce a variety of cognitive and behavioral deficits, including specific disturbances of language, memory, attention, perception, planning, and motor function. Some patients with compromised functions in these areas display impaired awareness of their deficits. Amnesic patients may insist that their memory is functioning normally, hemiplegic patients may deny any motor impairment, and aphasic patients may not be aware of their incoherent speech production (for review, see McGlynn & Schacter, 1989). Yet these deficits have profound effects on patients' everyday lives. Impaired awareness of deficits has obvious clinical implications in terms of treatment and management. Patients who are unaware of their impairment are unlikely to be motivated to participate in rehabilitation or benefit from any kind of treatment intervention. These patients also pose serious problems for caretakers because they may insist on engaging in activities that they can no longer perform safely or competently.

A variety of terms have been used to describe unawareness phenomena including *anosognosia*, *unawareness* or *impaired awareness of deficits*, *lack of insight*, and *imperception of disease*. These terms will be used interchangeably to refer to a neurologically based unawareness whereby patients are unable to become fully aware of their condition. Other descriptors such as *denial of illness*, *denial of deficit*, and *defensive denial* typically imply the involvement of the psychological defense mechanism of denial. Although defensive denial likely plays a role in some forms of awareness disturbances, it is not the focus of this discussion. Related terms such as *emotional indifference, lack of concern*, and *anosodiaphoria* refer to the diminished affective responses to impairment that often accompany awareness disturbances. This alteration in emotional behavior, however, can also be seen in patients who are well aware of their deficits and can therefore be conceptualized as an independent phenomenon.

Striking reports of awareness disturbances in neurological patients date back to the late 19th century. Among the first reports was Anton's description of a cortical lesion patient who was completely blind yet unaware of her visual defect (1899, cited in Redlich & Dorsey, 1945). This phenomenon was referred to as Anton's syndrome. In 1914 Babinski coined the term *anosognosia* to refer to unawareness of left hemiplegia after sudden brain insult. This term has since been used more generally to refer to unawareness of a variety of impairments. There were numerous reports of anosognosia in the first half of the 20th century with early interpretations focusing on the notion of a disturbed "body schema." An increasing emphasis on psychoanalytical ideas in the conceptualization of anosognosia culminated in the 1955 monograph entitled *Denial of Illness* by Weinstein and Kahn. Their use of the term *denial of illness* rather than anosognosia represented a conceptual shift from a neurobehavioral perspective to a psychodynamic explanation. There was a decline in reports of anosognosia in the neurological literature in the years following Weinstein and Kahn's publication, but interest in disturbances of awareness has been rekindled over the past two decades. Prigatano and Schacter (1991) proposed several factors to account for this reemergence of interest in anosognosia, including the decline of behaviorism, the importance of consciousness and self-awareness in neuropsychological theory, the limitations of rehabilitation with brain-injured patients due to impaired awareness, and the interest by behavioral neurologists in the theoretical implications of awareness disturbances for the organization of higher cerebral functions.

Although research concerned with impaired awareness has traditionally taken place in a medical setting with a focus on the neurological sequelae of brain injury or disease, there has been a growing interest in unawareness phenomena within a psychiatric context (Amador, Strauss, Yale, & Gorman, 1991). Patients with cognitive impairment due to various kinds of brain dysfunction often exhibit severe psychiatric symptoms that interfere with daily functioning and require psychiatric intervention. Unfortunately, these patients frequently exhibit impaired awareness of their deficits and, consequently, do not benefit from treatment efforts. Contemporary rehabilitation programs tend to include impaired awareness as a major focus of treatment. Several approaches to neuropsychological rehabilitation of impaired awareness have been based on a metacognitive perspective. Specifically, impaired awareness is viewed as a self-monitoring disturbance that prevents patients from acquiring knowledge of their cognitive and/or affective states. The results of these interventions are discussed wherever relevant in this chapter to help conceptualize unawareness phenomena and to make recommendations for future rehabilitation efforts. Awareness disturbances within a psychiatric context are most prominent in schizophrenic patients and elderly demented patients, although other psychiatric patient groups may also exhibit some degree of unawareness with respect to their symptoms. This paper presents empirical evidence for unawareness of deficits in various neuropsychological syndromes and discusses several theories that have been proposed to explain unawareness phenomena before turning to a review of the literature concerned with impaired awareness in dementia and schizophrenia. Finally, the clinical and theoretical implications of this body of research are addressed, and potential directions for future research are discussed.

UNAWARENESS OF DEFICITS IN NEUROPSYCHOLOGICAL/NEUROLOGICAL SYNDROMES

Most early case studies of unawareness of deficit described patients who were unaware of their left hemiplegia. Babinski (1914) coined the term *anosognosia* to refer to this phenomenon. These patients typically sustained an acute lesion in the right posterior region of the brain that resulted in paralysis on the left side of the body. Many early case reports of anosognosia for hemiplegia were characterized by the apparent absence of generalized confusion and intellectual deterioration (e.g., Babinski, 1914; Barré, Morin, & Kaiser, 1923). Several subsequent studies, however, indicated that unawareness of hemiplegia was often associated with intellectual impairment, disorientation, or confusion (e.g., Nathanson, Bergman, & Gordon, 1952; Weinstein & Kahn, 1955) and that increased awareness correlated with clearing of consciousness. The neuropathology associated with unawareness of hemiplegia varied from one case report to another but often involved the

parietal lobe, particularly the inferior parietal lobule, and the thalamoparie-
tal region (Nielsen, 1938).

A number of investigators have observed considerable specificity in
anosognosia phenomena. For example, Von Hagen and Ives (1937) described a 76-year old stroke patient who was well aware of her severe memory
impairment and paralysis of the left upper limb but denied paralysis of the
left leg (see Bisiach, Vallar, Perani, Papagno, & Berti, 1986; Cutting, 1978,
for similar results). An issue that has attracted considerable attention in
recent research concerns the relation between anosognosia for hemiplegia
and the phenomenon of unilateral neglect—unawareness of and inattention to the side of space contralateral to their lesion. Although anosognosia
and neglect may frequently appear together in the same patient, empirical
studies have found that they have different etiologies and can be dissociated
from one another (Bisiach et al., 1986). Some patients who completely
ignore the affected side of the body may be fully aware of their motor defect.
Others who continue to deny their hemiplegia, even when confronted with
evidence to the contrary, may attend normally to the left side.

Perhaps the most striking form of anosognosia is unawareness of blindness, or Anton's syndrome. Anton (1899, cited in Redlich & Dorsey, 1945)
and Von Monakow (1885, cited in Redlich & Dorsey, 1945) were the first
to describe patients who were unaware of their visual defect, though several
similar reports followed in the first half of the 20th century. Redlich and
Dorsey (1945) reported six cases of Anton's syndrome and summarized five
main features that characterized these patients as well as others in the
literature. First, the patients were unaware of their blindness, behaved as
though they could see, reported visual experiences, and denied their blindness when confronted with it. Second, all patients showed at least a
moderate amount of intellectual deterioration. Third, the patients were
generally disoriented, had impaired memory, and tended to confabulate.
Fourth, all six of Redlich and Dorsey's patients had amnestic aphasia
(word-finding deficit). Fifth, the blindness was usually, but not always,
caused by bilateral hemianopia due to occipital or temporoparietal lesions.
Despite the prevalence of intellectual impairment in patients with Anton's
syndrome, Redlich and Dorsey argued that intellectual deterioration alone
did not provide a satisfactory explanation of anosognosia for blindness.

Nobile and Dagata (1951, cited in Bisiach et al., 1986) described four
types of unawareness phenomena which may be associated with cortical
blindness. The first type is demonstrated by patients who do not explicitly
deny their visual defect but never mention it spontaneously and appear
unconcerned about it. The second type is observed in patients who actively

claim that they are not blind and attribute their inability to see to other causes (e.g., darkness in the room). The third form is seen in patients who are unaware of their blindness and lucidly describe what they apparently believe they can see. Finally, the fourth type involves anosognosia for blindness accompanied by confusion and mental deterioratin.

Anosognosia for visual loss is also seen in some patients with hemianopic field defects (Critchley, 1949). Hemianopia refers to blindness in one half of the visual field caused by a posterior cortical lesion in the opposite hemisphere. Unawareness of hemianopia is most often seen in cases of left hemianopia (Willanger, Danielsen, & Ankerhus, 1981) resulting from posterior right hemisphere damage. As with patients who are unaware of hemiplegia, unawareness of visual defect is often, though not always, associated with the neglect syndrome. The relation between unawareness of hemianopia and lesion site has been addressed by at least one study (Koehler, Endtz, Te Velde, & Hekster, 1986). The computerized tomography (CT) scans of 41 patients with homonymous hemianopia were examined and patients were asked several questions to establish their degree of awareness with respect to their visual impairment. Results indicated that lesions in the aware patients tended to be smaller and restricted to the occipital lobe whereas lesions in the unaware patients were more extensive and more anterior involving the occipito–temporal and occipito–parietal regions. The side of hemianopia was predominantly left in the unaware group, but this may have been attributable to the exclusion of aphasic patients in this study. Parietal lobe pathology has also been implicated in unawareness of visual defects by a study that found a strong association between unawareness of hemianopic field defects and a tendency to complete visual forms on a confrontation task (Warrington, 1962). Specifically, unaware patients reported seeing complete figures even though they were presented in such a way that only half of each form fell within the intact half field of vision. Since there was a close association between the presence of parietal lobe lesions in either hemisphere and presence of completion, Warrington concluded that unawareness of visual disability is related to parietal lobe disease. Others have not found any relation between impaired awareness and lesion site (e.g., Gassel & Williams, 1963). The specificity issue has also arisen in studies of impaired awareness of hemianopia. For example, Gassel and Williams (1963) indicated that some patients who lacked awareness of their visual defect had normal awareness of other physical defects. Similarly, Bisiach et al. (1986) reported that 4 of 10 patients in their study with severe anosognosia for hemianopia had very little, if any, unawareness of hemiplegia.

Whereas the forms of awareness disturbances discussed thus far have generally been associated with posterior lesions, unawareness of memory impairment in amnesic patients has been related to a different pattern of brain damage (McGlynn & Schacter, 1989; Schacter, 1991). Amnesic syndromes occur as a consequence of various types of neurological damage including viral encephalitis, anoxia, ruptured aneurysms, tumors, bilateral strokes, Korsakoff's syndrome, and head injuries, and patients generally exhibit intact intellectual functioning despite severe memory impairment. Lesions to medial temporal or diencephalic brain regions are necessary to produce amnesia (Squire, 1986). Evidence for impaired awareness in amnesic patients has been derived from clinical observations, questionnaire studies, and experimental paradigms. Impaired awareness in amnesic patients has most frequently been reported as a characteristic of Korsakoff's syndrome (Korsakoff, 1889; Victor, Adams, Collins, 1971). A prominent feature of Korsakoff's syndrome is the presence of neuropsychological signs of frontal lobe impairment (e.g., Schacter, 1987). Impaired awareness of memory disorder has been described in other patients with signs of frontal pathology. Specifically, patients with penetrating brain injuries affecting the frontal lobes, ruptured aneurysms of the anterior communicating artery (ACAA) resulting in frontal lesions, and frontal lobe tumors have been characterized by impaired awareness of their memory deficit (e.g., Vilkki, 1985). In contrast, intact awareness of memory deficit has been observed in a variety of other patients who do not exhibit any signs of frontal lobe pathology. For example, encephalitic patients with amnesia attributable to temporal lobe lesions generally appear aware of their memory impairment (Rose & Symonds, 1960), as do patients with transient global amnesia. The well known patient H.M., who became globally amnesic after medial temporal lobe resection, was also reported to be aware of his deficit (Milner, Corkin, & Teuber, 1968).

More recently, questionnaire measures and experimental paradigms have increasingly been used to assess the accuracy of patients' self-reports and performance predictions regarding various aspects of their own memory function. Questionnaire studies of head-injured patients have found that patients' subjective rating of their own memory function shows little if any correlation with either relatives' ratings or objective test performance (Sunderland, Harris, & Baddeley, 1983), whereas relatives' questionnaire ratings are often consistent with patients' actual test performance. Not all patients with memory impairment, however, report inaccurately on their memory abilities. Bennett-Levy, Polkey, and Powell (1980) found that patients with memory disorders attributable to temporal lobectomy provided generally accurate assessments of their memory problems on a question-naire. Head-injured patients typically have extensive frontal lobe damage, whereas the temporal lobectomy patients did not have significant frontal lobe impairment. Based on the results of these and other questionnaire studies, Schacter (1991) proposed that amnesic patients without frontal involvement may be able to provide reasonably accurate self-assessments on a memory questionnaire, whereas patients with frontal signs cannot.

This interpretation received further support from a study by McGlynn, Schacter, and Glisky (1989). Several new questionnaire measures were developed to investigate subjective assessment of memory impairment in two amnesic patients. Questionnaires were also administered to spouses who were asked to report on patients' memory abilities. Neuropsychological testing of patients was performed to provide objective measures of their cognitive abilities. The first patient, B.Z., suffered a ruptured anterior communicating artery aneurysm, producing damage in frontal regions and in the anterior cerebral artery. The second patient, H.D., became amnesic after contracting herpes simplex encephalitis, and damage was largely restricted to the left temporal lobe. Overall, results revealed that B.Z. significantly overestimated his memory abilities relative to both his spouse's estimates and objective measures of his memory performance. In contrast, the encephalitic patient H.D. expressed acute awareness of her memory problems (i.e., her ratings were generally consistent with both her spouse's ratings and objective measures of memory function). Importantly, B.Z. had a much higher IQ than did H.D. (126 versus 84), so his lack of awareness cannot be attributed to generalized intellectual impairment. In addition, his memory difficulties were no more severe than those of H.D., ruling out the possibility that his inaccurate self-report was related to a greater incidence of memory failure.

Experimental studies of awareness of memory deficit have generally involved asking patients to predict some aspect of their memory perform-ance. Shimamura and Squire (1986) examined the ability of amnesic patients to predict recognition of unrecalled information in the feeling-of-knowing paradigm, and found that Korsakoff amnesics have severe difficulty monitoring and predicting their memory performance, whereas non-Kor-sakoff patients do not. Schacter, McLachlan, Moscovitch, and Tulving (1986) found that Alzheimer patients, but not head-injured patients or those with ruptured ACAAs, significantly overpredicted their ability to recall word lists. Prediction of recall performance was also used in a study that examined whether awareness of deficit could be increased through training (see Schacter, Glisky, & McGlynn, 1990). The ACAA patient B.Z. described earlier was given repeated feedback regarding his predictions and actual performance on several recall tasks over a period of several days. Awareness training involved giving B.Z. lists of words and actions to remember, requiring him to predict his own recall performance, and then providing extensive feedback and discussion concerning the discrepancies between prediction and performance. This intervention was conducted for a total of 8 days and was followed by a 1-, 2-, and 6-week follow-up assessment and intervention. The self-report questionnaire measures used to assess awareness before treatment were also administered at the beginning and end of each day of training to determine whether there was any baseline shift in B.Z.'s awareness and to evaluate within-day changes in awareness. As expected, B.Z. initially overpredicted his performance on the recall tests. With extensive training, however, his predictions became more realistic, and his responses on many questionnaire items reflected increased awareness of memory problems. The changes in B.Z.'s ratings were most evident on general questions about his memory to which he continued to respond reasonably at the 1-, 2-, and 6-week followups. These findings suggest that with sufficient repetition amnesic patients may be able to develop some awareness of their current state of memory function, but it is not known whether the awareness training has any long-lasting effects. Results also revealed that although B.Z. learned through feedback that he had memory problems, he did not apply this knowledge to all appropriate situations. For example, his belief that he could return to his management level job persisted, despite his increased awareness of memory impairment.

There are a substantial number of studies that have examined unawareness of cognitive, social, and behavioral changes in head-injured patients. Many of these studies assessed awareness by examining discrepancies between patients' and relatives' (or staff members') reports on questionnaire measures. Overall, results have shown that in addition to lacking awareness of their cognitive impairment, head-injured patients are frequently unaware of significant personality and behavioral changes that are obvious to others (Fahy, Irving, & Millac, 1967; Prigatano & Fordyce, 1986). Hackler and Tobis (1983) reported on unawareness of deficits in young head-injured adults who were participants of a prevocational training program. Observations of patients in the social realm indicated that they could not understand the effects that their rage or other socially inappropriate behaviors had on people around them because they were incapable of judging when they were behaving in an unacceptable manner. Patients' inability to monitor their own behavior and their failure to remember what they had done were considered by families to be the most common cause of social isolation in the post-trauma years. Attempts to increase awareness in a rehabilitation program have had limited success. Prigatano and Fordyce (1986) included enhanced awareness as a primary rehabilitation target in their multidisciplinary neuropsychological rehabilitation program for head-injured patients. This program was based largely on behavioral principles. Awareness training involved a number of phases beginning with educational sessions to inform patients of the consequences of brain injury. Later, patients were instructed to record and chart their performances across a variety of behavioral domains. Finally, videotaping, public review, and the generation of individual problem lists that were openly discussed among program members became the focus of treatment. Patients were strongly reinforced by staff and other patients for any behavior indicating greater self-awareness and acceptance.

Fordyce and Roueche (1986) attempted to assess the awareness training aspect of this program by examining the degree to which patients exhibited increased awareness of their deficits. Twenty-eight seriously brain-damaged patients received awareness training as part of a 6-month intensive program. To assess any change in patients' awareness of deficits, patients and staff members were asked to judge the patient's competency on a rating scale of everyday activities. Objective measures of patients' functioning pre- and postrehabilitation were also recorded. Three groups of patients were identified based on staff-patient differences in perceived impairment. Group 1 ($n = 11$) rated their abilities similar to staff members' ratings both before and after rehabilitation. Patients in Group 2 ($n = 9$) and Group 3 ($n = 8$) underestimated their initial level of impairment. By the end of rehabilitation, Group 2 had become more consistent with the ratings of staff members. In contrast, patients in Group 3 rated significantly more improvement in their abilities than did staff. Fordyce and Roueche concluded that only some head-injured patients benefit from rehabilitation attempts to increase awareness of deficits. Ranseen & Bohaska (1987) found that patients with right-sided brain damage exhibited more marked awareness disturbances and less improvement during rehabilitation than those with left-sided or diffuse damage, suggesting that degree of impaired awareness is, at least partly, a function of lesion site.

It is clear from the study of aphasia that left-hemisphere lesions also can result in compromised awareness. Unawareness of language disturbance is most commonly seen in patients with jargon, stereotypy, or echolalia (e.g., Alajouanine, 1956), and can occur in the context of preserved intellectual functions (Kinsbourne & Warrington, 1963). Wernicke's aphasics, also known as jargon aphasics, are unaware of the fact that their own speech is incomprehensible, but they do notice errors in others' speech (Kinsbourne & Warrington, 1963). Several investigators have concluded that jargon aphasia only occurs in patients who sustain a left-hemisphere lesion plus some further neurological damage producing disturbed consciousness (Weinstein, Cole, Mitchell, & Lyerly, 1964).

Despite the wealth of published reports concerning impaired awareness in neurological patients, there have been few methodologically sound experimental studies in the literature (for review, see McGlynn & Schacter, 1989). A major problem is the absence of objective, quantitative measures of anosognosia. Many investigators have relied solely on their subjective observations of the patient to determine the presence of anosognosia or have used simplistic measures that do not adequately assess the complexity of awareness disturbances. Methodological shortcomings have not, however, prevented authors from proposing theoretical interpretations and explanations of the phenomenon. Most investigators support some form of neuroanatomical theory, attributing anosognosia to focal brain lesions or to diffuse brain damage. Proponents of the former view generally agree that anosognosia results from lesion sites in the right hemisphere, usually involving the parietal region and its connections, and often view anosognosia as a disorder of cognition arising from a defective body scheme (for review, see McGlynn & Schacter, 1989). This view can account for unawareness of a physical defect but other types of awareness disturbances (e.g., unawareness of cognitive or behavioral deficits) are difficult to understand within this framework. Bisiach et al. (1985) viewed anosognosia and related phenomena as "modality-specific disorders of thought" resulting from disruption of specific mechanisms that normally monitor the output of individual perceptual and cognitive modules. Stuss and Benson (1986) discussed the possible contribution of frontal lobe damage to the development of anosognosia, conceptualizing anosognosia as a deficit in self-monitoring. Similarly, a descriptive model provided by McGlynn & Schacter (1989) to account for anosognosia emphasized the role of a frontal executive system for maintaining awareness of complex functions. Others have viewed anosognosia as a manifestation of a general mental disorder associated with diffuse brain pathology (e.g., Sandifer, 1946), arguing that anosognosia only occurs in association with intellectual impairment. This view cannot explain cases of anosognosia where intellectual functioning is intact, nor does it account for the specificity of anosognosia.

In contrast to neurologically based theories, several investigators have proposed that anosognosia reflects primarily motivated use of the psychological defense mechanism of denial and that premorbid personality factors are critically involved in the development of anosognosia (Weinstein & Kahn, 1955). This psychodynamic account of anosognosia does not explain a number of empirical observations such as the specificity of anosognosia and the correlation between lesion site and unawareness.

IMPAIRED AWARENESS IN DEMENTIA

Patients with certain kinds of dementing illness have been described as lacking awareness or insight into their condition. Frederiks (1985) referred to this phenomenon as *anosognosia for dementia*. Unawareness of deficits is most frequently reported as a clinical feature of cortical dementias, such as Alzheimer's disease (AD) and Pick's disease (e.g., Gustafson & Nilsson, 1982; Neary et al., 1986; Reisberg, Gordon, Mc Carthy, & Ferris, 1985; Schneck, Reisberg, & Ferris, 1982), but has also been observed as part of the frontal-subcortical dementia syndrome of Huntington's disease (HD; Joynt & Shoulson, 1985; McHugh & Folstein, 1975). In contrast, patients with the predominantly subcortical disorder of Parkinson's disease (PD) have been described as exhibiting good comprehension of their illness, even in the most advanced stages of the disease (Danielczyk, 1983).

Clinical descriptions of the more advanced stages of AD often include loss of insight into one's illness as a major feature. Schneck et al. (1982) described a pattern of decreasing insight and knowledge with increasing severity of the disease process. During the early "forgetfulness" phase, patients are cognizant of and increasingly anxious about their memory difficulties. The second, "confusional," phase is characterized by clear signs of cognitive impairment and a loss of insight. In the most advanced "dementia" phase, patients appear extremely disoriented and may exhibit substantial anxiety despite the continued unawareness of their condition. Reisberg and colleagues (Reisberg, Gordon, McCarthy, & Ferris, 1985) assessed awareness of cognitive decline in normal aging and in AD. In this study, 35 community-residing couples consisting of a subject and a spouse were interviewed. The subjects were 60 to 85 years of age and consisted of 25 AD patients, 5 subjects with a primary diagnosis of age-associated cognitive decline consistent with "senescent forgetfulness," and 10 control subjects who had no memory impairment. Subjects were interviewed and questioned about their own functioning as well as their spouses' functioning. Spouses of subjects were similarly interviewed and questioned about their own functioning and the subject's functioning. Findings revealed that subjects with senescent forgetfulness rated their memory problems as somewhat worse than did the controls, and early "confusional phase" AD patients rated their problems as being considerably worse than did the "forgetfulness phase" AD patients. However, once beyond the early "confusional phase," AD patients tended to rate the degree of their memory impairment as progressively less severe, whereas objective measures of memory function provided evidence of progressive deterioration. Spouses' reports of patients' memory deficit increased consistently as patients' level of impairment increased on objective measures. Patients with moderate to severe memory impairent also tended to minimize their emotional difficulties. They rated their emotional problems as substantially less severe than did their spouses. Despite marked unawareness of their own deficits during the final phase, patients continued to display awareness of their spouses' cognitive functioning (i.e., patients' ratings of spouses' cognitive abilities closely matched the spouses' ratings of themselves). Based on the latter observation, Reisberg et al. concluded that AD patients were engaging in defensive denial, a mechanism "protecting" them against depressive symptoms.

There may be considerable variability in awareness among different subgroups of AD patients (Neary et al., 1986) and between different dementia populations. Some clinical reports have emphasized an early loss of insight in contrast to unawareness during the late stage (Frederiks, 1985; Joynt & Shoulson, 1985). For example, Frederiks (1985) indicated that the patient is usually unaware of the gradual onset of dementia occurring in both AD and Pick's disease. Gustafson and Nilsson (1982) found that early loss of insight is a useful dimension for differentiating between AD and Pick's disease, because patients with Pick's disease appear to lose insight significantly earlier in the disease process. Interestingly, both of these dementias are typically associated with signs of frontal lobe pathology (Kaszniak, 1986), and frontal degeneration is generally more severe in the early stages of Pick's disease than in AD.

The relation between depression and anosognosia in AD was investigated in a recent study by Migliorelli et al. (1995a). A group of patients (n = 103) with probable AD were examined with a structured psychiatric interview, and were assessed for the presence of cognitive impairment, deficits in activities of daily living, social functioning, and anosognosia. Anosognosia was evaluated with the Anosognosia Questionnaire–Dementia (AQ–D), a 30-item instrument administered to AD patients and their caretakers. Differences in patients' and caretakers' reports of cognitive functioning and behavioral changes in the AD patients provided a measure of unawareness. Findings indicated that patients with dysthymia were significantly more aware of their cognitive deficits than were patients with either major depression or no depression. Dysthymia usually started after the onset of dementia and was significantly more prevalent in the early stages of dementia, whereas major depression often began prior to the dementia and was equally prevalent across the different stages of the illness. Importantly, there were no significant neuropsychological differences between patients with major depression, no depression, or dysthymia. The authors concluded that dysthymia in AD may represent a realistic emotional response to their progressive cognitive decline, whereas major depression may be more related to biological factors. These investigators had earlier reported on a study of anosognosia and associated factors using the same sample of AD patients (Migliorelli et al., 1995b). Their analyses revealed a significantly longer duration of illness, more severe cognitive impairment, deficits in activities of daily living, and higher mania and pathological laughing scores in AD patients with anosognosia ($n = 21$) than AD patients without anosognosia ($n = 52$). These findings were interpreted to suggest that anosognosia in AD may be part of a neuropsychiatric syndrome characterized by "elevated mood and disinhibition of positive emotional display (Migliorelli et al., 1995b, p. 343)." Interestingly, AD patients with anosognosia have been found to have significantly decreased regional cerebral blood flow (rCBF) in the right frontal lobe (Reed, Jagust, & Coulter, 1993). Migliorelli et al. (1995b) proposed that this change in blood flow may account for the combination of elevated mood and anosognosia, because these behavioral changes have been reported in patients with right frontal lesions and right hemisphere damage, respectively.

Experimental evidence of unawareness of memory dysfunction in AD patients was provided by Schacter et al. (1986). Alzheimer's patients were given a categorized list and were asked to predict how many items they would be able to recall. Relative to control patients, AD patients substantially overestimated their ability to remember. McGlynn and Kaszniak (1991) also used a prediction paradigm to assess awareness of deficits in AD, and found that AD patients were inaccurate in predicting their performance on a variety of verbal and visual memory tasks when compared both to their actual performance and to relatives' predictions, despite generally accurate prediction of their relatives' performance on the same tasks. AD patients tended to overestimate their memory abilities, particularly on cognitive tasks in which their performance had changed most dramatically as a consequence of dementia. Results of a questionnaire measure indicated that AD patients rated their own difficulties with cognitive activities of daily life significantly lower than relatives rated patients' problems, and this discrepancy was related to patients' dementia severity. In other words, the discrepancy between AD patients' ratings of themselves and relatives' ratings of the patients increases as patients' cognitive functioning deteriorates. Based on these findings, McGlynn and Kaszniak proposed that a breakdown in metacognitive functions occurs with progressive AD, resulting in patients' failure to update knowledge about their own cognitive performance. This monitoring deficit appears to be restricted to the self, because AD patients were generally accurate when making judgments about their relatives' cognitive abilities.

Danielczyk (1983) included *insight into own illness* as a clinical parameter of a rating scale to assess mental deterioration in four groups of patients: PD, AD, atypical Parkinson's disease (AP) with signs of vascular disease, and multiple infarction dementia (MID). The specific scale for the *insight* parameter ranged from 0 to 3, where 0 indicates *no awareness disturbance* and 3 reflects a *severe disturbance*. Patients with PD were found to retain reasonably good insight into their illness, whereas those in the other three groups exhibited disturbed awareness of their deficits. The AD patients showed the least comprehension of their illness, followed by the AP group. The MID patients, although also lacking awareness of their condition, were significantly less impaired on this dimension than the AD group. It is important to note that the PD group showed little cognitive or behavioral disturbance on a number of measures relative to the other three groups (e.g., digit span, reading, writing, orientation, motivation, and initiative).

Lack of insight has been described as a prominent characteristic of the dementia associated with (HD), a hereditary neurological disorder affecting frontal-subcortical regions of the brain (Bruyn, 1968; Wilson & Garron, 1979). Two prominent deficits are evident relatively early in HD: choreiform movements and a severe memory impairment. The chorea consists of irregular, involuntary movements of certain muscles or muscle groups that cause considerable difficulty when performing everyday activities. These patients also demonstrate impaired cortical executive functions closely resembling that observed in classic frontal lobe patients (e.g., Caine, Hunt, Weingartner, & Ebert, 1978). Specifically, they have difficulty with planning, organizing, and sequential arrangement of information. Bruyn (1968) noted that, despite marked impairment of intellectual functioning, HD patients rarely exhibit confusional states, disorientation, or delirium. Thus, the unawareness could not be attributed to confusional disturbances in this population. Caine and Shoulson (1983) interviewed 30 HD patients to assess their insight into the process of their disease. Results revealed that 11 of the 30 patients lacked awareness of their deficits, and these were generally the patients who had been classified as moderately or severely impaired based on functional disability in everyday life. Consistent with these findings, Mahendra (1984) noted that insight may be preserved until more advanced stages of the disease process. The high frequency of suicide during the initial stages of the disease (Oltman & Friedman, 1961) in contrast to later stages may also be consistent with the notion that insight declines with progression of the disease. Other clinical reports of HD have described preservation of insight in most patients (Caine et al., 1978).

McGlynn and Kaszniak (1991) attempted to assess unawareness of deficits in HD patients using quantitative measures to determine the relation between cognitive impairment and development of unawareness. Because HD patients have both memory and motor deficits, differential awareness of the two impairments could also be evaluated. A questionnaire measure was administered to eight HD patients at various stages of the disease process. They were asked to rate, on a 7-point scale, the degree to which they currently experience difficulty performing a variety of cognitive and motor activities in everyday life compared to 5 years ago. They were also asked to rate their relatives on these items. Relatives were asked to rate their own and patients' abilities on the same questionnaire items. In the second part of the study, patients were asked to perform a variety of memory and motor tasks following prediction of their own performance on these tasks. Relatives of the HD patients served as controls and were also asked to predict their own and the patients' performance on these tasks. Patients' predictions were compared to both their actual performance and to relatives' estimates of patients' memory and motor abilities to determine the degree to which HD patients lack awareness of their deficits. Analysis of the questionnaire results revealed that patients' ratings of their own difficulties on both the motor and cognitive items were significantly lower than relatives' ratings of patients problems. In contrast, no difference was observed between patients' ratings of relatives and relatives' ratings of themselves. There was no evidence for differential awareness of motor versus cognitive problems. A significant interaction was found between degree of cognitive impairment and rater, indicating that patients who were relatively intact in terms of their cognitive functioning tended to rate themselves as more impaired than their relatives rated them, whereas more demented patients tended to rate themselves as less impaired than relatives reported.

Contrary to the lack of awareness evident on the questionnaire data, results from the task performance predictions suggested that HD patients are reasonably good at estimating their performance on specific motor and cognitive tasks. Based on these seemingly contradictory results of the questionnaire data and the task prediction data, McGlynn and Kaszniak proposed that these measures may be sensitive to different dimensions of awareness.

The clinical observations and experimental studies discussed in this section suggest that impaired awareness is frequently associated with dementing illnesses such as AD and HD. Diminished awareness typically occurs as the disease progresses and cortical functions, particularly those involving the frontal lobes, become increasingly compromised. Impaired awareness of deficit in dementia has been viewed as a breakdown in metacognitive functions, whereby patients are unable to monitor and reflect on their own cognitive performance. Consequently, they fail to alter knowledge of their own cognitive capacity despite marked changes over time. The next section focuses on impaired self-monitoring and unawareness of psychiatric symptoms in patients with schizophrenia and other psychiatric disorders.

IMPAIRED AWARENESS IN SCHIZOPHRENIA AND OTHER PSYCHOTIC DISORDERS

A number of clinical, neuropsychological, neuroradiological, and neurophysiological investigations have provided converging evidence for significant frontal system dysfunction in schizophrenics (Liddle & Morris, 1991; Seidman, 1983). It is not surprising, therefore, that schizophrenic patients frequently exhibit impaired awareness of their illness and its symptoms. Poor insight in schizophrenia was noted when the disorder was first named by Bleuler (Bertschinger, 1916). The gradual loss of insight characterizing schizophrenia was captured in the following description by Anscombe (1987):

> The loss of self is a gradual process attended by vagueness. As in other processes in which the intellect is affected, the patient goes through an early stage in which it is possible to deny the changes that are taking place, and a later stage in which the failings themselves prevent awareness. In between is a stage of alarm in which the person retains enough insight to be aware of what he is losing. (p. 255)

Many reports have documented disturbed awareness as a prominent feature of schizophrenia. Results of the World Health Organization's study of schizophrenia (Carpenter, Strauss, & Bartko, 1973) revealed that 85% of schizophrenics vehemently denied that they were emotionally ill. Lin, Spiga, and Fortsch (1979) reported that 69% of schizophrenic patients in their study showed no insight when asked about needing to be in a hospital or see a doctor. Van Putten, Crumpton, and Yale (1976) addressed the issue of medication compliance and insight. They found that 76% of drug refusers versus 40% of drug compliers had no insight into the presence of illness. In contrast, there have been other reports suggesting greater awareness of deficits in schizophrenics (e.g., Liddle & Barnes, 1988). The discrepant outcomes of these studies may be largely attributable to the different methods of defining and measuring impaired awareness.

Most studies concerned with assessing awareness of deficits in psychiatric patients have used subjective, unstandardized measures with no established reliability or validity. Furthermore, they have generally failed to assess the multidimensional nature of impaired awareness, the specificity of awareness disturbances, or the relation between cognitive impairment and unaware-ness. Amador and Strauss (1990) recognized the need for an objective, standardized, more complex measure of awareness disturbances in schizo-phrenia. They developed the Scale to Assess Unawareness of Mental Disorder (SUMD), a standardized scale on which ratings are made based on direct patient interviews to assess awareness of current and past illness. The scale attempts to measure specific and global aspects of awareness (e.g., awareness of a mental disorder and awareness of particular symptoms such as delusions and hallucinations). It also assesses patients' attributions about the cause or source of signs and symptoms. Patients may recognize the symptoms of illness, but make incorrect attributions to explain their expe-rience. Amador et al. (1993) have reported evidence of convergent and criterion validity as well as reliability for this instrument. In their analyses, Amador et al. noted that level of education was not associated with any insight score, suggesting that "educational background is not an important moderating variable in the assessment of insight" (p. 877). Similarly, meas-ures of delusions did not correlate with any of the insight scores on the SUMD, ruling out the possibility that poor insight simply reflects severity of delusions.

An abbreviated version of the SUMD was recently used to investigate the multiple dimensions of insight in schizophrenic patients relative to patients with schizoaffective or mood disorders with and without psychosis

(Amador et al., 1994). Scores for each of the nine items on this shortened version ranged from 1 to 3, with higher scores indicating poorer awareness. A sample of 412 patients with psychotic and mood disorders were evaluated in terms of their general awareness of having a mental disorder, awareness of the efficacy of pharmacotherapy, awareness of the social consequences of mental disorder, and awareness of six common symptoms of schizophrenia. The sample included 212 schizophrenic (SZ) patients, 49 patients with schizoaffective (SA) disorder, 40 patients with bipolar disorder (severely manic BP), 24 patients with major depressive disorder who were also psychotic (PMDD), and 14 nonpsychotic patients with major depressive disorder (MDD). Results revealed that impaired awareness was a common characteristic of the schizophrenic group. A variety of self-awareness deficits were more severe and pervasive in patients with schizophrenia than in patients with schizoaffective or major depressive disorders with or without psychosis and were associated with poorer psychosocial functioning. The BP group, however, scored as poorly as the SZ group on the majority of items with the exception of awareness of delusions. The BP patients were significantly more aware of currently having delusions than were patients with SZ. Some differences between these two groups may not have been detected due to limited statistical power. Among the schizophrenic group, 57.4% showed a moderate to severe lack of awareness of having a mental disorder, 31.5% exhibited severe unawareness of the social consequences of mental disorder, and 21.7% were rated as having severe unawareness of the efficacy of medication. The results suggested that impaired awareness in schizophrenia can be modality specific (i.e., one can be unaware of one symptom but maintain insight into other aspects of the illness).

Michalakeas et al. (1994) also assessed insight in various inpatient groups. They used a questionnaire measure (ITAQ; McEvoy, Apperson, & Appelbaum, 1989) to assess insight in 77 female inpatients (42 schizophrenic, 13 manic, 22 depressives) and to determine the relation between insight and psychopathology. The ITAQ consists of 11 questions, the responses of which can be scored on a scale of 0 to 2 (0 = *no insight*, 1 = *partial insight*, 2 = *good insight*). Psychopathology was assessed by the Brief Psychiatric Rating Scale (BPRS). These measures were administered upon admission, on the 15th, 30th, and discharge day. The data showed that depressive patients had good insight upon admission and did not change significantly during hospitalization. In contrast, acutely psychotic schizophrenic patients and acutely disturbed manic patients showed poor insight upon admission. Insight improved significantly in the course of hospitalization for schizophrenics and manics, but there was no consistent negative correlation of insight and psychopathology in the schizophrenic group, whereas this negative correlation was significant for the manic group. The authors concluded that psychopathology improves together with insight in manic patients, and the impaired awareness in mania is amenable to treatment. In the schizophrenic group, however, the data suggested that other factors besides psychopathology account for changes in insight in the course of treatment.

Other investigators have similarly questioned whether impaired awareness in schizophrenia may be a function of acute psychopathology. McEvoy et al. (1989) used the ITAQ and standard psychopathology rating scales (BPRS, Clinical Global Impressions) at various times during hospitalization of 52 acutely psychotic, schizophrenic patients to address this issue. They found no consistent relation between degree of insight and severity of acute psychopathology. The improvement in psychopathology that typically occurred over time was not consistently accompanied by improvement in insight. In fact, a significant proportion of patients (40%) showed little change in their levels of insight over the course of hospitalization. They concluded that the mechanism for impaired awareness of deficits may be resistant to treatment with neuroleptic medication. A followup study was performed with 46 of the same group of patients between 2 ½ and 3 ½ years after discharge to assess the relation between insight and several outcome variables. Results revealed that the association between insight and outcome approached statistical significance. Patients with more insight were significantly less likely to be readmitted over the course of followup, and tended to be more compliant with treatment 30 days after discharge. There was no interaction between aftercare environment and insight, suggesting that insight operates independently of aftercare environment on outcome.

Amador et al. (1994) emphasized the importance of remediating self-awareness deficits in schizophrenia as part of a comprehensive psychoeducational program. Related to this idea, Lysaker and Bell (1995b) found that measures of neuropsychological dysfunction in schizophrenics, including measures of frontal lobe impairment, were negatively correlated with improvement in insight following a vocational rehabilitation program. More recently, Lysaker and Bell (1995a) reported that schizophrenic patients with poor awareness and neuropsychological dysfunction of the frontal lobes showed no improvement in awareness following psychosocial treatment, whereas those with impaired awareness and intact frontal lobe functioning were able to benefit from this intervention. These findings suggest that patients with evidence of frontal lobe dysfunction may be unable to increase awareness of their condition despite rehabilitation efforts.

The relation between impaired awareness and frontal lobe functioning was addressed in a study by Young, Davila, and Scher (1993). They administered the SUMD, the Wisconsin Card Sorting Test (WCST), a test of verbal fluency, and Trails A and B to 31 patients with chronic schizophrenia. A WAIS–R IQ estimate was also obtained for each patient. The percentage of perseverative responses (tendency to repeat the same response rather than shift response set when the demands of the task change) on the WCST significantly correlated with the SUMD total awareness of symptoms score. The other tests did not correlate significantly with impaired awareness of illness. In addition, a discriminant function analysis found that a linear combination of WCST percent perseverative responses and average symptom severity correctly categorized 84% of the patients in "high" and "low" awareness groups. Importantly, IQ did not contribute significantly to the discrimination of patients with high versus low awareness, suggesting that impaired awareness could not be attributed to generalized cognitive impairment. These results supported the authors' hypothesis that "at least in some of its manifestations lack of awareness among chronic schizophrenics has an organic etiology probably mediated by the frontal lobes" (p. 117).

The poor performance of schizophrenics on the WCST in this study was consistent with the literature on self-monitoring and schizophrenia. Attempts to teach the WCST to chronic schizophrenics have generally failed because patients are unable to use feedback to alter their performance (Goldberg, Weinberger, Berman, Pliskin, & Podd, 1987). In addition to being unable to monitor their own cognitive behavior, schizophrenics are deficient in the ability to monitor and correct ongoing motor behavior on the basis of internal, self-generated cues (Malenka, Angel, Hampton, & Berger, 1982). Impaired self-monitoring characterizes a number of disturbances of self-awareness, self-consciousness, and self-control (Stuss & Benson, 1984) and may be a key factor in understanding why some patients are unaware of their deficits.

There is a body of literature concerned primarily with unawareness of tardive dyskinesia (TD) in schizophrenia. TD refers to the syndrome of abnormal involuntary movements often seen in patients with chronic schizophrenia. This motor disturbance has generally been attributed to the effects of long-term treatment with neuroleptic drugs. Alexopoulos (1979) found that of 18 schizophrenic outpatients diagnosed with TD, eight were entirely unaware of their movement disorders. Awareness was assessed by a psychiatric interview with each patient. Five of the unaware patients were actively delusional or hallucinating, whereas only 1 of the 10 aware patients was delusional. Surprisingly, none of the 10 aware patients had complained to their therapists of their symptoms, but they admitted the involuntary movements when questioned directly about them.

In another study by Smith, Kucharski, Oswald, & Waterman (1979), the presence and severity of abnormal movements was assessed in 377 psychiatric inpatients using a rating scale that includes items evaluating patients' reported awareness and distress as a consequence of disturbed movements (range 0 to 4). Of 113 patients who had an average rating of 3 (*moderate*) or 4 (*severe*) for any one item concerning symptoms of abnormal movements, only 9 (8%) had mean ratings indicating that they had awareness of their motor disturbance and only 4 (3.5%) expressed some degree of distress. The authors believed, however, that many patients were unwilling to report awareness and distress associated with the movements rather than being truly unaware of the symptoms. To address this issue, these patients were asked if they noticed any abnormal movements in other patients. A number of the patients were able to identify accurately the symptoms of TD in others. Smith and colleagues concluded that although these patients may have been unaware of their own tongue or mouth movements, it is unlikely that they did not notice their more obvious hand, feet, or leg movements. The self-other discrepancy observed in this study need not imply that patients are engaged in defensive denial. Rather, it may reflect a self-monitoring deficit that prevents patients from recognizing their own disturbed behavior while leaving intact the ability to make accurate observations and judgments about others' performance.

Rosen, Mukherjee, Olarte, Varia, and Cardenas (1982) found that only 23 of 70 patients with TD indicated an awareness of their abnormal movements, and their awareness increased with symptom severity. Factor analysis on the data revealed that these 23 patients seemed aware of their TD and were distressed by it when they experienced functional impairment, usually when their arms or legs were affected. Myslobodsky, Tomer, Holden, Kempler, and Sigal (1985) reported that 15 of the 17 schizophrenic patients with TD they studied were entirely unaware of or not concerned with their prominent orolingual symptomatology, despite the obvious disturbances of speech these symptoms produce. Patients with TD were also impaired on a picture recall test when compared to schizophrenic patients without the motor disturbance. Myslobodsky et al. conjectured that the mild memory impairment together with the lack of awareness or concern are suggestive of an insidious dementia disorder.

In a later study, Myslobodsky, Holden, and Sandler (1986) examined a group of 49 schizophrenic patients with TD, 38 of whom exhibited abnormal movements of the trunk, limbs, or both in addition to dyskinetic movements of the facial region. Only two patients (4%) complained about their motor incapacity when asked directly about the problem. The rest of the sample tended to minimize the motor disturbance or had absolutely no awareness of their motor abnormalities. As Myslobodsky (1986) pointed out, this lack of awareness may account for the fact that even grotesque dyskinesia does not result in social withdrawal but is particularly distressing for the patient's family. Myslobodsky (1986) related anosognosia in patients with TD to a dementing process attributable to a neuroleptic-induced deficiency within the dopaminergic circuitry in the right hemisphere.

The literature concerned with unawareness in schizophrenia does suggest that a variety of unawareness phenomena are prevalent in this population. Furthermore, the frontal lobe dysfunction associated with schizophrenia is consistent with evidence suggesting that unawareness of deficits in certain neuropsychological syndromes depends on patterns of brain impairment involving the frontal lobes.

IMPLICATIONS AND FUTURE DIRECTIONS

In summary, it appears that awareness disturbances are common within a psychiatric setting, particularly in patients with schizophrenia or dementia. Although limited experimental evidence is available for these patient populations, the literature suggests that compromised frontal lobe functions may play a significant role in producing impaired awareness. Of the various theoretical frameworks discussed earlier, those models that can account for the specificity of impaired awareness and that emphasize the role of a frontally based executive system for integrating complex information about the self may be most relevant for conceptualizing anosognosia in these psychiatric groups (Bisiach et al., 1985; McGlynn & Schacter, 1989; Stuss & Benson, 1986).

More importantly for the clinician, impaired awareness of deficits has a significant impact on management and treatment of patients. Elderly psychiatric patients with dementia who are unaware of their cognitive limitations may insist that they are capable of functioning independently and may attempt to engage in tasks that are unsafe given their severe cognitive impairment (e.g., driving, using household appliances, self-medicating). In these cases, it is critical that family members or other caretakers be educated regarding the patient's cognitive deficits, including the awareness disturbance, so they can make appropriate adjustments in the patient's living situation. The consequences of impaired awareness in younger psychiatric patients, particularly those with schizophrenia, are also serious. Treatment compliance (e.g., taking medication, keeping appointments with treatment providers, attending programs) is a major issue with schizophrenic patients, particularly when they do not recognize their symptoms or appreciate the impact of their psychiatric illness on daily functioning.

Rehabilitation potential may be severely limited by patients' lack of awareness. For example, Cicerone and Tupper (1986) noted that head-injured patients with severely impaired metacognitive functions had a far worse prognosis than individuals who were able to recognize deficits, learn new strategies, and apply these new strategies in the appropriate situations. Attempts to increase awareness of deficits in a rehabilitation setting have had limited success, and further research is needed to address the efficacy of this strategy for various patient groups. There are likely a complex array of variables that affect the outcome of awareness training. Patients with cognitive deficits may learn at a far slower rate than those without substantial cognitive problems, and as a consequence may require more intensive training over a longer period of time than is typically offered. Although some patients may learn about their deficits through repeated confrontation and feedback, there is little evidence to suggest that they appropriately generalize this knowledge to different situations or that the knowledge they acquire will have any long-term impact.

Patients with significant metacognitive disruption may not be capable of using their acquired knowledge spontaneously in different contexts. They may "know" in a general sense that they have memory problems, for example, but may not be able to abstract from this knowledge its consequences and implications. Alternatively, they may be able to describe the appropriate response given a particular scenario, but may not act accordingly when they are actually placed in the situation. It is unlikely that awareness training can rebuild the capacity for automatic, internally generated self-reflection and self-awareness, but patients may be able to acquire concrete, explicit knowledge of their limitations within a variety of stimulus situations in the context of rehabilitation. McGlynn (1990) noted that for patients with severe cognitive impairment, maintenance of rehabilitation effects may require that patients' relatives continue the treatment techniques in the home. By extending the therapeutic program to another setting for a longer period of time, there is more opportunity for overlearning and generalization to occur. Some organically based awareness disturbances may be completely intractable, and treatment may best focus on modifying the environment to allow for optimal functioning. There may also be an emotional component to the apparent unawareness that prevents patients from responding to training efforts (i.e., the unawareness could be partly a function of denial, an emotionally based inability to acknowledge the painful truth). Psychotherapy that focuses on strengthening the ego in preparation for integrating knowledge of deficits may be a critical component of treatment in these cases (Langer & Padrone, 1992).

In terms of future directions for research on impaired awareness, it is clear that more reliable, systematic assessment tools are needed to measure the degree and quality of unawareness in different patient groups. Another important area of study concerns the neuroanatomical basis of impaired awareness. Specifically, the relationship between frontal lobe pathology and unawareness and the role of generalized cognitive impairment to the development of awareness disturbances needs to be explored further with psychiatric populations. The use of brain imaging techniques, particularly positron emission tomography (PET) or functional magnetic resonance imaging (fMRI), may be particularly helpful for investigating the neuroanatomical correlates of disturbed awareness. The possibility that patients may be able to learn through training to become more aware of their deficits deserves further attention. Damasio (1994) pointed out that the distinction between patients' direct and indirect awareness of their condition is often overlooked. This distinction could be addressed by examining the effects of awareness training. For example, would acquisition of knowledge about the self from external sources be sufficient for altering one's behavior, or does awareness ultimately have to come from an automatic, direct, internal system to have any real impact? If the latter is true, then patients with impaired self-monitoring capacity will be less likely to benefit from awareness training. Finally, the relation between neurologically based unawareness and defensive denial needs to be investigated. The notion that all deficit unawareness in brain-damaged patients is partly or entirely attributable to defensive denial has been rejected, but it will be essential to develop criteria to differentiate the two (McGlynn & Schacter, 1989).

REFERENCES

Alajouanine, T. (1956). Verbal realization in aphasia. *Brain, 79*, 1–28.

Alexopoulos, G. S. (1979). Lack of complaints in schizophrenics with tardive dyskinesia. *Journal of Nervous and Mental Disorders, 167*, 125–127.

Amador, X. F., Flaum, M., Andreasen, N. C., Strauss, D. H., Yale, S. A., Clark, S. C., & Gorman, J. M. (1994). Awareness of illness in schizophrenia and schizoaffective and mood disorders. *Archives of General Psychiatry, 51*, 826–836.

Amador, X. F., & Strauss, D. H. (1990). *The Scale to Assess Unawareness of Mental Disorder.* New York: Columbia University & New York State Psychiatric Institute.

Amador, X. F., Strauss, D. H., Yale, S. A., Flaum, M. M., Endicott, J., & Gorman, J. M. (1993). Assessment of insight in psychosis. *American Journal of Psychiatry, 150,* 873–879.

Amador, X. F., Strauss, D. H., Yale, S. A., & Gorman, J. M. (1991). Awareness of illness in schizophrenia. *Schizophrenia Bulletin, 17,* 113–132.

Anscombe, R. (1987). The disorder of consciousness in schizophrenia. *Schizophrenia Bulletin, 13,* 241–260.

Babinski, M. J. (1914). Contribution à l'etude des troubles mentaux dans l'hémiplégie organique cerébralé (anosognosie) [Contribution to the study of mental disturbance in organic cerebral hemiplegia (anosognosia)]. *Revue Neurologique (Paris), 12,* 845–848.

Barré, J. A., Morin, L., & Kaiser, J. (1923). Étude clinique d'un nouveau cas d'anosognosie de Babinski [Clinical study of a new case of Babinski's anosognosia.] *Revue Neurologique, 29,* 500–504.

Bennett-Levy, J., Polkey, C. E., & Powell, G. E. (1980). Self-report of memory skills after temporal lobectomy: The effect of clinical variables. *Cortex, 16,* 543–557.

Bertschinger, H. (1916). Processes of recovery in schizophrenics. *Psychoanalysis Review, 3,* 176–188.

Bisiach, E., Meregalli, S., & Berti, A. (1985, June). *Mechanisms of production-control and belief-fixation in human visuospatial processing. Clinical evidence from hemispatial neglect.* Paper presented to the Eighth Symposium on Quantitative Analyses of Behavior, Harvard University, Cambridge, MA.

Bisiach, E., Vallar, G., Perani, D., Papagno, C., & Berti, A. (1986). Unawareness of disease following lesions of the right hemisphere: Anosognosia for hemiplegia and anosognosia for hemianopia. *Neuropsychologia, 24,* 471–482.

Bruyn, G. (1968). A historical, clinical and laboratory synopsis. In: P. Vinken & G. W. Bruyn, (Eds.), *Handbook of clinical neurology* (Vol. 6, pp. 298–378). Amsterdam: North Holland.

Caine, E. D., Hunt, R. D., Weingartner, H., & Ebert, M. H. (1978). Huntington's dementia. *Archives of General Psychiatry, 35,* 377–384.

Caine, E. D., & Shoulson, I. (1983). Psychiatric syndromes in Huntington's disease. *American Journal of Psychiatry, 140,* 728–733.

Carpenter, W. T., Strauss, J. S., & Bartko, J. J. (1973). Flexible system for the diagnosis of schizophrenia: Report from the WHO International Pilot Study of Schizophrenia. *Science, 182,* 1275–1278.

Cicerone, K. D., & Tupper, D. E. (1986). Cognitive assessment in the neuropsychological rehabilitation of head-injured adults. In B. P. Uzzell, & Y. Gross (Eds.), *Clinical neuropsychology of intervention* (pp. 59–83). Boston: Nartinus Nijhoff.

Critchley, M. (1949). The problem of awareness or non-awareness of hemianopic field defects. *Transactions of the Ophthalmological Society of U. K. , 69,* 95–109.

Cutting, J. (1978). Study of anosognosia. *Journal of Neurology, Neurosurgery, and Psychiatry, 41,* 548–555.

Damasio, A. R. (1994). *Descartes' error.* New York: Avon Books.

Danielczyk, W. (1983) Various mental behavioral disorders in Parkinson's disease, primary degenerative senile dementia, and multiple infarction dementia. *Journal of Neural Transmission, 56,* 161–176.

Fahy, T. J., Irving, M. H., & Millac, P. (1967). Severe head injuries. *The Lancet, 2,* 475–479.

Fordyce, D. J., & Roueche, J. R. (1986). Changes in perspectives of disability among patients, staff, and relatives during rehabilitation of brain injury. *Rehabilitation Psychology, 31,* 217–229.

Frederiks, J. A. M. (1985). Disorders of the body schema. In J. A. M. Frederiks, (Ed.), *Handbook of clinical neurology* (Vol. 1, pp. 373–393). Amsterdam: Elsevier.

Gassel, M. M., & Williams, D. (1963). Visual function in patients with homonymous hemianopia: Part III. The completion phenomenon: Insight and attitude to the defect; and visual functional efficiency. *Brain*, 86, 229–260.

Goldberg, T. E., Weinberger, D. R., Berman, K. F., Pliskin, N. H., & Podd, M. H. (1987). Further evidence for dementia of the prefrontal type in schizophrenia? *Archives of General Psychiatry*, 44, 1008–1014.

Gustafson, I., & Nilsson, L. (1982). Differential diagnosis of presenile dementia on clinical grounds. *Acta Psychiatrica Scandinavica*, 65, 194–207.

Hackler, E, & Tobis, J. S. (1983). Reintegration into the community. In M. Rosenthal, E. R., Griffith, M. R., Bond, & J. D. Miller, (Eds.), *Rehabilitation of the head injured adult* (pp. 421–424). Philadelphia: FC Davis.

Joynt, R. J., & Shoulson, I. (1985). Dementia. In: K. M. Heilman, E. Valenstein (Eds.), *Clinical neuropsychology* (2nd ed., pp. 453–479). New York: Oxford University Press.

Kaszniak, A. W. (1986). The neuropsychology of dementia. In I. Grant, & K. M. Adams, (Eds.), *Neuropsychological assessment of neuropsychiatric disorders* (pp. 172–220). New York: Oxford University Press.

Kinsbourne, M., & Warrington, E. K. (1963). Jargon aphasia. *Neuropsychologia*, 1, 27–37.

Koehler, P. J., Endtz, L. J., Te Velde, J., & Hekster, R. E. M. (1986). Aware or non-aware: On the significance of awareness for the localization of the lesion responsible for homonymous hemianopia. *Journal of the Neurological Sciences*, 75, 255–262.

Korsakoff, S. S. (1889). Étude mßdico-psychologique sur une forme des maladies de la mßmoire [Medical-psychological study of a form of diseases of memory]. *Revue Philosophique*, 28, 501–530.

Langer, K. G., & Padrone, F. J. (1992). Psychotherapeutic treatment of awareness in acute rehabilitation of traumatic brain injury. *Neuropsychological Rehabilitation*, 2, 59–70.

Liddle, P. F., & Barnes, T. R. E. (1988). The subjective experience of deficits in schizophrenia. *Comprehensive Psychiatry*, 29, 157–164.

Liddle, P. F., & Morris, D. L. (1991). Schizophrenic syndromes and frontal lobe performance. *British Journal of Psychiatry*, 158, 340–345.

Lin, I. F., Spiga, R., & Fortsch, W. (1979). Insight and adherence to medication in chronic schizophrenics. *Journal of Clinical Psychology*, 40, 430–432.

Lysaker, P., & Bell, M. (1995a). Impaired insight in schizophrenia: Advances from psychosocial treatment research. In X. F. Amador, & A. David, (Eds.), *Insight and psychosis*. Oxford, England: Oxford University Press.

Lysaker, P., & Bell, M. (1995b). Work rehabilitation and improvements in insight in schizophrenia. *The Journal of Nervous and Mental Disease*, 183, 103–106.

Mahendra, B. (1984). *Dementia*. Lancaster: MTP Press.

Malenka, R. C., Angel, R. W., Hamptom, B., & Berger, P. A. (1982). Impaired central error-correcting behavior in schizophrenia. *Archives of General Psychiatry*, 39, 101–107.

McEvoy, J. P., Apperson, L. S., & Appelbaum, P. S. (1989). Insight in schizophrenia. Its relationship to acute psychopathology. *The Journal of Nervous Mental Disease*, 177, 42–47.

McGlynn, S. M. (1990). Behavioral approaches to neuropsychological rehabilitation. *Psychological Bulletin*, 108, 420–441.

McGlynn, S. M., & Kaszniak, A. W. (1991). Unawareness of deficits in dementia and schizophrenia. In G. P., Prigatano, & D. L., Schacter, (Eds.), *Awareness of deficit after brain injury: Clinical and theoretical issues* (pp. 84–110). New York: Oxford University Press.

McGlynn, S. M., & Schacter, D. L. (1989). Unawareness of deficits in neuropsychological syndromes. *Journal of Clinical and Experimental Neuropsychology*, 11, 143–205.

McGlynn, S. M., Schacter, D. L., & Glisky, E. L. (1989). Unawareness of deficit in organic amnesia. *Journal of Clinical and Experimental Neuropsychology Abstracts*, 11, 50.

McHugh, P. R., & Folstein, M. F. (1975). Psychiatric syndromes of Huntington's chorea: a clinical and phenomenologic study. In D. F. Benson, & D. Blumer, (Eds.), *Psychiatric aspects of neurologic disease* (pp. 267–285). Orlando: Grune & Stratton.

Michalakeas, A., Skoutas, C., Charalambous, A., Peristeris, A., Marinos, V., Keramari, E., & Theologou, A. (1994). *Acta Psychiatrica Scandinavica, 90*, 46–49.

Migliorelli, R., Teson, A., Sabe, L., Petracchi, M., Leiguarda, R., & Starkstein, S. E. (1995a). Prevalence and correlates of dysthymia and major depression among patients with Alzheimer's disease. *American Journal of Psychiatry, 152*, 37–44.

Migliorelli, R., Teson, A., Sabe, L., Petracca, G., Petracchi, M., Leiguarda, R., & Starkstein, S. E. (1995b). Anosognosia in Alzheimer's disease: A study of associated factors. *Journal of Neuropsychiatry, 7*, 338–344.

Milner, B., Corkin, S., & Teuber, H. L. (1968). Further analysis of the hippocampal amnesic syndrome: 14 year follow-up study of H. M. *Neuropsychologia, 6*, 215–234.

Myslobodsky, M. S. (1986). Anosognosia in patients with tardive dyskinesia: A symptom of "tardive dysmentia" or "tardive dementia"? *Schizophrenia Bulletin, 12*, 1–6.

Myslobodsky, M. S., Holden, T., & Sandler, R. (1986). Parkinsonian symptoms in tardive dyskinesia. *South African Medical Journal, 69*, 424–426.

Myslobodsky, M. S., Tomer, R., Holden, T., Kempler, S., & Sigal, M. (1985). Cognitive impairment in patients with tardive dyskinesia. *Journal of Nervous and Mental Disorders, 173*, 156–160.

Nathanson, M., Bergman, P. S., & Gordon, G. G. (1952). Denial of illness: Its occurrence in one hundred consecutive cases of hemiplegia. *Archives of Neurology and Psychiatry, 68*, 380–387.

Neary, D., Snowden, J. S., Bowen, D. M., Sims, N. R., Mann, D. M. A., Benton, J. S., Northen, B., Yates, P. O., & Davison, A. N. (1986). Neuropsychological syndromes in presenile dementia due to cerebral atrophy. *Journal of Neurology, Neurosurgery, and Psychiatry, 49*, 163–174.

Nielsen, J. M. (1938). Disturbances of the body scheme. Their physiologic mechanism. *Bulletin of Los Angeles Neurological Society, 3*, 127–135.

Oltman, J. E., & Friedman, S. (1961). Combination of general paresis and Huntington's chorea. *Disorder of the Nervous System, 22*, 507–509.

Prigatano, G. P., & Fordyce, D. J. (1986). Cognitive dysfunction and psychosocial adjustment after brain injury. In G. P. Prigatano (Ed.), *Neuropsychological rehabilitation after brain injury* (pp. 1–17). Baltimore: Johns Hopkins University Press.

Prigatano, G. P., & Schacter, D. L. (1991). *Awareness of deficit after brain injury: Clinical and theoretical issues.* New York: Oxford University Press.

Redlich, F. C., & Dorsey, J. F. (1945). Denial of blindness by patients with cerebral disease. *Archives of Neurology and Psychiatry, 53*, 407–417.

Reed, B. R., Jagust, W. J., & Coulter, L. (1993). Anosognosia in Alzheimer's disease: Relationships to depression, cognitive function, and cerebral perfusion. *Journal of Clinical and Experimental Neuropsychology, 15*, 231–244.

Reisberg, B., Gordon, B., McCarthy, M., & Ferris, S. H. (1985). Clinical symptoms accompanying progressive cognitive decline and Alzheimer's disease. In V. L. Melnick, & N. N. Dubler, (Eds.), *Alzheimer's dementia* (pp. 19–39). Clifton, NJ: Humana Press.

Rose, F. C., & Symonds, C. P. (1960). Persistent memory defect following encephalitis. *Brain, 83*, 195–212.

Rosen, A. M., Mukherjee, S., Olarte, S., Varia, V., & Cardenas, C. (1982). Perception of tardive dyskinesia in outpatients receiving maintenance neuroleptics. *American Journal of Psychiatry, 139*, 372–373.

Sandifer, P. H. (1946). Anosognosia and disorders of body scheme. *Brain, 69*, 122–137.

Schacter, D. L. (1987). Memory, amnesia, and frontal lobe dysfunction. *Psychobiology*, *15*, 21–36.

Schacter, D. L. (1991). Unawareness of deficit and unawareness of knowledge in patients with memory disorders. In G. P. Prigatano, & D. L. Schacter, (Eds.), *Awareness of deficit after brain injury: Clinical and theoretical issues* (pp. 127–151). New York: Oxford University Press.

Schacter, D. L., Glisky, E. L., & McGlynn, S. M. (1990). Impact of memory disorder on everyday life: Awareness of deficits and return to work. In D. Tupper & K. Cicerone (Eds.), *The Neuropsychology of Everyday Life. Vol. I: Theories and Basic Competencies* (pp. 231–298). Boston: Kluwer Academic Publishers

Schacter, D. L., McLachlan, D. R., Moscovitch, M., & Tulving, E. (1986). Monitoring of recall performance by memory-disordered patients. *Journal of Clinical and Experimental Neuropsychology Abstracts*, *8*, 130.

Schneck, M. K., Reisberg, B., & Ferris, S. H. (1982). An overview of current concepts of Alzheimer's disease. *American Journal of Psychiatry*, *139*, 165–173.

Seidman, L. J. (1983). Schizophrenia and brain dysfunction: An integration of recent neurodiagnostic findings. *Psychological Bulletin*, *94*, 195–238.

Shimamura, A. P., & Squire, L. R. (1986). Memory and metamemory: A study of the feeling-of-knowing phenomenon in amnesic patients. *Journal of Experimental Psychology: Learning, Memory, and Cognition*, *12*, 452–460.

Smith, J. M., Kucharski, L. T., Oswald, W. T., & Waterman, L. J. (1979). A systematic investigation of tardive dyskinesia in inpatients. *American Journal of Psychiatry*, *136*, 918–922.

Squire, L. R. (1986). Mechanisms of memory. *Science*, *232*, 1612–1619.

Stuss, D. T., & Benson, D. F. (1984). Neuropsychological studies of the frontal lobes. *Psychological Bulletin*, *95*, 3–78.

Stuss, D. T., & Benson, D. F. (1986). *The frontal lobes*. New York: Raven Press.

Sunderland, A., Harris, J. E., & Baddeley, A. D. (1983). Do laboratory tests predict everyday memory? A neuropsychological study. *Journal of Verbal Learning and Verbal Behavior*, *22*, 341–357.

Van Putten, T., Crumpton, E., & Yale, C. (1976). Drug refusal in schizophrenia and the wish to be crazy. *Archives of General Psychiatry*, *33*, 1443–1446.

Victor, M., Adams, R. D., & Collins, G. N. (1971). *The Wernicke-Korsakoff syndrome*. Philadelphia: FA Davis.

Vilkki, J. (1985). Amnesic syndromes after surgery of anterior communicating artery aneurysms. *Cortex*, *21*, 431–444.

Von Hagen, K. O., & Ives, E. R. (1937). Anosognosia (Babinski), imperception of hemiplegia. Report of six cases, one with autopsy. *Bulletin of Los Angeles Neurological Society*, *2*, 95–103.

Warrington, E. K. (1962). The completion of visual forms across hemianopic field defects. *Journal of Neurology, Neurosurgery, and Psychiatry*, *25*, 208–217.

Weinstein, E. A., Cole, M., Mitchell, M. S., & Lyerly, O. G. (1964). Anosognosia and aphasia. *Archives of Neurology*, *10*, 376–386.

Weinstein, E. A., & Kahn, R. L. (1955). *Denial of illness: Symbolic and physiological aspects*. Springfield, IL: Charles C. Thomas.

Willanger, R., Danielsen, U. T., & Ankerhus, J. (1981). Visual neglect in right-sided apoplectic lesions. *Acta Neurologica Scandinavica*, *64*, 327–336.

Wilson, R. S., & Garron, D. C. (1979). Cognitive and affective aspects of Huntington's disease. *Advances in Neurology*, *23*, 193–201.

Young, D. A., Davila, R., & Scher, H. (1993). Unawareness of illness and neuropsychological performance in chronic schizophrenia. *Schizophrenia Research*, *10*, 117–124.

11

Training Programs to Improve Learning in Later Adulthood: Helping Older Adults Educate Themselves

John Dunlosky
University of North Carolina at Greensboro
Christopher Hertzog
Georgia Institute of Technology

The number of adults over the age of 65 will continue to increase over the next few decades, with some estimates indicating that one fifth of the U.S. population will be 65 or older by the year 2030. This represents a considerable increase from one eighth in 1990 (Roush, 1996)! Considering that the number of older adults seeking advanced education has been steadily increasing over the past decade, these demographics indicate that this trend is likely to continue far into the future. Educating and retraining older adults may provide a special challenge given the difficulties many will face relative to their younger peers. Older adults often require more time to learn new materials required in educational settings, such as the content of expository texts and even simple associations like foreign-language vocabulary or people's names and faces (for recent reviews, see chaps. 6, 7, 8, 12, & 15 in Blanchard-Fields & Hess, 1996). Older adults are also likely to have less confidence in their ability to learn new materials, a decrease in *memory self-efficacy* that may stop many adults from pursuing further education.

Given age-related declines in memory and in memory self-efficacy, a growing number of researchers have explored how older adults can be trained to improve their learning (for a variety of perspectives on adult life-span learning, see Sinnott, 1994). Much has been learned about the effectiveness of a number of intervention approaches, including training older adults to use mnemonics. However, our review of the literature suggests that an alternative approach offers possibilities for reframing past research and identifying new avenues for the future (for other reviews of the memory-training literature, see Kotler-Cope & Camp, 1990; Verhaeghen, Marcoen, & Goossens, 1992; West, 1995). In this chapter, we review research on memory training within a theoretical framework of self-regulated learning because effective self regulation is arguably central to achievement in educational settings (e.g., Pressley & El-Dinary, 1992). Although many investigators have trained older adults some skills necessary for self-regulated learning, critical skills involved in self-regulation—most notably, memory monitoring—have not yet been integrated into existing training programs. A major thesis developed in this chapter is the importance of training older adults to monitor their own learning, which we substantiate with rational arguments and with empirical evidence from research on metacognitive aging.

THEORETICAL FRAMEWORK OF
SELF-REGULATED LEARNING

The theoretical framework of self-regulated learning that guides our review of the memory-training research is illustrated in Fig. 11.1. The framework is composed of three interrelated sections that pertain to study preparation, on-going study, and tests on newly studied material (cf. Nelson & Narens, 1990). It includes many components from the area of metacognition, which is broadly defined as cognition about cognition. Metacognition has become an increasingly important concept in developmental and cognitive psychology (Metcalfe & Shimamura, 1994; Schneider & Pressley, 1989) and has been conceptualized as having multiple domains: declarative knowledge about cognition, beliefs about self and others regarding cognitive functioning, and monitoring and control of cognitive processes as they occur during behavior (Cavanaugh & Green, 1990; Hertzog & Dixon, 1994; Nelson & Narens, 1990). Each of these domains is represented in our framework.

This theoretical framework has guided our own research on paired-associate tasks and list-learning tasks (e.g., Dunlosky & Hertzog, 1997), and it also provides a vehicle for thinking about learning at the level of individual units of material, as in lists composed of individual words or sentences, sentences in connected discourse, or paragraphs in expository texts. A key assumption of this framework is that learning is often intentional and goal-directed, with individuals having a great deal of control of their own learning. Such control is presumably critical for effective learning because individuals need to regulate and adapt their learning to specific materials as well as to the progress they have already made.

Although the framework includes numerous components and relations among them, it is not meant to be comprehensive (for a more general framework, see Winne & Hadwin, chap. 12, this volume). Some aspects of self-regulated learning that may prove important do not appear in our framework (e.g., monitoring processes involved in emotion, Carver & Scheier, 1990; and memory-related affect, Hertzog & Dixon, 1994), and some plausible links are not shown (e.g., between memory self-efficacy and initial strategy selection, Rellinger, Borkowski, Turner, & Hale, 1995). Furthermore, the components are shown at a relatively coarsened level, without much heed being given to details of how some components interact during self-regulated learning (for refinements of components shown in Fig. 11.1 see Hertzog, Saylor, Fleece, & Dixon, 1994; Koriat & Goldsmith, 1996; Nelson & Narens, 1990; Reder & Ritter, 1992). Instead, the framework provides an overview of some components that arguably influence achievement in educational settings. In the remainder of this section, we briefly describe this framework, which is later used to organize a review of the memory-training literature.

The three sections of our framework include metacognitive components and cognitive components that may facilitate or constrain learning. In regard to a person's preparation for study, several components of metacognition may influence learning. Memory self-efficacy is an individual's belief in his or her own ability to successfully use memory in various situations (for recent reviews relevant to older adults, see Cavanaugh, 1996; Welch & West, 1995). A person's memory self-efficacy may affect appraisal of task difficulty. At one extreme, people with low memory self-efficacy may believe that many tasks involving memory are too challenging to undertake (Berry & West, 1993). Metacognitive knowledge, which is declarative knowledge about memory, may influence both task appraisal and the kinds of strategy that are selected for study (cf. Flavell's, 1979, account of task and strategy variables). Knowledge about different kinds of tasks and strategies may enable an individual to accurately appraise task demands affording an opportunity to match learning behavior with learning goals. By contrast, a person with little knowledge of memory strategies (e.g., interactive imagery, keyword mnemonic, etc.) is unlikely to select a strategy that will produce efficient

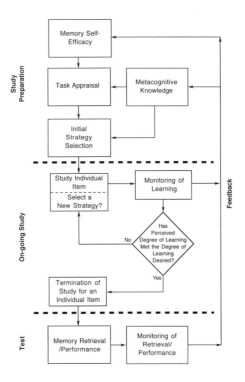

FIG. 11.1. Theoretical framework including metacognitive components and cognitive components that may interact during task preparation, ongoing study, and retrieval.

learning for a given situation. These three components (memory self-efficacy, knowledge of strategies, and strategy selection) of our framework have
already been the focus of numerous memory-training programs and are
discussed later in more detail.

The framework in Fig. 11.1 also highlights possible roles of monitoring
in self-regulated learning. During on-going study, a person may monitor
how well an individual item has been learned. This perceived degree of
learning may then be compared to the degree of learning the person
desires for the item, which is called the norm of study (see Nelson &
Narens, 1990, for further discussion of this decision criterion). If the
perceived degree of learning is less than the norm of study, the person
presumably will continue to study the item or will select a new study
strategy to use. If the perceived degree of learning meets or exceeds this

norm of study, the person will terminate study of that item and proceed to another. One implication of this discrepancy-reduction mechanism of self-paced study is that a person's perceived degree of learning will be inversely related to subsequent study time. This prediction has received empirical confirmation (Dunlosky & Connor, in press; Mazzoni & Cornoldi, 1993; Nelson & Leonesio, 1988). Another implication is that highly accurate monitoring, if utilized, will lead to effective regulation of on-going study. If people perfectly assess which items have (vs. have not) been well learned, they will be able to devote restudy to only items that require it. However, if monitoring of memory is inaccurate, they may inappropriately allocate study to items (e.g., spending too little time studying less well-learned items), which may lead to poor test performance.

Metacognitive components can influence retrieval as well. During the eventual test of memory, people may monitor their attempts to retrieve items and then utilize this monitoring to guide both retrieval and restudy. For example, people may allocate more time to retrieve items that they are confident that they can remember versus those they are confident that they will not remember (for further discussion, see Miner & Reder, 1994). Thus, if one's confidence is inaccurate, regulation of retrieval may be relatively ineffective because too much time may be spent trying to retrieve answers that are actually not known (Koriat & Goldsmith, 1996). By contrast, individuals who accurately monitor the outcome of retrieval may effectively control retrieval: Individuals who fail to retrieve an answer to a question but experience a tip-of-the-tongue state due to inaccessibility of the answer may engage in retrieval strategies that will help resolve the retrieval block. However, to the extent that the tip-of-the-tongue state is not induced by a retrieval block, but instead is an inference based on familiarity with the topic (Metcalfe, Schwartz, & Joaquim, 1993), individuals may be misled into trying to resolve a retrieval block instead of attempting to relearn the answer.

Figure 11.1 contains a number of feedback loops in which information gained from monitoring has broader effects than merely influencing control per se. Monitoring that occurs during both study and test may also be involved in updating metacognitive knowledge. This updating can occur when the output from monitoring is used to compare the effectiveness of two different strategies, with the person maintaining or switching to strategies that are perceived to produce the most effective learning (for further discussion, see Borkowski, Carr, Rellinger, & Pressley, 1990). Thus, monitoring may have relatively direct effects on test performance, such as by influencing self-paced study or retrieval, as well as more indirect but long-term effects on test performance, such as by influencing a person's metacognitive knowledge.

SELECTIVE REVIEW OF MEMORY-TRAINING LITERATURE

How is the model of Fig. 11.1 relevant to training older adults to improve their learning skills? A fundamental assumption of our approach is that individual differences inevitably occur in each of the aforementioned components of self-regulated learning. Some people will have detailed knowledge about multiple study strategies, whereas others will have little knowledge about which strategies support effective learning. Some people will often utilize monitoring to regulate learning, whereas others may not even attempt to monitor on-going learning. Training programs typically target deficiencies expected in specific components of learning, such as training older adults to use effective strategies that they do not use. The success of training programs has been mainly assessed with respect to answering questions such as: Did training have the desired effect on the components that were targeted? Did this training also boost the memory performance of the trained group in comparison to the performance of some control group? If memory performance was enhanced, how long was this maintained: a few days, weeks, or years?

In this review, we focus on research involving older adults that has relevance for our framework of self-regulated learning (Fig. 11.1) and that provides empirical answers to one or more of the questions posed earlier. This review is not meant as a step-by-step guide on how to develop a training program. However, we do highlight some training techniques that show promise in helping older adults educate themselves (for discussions on how to develop training programs, see Treat, Poon, Fozard, & Popkin, 1978; West, 1985, 1989; and for other perspectives on cognitive training with older adults, see Camp and McKitrick, 1992; Willis, 1987).

Memory Self-Efficacy

Memory self-efficacy can influence one's memory performance in a variety of ways. Many older adults believe their ability to learn has declined (Hertzog & Dixon, 1994), and as explained by West and Berry (1994), such "low self-evaluation could result in self-limiting actions that further reduce competence" (p. 427). For instance, older adults with lower memory self-efficacy (a) may be unlikely to use effortful but effective strategies to learn new materials (i.e., link between memory self-efficacy and strategy selection in Fig. 11.1), (b) may not attempt to learn new strategies that would otherwise compensate for memory problems, or (c) may set lower goals for learning individual items (i.e., link between memory self-efficacy and norm of study) and hence will terminate study prior to mastery (Berry & West, 1993). An idea common to these possibilities is that memory self-efficacy limits memory performance by disrupting self-regulated processes, such as strategy selection and the allocation of study time (for other possibilities, see Bandura, 1989). Thus, improving older adults' memory self-efficacy may also be necessary for training them to maintain the use of strategies. Even if older adults are taught to use an effective strategy, low memory self-efficacy could inhibit subsequent strategy utilization. That is, improving memory self-efficacy may be critical for maintaining use of skills learned during training. Without skill maintenance, training programs are unlikely to improve older adults' learning in naturalistic settings.

Given this rationale, a variety of training programs have focused on changing memory self-efficacy. Research in this area differs in regard to whether training directly or indirectly attempts to change memory self-efficacy. Lachman and colleagues (e.g., Lachman, 1991; Lachman, Weaver, Bandura, Elliott, & Lewkowicz, 1992) have championed one approach in which training is aimed at improving older adults' memory self-efficacy by teaching them that they can successfully complete memory tasks. Such a direct approach, however, may be sufficient but not necessary to enhance memory self-efficacy. Training older adults to use a strategy effectively may in itself improve memory self-efficacy, such as by providing experience with mastering a memory task (Welch & West, 1995). Thus, we also discuss attempts to improve memory self-efficacy by training memory skills alone.

Lachman (1986, 1991) and others (e.g., Hultsch, Hertzog, & Dixon, 1987) have reported that age differences exist in beliefs about one's ability to control memory, with older adults believing that they have less control. As already discussed, such negative beliefs about one's memory abilities may limit the effectiveness of training programs and memory performance. A goal of two studies reported by Lachman (1991) was to investigate whether low memory self-efficacy of older adults could be improved, and if so, whether such improvements were associated with better memory performance. The training program to enhance memory self-efficacy consisted of *attributional retraining* in which participants were given information "that memory failures in later life are not inevitable and irreversible. Further, they were informed that many people, but not all people, experience memory problems, and that memory can be improved through training and the use of specific strategies" (p. 167). Results across the two studies indicated that memory self-efficacy could be boosted through training, although attributional retraining itself may not have been critical: All groups that had received feedback about test performance showed a boost in memory self-efficacy, even if they did not receive attributional retraining. Memory performance also tended to improve for all groups.

Lachman, Weaver, Bandura, Elliott, and Lewkowicz (1992) sought to improve older adults' beliefs about memory via a program of training called *cognitive restructuring*, which involves teaching older adults that memory is controllable and how to "shift from maladaptive to adaptive cognitions, to foster motivation and task orientation" (p. 296). A group receiving both cognitive restructuring and training in memory skills showed the greatest boost in memory self-efficacy, although these effects were somewhat diminished 3 months after training. As important, all groups (even a no-contact control group) showed improved memory performance. Similarly, the training program used by Best, Hamlett, and Davis (1992) challenged negative beliefs that older adults have about aging and memory ability. Older adults who received this attributional training had fewer memory complaints after training, an effect that was even maintained for 2 weeks. However, this group did not show improved memory performance, whereas a group that had been trained to use strategies (e.g., interactive imagery and verbal mnemonics) did not have fewer complaints after training but did show improved memory performance.

Finally, Caprio-Prevette and Fry (1996) recently reported that cognitive restructuring alone boosted both memory self-efficacy and memory performance, whereas training only memory skills did not significantly influence either variable. Caprio-Prevette and Fry's (1996) outcomes—such as the lack of an effect of memory-skills training on memory performance—are somewhat discrepant with findings reported elsewhere (e.g., see review in a later section, "Training People to Use Study Strategies"). Leaving such discrepancies aside, however, outcomes from these studies demonstrate that memory self-efficacy can be improved with training.

Is some kind of attributional retraining necessary to improve memory self-efficacy? Perhaps not. In a study by West, Bellott, Bramblett, and Welch (1993), older adults' training included experience with mastering memory exercises, which included first mastering easy exercises followed by mastering progressively more difficult ones. This training technique may influence older adult's negative attributions by demonstrating that they can complete difficult memory tasks. Training that involved these mastery experiences boosted memory self-efficacy, but so did training that involved teaching strategy use without providing mastery experiences (cf. Lachman, 1991). Zarit, Cole, and Guider (1981, Study 2) found that training strategies alone enhanced memory self-efficacy (as measured by memory complaints) in comparison to a no-contact control group (cf. Zarit, Gallagher, & Kramer, 1981). Zarit, Cole, and Guider (1981) noted, however, that "an important facet of the training was the initial screening for severe memory loss associated with senile dementia. This permitted trainers to *reassure participants about their abilities to learn* [italics added] and that occasional forgetting did not indicate senility" (p. 163). Perhaps this kind of reassurance contributed to improvements in memory self-efficacy.

Unfortunately, training strategies alone may not always improve memory self-efficacy. Scogin, Storandt, and Lott (1985) had their participants complete 16 hours of training, which involved learning strategies to remember name–face associations and other materials. In contrast to the research discussed earlier in which someone taught the older adults, each participant taught himself or herself strategies using a manual provided by the experimenter. As compared to a no-contact control, training had no effect on memory self-efficacy, although training did improve memory performance. Two other studies (Best et al., 1992; Caprio-Prevette & Fry, 1996) also found that training strategies alone did not significantly affect memory self-efficacy.

In conclusion, researchers have demonstrated that people's memory self-efficacy can be improved, although success in improving memory self-efficacy may depend on the kind of training program used. Memory training alone has inconsistently affected memory self-efficacy (see also, Verhaeghen, Van Ranst, & Marcoen, 1993), although the positive effects of West et al.'s (1993) memory training were maintained a month after training. Attributional retraining significantly boosted memory self-efficacy in some situations (e.g., Best et al., 1992; Caprio-Prevette & Fry, 1996) but not in others (Lachman et al., 1992). By contrast, a combination of attributional retraining and strategy training has consistently enhanced memory self-efficacy (e.g., Lachman, 1991; Lachman et al., 1992; McEvoy & Moon, 1988; West et al., 1993). In a recent meta-analysis of this literature, Floyd and Scogin (1997) arrived at the same conclusion independently: Older adults' beliefs about their memory can be improved, and this improvement is "best accomplished by addressing both the improvement of skills (mnemonic training) and the development of more adaptive attitudes towards memory performance (expectancy modification)" (p. 160). Thus, one metacognitive component, memory self-efficacy, that presumably influences self-directed learning (Fig. 11.1) can be reliably improved through training.

This conclusion is encouraging, especially when the primary goal of a training program is to change older adults' beliefs about their own memory. However, if the goal of training is to help older adults improve learning, the promise of training memory self-efficacy per se may be tempered because improving it may have had a minor impact on memory performance: Some training has improved memory self-efficacy but not memory performance (e.g., Best et al., 1992). Furthermore, when training improves both memory self-efficacy and memory performance, improvements in memory performance may often be determined more by practice effects than by enhanced memory self-efficacy (for discussion, see Lachman et al., 1992).

Why may improving memory self-efficacy not always produce improvements in memory performance? One possible answer concerns the resistance to change in beliefs about one's own memory functioning. Questionnaire measures of memory self-efficacy often measure a higher order (or generalized) set of beliefs regarding self-as-rememberer (Hertzog & Dixon, 1994) as opposed to task-specific memory self-efficacy (Berry, West, & Dennehey, 1989). Generalized memory self-efficacy has shown high stability across individual differences over time: McDonald-Miszczak, Hertzog, and Hultsch (1995) found that the stability of memory self-efficacy, as measured by the Metamemory-in-Adulthood Capacity scale, was almost perfect in two separate samples (across a 2-year retest interval in one sample and a 6-year retest interval in the other). Although the cognitive-restructuring interventions described earlier have affected task-specific measures of memory self-efficacy, these effects may have been too small and too specific to the task context to have a substantive long-term impact. Moreover, improvements in task-specific efficacy may dissipate over time, with self-efficacy beliefs reverting to levels determined by generalized memory self-efficacy. For example, Lachman et al. (1992) found that measures of self-efficacy moved back toward baseline at a 3-month follow-up.

In general, more knowledge is needed about the convergent and divergent validity of the numerous measures of memory self-efficacy (cf. Hertzog, Hultsch, & Dixon, 1989). Inconsistent results in the literature on training memory self-efficacy may be due in part to variations in how memory self-efficacy has been operationalized. Furthermore, the existing studies have yet to deal with the vexing problem of demand characteristics. After cognitive restructuring, older adults may believe that they should report having greater memory self-efficacy, even though their underlying beliefs have not changed. That is, individuals may change their questionnaire responses after the intervention, but this change may not accurately reflect an actual increase in memory self-efficacy.

Another reason why memory self-efficacy may have a minor impact on memory performance is provided by our framework of self-regulated learning. Namely, memory self-efficacy may affect memory performance indirectly through changes in some other component(s) of self-regulated learning. For instance, improvements in memory self-efficacy may indirectly influence memory performance by directly increasing the likelihood that multiple strategies are used or by increasing persistence in trying to complete a task. If so, the observed effects of memory self-efficacy on memory performance may be limited because methods used to evaluate memory performance often short-circuit these components of self-regulated learning (for discussion of some exceptions, see Storandt, 1992). For instance, presentation rate of material is often fixed (vs. self-paced) and occurs during a single study trial (vs. multiple trials), which may short-circuit differential allocation of study time, the use of more effortful strategies, or the use of multiple strategies. Given that the target of many training programs is performance on self-regulated tasks, an avenue for future research will be to explore the degree to which improving older adults' memory self-efficacy also improves self-regulated learning (Hertzog & Dunlosky, 1996).

Finally, the relation between memory self-efficacy and memory performance may be moderated by a third, intervening variable. For instance, Baldi and Berry (1996) found a positive relation between memory self-efficacy and memory performance in a group of older adults who complained about memory problems, whereas this relation was less evident for a group of older adults who had fewer memory complaints. This relation between memory self-efficacy and memory performance (for the high-complaint group) was also partially mediated through differences in self-paced study and reported strategy use. Regardless of why memory complaint may moderate these effects, this evidence suggests that the relation between memory self-efficacy and memory performance may be suppressed by other intervening variables. Identifying these variables may help further the development of more effective training programs.

Training People to Use Study Strategies

Most training programs have attempted to improve older adults' learning by teaching them to use a new strategy during on-going study. Excellent reviews of this research are already available (e.g., Kotler-Cope & Camp, 1990; Verhaeghen, Marcoen, & Goossens, 1992; West, 1995), so we focus only on a subset of articles to illustrate some key points. In relation to our framework of self-regulated learning (Fig. 11.1), this research pertains mainly to strategy selection that occurs either during study preparation or during on-going study. The critical influence that strategy selection can have on learning is uncontested (Pressley & El-Dinary, 1992). For instance, learning may be limited if an individual selects merely to repeat paired associates when the characteristics of the pairs afford the use of a normatively more effective strategy, such as interactive imagery. Thus, questions arising from our framework include, "Do older adults select normatively effective strategies when studying new material?" And if not, "Will training them to use a normatively effective strategy improve their memory performance?"

Intervention research often implicitly assumes that the answer to the first question just posed is "No." Although this answer may not be completely justified (e.g., Camp, Markley, & Kramer, 1983), older adults do appear to under-utilize strategies that involve mental imagery and/or do not know about more complex—but effective—kinds of imagery-based strategies (e.g., Method of Loci or the peg system). Because these imagery-based strategies often yield high levels of memory performance, many interventions involve training older adults to use them. Yesavage and colleagues (e.g., Yesavage, 1984; Yesavage & Rose, 1983; 1984) have programmatically investigated the benefits of training older adults to use imagery-based strategies, such as the Method of Loci. In their investigations, memory performance after training has rarely been on the ceiling; however, gains in performance have been greater for adults who were trained to use imagery-based strategies than for those in control groups. This and other research highlights the plasticity of memory performance for older adults (see also Kliegl, Smith, & Baltes, 1989): With proper training, older adults can increase their capacity to learn new material.

In their meta-analysis of the literature, Verhaeghen et al. (1992) analyzed data from 49 groups of older adults involved in memory-training programs. Most important, the outcome of their meta-analysis indicated that training older adults to use study strategies improved their memory performance. Verhaeghen et al. also concluded that several other factors contributed to the success of training programs: Improvements in performance were negatively related to chronological age, suggesting that plasticity in memory declines with aging (as in Kliegl et al., 1989). By contrast, improvements in performance were positively related to whether older adults had (vs. did not have) pretraining prior to any memory-training session. Pretraining sessions that involved training relaxation skills or that involved training participants to judge the pleasantness of visual images contributed to gains in memory performance. Thus, training skills other than memory mnemonics per se may contribute to the plasticity of memory performance.

In contrast to the great number of investigations that have examined short-term improvements in memory performance after training, few investigators have examined whether training provides long-term maintenance of these improvements. Several exceptions are noteworthy. Stigsdotter and Bäckman's (1989) training program involved training older adults to use strategies (e.g., Method of Loci), to relax, and to focus attention while studying new material. Older adults who received this multifactorial training showed improved learning on the selective-reminding task, but not on a digit span task or on visual retention tests. As argued by Stigsdotter and Bäckman, these findings suggest "that improvement from training of particular memory-related skills does not generalize to other domains of memory functioning" (p. 265), a conclusion also supported by Verhaeghen et al.'s (1992) meta-analysis. Perhaps most impressive, Neely and Bäckman (1993) found that the benefits of training were maintained 3 ½ years after training!

Other research has failed to find such long-term maintenance. Scogin and Bienias (1988) conducted a 3-year follow-up to the training program by Scogin et al. (1985). Although training memory skills had initially improved the memory performance of older adults, 3 years later the performance of this group was not reliably different than performance of a control group. Anschutz, Camp, Markley, and Kramer (1987) trained older adults to use the Method of Loci, which improved their memory performance shortly after training. In a 3-year follow-up, however, the participants' mean level of memory performance was no better than it had been prior to training. Why did older adults in these two investigations fail to maintain original improvements in memory performance? Anschutz et al. (1987) reported that 3 years after training, their participants retained most of the loci that had been originally learned during training. Thus, failure to remember a given strategy may not underlie lack of maintenance. Another possibility is that these strategies are not useful in many everyday situations and hence will not be practiced after the original training sessions. As argued by McEvoy and Moon (1988), "although these well-established mnemonic devices can be applied to everyday problems, the application is not obvious to most people and requires considerable practice to be useful in non-laboratory settings" (p. 156; see also Lachman et al., 1992; Park, Smith, & Cavanaugh, 1990).

If lack of maintenance occurs in part because a given strategy is not useful in non-laboratory settings, perhaps older adults will maintain strategies that are readily applicable to everyday learning. For instance, Meyer, Young, and Bartlett (1989) have developed a technique to enhance people's memory for text material. Older adults were taught to guide their reading by discovering the organizational structure of a passage. This structure was then used to identify the main topic of the passage as well as to guide recall of the passage. Before training, the majority of older adults did not use this strategy, whereas after training, this strategy was used by most of the older adults and resulted in improved memory performance. Perhaps this organizational strategy will show long-term maintenance because it presumably would be applicable to everyday settings, such as in comprehending newspaper and magazine articles. Long-term maintenance also seems likely for older adults seeking advanced education because they will have the chance to regularly use various study strategies to learn class materials. Given the importance of long-term maintenance of skills targeted by training programs, determining which conditions are necessary and sufficient for long-lasting maintenance is essential.

Memory Monitoring

To the best of our knowledge, memory monitoring has never been the main focus of a training program. Indeed, training older adults to monitor memory has played at most a minor role in the programs mentioned previously. In most cases, however, training people to use monitoring skills could have been included as a component of training without great cost or difficulty. We briefly describe two illustrative instances. Lachman et al. (1992) trained older adults to use a four-step procedure to develop their own strategies. During the fourth step, older adults "were asked to try the strategies and *to determine whether or not they helped* [italics added]" (p. 296; see also, West, 1985, chap. 6). This procedure is represented in Fig. 11.1 by monitoring of learning and by the feedback loop in which monitoring is used to update metacognitive knowledge. McEvoy and Moon (1988) taught older adults to use check lists "for remembering when a task was to be done, and for recording that it had been completed" (p. 157), which is an external aid for monitoring the successful completion of the task. In both training programs, monitoring skills were taught in relation to a subset of strategies, even though monitoring could have been used to support the effective use of most—if not all—of the strategies that had been trained.

In their meta-analysis of the literature, Verhaeghen et al. (1992) also mentioned that some memory-related interventions included the training of self-monitoring (p. 243, under Method). The effect of this specific kind of memory-related intervention was not considered further in their review, perhaps because monitoring was not taught in enough interventions to adequately evaluate its effects. Thus, it appears that the benefit of teaching older adults to use monitoring skills has not been systematically evaluated, and at best, training these skills appears to have played a minor role in previous research.

Conclusions

Training programs have influenced some components of the framework shown in Fig. 11.1. These training programs have been successful in the short-term, with reliable gains being shown by older adults both in memory self-efficacy (Floyd & Scogin, 1997) and in memory performance (Verhaeghen et al., 1992). The success of these programs, however, has not been impressive. With one exception (Neely & Bäckman, 1993), long-term maintenance of these skills has not been demonstrated. Furthermore, mastery of to-be-learned materials after training is rarely attained: Even when older adults pace the study of a relatively short list of to-be-learned items, many adults terminate study prior to mastering the list (Scogin et al., 1985). None of the training programs have systematically trained memory-monitoring skills. Perhaps training older adults to use these and other skills will provide further advances toward mastery.

TRAINING AND MEMORY MONITORING

The idea that older adults will benefit from training them to monitor memory is by no means novel. Consistent with rationale already provided, West and Tomer (1989) observed that "if older adults are to apply training consistently in practical memory situations, they may need additional metacognitive knowledge. If an individual is unaware of not having learned an item, he or she is not likely to make an effort to learn it through strategic processing" (p. 88; see also West, 1989). Nevertheless, we are not aware of a training program for older adults that has systematically trained them either to monitor their memory or to utilize the output from monitoring to regulate study. In light of the central role of monitoring in self-regulated learning, a reasonable question to ask is "Why haven't these monitoring skills been trained?"

Accuracy of Global Predictions of Memory Performance

A possible answer to this question is provided by research that has evaluated whether age-related differences occur in people's ability to predict future memory performance. One way the accuracy of memory predictions has been evaluated is by having people make global predictions. In particular, prior to studying the to-be-learned items, each participant makes a *global prediction* about the number of items that he or she will remember on the eventual test. Next, the items are presented for study, which is followed by a test of memory. Predictive accuracy is then assessed by examining how close people's predictions are to the actual number of items correctly remembered on the eventual test, such as by computing a difference between the number of items predicted and the number of items actually recalled. Age-related differences in predictive accuracy favoring younger adults has often been obtained. In these cases, younger adults' predictions were relatively close to actual performance, whereas older adults' predictions tended to overestimate actual performance. Thus, early skepticism about the accuracy of older adults' memory monitoring may have diverted attention from the utility of training monitoring skills (Murphy, Sanders, Gabriesheski, & Schmitt, 1981; West & Tomer, 1989). After all, if older adults overestimate memory performance, training them to make these predictions may subsequently reduce study time and memory performance.

Connor, Dunlosky, and Hertzog (1997) recently argued that the aforementioned age-related differences were not due to underlying differences in metamemory per se, but were determined in part by age-related differences in recall performance. This may occur because recall performance is typically near 50% for younger adults and lower for older adults, whereas both age groups anchor their global predictions around 50%. Keren (1991) described one reason why such anchoring may occur: "The laboratory setting creates an expectation of an intermediate level of difficulty. The two extremes, namely a task that is either so difficult that performance is on a chance level or a task that is so easy that performance will always be perfect or close to perfect, are assumed unlikely. Consequently, subjects may anchor on a probability estimate that would reflect intermediate performance" (p. 255).

Connor et al. (1997) provide evidence for an anchoring hypothesis by illustrating the possible relation between predictive accuracy and overall levels of recall performance. Each participant made a global prediction prior to study, studied a list of paired-associate items, and then received a test of paired-associate recall. First consider the results from Experiment 1, which are presented in the top-most panel of Fig. 11.2. For both age groups, global predictions were intermediate, whereas recall performance was intermediate for younger adults but only 20% for older adults. These results replicate the aforementioned pattern of age-related differences in which younger adults are relatively accurate and older adults overestimate recall.

In Experiment 2 (bottom panel), we attempted to boost older adults' performance by having participants study each item twice. Global predictions were still intermediate, but recall performance was 45% for older adults and near 70% for younger adults. Thus, in contrast to results from Experiment 1, global predictions appeared closer to actual recall performance for older than younger adults (as in Hertzog et al., 1994). Although other results from these experiments are not completely consistent with our anchoring hypothesis, the results shown in Fig. 11.2 suggest that age-related differences in predictive accuracy are determined more by levels of recall performance than by true age-related differences in some aspect of metamemory (e.g., monitoring memory, metacognitive knowledge, etc.). More important for training is that predictive accuracy for both age groups varied widely across experiments. Therefore, unless a technique is discovered to ensure consistently high predictive accuracy, training people to make global judgments (prior to study) may often contribute to ineffective self-regulated study.

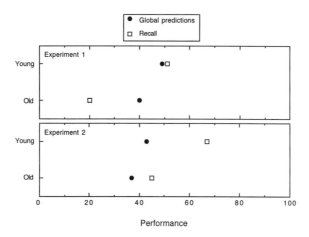

FIG. 11.2. Mean level of global predictions (made prior to the critical study trial) and mean level of recall performance plotted in a dot chart, illustrating that age-related differences in predictive accuracy appear to be determined more by age-related differences in recall performance than by age-related differences in global predictions. Values were taken from Connor, Dunlosky, and Hertog (1997).

Other Evidence for Age Equivalence in the Accuracy of Memory Monitoring

When global judgments are made after recall attempts and involve postdicting how many items had been correctly recalled, accuracy is typically high for both age groups (Connor et al., 1997; Devolder, Brigham, & Pressley, 1990; Hertzog et al., 1994). This outcome suggests that people are able to accurately monitor retrieval and performance, and it also undermines previous skepticism about the utility of training older adults to monitor memory. That is, even if global predictions made before study are not useful in regulating study, perhaps older adults will benefit by making global postdictions by testing themselves after study. These accurate postdictions may then be used to effectively regulate restudy. Although this possibility seems promising (e.g., Murphy, Schmitt, Caruso, & Sanders, 1987), the degree to which older adults' will benefit from this kind of training has not been investigated.

Global postdictions may be most useful in guiding people's decisions about the overall amount of material to be restudied. For instance, if a person postdicts that only 5 of 12 items of a list had been correctly retrieved, she may decide to restudy only 7 items. In deciding which 7 items to restudy, global postdictions may be less useful. To decide which items to restudy, an individual may instead use item-by-item judgments of learning (JOLs), which are predictions about the likelihood that recently studied items will be correctly remembered at a later time. If the individual's goal is to master the entire list of items, she presumably will select the 7 items that had been judged as least likely to be remembered. Accordingly, the accuracy of these item-by-item judgments of learning also will influence the effectiveness of learning. If people are highly accurate at judging which items are least likely to be remembered, they will be able to isolate those items for restudy (Nelson, Dunlosky, Graf, & Narens, 1994). By contrast, if the accuracy of the judgments is poor, they may inappropriately choose to restudy items that will be remembered or fail to choose items that will not be remembered.

One implication of this rationale for training programs is straightforward. If older adults are unable to accurately judge their learning of one item relative to another, they may not benefit (or may even be hurt) by utilizing item-by-item judgments of learning to guide self-regulated study. Fortunately, older adults are not deficient at making these JOLs: Not only is age equivalence the norm in the accuracy of item-by-item JOLs, adults from both age groups can have near-perfect accuracy when monitoring is based on delayed retrieval of the to-be-learned items (Connor et al., 1997; Nelson & Dunlosky, 1991). In particular, consider two ways older students could judge how well they have learned foreign-language translation equivalents (e.g., *Hund*–dog, *Löffel*–spoon, etc.). They may study an item (*Hund*–dog), and then immediately cover the English equivalent (e.g., *Hund*–?) so as to make a JOL for that item. By contrast, they may study the item and then study others. After a minute or so has passed studying other items, they would then go back to the item, cover its English equivalent, and then judge how well the item had been learned.

The first case involves what has been called an immediate JOL because it is made immediately after each item is studied. The accuracy of immediate JOLs is above chance but far from perfect, with gamma correlations between these JOLs and subsequent recall falling between +.30 and +.50. In the case where the judgments are delayed after study, predictive accuracy is typically above +.75 (Connor et al., 1997). Regardless of why delayed JOLs are highly accurate (for alternative hypotheses, see Dunlosky & Nelson, 1997), the results demonstrate that people can be highly accurate at predicting future memory performance. However, even if people are trained to accurately monitor memory, will they utilize this kind of monitoring (e.g., from delayed JOLs) to regulate learning?

Utilization of Monitoring to Regulate Learning

According to the theoretical framework in Fig. 11.1 (see On-Going Study), people will utilize monitoring by allocating more study time to items judged less well-learned than to items judged well-learned. Nelson et al. (1994) provided a test of this prediction by investigating how people select items for restudy. They had younger adults study a list of paired associates and make delayed JOLs as just described. After making JOLs, participants selected which items they wanted to restudy. Consistent with the prediction, younger adults were more likely to select items that they had judged least well-learned than items judged most well-learned. As important, this selection algorithm yielded learning that was statistically equivalent to a group whose restudy was allocated (by a computer) to maximize learning.

Using the procedure developed by Nelson et al. (1994), we investigated whether older adults would utilize the same algorithm to select items for restudy (Dunlosky & Hertzog, 1997). Without any training, the majority of older adults also selected to restudy the items that they had judged least well-learned. Older adults' successful utilization of monitoring to select items for restudy was also independently demonstrated by Baldi (1996), who used a slightly different procedure than the one described here. Thus, when older and younger adults are required to monitor their learning by making delayed JOLs, individuals from both age groups utilize monitoring in a way that supports effective learning.

In contrast to selecting items for restudy, age-related differences have been found in the degree to which monitoring is utilized in other aspects of self-regulated study. Dunlosky and Connor (in press) had older adults and younger adults study a list of paired associates. During each study trial, a given participant paced his or her own study and made a delayed JOL for each item. After all items had been studied and judged, paired-associate recall occurred for a subset of the items. This procedure was repeated multiple times. Both age groups allocated more restudy time to items that had been judged less well-learned than to those that had been judged more well-learned. That is, JOLs made on one trial correlated negatively with self-paced study time on the next trial. However, the magnitude of this correlation was lower for older adults than for younger adults, suggesting that older adults did not use their (highly accurate) monitoring to the same degree as did younger adults. Results from regression analyses suggested that such differences in allocating study time partially mediated age differences in memory performance. Thus, perhaps older adults' learning could be improved if they were trained to utilize monitoring to a greater degree.

Murphy et al. (1987) also found that older adults underutilized self-testing during study. Older and younger adults paced their study in an attempt to master a list of single words. As compared to younger adults, older adults used less study time and recalled fewer words. Further analyses indicated that the younger adults spontaneously monitored memory via self-testing and utilized this information to regulate study, whereas older adults were much less likely to test themselves and hence could not utilize this information to regulate study. More important for training programs, Murphy et al. (1987) instructed another group of older adults to test themselves prior to terminating study. Although age differences still remained in memory performance, older adults instructed to self-test used more study time and recalled more words than did a control group of same-age cohorts. Thus, relatively minimal training may be required for older adults to benefit from self-testing because they utilize this kind of monitoring spontaneously in ways that can improve learning (cf. Dunlosky & Hertzog, 1997).

CONCLUSIONS

Results from the research just described indicate that older adults can accurately monitor their on-going learning, but they may fail to monitor their memory in effective ways, such as by self-testing. Thus, although research is still needed to specify more fully the relations among monitoring, the utilization of monitoring, and age differences in self-regulated learning, a conclusion from the present research is that training older adults to monitor their memory will improve their self-regulated learning. This kind of training may be incorporated into the programs discussed here, and it appears readily applicable to a new training program based on compact disc-interactive (CD-i) technology, which can incorporate a self-regulated, multitrial approach to learning (see Plude & Schwartz, 1996, for a primer on the benefits of using CD-i technology and for research in using this technology in memory training for older adults). Perhaps most impressive, little training may be required to attain improvements in learning because older adults spontaneously utilize the output of monitoring when they are instructed or required to monitor learning (either by having them test themselves or by having them make delayed JOLs). The extent to which these conclusions will generalize to other domains (e.g., learning text material or completing other kinds of cognitive tasks) is an important avenue for future training research.

Teaching older adults to monitor their learning may provide other benefits as well. Self-testing can be used in conjunction with a wide variety of strategies, so it can be trained as a general skill that will complement many other kinds of training (Murphy et al., 1987). And even if an individual fails to use an effective study strategy, mastery may still be attained via the judicial use of monitoring skills in reallocating study to less well-learned items. Finally, training older adults to use monitoring skills may support development of metacognitive knowledge about which strategies yield effective learning (West, 1985), such as those illustrated by the feedback loop in Fig. 11.1.

Basic and applied research is needed to systematically answer many questions relevant to training older adults to monitor memory. When is this kind of training most likely to improve performance, and when will it fail? Will monitoring skills trained in conjunction with one kind of study strategy generalize to other study strategies without extra training? How long will monitoring skills be maintained without extra training sessions? And if such "booster" sessions are required, what kind of schedule of retraining will ensure long-term maintenance (see Landauer & Bjork, 1978)?

Future research will undoubtedly uncover limitations of the approaches outlined here. Even if older adults can be trained to use monitoring effectively, this kind of training may not be a panacea for all situations. In some domains, monitoring alone may fall short of producing gains in learning. This limitation may occur if an individual cannot develop a technique to accurately test memory or comprehension of to-be-learned material. People's JOLs often show far from perfect accuracy even for less complex material (such as in the case of immediate JOLs for paired associates), perhaps because JOLs are partly based on the fluency of item-by-item processing that is not always indicative of subsequent memory performance (Benjamin & Bjork, 1996; Koriat, in press). Our main point here is that training individuals to monitor their learning will provide little benefit when the accuracy of that monitoring is poor (Koriat & Goldsmith, 1996). Accordingly, an important area of research is to continue developing techniques to enhance the accuracy of monitoring across multiple domains.

Monitoring will be less useful under circumstances in which situational constraints (usually task characteristics) make it difficult or impossible for people to regulate study. These situations may occur quite often, such as if not enough time is available to study, if the presentation of material is not self-paced (e.g., during video presentations), and so forth. Other limitations may also be discovered. However, given the promise of training older adults to monitor their learning, such limitations should not stifle researchers from exploring these issues, but instead will pose challenges with regard to developing theory that delineates when training these skills will (vs. will not) improve learning.

In summary, much has been learned about the characteristics that are required for effective memory-training programs for older adults. A variety of training programs have shown at least short-term success at enhancing the memory performance of older adults: Lachman's attributional retraining, Neely and Bäckman's multi-factorial program, Meyer's organizational training, and Scogin and Storandt's self-training program, to name a few. Yet it is also evident that the magnitude of training gains has not been substantial and that much work is needed to develop individually tailored programs that identify a person's specific deficiencies and then target those for training. We have offered a theoretical perspective on self-regulated learning that identifies several loci for new interventions. Our main argument is that interventions focused on training monitoring skills will complement the study strategies that are central to any of the existing training programs. In training these skills, a new emphasis must be placed on the dynamic interplay between monitoring processes and control processes that are critical for effective self-regulated learning.

ACKNOWLEDGMENTS

This research was supported by a grant from the National Institute on Aging (R01-AG13148-01). We thank Robin West for providing valuable comments and discussion about a draft of this chapter.

REFERENCES

Anschutz, L., Camp, C. J., Markley, R. P., & Kramer, J. J. (1987). Remembering mnemonics: A three-year follow-up on the effects of mnemonics training in elderly adults. *Experimental Aging Research, 13*, 141–143.

Baldi, R. (1996). *The effects of self-referent beliefs, memory complaints, and depression on judgments of learning in young and older adults.* Unpublished doctoral dissertation. University of Maryland, College Park.

Baldi, R., & Berry, J. M. (1996). *Memory self-efficacy and memory performance in older adults: Anchoring and choice effects.* Manuscript under review.

Bandura, A. (1989). Regulation of cognitive processes through perceived self-efficacy. *Developmental Psychology, 22*, 729–735.

Benjamin, A. S., & Bjork, R. A. (1996). Retrieval fluency as a metacognitive index. In L. M. Reder (Ed.), *Implicit memory and metacognition* (pp. 309–338). Mahwah, NJ: Lawrence Erlbaum Associates.

Berry, J. M., & West, R. L. (1993). Cognitive self-efficacy in relation to personal mastery and goal setting across the life span. *International Journal of Behavioral Development, 16*, 351–379.

Berry, J. M., West, R. L., & Dennehey, D. M. (1989). Reliability and validity of the memory self-efficacy questionnaire. *Developmental Psychology, 25*, 701–713.

Best, D. L., Hamlett, K. W., & Davis, S. W. (1992). Memory complaint and memory performance in the elderly: The effects of memory-skills training and expectancy change. *Applied Cognitive Psychology, 6,* 405–416.

Blanchard-Fields, F., & Hess, T. M. (Eds.). (1996). *Perspectives on cognitive change in adulthood and aging.* New York: McGraw–Hill.

Borkowski, J. G., Carr, M., Rellinger, E., & Pressley, M. (1990). Self-regulated cognition: Interdependence of metacognition, attributions, and self-esteem. In B. F. Jones & L. Idol (Eds.), *Dimensions of thinking and cognitive instruction* (pp. 53–92). Hillsdale, NJ: Lawrence Erlbaum Associates.

Camp, C. J., Markley, R. P., Kramer, J. J. (1983). Spontaneous use of mnemonics by elderly individuals. *Educational Gerontology, 9*, 57–71.

Camp, C. J., & McKitrick, L. A. (1992). Memory interventions in Alzheimer's-type dementia populations: Methodological and theoretical issues. In R. L. West & J. D. Sinnott (Eds.), *Everyday memory and aging* (pp. 155–172). New York: Springer-Verlag.

Caprio-Prevette, M. D., & Fry, P. S. (1996). Memory enhancement program for community-based older adults: Development and evaluation. *Experimental Aging Research, 22*, 281–303.

Carver, C. S., & Scheier, M. F. (1990). Origins and functions of positive and negative affect: A control-process view. *Psychological Review, 97*, 19–35.

Cavanaugh, J. C. (1996). Memory self-efficacy as a moderator of memory change. In F. Blanchard-Fields & T. M. Hess (Eds.), *Perspectives on cognitive change in adulthood and aging* (pp. 488–507). New York: McGraw-Hill.

Cavanaugh, J. C., & Green, E. E. (1990). I believe, therefore I can: Self-efficacy beliefs in memory aging. In E. A. Lovelace (Ed.), *Aging and cognition: Mental processes, self-awareness and interventions* (pp. 189–230). Amsterdam: North Holland.

Connor, L. T., Dunlosky, J., & Hertzog, C. (1997). Age-related differences in absolute but not relative metamemory accuracy. *Psychology and Aging, 12,* 50–71.

Devolder, P. A., Brigham, M. C., & Pressley, M. (1990). Memory performance awareness in younger and older adults. *Psychology and Aging, 5,* 291–303.

Dunlosky, J., & Connor, L. T. (in press). Age differences in the allocation of study time account for age differences in memory performance. *Memory & Cognition.*

Dunlosky, J., & Hertzog, C. (1997). Older and younger adults use a functionally identical algorithm to select items for restudy during multi-trial learning. *Journal of Gerontology: Psychological Sciences, 52B,* 178–186.

Dunlosky, J., & Nelson, T. O. (1997). Similarity between the cue for judgments of learning (JOLs) and the cue for test is not the primary determinant of JOL accuracy. *Journal of Memory and Language, 36,* 34–49.

Flavell, J. H. (1979). Metacognition and cognitive monitoring: A new area of cognitive-developmental inquiry. *American Psychologist, 34,* 906–911.

Floyd, M., & Scogin, F. (1997). Effects of memory training on subjective memory functioning and mental health of older adults: A meta-analysis. *Psychology and Aging, 12,* 150–161.

Hertzog, C., & Dixon, R. (1994). Metacognitive development in adulthood and old age. In J. Metcalfe & A. P. Shimamura (Eds.). *Metacognition: knowing about knowing* (pp. 227–251). Cambridge, MA: MIT Press.

Hertzog, C., & Dunlosky, J. (1996). The aging of practical memory: an overview. In D. Herrmann, C. McEvoy, C. Hertzog, P. Hertel, & M. K. Johnson (Eds.) *Basic and applied memory research: Theory in context.* (Vol. 1, pp. 337–358). Mahwah, NJ: Lawrence Erlbaum Associates.

Hertzog, C., Hultsch, D. F., & Dixon, R. A. (1989). Evidence for the convergent validity of two self-report metamemory questionnaires. *Developmental Psychology, 25,* 687–700.

Hertzog, C., Saylor, L. L., Fleece, A. M., & Dixon, R. A. (1994). Metamemory and aging: Relations between predicted, actual and perceived memory task performance. *Aging and Cognition, 1,* 203–237.

Hultsch, D. F., Hertzog, C., & Dixon, R. A. (1987). Age differences in metamemory: resolving the inconsistencies. *Canadian Journal of Psychology, 41,* 193-208

Keren, G. (1991). Calibration and probability judgments: Conceptual and methodological issues. *Acta Psychologica, 77,* 217–273.

Kliegl, R., Smith, J., & Baltes, P. B. (1989). Testing-the-limits and the study of adult age differences in cognitive plasticity of a mnemonic skill. *Developmental Psychology, 25,* 247–256.

Koriat, A. (in press). Monitoring one's own knowledge during study: A cue-utilization approach to judgments of learning. *Journal of Experimental Psychology: General.*

Koriat, A., & Goldsmith, M. (1996). Monitoring and control process in the strategic regulation of memory accuracy. *Psychological Review, 103,* 409–517.

Kotler-Cope, S., & Camp, C. J. (1990). Memory interventions in aging populations. In E. A. Lovelace (Ed.), *Aging and cognition: Mental processes, self-awareness and interventions* (pp. 231–261). Amsterdam: North Holland.

Lachman, M. E. (1986). Locus of control in aging research: A case for multidimensional and domain-specific assessment. *Psychology and Aging, 1,* 34–40.

Lachman, M. E. (1991). Perceived control over memory aging: Developmental and intervention perspectives. *Journal of Social Issues, 47,* 159–175.

Lachman, M. E., Weaver, S. L., Bandura, M., Elliott, E., & Lewkowicz, C. J. (1992). Improving memory and control beliefs through cognitive restructuring and self-generated strategies. *Journal of Gerontology: Psychological Sciences, 47,* 293–299.

Landauer, T. K., & Bjork, R. A. (1978). Optimum rehearsal patterns and name learning. In M. M. Gruneberg, P. E. Morris, & R. N. Sykes (Eds.), *Practical aspects of memory* (pp. 625–632). London: Academic Press.

Mazzoni, G., & Cornoldi, C. (1993). Strategies in study time allocation: Why is study time sometimes not effective? *Journal of Experimental Psychology: General, 122*, 47–60.

McDonald-Miszczak, L., Hertzog, C., & Hultsch, D. F. (1995). Stability and accuracy of metamemory in adulthood and aging. *Psychology and Aging, 10*, 533–564.

McEvoy, C. L., & Moon, J. R. (1988). Assessment and treatment of everyday memory problems in the elderly. In M. M. Gruneber, P. M. Morris, & R. N. Sykes (Eds.), *Practical aspects of memory: Current research and issues* (Vol. 2, pp. 155–160). Chichester, England: Wiley.

Metcalfe, J., Schwartz, B. L., & Joaquim, S. G. (1993). The cue-familiarity heuristic in metacognition. *Journal of Experimental Psychology: Learning, Memory, and Cognition, 19*, 851–861.

Metcalfe, J., &, Shimamura, A. P. (Eds.). (1994). *Metacognition: Knowing about knowing.* Cambridge, MA: MIT Press.

Meyer, B. J. F., Young, C. J., & Bartlett, B. J. (1989). *Memory improved: Reading and memory enhancement across the lifespan through strategic text structures.* Hillsdale, NJ: Lawrence Erlbaum Associates.

Miner, A. C., & Reder, M. L. (1994). A new look at feeling of knowing: Its metacognitive role in regulating question answering. In J. Metcalfe & A. P. Shimamura (Eds.), *Metacognition: Knowing about knowing* (pp. 47–70). Cambridge MA: MIT Press.

Murphy, M. D., Sanders. R. E., Gabriesheski, A. S., & Schmitt, F. A. (1981). Metamemory in the aged. *Journal of Gerontology, 36*, 185–193.

Murphy, M. D., Schmitt, F. A., Caruso, M. J., & Sanders, R. E. (1987). Metamemory in older adults: The role of monitoring in serial recall. *Psychology and Aging, 2*, 331–339.

Neely, A. S., & Bäckman, L. (1993). Long-term maintenance of gains from memory training in older adults: Two 3 ½-year follow-up studies. *Journal of Gerontology: Psychological Sciences, 48*, 233–237.

Nelson, T. O., & Dunlosky, J. (1991). When people's judgments of learning (JOLs) are extremely accurate at predicting subsequent recall: The "delayed-JOL effect." *Psychological Science, 2*, 267–270.

Nelson, T. O., Dunlosky, J., Graf, A., & Narens, L. (1994). Utilization of metacognitive judgments in the allocation of study during multitrial learning. *Psychological Science, 5*, 207–213.

Nelson, T. O., & Leonesio, R. J. (1988). Allocation of self-paced study time and the "labor-in-vain effect." *Journal of Experimental Psychology: Learning, Memory, and Cognition, 14*, 676–686.

Nelson, T. O., & Narens, L. (1990). Metamemory: A theoretical framework and new findings. In G. H. Bower (Ed.), *The psychology of learning and motivation* (Vol. 26, pp. 125–173). New York: Academic Press.

Park, D. C., Smith, A. D., & Cavanaugh, J. C. (1990). Metamemories of memory researchers. *Memory & Cognition, 18*, 321–327.

Plude, D. J., & Schwartz, L. K. (1996). Compact disc–interactive memory training with the elderly. *Educational Gerontology, 22*, 507–521.

Pressley, M., & El-Dinary, P. B. (1992). Memory strategy instruction that promotes good information processing. In D. J. Herrmann, H. Weingartner, A. Serleman, & C. McEvoy (Eds.), *Memory improvement: Implications for memory theory* (pp. 79–100). New York: Springer-Verlag.

Reder, L. M., & Ritter, F. E. (1992). What determines initial feeling of knowing? Familiarity with question terms, not with the answer. *Journal of Experimental Psychology: Learning, Memory, and Cognition, 18*, 435–451.

Rellinger, E., Borkowski, J. G., Turner, L. A., & Hale, C. A. (1995). Perceived task difficulty and intelligence: Determinants of strategy use and recall. *Intelligence, 20*, 125–143.

Roush, W. (1996). Live long and prosper? *Science, 273*, 42–46.

Schneider, W., & Pressley, M. (1989). *Memory development between 2 and 20*. New York: Springer.

Scogin, F., & Bienias, J. L. (1988). A three-year follow-up of older adult participants in a memory-skills training program. *Psychology and Aging, 3*, 334–337.

Scogin, F., Storandt, M., & Lott, L. (1985). Memory-skills training, memory complaints, and depression in older adults. *Journal of Gerontology, 40*, 562–568.

Sinnott, J. D. (Ed.). (1994). *Interdisciplinary handbook of adult lifespan learning*. Westport, CT: Greenwood Press.

Stigsdotter, A., & Bäckman, L. (1989). Multifactorial memory training with older adults: How to foster maintenance of improved performance. *Gerontology, 35*, 260–267.

Storandt, M. (1992). Memory–skills training for older adults. In J. J. Berman & T. B. Sonderegger (Eds.), *Psychology and aging: Nebraska Symposium on Motivation 1991* (pp. 38–62). Lincoln: University of Nebraska Press.

Treat, N. J., Poon, L. W., Fozard, J. L., & Popkin, S. J. (1978). Toward applying cognitive skill training to memory problems. *Experimental Aging Research, 4*, 305–319.

Verhaeghen, P., Marcoen, A., & Goossens, L. (1992). Improving memory performance in the aged through mnemonic training: A meta-analytic study. *Psychology and Aging, 7*, 242–251.

Verhaeghen, P., Van Ranst, N., Marcoen, A. (1993). Memory training in the community: Evaluations by participants and effects on metamemory. *Educational Gerontology, 19*, 525–534.

Welch, D. C., & West, R. L. (1995). Self-efficacy and mastery: Its application to issues of environmental control, cognition, and aging. *Developmental Review, 15*, 150–171.

West, R. L. (1985). *Memory fitness over 49*. Gainsville, FL: Triad Publishing.

West, R. L. (1989). Planning practical memory training for the aged. In L. W. Poon, D. C. Rubin, & B. A. Wilson, (Eds.), *Everyday cognition in adulthood and late life* (pp. 573–597). New York: Cambridge University Press.

West, R. L. (1995). Compensatory strategies for age associated memory impairment. In B. A. Wilson & F. Watts (Eds.), *Handbook of memory disorders*. London: Wiley.

West, R. L., Bellott, B. P., Bramblett, J. P., & Welch, D. C. (1993, November). *Memory training and memory self-efficacy interventions*. Paper presented at the Gerontological Society of America, New Orleans.

West, R. L., & Berry, J. M. (1994). Age declines in memory self-efficacy: General or limited to particular tasks and measures? In J. D. Sinnott (Ed.), *Interdisciplinary handbook of adult lifespan learning* (pp. 426–445). Westport, CT: Greenwood Press.

West, R. L., & Tomer, A. (1989). Everyday memory problems of healthy older adults: Characteristics of successful intervention. In G. C. Gilmore, P. J. Whitehouse, & M. L. Wykle (Eds.), *Memory, aging, and dementia: Theory, assessment and treatment* (pp. 74–98). New York: Springer.

Willis, S. L. (1987). Cognitive training and everyday competence. In K. W. Schaie (Ed.), *Annual review of gerontology and geriatrics* (Vol. 7, pp. 159–188). New York: Springer-Verlag.

Yesavage, J. A. (1984). Relaxation and memory training in 39 elderly patients. *American Journal of Psychiatry, 141*, 778–781.

Yesavage, J. A., & Rose, T. L. (1983). Concentration and mnemonic training in elderly subjects with memory complaints: A study of combined therapy and order effects. *Psychiatry Research, 9,* 157–167.

Yesavage, J. A., & Rose, T. L. (1984). Semantic elaboration and the method of loci: A new trip for older learners. *Experimental Aging Research, 10,* 155–159.

Zarit, S. H., Cole, K. D., & Guider, R. L. (1981). Memory training strategies and subjective complaints of memory in the aged. *The Gerontologist, 21,* 158–164.

Zarit, S. H., Gallagher, D., & Kramer, N. (1981). Memory training in the community aged: Effects on depression, memory complaint, and memory performance. *Educational Gerontology, 6,* 11–27.

12

Studying as Self-Regulated Learning

Philip H. Winne and Allyson F. Hadwin
Simon Fraser University

Asked what they are doing as they engage in school- or university-related activities, students might say, "I'm working on my project," "I'm doing homework," or, commonly, "I'm studying." Charting the boundaries of studying is a fuzzy task. Colloquially, the range of activities it encompasses is nearly synonymous with all the activities that probabilistically lead to "a relatively permanent change in cognitive structure."[1] However, several features may distinguish studying from the subsuming category of learning activities. In particular, studying:

1. Rarely includes direct or frequent intervention by a teacher.
2. Is often a solo activity, although peer mediation is also common.
3. Often originates with a general goal set by a teacher that the student subsequently interprets at the studying session's outset and refines in a recursive way as studying unfolds.
4. Quite often involves searching in and synthesizing information from multiple sources, for example; a text book, notes taken in a class or borrowed from a friend, a volume of an encyclopedia, a video or TV show, or online databases (e.g., PsychLit).
5. Quite often occurs in settings where the student can engineer the studying environment to satisfy personal preferences (e.g., studying with or without the radio turned on, automatic calls that check email, or stimulants supplied by tea or coffee).

---

[1] We use the phrase *cognitive structure* rather than the term *knowledge* because we include some topics that are not typically included in the category labeled by the term knowledge. In particular, these topics include propositions about motivation (e.g., an efficacy expectation about competence to enact a study tactic under current conditions) and about affect (e.g., positive feelings about applying a study tactic).

6. Almost always produces observable traces (Winne, 1982) of cognitive processing in forms such as notes in a notebook or in the margins of a textbook's
   pages, outlines, summaries, self-generated questions, diagrams, records of
   attempts to solve problems, and especially highlighted (or underlined) text.

Studying has been a topic of research for nearly a century. The dominant
form of research has been to compare unknown "normal" studying activities
to a specific study tactic—underlining, outlining, making notes as a spatial
display of nodes and labeled links (concept maps or webs), generating
questions, and so forth—that is described in terms of observable traces or
what students were trained to use. Less common is research in which
students are observed or trained to use a set of study tactics that are
coordinated into a strategy, such as the 6-step method of previewing,
questioning, reading, reflecting, reciting, and reviewing (PQ4R; Thomas &
Robinson, 1972). Reynolds and Shirey (1988) judged that both kinds of
research on studying skills, tactics, and strategies overshadow work investigating more basic and generative issues about how to model cognitive
processing that underlies studying. Hence, too little is known about cognitive processes that are the proximal causes of whatever effects may be
observed when students enact specific study tactics or strategies. We concur.

PROSPECTUS FOR THE CHAPTER

The six features just enumerated that distinguish studying from learning in
general describe circumstances that essentially compel students to engage
in complex bundles of goal-directed cognitive and motivational processes
that "get studying done." We view these bundles as instances of metacognitively powered self-regulated learning (Winne, 1995a, 1995b, 1996).

As a first step toward examining studying through metacognitive lenses,
we present a general typology that delineates facets of academic tasks in
general, including studying tasks. Then, we use this typology to characterize
four distinguishable but recursively linked stages of studying: task definition,
goal setting and planning, enacting study tactics and strategies, and metacognitively adapting studying. Next, we develop connections between our
typology for studying and models of metacognitive monitoring, metacognitive control, and self-regulated learning (Butler & Winne, 1995; Winne,
1995a, 1995b). With this backdrop, we then survey select research that
highlights metacognitive activities in each of the four stages of studying.
Finally, we summarize our model of studying and offer suggestions for next
steps in research on studying as a complex, self-regulated learning event.

THE COPES MODEL OF STUDY TASKS

Studying tasks vary enormously. We use a 5-facet typology as a schema to characterize instances of studying in terms of common dimensions: conditions, operations, products, evaluations (of products), and standards (for products). The typology, presented in Table 12.1, is referred to by the first-letter acronym COPES because it identifies facets of tasks that a student copes with in studying and learning (see Winne, 1997; Winne & Marx, 1989). In Table 12.1, we offer four instances of COPES facets that correspond to each of four stages of studying described next.

Four Stages of Studying

We theorize that a complete model of studying has four basic stages: *task definition, goal setting and planning, enactment,* and *adaptation* (see also Simpson & Nist, 1984). In the task definition stage, the student generates a perception about what the studying task is, and what constraints and resources are in place. Based on this perception or definition of the task, at Stage 2, the student selects or generates idiosyncratic goal(s) and constructs a plan for addressing that study task. In the enactment stage, the plan of study tactics that was created in Stage 2 is carried out. In Stage 4, based on the overall experience of this studying event at the first three stages, the student makes changes to cognitive structure that will affect future studying tasks. This forward planning changes knowledge, skills, beliefs, dispositions, and motivational factors that the student predicts will play important roles in future studying tasks.

All four stages of studying have the same general cognitive architecture (see Fig. 12.1). A collage of environmental factors and cognitive information constitutes the *conditions* within which cognitive activities occur. Single cognitive *operations* and coordinated sets of them (tactics, strategies) create internal *products* by transforming conditions (Winne, 1989). For example, previously inert information in long-term memory may be stimulated and made available to working memory, information that is not organized may be assembled into a structured form, information represented in one medium (e.g., words) may be translated into another medium (e.g., algebraic symbols, an image), an inference or an attribution may be generated, and so forth. Operations also can create external *performance*, behaviors the student enacts that others can observe. Our four stages of studying are distinguished by the product created at each stage.

TABLE 12.1

Facets in the COPES Typology of Tasks

Facet	Definition	Stage 1: Task Definition	Stage 2: Goals & Plan	Stage 3: Enactment	Stage 4: Adaptation
Conditions	conditions that affect how the task will be engaged, including conditional knowledge (IFs in IF–THEN rules that filter which operations are enacted)	• interest • goal orientation • learning styles • time constraints • available resources • knowledge of tactics • task knowledge • subject matter expertise	• Stage 1 conditions + • Stage 1 products	• Stage 1 & 2 conditions + • Stage 2 products	• Stage 1–3 conditions + • Stage 1–3 products
Operations	cognitive processes, tactics, and strategies the student engages to address the task	• searching • monitoring (including tactics such as self-questioning, charting similarities and differences) • assembling (including tactics such as elaborating, integrating) • rehearsing (including tactics such as copying notes, rereading) • translating (including tactics such as making diagrams, 1st-letter mnemonics)			
Products	information created by operations	• Perception of what the task is, its COPES	• standards for the task as in Stage 1 or reframed in light of individual differences (e.g., learning style) • plan for coordinating study tactics • standards for enacting tactics (e.g., speed)	• traces of study tactics (e.g., margin notes, answers to questions, concept map) • new/reorganized subject matter knowledge	Updates to: • COPES that distinguish tasks • motivation, beliefs • conditional knowledge and study tactics • standards for judging qualities of tactics
Evaluations	feedback about products, either generated internally by the student or provided by external source(s)	Judgments about: • task understanding • COPES of the task Comparisons with other sources of information	Judgments about: • complexity/difficulty • incentive of goal • ability to carry out plan • effort required	Judgments about: • learning (calibration) • utility of tactics • efficacy • attributions	Judgments about: • "distance" between prior version and adaptation • predicted effects of adaptation Other evaluations must await future tasks
Standards	criteria against which products are monitored	• grading criteria • past performance	• Stage 1 standards & products • effort/utility thresholds • motivation orientation	• Stage 2 standards and products + object-level standards & meta-level standards	• Stage 1–3 standards and products

We adopt the common assumption that studying, like other forms of behavior, is a goal directed activity (Winne, 1995a). In our model of studying, goals are represented as a multivariate profile of standards. Standards characterize ideal, optimal, or satisficing states. For example, a student may hold standards to study a chapter (a) in 30 minutes, (b) so that a judgment of comprehension about the whole chapter is high, while (c) allowing that judgments of learning for specific bits of information are low (e.g., see Schraw, 1994).

We theorize that products take two forms. Cognitively, products are represented as a multivariate profile of attributes. For example, at the stage of defining the studying task, a student with a performance motivational orientation might perceive an assignment to study a chapter as a task that involves reading (a) without deep processing while (b) marking (highlighting) definitions and principles for future review. We hypothesize that, if students were asked to describe what they perceived or understood about informational products they create within a stage of studying, they would name such attributes and report levels for them. Externally, products can be manifested as behavior or performance.

When students monitor a product's profile of attributes against the profile of standards, cognitive evaluations are generated that mark whether an attribute is on target, how much off target an attribute is, and whether there is a discrepancy between items listed as standards and attributes of a product. External evaluations also can be created by performance when, for instance, a statistics package for the social sciences (SPSS) program has an error or a friend complains that a summary is off target. If the student acts on evaluations, this is control by which elements in the collage of cognitive conditions may be altered; standards may be adjusted, added, or abandoned; and, operations of new kinds may be carried out.

Our 4-stage model, like models of self-regulated learning (Butler & Winne, 1995; Nelson & Narens, 1994; Winne, 1995a, 1995b, 1996), is a recursive, weakly sequenced system. In recursive systems, products of earlier stages (or steps within a stage) update conditions on which operations work during the next cycle of activity. For example, the product of Stage 1, a definition of the studying task, updates cognitive conditions that establish the information and resources used in Stage 2, generating goals and plans. Although studying generally proceeds from Stage 1 to 2 to 3 to 4, stages are weakly sequenced and do not necessarily unfold in order. Some studying tasks may be so familiar that defining the

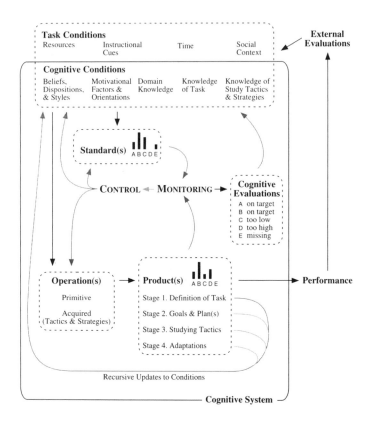

FIG. 12.1. The COPES model of metacognitive monitoring and control in four stages of studying.

task (Stage 1) is virtually skipped. Students who practice means–ends analysis will oscillate frequently between generating goals and plans (Stage 2) and enacting study tactics (Stage 3). Making adaptations can occur at practically any point.

Stage 1: Task Definition.   In this stage, the student develops a perception about features of the task, charting the task as a "study space." As we noted earlier, most study tasks are indeterminate with respect to one or several COPES facets. Thus, the student must make inferences about the nature of these facets. An important element in the product of this stage is the student's perception of a goal for the task. A goal is a set of standards by which the task can be judged. The student's perceived goal may be the same goal that the teacher or the text set. Or, it may be a goal that the student frames. Grade school students' questions about whether the assigned summary of a science chapter will be handed in or whether they can collaborate on book reports are evidence of inferences about standards by which the task will be judged. In the next stage of studying, the student may include these standards in conditional knowledge that sets new goals, for example, to create neat work or to avoid behavior that will result in points deducted for "cheating."

Latitude for students to develop perceptions about study tasks also characterizes interventions in experimental research. When students study a text, typical instructions might be: "Read the material and, if you have time, review. Don't try to memorize every word, but be prepared for a test in 20 minutes." Although students are explicitly instructed not to use tactics that create verbatim recall of the entire text (e.g., cumulative rehearsal), they may interpret the instructions as allowing main ideas to be rehearsed. They also are free to infer, for example, whether the text will be available during recall (a condition; probably not), whether they are allowed to underline or make marginal notes (modest sets of cognitive operations that comprise study tactics; if they have a pencil in a pocket, the inference is a 50–50 guess), and what kind of test will be administered (a standard; for veterans in subject pools, perhaps inferred to be free recall rather than multiple choice). Individual differences between students and intraindividual differences within a student over time practically ensure that there will be variance in perceptions about what a "given" study task is.

Stage 2: Goal Setting and Planning. In Stage 2 of studying, students may re-frame the goal(s) that were products of Stage 1 if the student's personal standards differ from those that were first perceived for the task. For example, students with a performance motivational orientation that views tasks as just jobs to complete may judge that the goal they understood their teacher set is at too high a level or requires too much effort. Therefore, they adjust or alter standards for summarizing the science chapter to levels where "just getting by" is adequate. In light of this re-framed goal, the student now builds a plan to approach it. This student will probably plan simplistic tactics, such as paraphrasing headings and monitoring surface features of typography to insure that every bold phrase and every scientist's name (standards) is reproduced in the finished product.

A student participating in the fictitious experiment we introduced in Stage 1 may set a goal to preserve time for deeply processing (a standard) sections of the text that are novel or complex (conditions). The plan for deep processing is to select that material (operation) and use a concept

mapping tactic (operation) that creates detailed views of the organization
and elaborations (standards) described in the text. An enabling plan supports the student's first intention. It involves developing a general representation of the text's structure (product) using a tactic that can be applied
quickly (a standard). That tactic is reading (operation) headings plus each
paragraph's first and last sentences (task conditions).

Stage 3: Enacting Study Tactics and Strategies.   Stage 3 of studying is enacting study tactics and strategies that the student has planned in
Stage 2. Study tactics, such as making summaries, using first-letter mnemonics, underlining, and reviewing by re-reading headings are composites
of operations by which the student addresses whatever task(s) the student
perceived to be focal. As these operations are applied, evaluations (feedback) are generated internally. For instance, the grade school student may
falter in paraphrasing the textbook's outline. Perhaps the student lacks
vocabulary for expressing that content or has only shallow understanding
about concepts in the subject matter domain. Monitoring this deficiency,
the student may generate an attribution (evaluation): The task may be
judged too difficult; or, if the student holds an entity belief about ability
(condition), the student may attribute the deficiency to low ability.

For the university student participating in the experiment we introduced
earlier, an unexpected announcement that "Only one quarter of the study
period has lapsed" updates conditions. The student may monitor that,
because deep processing is now in progress at the middle region of the text,
too little time was spent developing a representation of the text's macrostructure (evaluation). There is spare time to add to the initial plan
additional study tactics that consolidate the macrostructure and elaborate
it with some details.

In this stage of studying, monitoring the products of study tactics may
result in dynamically sensitive changes to the plan for studying. Our university student activated new study tactics not previously part of the plan
generated in Stage 2 to take advantage of the situation as it had unfolded.
In general, these kinds of instantaneous adaptations to the changing land-
scape of the task serve to repair gaps or errors in the student's evolving
domain knowledge. An alternative adaptation in Stage 3 is that, if the
student judges that there are no study tactics available to achieve goals, the
student may quit the task.

Stage 4: Metacognitively Adapting Studying.   In Stage 4, the student inspects products created in preceding stages, monitoring them relative

to metaknowledge that characterizes standards for those events. Monitoring at this stage is not about fine-tuning the process within just Stage 1 or 2 or 3. Rather, decisions made in Stage 4 take one of two forms. In one form, they address how activities coordinate across several stages of studying. Acting on these decisions results in large scale adjustments to the student's understandings about the task, goals, plans, and tactical engagement. The second form of adaptive decision making reaches beyond the boundaries of the present studying task to change the conditions for studying in the future. Acting on these latter decisions results in relatively permanent changes to cognitive conditions that will be in force for future studying tasks. A change like this might reshape motivational orientation from task-based to mastery-based. Or, the student may lower personal standards for success. Alternatively, by adding constraints to the conditional knowledge that triggers a tactic, the student may specialize the tactic's use for the future.

When students make deliberate changes to studying "on the fly," at any of the four stages of studying, they are engaging in metacognition. We now turn our focus to this topic.

METACOGNITION IN STUDYING

We propose that each stage of studying should be considered in terms of two main factors. The first factor is the student's expertise in the subject matter domain. Students' subject matter expertise reduces the need to allocate substantial cognitive resources to studying because domain knowledge itself is sufficient to make progress or achieve success (Schneider, 1993). For example, Körkel (1987; cited in Schneider, 1993) found that students' metacognitive knowledge about generic cognitive tactics for studying text combined linearly with the extent of domain knowledge in accounting for amount recalled. Domain novices (in soccer) with more metacognitive knowledge about generic studying tactics recalled more than novices with less metacognitive knowledge. The same benefit of metacognitive knowledge was observed among domain experts. Experts with less knowledge about cognitive tactics recalled less about what they had studied than experts with more knowledge of study tactics. Thus, when experts study material in their domain, although metacognition may be less frequent because it is less necessary (McKoon & Ratcliff, 1992; see also Wyatt, Pressley, El-Dinary, Stein, Evans, & Brown, 1993), metacognition can still benefit experts' studying.

The second factor to be considered in modeling studying is the degree to which the student is metacognitively active. Models of metacognition (Nelson & Narens, 1990, 1994) distinguish two "levels" of information—the object-level and the meta-level—and two operations—monitoring and control. In our 4-stage model of studying, *object-level information* corresponds to the products of cognitive operations that are created in each stage of studying: a definition of the task, goals and plans, tactics and strategies, and adaptations. *Meta-level information* in our model has two elements. Metastandards describe object-level conditions, operations, products, and standards. They constitute the student's model of studying and provide the basis for metacognitively monitoring studying. The second element of meta-level information consists of cognitive operations that change object-level elements. This is metacognitive control.

Metacognitive Monitoring

Metacognitive monitoring is a cognitive operation that has two inputs and creates one product. One input is an object-level multivariate profile of attributes for a product of studying. The second input is a meta-level multivariate profile of attributes that constitutes a standard for that product. The product that metacognitive monitoring creates is a third multivariate profile of attributes, one that records discrepancies between the object-level information and the meta-level information. In our COPES typology, this cognitively generated product is an evaluation that serves as feedback.

For example, suppose a student is in Stage 3 of studying, enacting a study tactic. The tactic is mapping the correspondence between features of a principle that has been presented in a text and an example that the student is now studying (e.g., Walczyk & Hall, 1989). This is a monitoring tactic. It compares attributes that describe two forms of domain information, the principle and the example. The product this monitoring generates is a list of matches and non-matches. This is non-metacognitive monitoring. The standards that monitoring uses are neither a meta-level model of a principle nor a description of how to apply the study tactic.

However, suppose the student has a meta-level model that describes general standards for using study tactics. For a student who holds the epistemological view (cognitive condition) that learning should be quick and effortless (Schommer, 1994), three meta-level standards for studying would be: (a) time spent should be minimal, (b) effort (ease of learning judgments, Nelson & Narens, 1990; depth of search; see Winne, 1997) required to apply a study tactic should be minimal, and (c) the judgment of learning (Nelson & Narens, 1990) that follows using a study tactic should be high. Monitoring other attributes that describe studying, such as actual time taken, effort spent, and strength of the judgment of learning contrasts this profile of meta-level standards to attributes that describe the product created by using the tactic. This is metacognitive monitoring. The product it creates is a profile of differences that describes how closely the study tactic as enacted matches meta-level standards for using study tactics in general.

Metacognitive Control and Self-Regulated Studying

Metacognitive control changes the task space at the object-level. The discrepancies created by metacognitive monitoring can be modeled as IFs in an IF–THEN (condition–action) rule. The THEN component of these rules is a cognitive operation (or a set of operations, a production system), such as a study tactic, that changes object-level information in the task space.

Suppose the student with the epistemological stance that learning should be quick and effortless monitors that, although time and effort are within tolerance of the meta-level standards, the judgment of learning is weak relative to the meta-level standard. This profile of attributes may trigger a 2-step production system:

1. IF time and effort spent are on target and
   IF judgment of learning is below standard,
   THEN attribute the negative difference to high task difficulty.
2. IF task difficulty is high,
   THEN quit the task.

This is self-regulated studying, task engagement in which students adapt2 their approach to studying to reduce discrepancies revealed by metacognitive monitoring. Our example illustrates a form of self-regulation that is almost surely academically counterproductive (Winne, 1995a) because, based on idiosyncratically rational criteria (Anderson, 1991), it leads the student to quit the task for the "wrong" reasons. In parallel to negative effects of subject matter misconceptions (Pintrich, Marx, & Boyle, 1993) on learning in general, meta-level misconceptions (e.g., the double-edged sword; see Covington, 1992) can also interfere with studying.

Forms of Metacognitive Control. We suggest a distinction between

---

[2]On rational grounds (Anderson, 1991; see also Winne, 1995a), adaptation can include (a) maintaining forms of cognition that are presently being applied rather than changing them, and (b) quitting the task.

two forms of metacognitive control that exercises self-regulation, toggling and editing. With toggling, the student turns studying tactics or other cognitive operations on and off. Toggling immediately changes the task space by shaping the mix of operations carried out in a stage of studying.

With the second form of metacognitive control, editing, the student does more than just toggle operations on and off. In editing, changes are made to object-level cognitive conditions and study tactics. If changes are extended to meta-level standards for metacognitive monitoring, the student engages in mindful abstraction (Salomon & Perkins, 1989). Following Rumelhart and Norman (1978), we suggest that three kinds of changes can be made by editing:

1. Accreting: adding or subtracting (specializing or generalizing) (a) propositions in conditional knowledge that trigger study tactics, (b) component operations that enact study tactics, and (c) propositions that constitute standards for metacognitive monitoring.
2. Tuning: adjusting weights and thresholds that govern how propositions in conditional knowledge articulate in metacognitive monitoring; or, changing the sequence for performing operations in a study tactic.
3. Restructuring: substantially reconstituting conditional knowledge and significantly changing the mix of operations that make up studying tactics, including inventing new components.

Although toggling and all three of kinds of editing can be topics of explicit deliberation, very extended practice plus evaluations can make them automatic, pushing features of their use beneath reportable levels of attention (McKoon & Ratcliff, 1992). When this state is achieved, previously separate metacognitive activities have become composed as one smoothly running unit, and the student studies on self-regulated "auto-pilot." We note explicitly that the student's self-regulation may be judged by others' standards as deficient. Like other cognition, metacognitive aspects of studying are rationally adaptive (Anderson, 1991) in relation to criteria the individual adopts rather than criteria that others may hold "for" a student.

Summary

We model studying as an activity that generally follows a 4-stage sequence. First, the student forms a perception of what the task is. Goals and plans are then created, followed by enacting study tactics that the student predicts can achieve those goals. As operations are performed in each of these stages, evaluations are generated that the student may metacognitively monitor. Metacognitive monitoring also can occur at the end of a study session.

When a student metacognitively examines studying, metacognitive control can be exercised to toggle study tactics on and off, or editing may be done to adapt the conditions, operations, or standards in cognitive structure that describe studying. Toggling and editing are forms of self-regulated studying, but not all forms of self-regulation are productive (Winne, 1995a, 1997).

METACOGNITION IN STUDYING

A complete view of metacognitive engagement in studying at all four stages of studying encompasses several large classes of variables, as identified in Fig. 12.1. If the number and scope of these variables were not enough to make models of studying inherently complicated, our modeling of studying as a recursive event will. Although such models need not be chaotic, they can quickly explode in complexity.

Conditions in the external environment, including opportunities to receive external evaluations (Kluger & DeNisi, 1996), have been widely investigated in descriptive studies (e.g., questionnaire studies) and experiments. Conditions in the cognitive system, including feedback generated internally (see Butler & Winne, 1995) and variables that we loosely categorized as capacity or capability, are individual differences in cognitive structure. These also shape or, in the case of study tactics, are engines of studying and metacognition during studying.

Students' Definitions of Studying Tasks

A few studies investigate what students perceive about studying tasks. That researchers and students can differ in their respective perceptions is illustrated in a study by Cordón and Day (1996). They observed that students do use reading comprehension tactics while taking standardized readings tests, a possibility that some researchers had ruled out. Little research documents correspondences between how students study at home, in study halls, or in their dorms versus how they report or have been observed to study in research settings. Because conditions within each stage of studying can vary widely as a function of differences in studying environments, it would be prudent to generalize cautiously from the research we report.

Some individual differences that color perceptions of studying tasks may be global and quite unresponsive to task conditions. Schommer (1994) reviewed research on learner's systems of epistemological "beliefs about the nature of knowledge and learning ... [that] are likely to affect reasoning, learning, and decision making" (p. 293). Her model describes five basic dimensions of such systems: source (handed down from authority vs. personally reasoned out), certainty (fixed vs. subject to revision), organization of knowledge (simple and compartmentalized vs. interwoven), control (predetermined vs. self-guided), and speed of learning (p. 301). These beliefs establish cognitive conditions that may lead students to adopt perceptions of tasks that pervade studying.

In one study (Schommer, 1990), undergraduates studied controversial texts that were missing a concluding paragraph on the resolution of the controversy, and then wrote a concluding paragraph. Qualities of their conclusions were predicted by epistemological beliefs. Undergraduates with stronger beliefs in quick learning tended to oversimplify the controversy. Those holding stronger beliefs in the certainty of knowledge were less likely to acknowledge that issues they had studied were indeterminate.

In another study (Schommer, Crouse, & Rhodes, 1992), undergraduates studied a text about statistics and were told to prepare for a multiple-choice test that contained items requiring both recognition and reasoning. After reading, but before the test, students estimated confidence in their understanding. Students' belief in simple-compartmentalized knowledge correlated negatively with learning but positively with overconfidence (relative to actual levels of performance). Students who held stronger beliefs in quick learning were more likely to report using shallow cognitive tactics for studying. A path analysis showed both direct and indirect effects on learning of the epistemological belief in simple knowledge.

Other studies suggest that not all perceptions of studying are inflexible. For example, Van Meter, Yokio, and Pressley (1994) interviewed college students about taking notes in lectures and how the students used notes to study subsequently. We report only a few illustrative findings. In general, these students perceived that forms of notetaking must adapt to task conditions, such as variations in lecturers' delivery speed and organization, and to cognitive conditions, such as their domain knowledge. Knowledge of notetaking tasks also was found. Notes record particular types of information, for example, material that is redundant with the text or that the professor stresses, but notes do not include information introduced by guest lecturers or in films. The students also were aware that the extent to which notes vary on a continuum from verbatim to paraphrase depends on how detailed the content is and their familiarity with the domain. Overall, Van Meter et al.'s findings suggest that these mature students have elaborate schemata for notetaking. Some slots in their schemata describe interactions among external task conditions and internal cognitive conditions.

It seems a logical necessity that metacognitive monitoring is engaged when a task is ambiguous. Because domain knowledge cannot be relied on to guide a definition of the task in this case, the student must infer features of the task before engaging with it. Making such inferences involves a meta-level model (standard). A study by Wong, Wong, and LeMare (1982) illustrates this hypothesis in the context of a reading comprehension task. Some students were given paragraphs to read and "think about what the story is about." Other students received a text including pre-paragraph questions and were told those questions illustrated kinds of questions they would be asked after the study period. Pre-paragraph questions provide standards for monitoring two products: comprehension of each paragraph and perceptions about the reading comprehension task, namely, that comprehension meant learning only a subset of the information rather than all of it. Not surprisingly, students who received this explicit guidance performed better on comprehension and recall tests than students who did not receive pre-questions. Students who studied texts without pre-questions expressed frustration. They complained that there "was too much too learn." Their meta-level model of reading led them to infer they should learn everything. That standard did not align with the task. Not only did they perform less well, they also experienced emotional distress.

Study tasks may be ambiguous because they are not familiar to students. We know of no research that explicitly links familiarity to metacognition in studying. There is indirect evidence, however, that students do engage metacognitively in forming perceptions about learning tasks. For example, Winne and Marx (1982) interviewed elementary school students about what they perceived their teacher wanted them to do after the teacher had issued an instructional cue in a lesson. Their descriptions indicated that students do judge the familiarity of brief instructional episodes and, on that basis, the students exercised metacognitive control over how they engaged in classroom activities. Another illustration is provided by Briggs' (1990) investigation of the questions students asked when assigned a simple letter-copying task using an unfamiliar word processing system. Only students with considerable experience in word processing asked questions, presumably products of metacognitive monitoring, that were relevant to the task. Briggs concluded that many students lacked appropriate standards against which to metacognitively monitor what the task was and, thus, were unable to frame useful questions about the task.

In instances where tasks are ambiguous, it seems safe to hypothesize students will set their own goals and build plans on that basis. As our example of the grade school student suggested, students also may reframe goals that are explicit and clear before generating a plan for studying. Goal setting and plan building is our next topic.

Setting Goals and Devising Plans

Most models of learning in the contemporary literature characterize learning as goal directed. This is logically necessary when studying is metacognitively directed because metacognitive monitoring entails using meta-level models as standards (Paris & Byrnes, 1989). A spate of correlational studies link students' motivational orientations and self-reports of how they set goals and plans for studying. For example, Ainley (1993) classified high-school students' in terms of three motivational orientations: striving for mastery and understanding, enhancing ego by demonstrating ability, or just meeting task demands. Motivational orientation predicted students' reports of using deep approaches to studying in which they strove to select cognitive operations that linked new information to prior knowledge versus using surface approaches that committed to memory surface features of information as relatively discrete items (e.g., Biggs, 1991). Woulters, Yu, and Pintrich (1996) report stronger findings. Motivational orientation accounted for approximately 22% to 29% of the variance in 7th and 8th grade students' reports about studying tactics they used in English, mathematics, and social studies, and 18% to 20% of the variance in students' reports about metacognitively monitoring and controlling their studying tactics in these subjects.

Several lines of work suggest that having specific goals can be deleterious to productive metacognition, particularly when domain knowledge is weak and the learning task is complex (Kanfer & Ackerman, 1989; Sweller, 1989). The common explanation is that metacognition can be engaged "too early," straining cognitive capacity to the point where metacognition interferes with learning the domain's rules (Kanfer & Ackerman) or schemata (Sweller). Other research (e.g., Catrambone, 1995) reveals that, when studying complex procedures (using the Poisson distribution in word problems), students fare better when subgoals are explicitly labeled for them than when they must locate those subgoals on their own.

A study by Morgan (1985) suggests that, even if students do set goals when they study, they may not be very good at it. He provided brief training for undergraduate education students to set one of three forms of goals in a year-long educational psychology course: (a) setting proximal subgoals for each study session in "behavioral" terms and planning to record at the end of each study session which goals were met to criterion, (b) setting one overall (distal) goal for each study session, and (c) setting a goal for the amount of time that would be spent at the beginning of each study session. All three groups and a control group, who studied "normally," recorded how long they studied during each of three randomly but spaced weeks over the year.

Morgan checked whether students complied with training and observed four main findings. First and second, students who set specific subgoals for each session and monitored their achievement scored higher on a final examination and reported more intrinsic interest for the subject than did students in the other three groups, who did not differ from one another. Third, students who set goals to study for set times studied longer than other students. Finally, on marks in other courses where, presumably, all the students studied "normally," there were no differences in achievement. In other words, students who profited by setting proximal subgoals for each study session in one course did not transfer the effect (and, presumably, the goal setting procedure) to those courses.

Not all goals are devised by students. Nolen and Haladyna (1990) distinguished between teacher goals and student goals. They suggested that, since teachers have the final say in student grades, students need to "figure out what the teacher wants" and study accordingly. Other research shows that when goals are set by others (teachers) and students adopt those goals, studying and resulting achievement improve if the goals target the process of learning rather than just producing acceptable outcomes (e.g., Schunk, 1996).

A study by Elbaum, Berg, and Dodd (1993) shows that the plans students build for studying are influenced by beliefs. They asked undergraduate students to allocate hours of instruction to either formal studying tasks that focus on the language per se (listening to and repeating sentences from an audiotape, and memorizing vocabulary and idioms, and having a native speaker correct errors in conversation) versus functional tasks that emphasize using the foreign language for communicative purposes (reading foreign language newspapers, keeping a diary written in the foreign language, and having conversations with native speakers who do not correct errors but encourage expression). The more students favored functional tasks, the less they perceived that knowledge of vocabulary and grammar were important goals, and the more they emphasized knowledge of sociolinguistic factors that shape language use and communication strategies that help new speakers compensate for linguistic limitations. If we speculate about causal relations, students whose beliefs lead them to set goals for learning about sociolinguistic factors and communication strategies will opt to study in functional formats. Students whose beliefs lead them to set goals for gaining competence in vocabulary and grammar will prefer formal tasks as the way to study a new language.

We observe two notable gaps in the literature. First, we know little about how students form goals (Winne, 1997). A very general answer is provided by Carver and Scheier's (1990) model of self-regulated behavior. They postulate a 3-tier hierarchy of feedback loops, headed by an idealized concept of self, followed by general principles that govern behavior and, at the lowest level, behavior programs. When monitoring reveals that the profile of products at a level differs from the standard for that level, control is exercised by the next higher level. It resets standards at the lower level where the discrepancy was perceived. Our earlier example of the student who held an epistemological belief in quick and effortless learning matches this description for producing goals.

Second, research that illuminates when and how a student might engage in metacognition during the first two stages of studying where tasks are perceived and where goals and plans are set, is scant. We hypothesize that metacognitive activity in these stages will be proportional to two factors: (a) the degree to which COPES facets are unspecified, and (b) the student's familiarity with the task.

Enacting Study Tactics and Strategies

It seems logical that students must know about and have at least minimal skill in enacting study tactics and strategies for metacognitive control to enhance studying. Without tactics and strategies, there is little to control. The literature, however, is replete with experiments that demonstrate gains when students are trained to use a study tactic and compared to peers who study "normally." The consistency of findings that "normal" studying is relatively ineffective suggests that students may be very undereducated about study tactics and strategies (cf. Pressley, Van Etter, Yokoi, Freebern, & Van Meter, Chap. 14, this volume).

Some knowledge about tactics is, however, subtle and might not be expected to be apparent to students without direct instruction or supportive scaffolding (Winne, 1995a, 1995b, 1997). For example, Dempster (1988) argues that even educators are undereducated about the robust spacing effect, that is, that learning can be improved by distributing study sessions. Students who do not metacognitively monitor against a standard that describes spacing of study sessions may well learn less. They may also draw invalid conclusions about the utility of some tactics by misattributing weak effects to otherwise effective tactics because they did not engage in spaced study sessions (e.g., Krug, Davis, & Glover, 1990).

A study by Spurlin, Dansereau, O'Donnell, and Brooks (1988) shows that students also need to understand how tactics affect learning. Summarizing has a solid history as an effective study tactic (see Foos, 1995) because, in broad strokes, students engage in varied forms of deeper processing of information as they construct summaries. For example, to select which information to include in a summary, the student must judge which ideas are central and which are less so. Making this determination can uncover instances where comprehension has failed, thereby inviting the student to make a repair for lack of comprehension. Another form of deeper processing can arise if summarizing occurs at the end of reading a text. In this case, effort spent in retrieving, selecting, and organizing information for the summary enhances retrieval paths and builds organizational structures that can support post-study retrieval based on partial cues (King, 1992).

Spurlin and colleagues compared students who generated four summaries, one for each fourth of a relatively large text (approximately 2,500 words), students who generated two summaries, one for each half of the text, and students who did not summarize. Results showed no differences in recall between students who generated four summaries and those who did not summarize at all, and both these groups recalled less than students who generated two summaries. Foos (1995) replicated this same pattern of findings, comparing one group who made two summaries of a 2,800 word text, one for each half, a second group who made one summary for the whole text, and a third group who made no summary. The common interpretation is that integrating all to-be-learned information in a single summary involves deeper processing and builds more useful retrieval cues than separately integrating information in several independent summaries. Hence, unless students use standards for judging whether tactics have been enacted appropriately, they may reach biased judgments about the effects of a tactic.

Research on experts' studying suggests that conditional knowledge that toggles tactics is probably sub rosa (McKoon & Ratcliff, 1992) in the sense that it is enfolded within an expert's domain knowledge rather than occupying separate status in long-term or working memory. However, Wyatt et al.'s (1993) study of domain experts (professors of social sciences) studying complex material outside their domain (a journal article on reading strategies) aligns with other research (e.g., Voss, Blais, Means, Greene, & Ahwesh, 1989) in demonstrating that experts deliberately monitor and control study tactics when domain expertise is challenged.

Some students metacognitively monitor the use of tactics using standards that refer to breadth of understanding and growth in knowledge. In contrast to these students who monitor with learning orientation, other students metacognitively measure studying in units that count the tasks they complete (Dweck & Leggett, 1988), a so-called performance orientation. A study by Tuckman (1996) shows that students can be guided by external conditions to favor one orientation over the other in metacognitively monitoring how they study.

Tuckman (1996) hypothesized that weekly quizzes administered at the start of every lecture would prompt students to study often, and that students trained to use two study tactics proven in experimental settings—identifying key terms and defining them, and elaborating each term with an example—would improve their comprehension of course material. To make each intervention "meaningful," he based part of students' grades on their quiz scores or scores awarded to glossary entries, respectively. In Experiment 2, students trained to use (and who were observed to use) the study tactics spent an average of 38 minutes more studying each week but had lower scores on the final exam compared to students who studied for frequent quizzes. Tuckman's conversations with students revealed that those using the study tactics to generate elaborated glossaries adopted a performance goal to add items to glossaries rather than a learning goal of enhancing knowledge. Hence, those students' metacognitive monitoring included a standard that was misaligned with elevating their achievement.

Finally, we note that it is not common for research on metacognition to investigate relatively global, personality-like dispositions that may infuse tactic's conditional knowledge. However, several lines of research strongly implicate such variables as potent IFs included in metacognitive monitoring. Cacioppo, Petty, Feinstein, and Jarvis (1996) reviewed wide-ranging research concerning one such individual difference, need for cognition. This is a tendency for people to "seek, acquire, think about, and reflect back on information to make sense of stimuli … [rather than] rely on others (e.g., celebrities and experts), cognitive heuristics, or social comparison processes" (p. 198). In their meta-analyses, people high in need for cognition, whom Cacioppo et al. call "cognizers," substantially outperformed "cognitive misers" in recalling information they had studied (mean $d = 3.55, p < .001$), were more likely to assess arguments for substantive merits and engage in scrutinizing information (mean $d = .312, p < .010$), were more likely to be metacognitively aware of cognitive effort spent (mean $d = .272, p < .001$), and in general, were more likely to engage in metacognitive control to correct initial misperceptions or biases (though such attempts are not necessarily successful). Need for cognition has not yet been examined in terms of traces obtained during studying, but it seems a good candidate for inclusion as a pervasive yet probably tacit dispositional IF that affects metacognitively guided studying.

Adapting Studying

As a result of metacognitive monitoring in Stage 3, students make changes to domain knowledge by adapting studying. Self-regulated learning, or metacognitive control of study tactics and strategies, is commonly viewed as occurring within the temporal boundaries of a study session. The methodological requirements for observing online, within-session self-regulation, however, are just now being conquered by advances in using computer technologies to trace how students study (Winne, Gupta, & Nesbit, 1994; Winne & Nesbit, 1995). Studies that use multiple-session designs, however, also demonstrate that students make forward reaching adaptations to studying tactics across study sessions as a result of metacognition about just-experienced (or prior) studying.

In one study, Rabinowitz, Freeman, and Cohen (1993) demonstrated an interaction between domain knowledge, first attempts to use studying tactics, and adapting approaches to study in a following study period. Students studied lists of randomly ordered words drawn from common categories (e.g., fruits, musical instruments). In a first session, students were told to use categorizing as a study tactic. One group studied items that were highly typical of the categories—domain knowledge was relevant here—whereas another group studied words low in typicality, making domain knowledge less useful. In a second study session, all students studied the same new list of medium typicality words using whatever study tactic(s) they preferred; no instructions were given to use categorizing as a study tactic. After recall of the new list, students were asked to describe study tactics they had used to study. And, after each of the two sessions, all students had rated how difficult, effortful, and useful it was to categorize words while studying.

The interesting finding concerns how students studied the second list. Recall of moderately typical words on the second list was the same for both groups, and it didn't differ from recall of the first list. Whatever study tactics students used in the second session were as effective as the categorizing tactic they were instructed to use studying the first list. Did students use a categorizing tactic on the second list? Among students who studied highly typical items in the first session, 96% reported they used categorizing only or categorizing plus another tactic on the second list. Only one student abandoned categorizing outright. Among students who had studied less typical words in the first session, only 53% reused categorizing alone or supplemented it with another study tactic; the rest abandoned categorizing. Students' perceptions of whether they used categorizing as a study tactic were verified by clustering scores. Thus, students who first tried a study tactic that was ill-matched to the task, because domain knowledge of categories was not well-matched to categorizing the atypical words they were studying, were not likely to use that same tactic in a second task where it was more likely to be helpful because medium typicality words are more readily categorized.

In Rabinowitz et al.'s (1993) study, learners did not differ in the effort they said they applied to studying. Other research, however, suggests that effort is a condition that students metacognitively monitor and use in exercising metacognitive control. Eisenberger (1992) has reviewed research on the transfer of effort, characterizing such transfer as learned industriousness. In a typical study (Eisenberger, Masterson, & McDermitt, 1982), undergraduate women tackled problems involving addition, anagrams, and differences between pairs of cartoon pictures. One group of women experienced all three types of problems. Three other groups were asked only one kind of problem each. Within each of these four groups, half the students were given easy problems that required little effort (e.g., adding 2-digit numbers) and half were given difficult problems that required high effort (e.g., adding 7-digit numbers). In a second session, all the students were set a completely different task, writing an essay about a controversial topic. To gauge effort applied in writing essays, their compositions were scored for length, a direct measure of effort applied, and quality, an indicator of effort that probably reflects students' use of writing tactics and strategies as "the substance of effort, the means by which effort is applied" (Winne, 1995a, p. 176).

Among students who solved only one type of problem in the first session, regardless of whether problems required more or less effort, the effort they said they invested was not associated with length or quality of essays. Students who solved a variety of easy problems wrote the shortest and lowest quality essays, whereas those who solved varied and hard problems wrote the longest and highest quality essays. According to Eisenberger's concept of learned industriousness, students in the varied problems group who were posed difficult problems abstracted a general perception that effort was an inherent part of tasks, and that perception became a standard they used to metacognitively monitor work when they wrote essays.

These studies indicate that, across study sessions and across tasks, students exercise metacognitive control that changes conditions in Stage 1 of subsequent studying cycles or sessions. Given our hypothesis about the recursive properties of studying, these changes will percolate throughout that subsequent cycle or session.

SUMMARY

Our model depicts studying as metacognitively powered self-regulated learning that spans four recursively linked and weakly sequenced stages: defining the task, goal setting and planning, enacting study tactics and strategies, and metacognitively adapting studying for the future (see Table 12.1). Each stage of studying is modeled by a single cognitive architecture in which environmental factors and individual differences (conditions) constitute a temporary state of a task space. Students engage in activities (operations) that create information (products) that can be monitored in relation to standards (see Fig. 12.1). At each stage, students generate internal feedback and may be provided with external feedback (evaluations). This updates their understanding of a task, goals and plans they create, the study tactics they enact, and produces relatively permanent adaptations to cognitive structures that describe tasks and studying. When models of tasks and studying are used as the basis for examining information at each stage, students engage in metacognitive monitoring. When students toggle tactics on and off or when they edit tactics, this metacognitive control effects self-regulating learning. We examined research that illustrates metacognition in each stage.

FUTURE RESEARCH ON STUDYING AS SELF-REGULATED LEARNING

Research demonstrates individual differences in students' perceptions of a task, and we noted that a teacher's (or researcher's) perception of an assigned task may not align with students' understandings of "the" task. These differences originate with variance in students' beliefs, motivation, and prior knowledge, all of which, according to our model, are products of prior engagement with previous study tasks. Though we speculated about metacognition in Stage 1 of studying, we do not find that research has directly investigated how students exercise metacognitive monitoring and control when they generate an understanding about a study task.

It is frequently assumed that students' perceptions of goals (standards) for a study task match assigned goals. At least, when there is no check on this correspondence, it seems this assumption is made. There may be adequate equivalence between goals assigned and students' perceptions; however, our model allows that, at Stage 2, students can add to or modify goals that they may accurately acknowledge as having been set for them. Although there are studies that document disparities between assigned goals and adopted goals, we know of none that explicitly investigates roles played by metacognitive monitoring and control in goal setting and subsequent planning.

Metacognition is a driver for online changes that students make to tactics they use to study. This stage of studying has more frequently been a focus for research, and there is considerable evidence that metacognition is a powerful influence here. However, the field needs to know more about kinds of meta-level knowledge that students use in metacognitive monitoring and about students' editing study tactics.

Finally, the field is struggling with issues of how students maintain, transfer, and adapt their approaches to studying. These are questions about Stage 4 of our model. The backward- and forward-reaching nature of metacognitive monitoring and control in this larger scale adaptive work is clearly more complicated than the local adaptations addressed in Stage 3, where students enact and control tactics. Perhaps progress in understanding these larger scale adaptations requires developing more adequate views about metaknowledge per se. As clarified by Alexander, Schallert, and Hare (1991) in their review of terms researchers use to describe knowledge, this is a formidable task.

We have three major recommendations for future research about any stage or stages of studying. First, traces (Winne, 1982) of metacognitive monitoring and control should be a standard feature. Without such data, we have only indirect evidence about metacognitive events and their recursive and forward reaching features. Trace data can chart how students metacognitively monitor and regulate within and between stages of studying. In addition, because traces operationally define metacognition, they provide clear guidelines for framing objectives about metacognition and for assessing those achievements in study skills training and other instructional interventions.

Second, studies should be designed with explicit options for students to toggle and edit study tactics. In many experiments, the control group meets our criterion of allowing students to exercise toggling. They are expressly told to study as they wish. In contrast, students who experience or take part in an intervention, such as training to use concept maps for organizing information during a study period, implicitly have toggling and editing curtailed. The experimenter does not want students to substitute outlining or point-form notetaking for concept mapping, although the process of examining whether to make such a substitution and how that decision-making process itself may be adapted is the substance of metacognition. In this context, trace data will be essential in revealing whether and how students toggle and edit.

Finally, studies should generate data that allow direct inspection of students' perceptions of conditions, operations, products, evaluations, and standards. These are the inputs to metacognitive monitoring and the products that are updated by metacognitive control. Our model suggests two implications. First, prior knowledge is not a static condition. It is potentially updated throughout a task. Second, though we labeled broad categories of "prior knowledge," it remains a challenge to understand how students "collapse" or "integrate" the information in these multivariate profiles to effect self-regulation.

ACKNOWLEDGMENT

Support for this research was provided by a grant to the first author from the Social Sciences and Humanities Research Council of Canada (#410-95-1046).

REFERENCES

Ainley, M. D. (1993). Styles of engagement with learning: Multidimensional assessment of their relationship with strategy use and school achievement. *Journal of Educational Psychology, 85,* 395–405.

Alexander, P. A., Schallert, D. L., & Hare, V. C. (1991). Coming to terms: How researchers in learning and literacy talk about knowledge. *Review of Educational Research, 61,* 315–343.

Anderson, J. R. (1991). The adaptive nature of human categorization. *Psychological Review, 98,* 409–429.

Biggs, J. B. (1991). Student learning in the context of school. In J. B. Biggs (Ed.), *Teaching for learning: The view from cognitive psychology* (pp. 7–29). Hawthorn, Victoria, Australia: Australian Council for Educational Research.

Briggs, P. (1990). Do they know what they're doing? An evaluation of word-processor users' implicit and explicit task-relevant knowledge, and its role in self-directed learning. *International Journal of Man–Machine Studies, 32,* 385–398.

Butler, D. L., & Winne, P. H. (1995). Feedback and self-regulated learning: A theoretical synthesis. *Review of Educational Research, 65,* 245–281.

Cacioppo, J. T, Petty, R. E., Feinstein, J. A., & Jarvis, W. B. G. (1996). Dispositional differences in cognitive motivation: The life and times of individuals varying in need for cognition. *Psychological Bulletin*, *119*, 197–233.

Carver, C. S., & Scheier, M. F. (1990). Origins and functions of positive and negative affect: A control-process view. *Psychological Review*, *97*, 19–35.

Catrambone, R. (1995). Aiding subgoal learning: Effects on transfer. *Journal of Educational Psychology*, *87*, 5–17.

Cordón, L. A., & Day, J. D. (1996). Strategy use on standardized reading comprehension tests. *Journal of Educational Psychology*, *88*, 288–295.

Covington, M. V. (1992). *Making the grade. A self-worth perspective on motivation and school reform.* Cambridge, England: Cambridge University Press.

Dempster, F. N. (1988). The spacing effect: A case study in the failure to apply the results of psychological research. *American Psychologist*, *43*, 627–634.

Dweck, C. S., & Leggett, E. L. (1988). A social-cognitive approach to motivation and personality. *Psychological Review*, *95*, 256–273.

Eisenberger, R. (1992). Learned industriousness. *Psychological Review*, *99*, 248–267.

Eisenberger, R., Masterson, F. A., & McDermitt, M. (1982). Effects of task variety on generalized effort. *Journal of Educational Psychology*, *74*, 499–506.

Elbaum, B. E., Berg, C. A., & Dodd, D. H. (1993). Previous learning experience, strategy beliefs, and task definition in self-regulated foreign language learning. *Contemporary Educational Psychology*, *18*, 318–336.

Foos, P. W. (1995). The effect of variations in text summarization opportunities on test performance. *Journal of Experimental Education*, *63*, 89–95

Kanfer, R., & Ackerman, P. L. (1989). Motivation and cognitive abilities: An integrative/aptitude-treatment interaction approach to skill acquisition. *Journal of Applied Psychology* [Monograph], *74*, 657–690.

King, A. (1992). Comparison of self-questioning, summarizing, and notetaking-review as strategies for learning from lectures. *American Educational Research Journal*, *29*, 303–323.

Kluger, A. N., & DeNisi, A. (1996). The effects of feedback interventions on performance: A historical review, a meta-analysis, and a preliminary feedback intervention theory. *Psychological Bulletin*, *119*, 254–284.

Körkel, J. (1987). *Die entwicklung von gedächtnis—und metagedächtnisleistungen in abhängigheit von bereichsspezifischen vorkenntnissen* [The development of memory and metamemory performance in relation to domain-specific prior knowledge]. Frankfurt/Main: Lang.

Krug, D., Davis, T. B., & Glover, J. A. (1990). Massed versus distributed repeated reading: A case of forgetting helping recall? *Journal of Educational Psychology*, *82*, 366–371.

McKoon, G., & Ratcliff, R. (1992). Inference during reading. *Psychological Review*, *99*, 440–466.

Morgan, M. (1985). Self-monitoring of attained subgoals in private study. *Journal of Educational Psychology*, *77*, 623–630.

Nelson, T. O., & Narens, L. (1990). Metamemory: A theoretical framework and new findings. In G. H. Bower (Ed.), *The psychology of learning and motivation*, Vol. 26, pp. 125–173). New York: Academic Press.

Nelson, T. O., & Narens, L. (1994). Why investigate metacognition? In J. Metcalfe & A. P. Shimamura (Eds.), *Metacognition: Knowing about knowing* (pp. 1–25). Cambridge, MA: MIT Press.

Nolen, S. B., & Haladyna, T. (1990). Personal and environmental influences on students' beliefs about effective study strategies. *Contemporary Educational Psychology*, *15*, 116–130.

Paris, S. G., & Byrnes, J. P. (1989). The constructivist approach to self-regulation and learning in the classroom. In B. J. Zimmerman & D. H. Schunk (Eds.), *Self-regulated learning and academic achievement: Theory, research, and practice* (pp. 169–200). New York: Springer-Verlag.

Pintrich, P. R., Marx, R. W., & Boyle, R. A. (1993). Beyond cold conceptual change: The role of motivational beliefs and classroom contextual factors in the process of conceptual change. *Review of Educational Research, 63,* 167–199.

Rabinowitz, M., Freeman, K., & Cohen, S. (1993). Use and maintenance of strategies: The influence of accessibility to knowledge. *Journal of Educational Psychology, 84,* 211–218.

Reynolds, R. E., & Shirey, L. L. (1988). The role of attention in studying and learning. In C. E. Weinstein, E. T. Goetz, & P. A. Alexander (Eds.), *Learning and study strategies: Issues in assessment, instruction, and evaluation* (pp. 77–100). San Diego: Academic Press.

Rumelhart, D. E., & Norman, D. A. (1978). Accretion, tuning, and restructuring: Three modes of learning. In J. W. Cotton & R. Klatzky (Eds.), *Semantic factors in cognition* (pp. 37–53). Hillsdale, NJ: Lawrence Erlbaum Associates.

Salomon, G., & Perkins, D. N. (1989). Rocky roads to transfer: Rethinking mechanisms of a neglected phenomenon. *Educational Psychologist, 24,* 113–142.

Schneider, W. (1993). Domain-specific knowledge and memory performance in children. *Educational Psychology Review, 5,* 257–273.

Schommer, M. (1990). Effects of belief about the nature of knowledge on comprehension. *Journal of Educational Psychology, 82,* 498–504.

Schommer, M. (1994). Synthesizing epistemological belief research: Tentative understandings and provocative conclusions. *Educational Psychology Review, 6,* 293–319.

Schommer, M., Crouse, A., & Rhodes, N. (1992). Epistemological beliefs and mathematical text comprehension: Believing it is simple does not make it so. *Journal of Educational Psychology, 84,* 435–443.

Schraw, G. (1994). The effect of metacognitive knowledge on local and global monitoring. *Contemporary Educational Psychology, 19,* 143–154.

Schunk, D. H. (1996). Goal and self-evaluative influences during children's cognitive skill learning. *American Educational Research Journal, 33,* 359–382.

Simpson, M. L., & Nist, S. L. (1984). PLAE: A model for independent learning. *Journal of Reading, 28,* 218–223.

Spurlin, J. E., Dansereau, D. F., O'Donnell, A., & Brooks, L. (1988). Text processing: Effects of summarization frequency on text recall. *Journal of Experimental Education, 56,* 199–202.

Sweller, J. (1989). Cognitive technology: Some procedures for facilitating learning and problem solving in mathematics and science. *Journal of Educational Psychology, 81,* 457–466.

Thomas, E. L., & Robinson, H. A. (1972). *Improving reading in every class: A sourcebook for teachers.* Boston: Allyn & Bacon.

Tuckman, B. W. (1996). The relative effectiveness of incentive motivation and prescribed learning strategy in improving college students' course performance. *Journal of Experimental Education, 64,* 197–210.

Van Meter, P., Yokio, L., & Pressley, M. (1994). College students' theory of note-taking derived from their perceptions of note-taking. *Journal of Educational Psychology, 86,* 323–338.

Voss, J. F., Blais, J., Means, M. L., Greene, T. R., & Ahwesh, E. (1989). Informal reasoning and subject matter knowledge in the solving of economics problems by naive and novice individuals. In L. Resnick (Ed.), *Knowing, learning, and instruction: Essays in honor of Robert Glaser* (pp. 217–249). Hillsdale, NJ: Lawrence Erlbaum Associates.

Walczyk, J. J., & Hall, V. C. (1989). Effects of examples and embedded questions on the accuracy of comprehension self-assessments. *Journal of Educational Psychology, 81,* 435–437.

Winne, P. H. (1982). Minimizing the black box problem to enhance the validity of theories about instructional effects. *Instructional Science, 11,* 13–28.

Winne, P. H. (1989). Theories of instruction and of intelligence for designing artificially intelligent tutoring systems. *Educational Psychologist, 24,* 229–259.

Winne, P. H. (1995a). Inherent details in self-regulated learning. *Educational Psychologist, 30,* 173–187.

Winne, P. H. (1995b). Self regulation is ubiquitous but its forms vary with knowledge. *Educational Psychologist, 30,* 223–228.

Winne, P. H. (1996). A metacognitive view of individual differences in self-regulated learning. *Learning and Individual Differences, 8,* 327–353.

Winne, P. H. (1997). Experimenting to bootstrap self-regulated learning. *Journal of Educational Psychology, 89,* 397–410.

Winne, P. H., Gupta, L., & Nesbit, J. C. (1994). Exploring individual differences in studying strategies using graph theoretic statistics. *Alberta Journal of Educational Research, 40,* 177–193.

Winne, P. H., & Marx, R. W. (1982). Students' and teachers' views of thinking processes for classroom learning. *Elementary School Journal, 82,* 493–518.

Winne, P. H., & Marx, R. W. (1989). A cognitive processing analysis of motivation within classroom tasks. In C. Ames & R. Ames (Eds.), *Research on motivation in education* (Vol. 3, pp. 223–257). Orlando, FL: Academic Press.

Winne, P. H., & Nesbit, J. C. (1995, April). *Graph theoretic techniques for examining patterns and strategies in students' studying: An application of LogMill.* Paper presented at the meeting of the American Educational Research Association, San Francisco.

Wong, B. Y. L., Wong, R., & LeMare, L. (1982). The effects of knowledge of criterion task on comprehension and recall in normally achieving and learning disabled children. *Journal of Educational Research, 76,* 119–126.

Woulters, C. A., Yu, S. L., & Pintrich, P. R. (1996). The relation between goal orientation and students' motivational beliefs and self-regulated learning. *Learning and Individual Differences, 8,* 211–238

Wyatt, D., Pressley, M., El-Dinary, P. B., Stein, S., Evans, P., & Brown, R. (1993). Comprehension strategies, worth and credibility monitoring, and evaluations: Cold and hot cognition when experts read professional articles that are important to them. *Learning and Individual Differences, 5,* 49–72.

13

SMART Environments That Support Monitoring, Reflection, and Revision

Nancy J. Vye
Daniel L. Schwartz
John D. Bransford
Brigid J. Barron
Linda Zech
The Cognition and Technology Group at Vanderbilt
Vanderbilt University

Recently, we had the opportunity to participate in a focus group with fifth-and sixth-grade teachers from a school in our local area. One of the goals of the meeting was to discuss their perceptions concerning the learning needs of their students. The teachers were confident that their students had the potential to become excellent learners, but they were dismayed that so many of them entered the fifth and sixth grades unprepared to learn effectively. Following are excerpts of the comments made by teachers:

> My students can memorize facts, but they can't tell you why these facts are significant ... they haven't had to take in facts and try to assimilate or synthesize and spit it back out into some form that has meaning. They are not used to having to attach meaning to what they are doing. (Tracie Pennington, fifth-grade teacher)

> It seems if I have students in a whole group and I say, "Oh gosh, what do we need to know about to find the answer to this question?" And they can say, "We would need to know X, Y, or Z." And then I'll say, "Let's look right in this section here. Does anybody spot something that might be related?" If I am prompting, they'll do a better job. But if they are working independently,

they won't pull it out. You have to prompt so much to get them to do it. (Suzanne Cassel, fifth-grade teacher)

After my students print out their first drafts, they are supposed to go proofread. They'll go read, read, read, "Sounds good to me." Or if I get peers to read each other's, it's like they say to each other, "Okay, I'll say yours is okay if you'll say mine's okay." (Babs Bertotti, fifth-grade teacher)

Most of the needs identified by the teachers in our focus group were metacognitive in nature. Some 20 years ago, Brown (1975, 1978) and Flavell (1976, 1985) defined metacognition as "the active monitoring and consequent regulation and orchestration of [cognitive] processes" (Flavell, 1976, p. 232). Later, Brown (1978) distinguished between two clusters of metacognitive activities: knowledge about cognition (e.g., that one's memory for a new phone number may only be short-term), and activities used to regulate and oversee cognition (e.g., that one needs to actively rehearse information to maintain it in working memory). Both of these areas were mentioned by the teachers, although they focused primarily on issues of monitoring and regulation. They were concerned that their students had difficulties executing research and comprehension strategies on their own, did not know what it means to understand something deeply, were not effective at monitoring when they did not understand something, and so forth. From this perspective, a major challenge facing educators and researchers alike continues to be to help students learn important metacognitive habits and skills.

Traditionally, research on metacognition has focused on teaching the individual learner a control structure or strategy for enhancing problem solving, memory, and comprehension (e.g., Bransford et al., 1982; Brown, Bransford, Ferrara, & Campione, 1983; Chi, Bassok, Lewis; Glaser, 1989; Chi, deLeeuw, Chiu, & LaVancher, 1994; Pressley, Woloshyn, Lysynchuk, Martin, Wood, & Willoughby, 1990; Scardamalia & Bereiter, 1985). Data from many of the metacognitive training studies illustrate phenomena similar to ones described by the teachers in our focus group, for example, that students do well when explicitly prompted but often fail to spontaneously use useful control strategies in new settings. Brown et al. (1983) showed that different ways to teach control strategies have different effects on transfer. For example, *blind* training refers to situations where students are taught new strategies without information about why, when, and how they are useful; this type of training usually resulted in very poor spontaneous transfer. In contrast, *informed training* and *informed training plus opportunities to exercise self-control of strategies* usually were much more successful in promoting spontaneous transfer (Brown et al., 1983).

In this chapter, we describe an approach to the development of metacognition that builds on the metacognitive training literature but also looks at the phenomena of metacognition more broadly. In particular, rather than focus solely on strategy training with individuals, we attempt to create a social environment that provides support for metacognitive activities such as reflection, self-assessment, and revision. Like many researchers trained in a brand of cognitive psychology that focused solely on individuals, we have only gradually begun to appreciate the importance of extending our theorizing by explicitly attempting to analyze the nature of the social environments within which people operate (e.g., Barron et al., 1995; Bransford, 1981). Our movement in this direction has been strongly influenced by our own experiences in classrooms (e.g., Cognition and Technology Group at Vanderbilt [CTGV], 1997), and by the work of a number of theorists including Brown and Campione (1994), Cobb (1994), Cole and Griffin (1987), Greeno, Collins, and Resnick (1996), Lave (1988), and Rogoff (1990).

LEARNING ABOUT RIVERS AS ECOSYSTEMS

We organize our discussion of metacognition around the goal of helping students learn about a precise subject matter; in particular, about interdependence and ecosystems in the context of monitoring rivers for pollution. Our assumption is that the ideas about individual and social support for metacognition that we discuss are applicable to all domains—not just river monitoring (see especially Barron et al., 1995, in press; CTGV, in press; Zech et al., in press). Nevertheless, we believe that many aspects of successful metacognitive monitoring require deep knowledge of the domain in which one is working; hence we situate our discussion in a particular content domain rather than attempt to discuss metacognition as a "domain general" set of competencies and skills.

Therefore, please imagine the goal of helping fifth graders learn about ecosystems in the context of a project that focuses on monitoring rivers for pollution. At the end of the project (which may last for approximately 10 to 12 weeks), students should understand procedures for determining the health of a river (e.g., sampling macroinvertebrates and measuring dissolved oxygen) and why these are appropriate measures, plus understand the effects of pollutants on the ecosystem (e.g., that these ultimately affect the degree of dissolved oxygen that is needed to support the life of macroinvertebrates and fish). Hundreds of classrooms throughout the country engage in river monitoring projects, and they take a variety of approaches.

We discuss two possible instructional approaches to a project on river monitoring and contrast them with the approach that we describe in this chapter. The two instructional approaches that we discuss are extreme; we are not claiming that teachers would actually use them. Nevertheless, a discussion of these extremes is useful because they provide contrasting examples that help us articulate some of the major metacognitive implications of different types of instruction. This should become clearer in the discussion that follows.

Total Student Control of Learning

One possible approach to learning about river monitoring is to announce that students will be taking a trip to a river and that everyone needs to be prepared to know how to monitor the river for pollution and understand why these procedures work, explain the effects of pollution on the ecosystem, plus write a report on their findings. Students can confer with one another and read whatever they wish to read. However, they are left on their own to decide what they need to learn and then to learn it.

This type of assignment places a great deal of responsibility on students to continually monitor their learning and assess their preparedness for the task of monitoring the river, and to define learning goals for themselves. No fifth-grade teacher we know would expect such an assignment to work for his or her students. It would even be difficult for college students. It is useful to understand some of the reasons why.

We contend that the idea of assessing one's level of preparedness for monitoring a river requires students to construct a relatively detailed mental model (cf. Johnson-Laird, 1983; McNamara, Miller, & Bransford, 1991) of what it means to monitor a river. Without such a model, they cannot assess whether their learning activities are moving them toward preparation. This view of monitoring as being dependent on knowledge is very different from a view of monitoring as based on a knowledge-independent "metacognitive" skill.

Several sources of evidence illustrate how the ability to create a clear mental model of one's testing situation is necessary for effective monitoring. In a study of new vocabulary acquisition conducted by Nitsch (see Bransford, 1979), one group of college students did an excellent job of predicting whether they were ready for a test. A second group—selected randomly from the same population as the first group—did an extremely poor job. They felt prepared but were not. The reason is that their method of training led them to develop expectations about the testing situation that were violated. Once students had experienced the testing situation, they had a much better idea of how to change their learning strategies and monitor their preparedness for the test.

Anyone who has expected a multiple choice test and then been surprised by an essay test knows the importance of being able to accurately imagine a testing situation in order to assess his or her degree of preparation (e.g., Bransford, 1979). Similarly, anyone who has given speeches to different groups of individuals (e.g., academics, business leaders, school administrators) knows the importance of being able to anticipate the kinds of questions they are likely to be asked at the end of their presentations (e.g., Bransford & Stein, 1993). The better individuals can imagine (model) the situation in which they must use their knowledge, the easier it is for them to assess their level of preparation. Increasing experience with particular situations (e.g., with talking to particular kinds of audiences) increases the accuracy with which one can anticipate the kinds of knowledge and skills necessary to perform adequately.

The idea that monitoring is highly knowledge dependent creates a "Catch-22" situation for novices. How can they assess whether their learning activities are leading them in the direction of "adequate preparation" if they do not already have a clear mental model of their ultimate testing situation? One of our major strategies to support assessments of preparedness is to give students experiences (often simulated experiences) of the nature of the situations in which they will eventually be interacting—*and to do this as close to the beginning of instruction as possible*. We say more about this later.

Total Teacher Control of Learning

A second approach to teaching about rivers as ecosystems allows the teacher to control the learning. Students can be helped to learn facts, such as why one might sample for macroinvertebrates to assess water quality, how pollution can effect the degree of dissolved oxygen in the river, and so forth. One possibility is to write or assign a textbook chapter that explains all this information and give students periodic quizzes on the materials. If students show mastery of a section of a text, they can proceed to new sections. If they need to study further, they go back to the text until they reach some level of mastery. Eventually, one should be able to get students to do very well on an overall test.

This approach to instruction has very few metacognitive require-ments. Tests provided by the teachers are used to check students' levels of preparation. If they need help, they return to the relevant sections and restudy the materials. If one's instruction were computer based, it could return students to exactly the relevant section with the needed materials. Under these conditions, the tests do the monitoring and the computers provide important support for regulative strategies, such as returning to the relevant information and reading it again.

In most fifth-grade classrooms, implementation of this Total Teacher Control instruction would probably result in better test performance than implementation of the Total Student Control instruction. Never-theless, we believe that there is a serious downside to Total Teacher Control: Students do not acquire the knowledge and strategies necessary to assess their own levels of understanding and revise them when needed. Experiences with opportunities for self-assessment seem to be fundamen-tally important for success outside of school environments. The more that people or groups work on the cutting edge of their knowledge, the more important it becomes to identify gaps between their present states and their goal states (e.g., Newell & Simon, 1972), and the less probable it will be that someone will be available to provide the perfect textbook, tests of mastery, and guidance for repairing one's learning. People must learn to build their own knowledge (Bereiter & Scardamalia, 1989), and this means that they must learn to assess what they currently understand and what they further need to know.

One might argue that students can be taught metacognitive skills in other courses that focus specifically on these kinds of activities. A number of courses in "thinking skills" have been designed and studied, and there is certainly reason to believe that they can be helpful (e.g. Bransford, Arbitman-Smith, Stein, & Vye, 1985). Nevertheless, courses such as these confront the "inert knowledge" problem (Whitehead, 1929), where general skills and concepts learned in one context do not transfer to others. We discuss examples elsewhere (Bransford, Franks, Vye, & Sherwood, 1989). We choose to integrate our work on metacog-nition with opportunities to learn about specific content for several reasons. One is that students need to experience what it is like to understand an area deeply; otherwise they do not know the difference between deep and shallow understanding. A second is that students need to understand the powerful role that knowledge plays in affecting their abilities to assess their own learning and transfer to new situations.

Environments That Support Self-Assessment

The model that we discuss in this chapter is based on a form of "anchored" instruction and formative assessment that is designed to support self-assessment, reflection, and revision in the context of learning important curriculum content. As a metaphor for anchored instruction, imagine a ship sailing across the surface of the ocean. This is similar to many curricula that simply skim the surface of disciplines and fail to provide students with any in-depth understanding of the domain. Our approach to instruction anchors the ship in one place so that people can engage in deep exploration and inquiry, and we provide resources that facilitate this exploration. Eventually, people can sail to a new destination and again engage in anchored inquiry. Ideally, knowledge and skills acquired from previous inquiry experiences will make their new inquiry more efficient and useful.

We attempt to facilitate the process of in-depth inquiry by supplementing anchored instruction with SMART environments, where SMART stands for Scientific and Mathematical Arenas for Refining Thinking (Barron et al., 1995; CTGV; 1997; Zech et al., in press). A fundamental principle guiding the design of SMART has been to use anchored instruction to give students a vision of the kinds of authentic problem-solving environments in which they will need to use their knowledge, and to then provide SMART resources that encourage self-assessment, reflection, and revision by students as they pursue the goal of preparing to function in these environments.

SMART environments include a number of components that are designed to function as a "system" in the sense that they are mutually supportive of its underlying goals (Brown & Campione, 1996). Barron et al., (in press) discuss the following components:

- A focus on learning goals that emphasize deep understanding of important subject-matter content (e.g., understanding rivers as ecosystems and how and why to monitor their health).
- The use of scaffolds to support both student and teacher learning.
- Frequent opportunities for formative self-assessment, revision, and reflection.
- Social organizations that promote collaboration and a striving for high standards.

These components are discussed in more detail in Barron et al. (in press). Rather than attempt to discuss each component separately, we embed them together as we discuss our attempts to design SMART environments that help students learn about rivers and ecosystems. We divide our curriculum into four phases to help students acquire the content. Each phase is discussed here.

PHASE I OF THE RIVER PROJECT

As noted earlier, students need to have a mental model of the contexts in which they must use their knowledge. Without such a model, they cannot assess where they are in the learning processes. We begin the process of helping students develop a mental model of river testing by exposing them to the first part of *Stones River Mystery*, one of the Scientists in Action adventures developed by Bob Sherwood and his colleagues at Vanderbilt (e.g., see Sherwood, Petrosino, Lin, Lamon, & CTGV, 1995). An alternate way to begin with an anchor would be to have students actually visit a river and attempt to find out about its health. This is very difficult and expensive for the schools in which we are working because it requires buses, extra help to monitor the students, and constant worries about the weather. Therefore, we begin with a simulated video anchor. Unlike a one-shot field trip, the video also provides unlimited opportunities to return easily to particular scenes and re-explore them as needed.

The Anchor for Phase I

Stones River Mystery tells the story of a team of high-school students who are working with a hydrologist and a biologist to monitor the quality of the water in Stones River. The team travels in a specially equipped van to different testing sites along the river. The van contains devices that enable the team to electronically transmit the results of their tests to students back at school who are charged with compiling and interpreting the incoming data.

The video shows the team conducting various water quality tests. We observe them collecting and sorting samples of macroinvertebrates from the river's bottom and measuring the dissolved oxygen in the water. They also measure pH, temperature, turbidity, and ammonia, and visually inspect the river and riverbank. The anchor poses two challenges to students. The first challenge appears about halfway through the story. Students in the video are asked to test the quality of the water at Site B along Stones River and to interpret the data. We stop the video at this point to help students in the classrooms deal with the part of the challenge that involves sampling for macroinvertebrates. This constitutes Phase I of the project. After students work on this challenge, they move into Phase II where they return to the video and continue the adventure. We describe Phase II later.

Contrasting Cases That Help Students Begin Their Own Inquiry

Opportunities to see the video anchor are useful and motivating to students, but they need additional help to develop more in-depth understanding of the situation. For example, students watching the video see actors using a net to catch macroinvertebrates, but they do not notice the details of the net (e.g., the size of the holes in it), and they do not necessarily understand exactly how and why macroinvertebrates are used to assess water quality. Furthermore, the video does not help students think about alternative methods of sampling.

When we began our work, we assumed that teachers would quite naturally structure classroom activities in ways that helped students build an understanding of these testing procedures. Some teachers engaged their students in question generation and collaborative inquiry, but many others did not. Instead, they tended to hold whole-class discussions about procedures for solving the problems, and the discussions were more teacher-directed than we would have hoped.

Our collaborations with teachers have enabled us to better understand their challenges. Many teachers' educational and practical experiences leave them feeling unprepared to engage students in deep inquiry related to concepts, especially in mathematics and science. In particular, most of the middle-school teachers with whom we worked did not begin the project with an in-depth understanding of ecosystems and rivers. As a result, they reported not always knowing what to talk about or how to guide discussions with their students. In addition, they reported worrying that the discussions would get into areas where they did not know "the answers." Teachers' lack of knowledge about principles of ecosystems and rivers also made it difficult for them to evaluate what their students understand because their own mental models are fuzzy. Our collaboration with teachers helped us realize that we needed additional scaffolds to help both students and teachers assess their current levels of understanding and generate appropriate learning goals.

We have found it useful to use *contrasting cases* to scaffold students' thinking about monitoring for river quality. We do this by creating catalogs of items that students must choose to monitor the river for macroinvertebrates. The design of our catalogs is based on contrasting cases theories of noticing and understanding (e.g., see Bransford, Franks, Vye, & Sherwood,

1989; Bransford et al., in press; Garner, 1974; Gibson & Gibson, 1955) to create catalogs about which students make decisions. Figures 13.1a and 13.1b contain examples of catalog items that students might choose in order to sample macroinvertebrates in a river. Some of the items will work; others are bogus. Students first make their own choice and then work in groups to discuss which catalog item to choose, and why. They are also asked to indicate why they did not select the other options.

We attempt to create contrasts in the catalog that help students notice gaps in their knowledge. For example, the tools in 13.1a and 13.1b differ from each other in a very important way. The TetraBen Laser Counter tallies the *number* of macroinvertebrates in the area scanned, whereas the .5mm Hockmeister Dip Net enables the user to identify the *types* of macroinvertebrates in the area. These instruments were designed to highlight important issues associated with macroinvertebrate sampling. To use macroinvertebrates as an indicator of water quality, it is important to determine the types that are in the river. Certain types of macroinvertebrates are more sensitive than others to the effects of pollution (i.e., they will die first if dissolved oxygen levels decrease). In general, the more types of pollution-sensitive macroinvertebrates in a river, the better the water quality. Therefore, the TetraBen Laser Counter is not a good choice.

Students also have access to text resources containing information that will help them make better choices. Fifth-grade students' reactions to the catalogs and text resources during Phase I have been very revealing. When they first broke into small groups to discuss their individual choices of items, everyone tended to acknowledge everyone else's choice as okay. Despite being warned that not all the items in the catalog were legitimate, students did not show an inclination to read the catalog items critically. Instead, each tended to express a preference much as one might pick a favorite song or pair of shoes.

In one group, a student eventually remembered something from a previous Jasper adventure the class had solved that involved analysis of arguments made by video-based "hucksters" (see CTGV, 1997). This recollection of the Jasper hucksters took place in a context where a student (S1) said: "I want this Super Collector Cone":

S2: You just want to get that because it comes with a free magnifying glass.

S3: That's why they did it! To fool us. That's why they did it! You have to know these sales things. Because if you had been there when we had Jasper, then you would know that. This man was trying to fool us into getting his sales plan, but we didn't because we knew the tricks. And that's why they put in that free magnifying glass, so you would buy it.

The Original
0.5 mm Mesh
Hockmeister Dip Net

AquaScientific
for accurate macroinvertebrate testing

0.5 mm

Everyone knows you can't get a macroinvertebrate sample to test for pollution without a good net. The 0.5 mm Hockmeister has been a standard for years. It provides a quick and easy way to check whether there is water pollution — almost any kind of pollution — without having to do hundreds of water tests. Because of its convenient size, the Hockmeister Net is the right size for small teams of people. A single person can hold the net while another person dislodges the macroinvertebrates from the bottom of the stream and directs them into the net. This net is guaranteed to catch all of the different types of macroinvertebrates that are in your sample area.

Catalog Item 7325: 0.5 mm Mesh Hockmeister Dip Net

TetraBen™
Laser Counter

Knowing the number of macroinvertebrates in your water is an important way to determine the health of your river. Collecting and counting these organisms can be a slow, tedious process. Modern science has revolutionized this process. The TetraBen Laser Counter lets you count macroinvertebrates without getting your hands wet! Simply scan the laser beam slowly over the water. The laser beam automatically counts the macroinvertebrates, and shows the total number on a built-in screen. The laser is completely water-proof and won't harm anything, living or non-living (and that includes macroinvertebrates and humans!). Simple, safe and completely accurate!

Catalog Item 2612: TetraBen Laser Counter

FIG. 13.1/a and b . Sample items from macroinvertebrate catalog.

This comment helped group members change their orientation toward reading the catalog. Nevertheless, the preferred mode was still to accept everyone's choice as okay.

Some groups entered into discussions that were a little deeper than "my choice is okay and so is yours." The following represents an excerpt of a discussion on the macroinvertebrate catalog by one group of fifth graders trying to make a single choice of a tool for their group:

S1: I think we should get the Hock [Cray] Fish Trap because we need to catch the crayfish fish.

S3: We don't need to catch the crayfish fish. What we are doing is catching ...

S2: The macroinvertebrates.

S3: Which they are crayfish fish, but all these other insect things are, too.

S1: Okay.

S2: I think we should get the Laser Counter.

S1: Why?

S2: Because if we ... you all you got to do is point it down at the water and the count is what is important.

S1: Okay. Do you think we should get the net or something else [directed to S3]?

S3: I think we should get the net because the Crayfish Trap might not catch all the macroinvertebrates and we need to catch all the macroinvertebrates.

This segment illustrates how the contrasting cases can help students focus on important goals and features related to macroinvertebrate sampling. For example, the students began by clarifying whether they need to catch crayfish only or other types of macroinvertebrates as well. The group then discussed two tools designed to give them information about all macroin-vertebrates in the water—the Laser Counter and the Hockmeister Net. S2 believes that the former tool is best because "the count is what is important." S3 believes that the Net is best because "we need to catch all of the macroinvertebrates." These kinds of discussions can help students define learning goals. Additional text resources provided in SMART environments are designed to help them meet these goals.

Early in the project, students' uses of the resources were also quite telling. Initially, they almost never consulted their resources and simply argued from their existing knowledge. When prompted by their teachers to use the resources, they often used very inefficient strategies. In particular, many students started at the beginning of the resources, presumably with the intention of reading all the way through. This is a very inefficient strategy because the resource book was over 50 pages in length! Students who tried this approach never reached the end of the text and were frustrated by the task. Even when teachers tried to remedy the situation by modeling the use of the table of contents and subject index, they found that students did not easily grasp the idea. Most students seemed used to the idea of being given passages that they always read from beginning to end. They had almost no experience in first setting learning goals and then choosing resources that might help them accomplish those goals.

Opportunities for Feedback, Reflection, and Revision in Phase I

We were not surprised that students initially had difficulty engaging in effective discussions that resulted in the articulation of new learning goals followed by a search for relevant resources. Activities such as these are rare in many classrooms. SMART is designed to help students develop expertise in these areas by allowing them to experience several cycles of work, feedback, and revision.

In traditional school settings, it is surprisingly rare for students to receive formative feedback and for them to revise their work. When we asked a random sample of fifth-grade students if and when they revise in school, 24% indicated that they never do. Of those who were able to describe a revision experience, 63% of the time the revision was a low-level task, such as checking spelling or punctuation, or copying something over to make it neater.

Providing support for revision is particularly important with respect to metacognition. There is little motivation to monitor one's current level of understanding and preparedness if there are no opportunities to revise based on one's assessment. Classroom structures often do not lend themselves to opportunities to revise for an important "consequential task." Consequently, students do not get to experience some of the powerful benefits of reflection, and this, we suspect, reduces their inclination to monitor their learning.

Feedback From the WWW. In *Stones River Mystery*, students input their choices of catalog items to a World Wide Web (WWW) site that we developed, and the site automatically produces formative feedback for them. Students use SMART WWWeb to "order" a sampling tool. Figures 13.2a and 13.2b contain items from the Web order form. As can be seen, students are asked to justify their choice of tool and their rejection of others. After completing their orders, students submit them and receive feedback over the Web. Figure 13.3 contains a segment of the feedback. If students select the Laser Counter, for example, they are told that the *number* of macroinvertebrates is not the information that they need to know. The feedback also suggests sections in their text resources to read that will help them learn more about how macroinvertebrates are used as indicators of water quality. Students are enthusiastic about receiving feedback from the Web and are anxious to print and read it. Teachers report that students seem much more interested to receive feedback from the Web than feedback from them, even when the teachers' feedback is computer-generated and looks ostensibly the same.

The Web site also provides teachers with information about students' choices and justifications. These data are collected in a log that teachers can access and print out. Teachers can also access graphs that summarize tool choice and justifications for their own classes and for all participating classes (we discuss this feature in more detail later). In this way, teachers are privy to information at the individual and the class level on current conceptions and misunderstandings concerning macroinvertebrate sampling.

SMART Lab: Support for Reflection.   After working with the contrasting cases and accessing the WWW for feedback, students use two additional, Web-based resources: SMART Lab and Kids Online. SMART Lab is comprised of graphs that summarize the choices (e.g., of water quality testing tools or pollution clean-up plans) and justifications entered by students. Input from students is stored in a database on our server. A computer program interfaces this database with a graphing program. Teachers can decide to discuss data that have been aggregated across all participating classes or can examine the data for each class separately. SMART Lab was designed as a tool for teachers to help them engage their students in conversations on different ways of solving problems, and in so doing, to help students reflect more about important concepts. For example, the class might talk about which testing tools or pollution clean-up plans were selected most often, and why these options were chosen. Our observations in classrooms suggest that an excellent way for teachers to gain insight into students' misconceptions and to motivate students to rethink their choices is to discuss a tool or plan that the teacher knows is *not* a good one. The class might also discuss their data relative to the data from other classes.

Kids Online.   Another page in the Web site is Kids Online. In Kids Online, students are asked as a class to provide feedback to students who are working on the same problem. Their feedback and the feedback from other classes is published online, and students receive responses from the

---

Catalog Item 2612
TetraBen Laser Counter

Do you want to select this item?   Yes ○   No ○
If no, why not select it?

○   (a) because there is no way to know if the laser counted correctly

○   (b) because it doesn't tell you what types of macroinvertebrates are in the sample

○   (c) this would work but I chose to use something else to test macroinvertebrates

If yes, why select it?

○   (a) because it will not hurt the macroinvertebrates that you count

○   (b) because it is safe for the environment

○   (c) because it is an easy way to count macroinvertebrates

---

Catalog Item 7325
0.5 mm
Mesh Hockmeister Dip Net

Do you want to select this item?   Yes ○   No ○
If no, why not select it?

○   (a) the holes in the mesh are too big; some of the macroinvertebrates might slip through the holes in the mesh

○   (b) fish might get caught up in the net

○   (c) this would work but I chose to use something else to test macroinvertebrates

If yes, why select it?

○   (a) the holes in the mesh are small enough to catch even the smallest macroinvertebrate

○   (b) because of its convenient size, the net is the right size for small teams

○   (c) because it is an easy way to count macroinvertebrates

---

FIG. 13.2a (top) and b (bottom). Sample items from SMART WWWeb macroinvertebrate catalog order form.

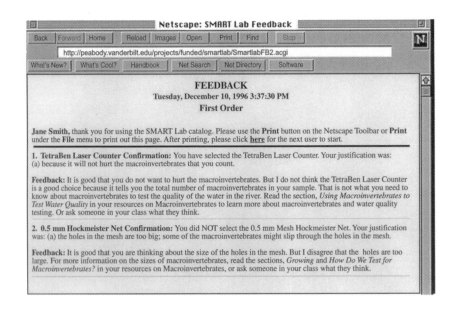

FIG. 13.3. Segment of SMART WWWeb feedback.

online student. Students are extremely motivated to help their peers, and Kids Online motivates some rich classroom discussions. To facilitate this process, we suggest to teachers that they first have individual students write feedback to the online students, have students then share their feedback, and finally have the class discuss and come to consensus on feedback that they will send. The following is an excerpt from Kids Online. The student, AJ, is discussing macroinvertebrate testing:

When I first read the catalog, I liked the TetraBen Lasers 'cause they're easy to use and lasers are cool. But some of the other tools looked pretty good too. You know, I realized that I didn't really know how to pick the best one. I mean, I didn't know how I was going to use the macroinvertebrates to test for pollution. So I did some research in my Resource book.

I looked in the index and found the section on how to use macroinvertebrates to test water pollution. I learned that to test for pollution I need to know the names of all the different macroinvertebrates that are in the river. The more types that live there, the healthier the water is. When water is polluted, some types die before other types do. Like, if the water is polluted, the mayflies will die before the earthworms do. The ones that die first in polluted water are the ones that need a lot of dissolved oxygen to live because polluted water doesn't have much dissolved oxygen.

So, I think that we should order the Plastic Super Collector Cone because it catches everything in the river. Both of the Hockmeister Nets would work too—you could use them to catch all of the macroinvertebrates in the river. But the Super Collector Cone is even better because it is solid plastic, so it collects bacteria too. Bacteria are bad for rivers, and if you catch a lot of different types of bacteria, your river is pretty polluted.

And the Collector Cone comes with a magnifying glass. I can use it to look at the bacteria.

That's the way I see it. Do you think I am on the right track? Send me your feedback.

Note that classes can use Kids Online to reflect on the process and form of AJ's thinking (i.e., he explains himself well, and even models the process of using text resources to find) as well as its content (i.e., AJ has some misconceptions about bacteria and the sizes of macroinvertebrates). Here is some feedback that one fifth-grade class sent to AJ:

We disagree with your choice of the Super Plastic Collector Cone. It collects bacteria, and we are not talking about bacteria, we are talking about macroin-vertebrates. We also think that it will be too heavy, and it might break. We think it will collect more water than macroinvertebrates. A good tool will help us put the macroinvertebrates into 3 groups—pollution tolerant, pollution intolerant, and sort of pollution tolerant.

Here's what another class sent to AJ:

We do not agree with your choice of the Super Collector Cone. We did an experiment with a cup and pieces of paper towels that were the macroinver-tebrates. The macroinvertebrates went in the cup with the water. As water rushes in the cup, water, macroinvertebrates and bacteria would come out. We would lose some of the macroinvertebrates and not have all of the macroinvertebrates to count. We think that you need to revise your order.

The activities related to SMART Lab and Kids Online give students a chance to hear how other students are thinking and why. They use the information they have learned, along with their feedback, to revise their work. During revision they can also access the text resources on river ecosystems that we developed. After revising their thinking, students again visit SMART WWWeb and make new choices of catalog items and new

322   VYE ET AL.

justifications. They can then see summarized data from their class and other classes and see how the data have changed.

Additional Supports for Learning

As noted earlier, the students' challenge is to decide if Stones River is polluted. Once students have learned about how and why scientists sample macroinvertebrates, they "test" Stones River and interpret the data. For example, for macroinvertebrates they use a simulation that enables them to collect and sort a sample of macroinvertebrates and derive a water-quality index. Figure 13.4 shows a sample of macroinvertebrates. Students can click on any of the pictures to see an enlarged view of the macroinvertebrate. They use a Field Guide to identify the macroinvertebrate and its pollution tolerance category. They enter this information into the computer and if they are correct, they are asked to click and drag the macroinvertebrate into the appropriate pollution tolerance "tray" that is seen at the bottom of Fig 13.4. Once students have identified and sorted all of the macroinvertebrates in their sample, they calculate a water quality index, and compare their results to previous data from Stones River (see Figure 13.5). Clicking on any one of the data points displays the sample of macroinvertebrates comprising

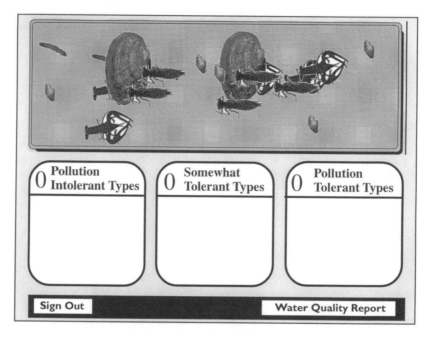

FIG. 13.4. Sample of macroinvertebrates as displayed in water-quality-testing software.

that water quality index. By comparing the content of previous samples with their current sample, students are able to "see" how the biodiversity of the river has changed. Although each student using the simulation gets a different sample of macroinvertebrates, each set of data shows that there is a serious absence of pollution sensitive macroinvertebrates in Stones River.

A RETURN TO THE ANCHOR VIDEO: PHASE II

Having discovered that some of the macroinvertebrates have died, students are encouraged to conduct further tests of the river to help them determine why they might have died and if the water is polluted. In particular, students focus on dissolved oxygen testing. Testing dissolved oxygen constitutes Phase II of the instructional sequence.

Dissolved oxygen is a pivotal concept in understanding pollution and ecosystems. Virtually every living animal, including micro-organisms like bacteria, require oxygen to live, and almost all forms of pollution will affect the amount of dissolved oxygen in the water available to nonplants. To

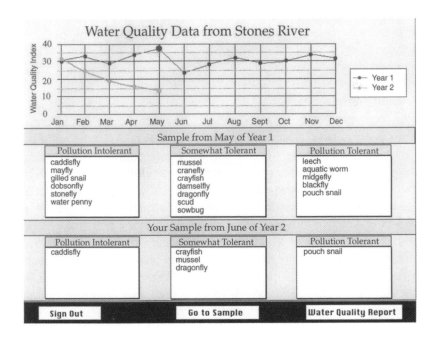

FIG. 13.5. Normative data as displayed in water-quality-testing software

understand the role of dissolved oxygen at the level of the ecosystem, we believe that it is important for students to understand dissolved oxygen at the molecular level as well. For example, to understand thermal pollution, students must understand how heat affects molecules (i.e., molecules of water and dissolved oxygen move faster and farther apart, and some escape into the air.).

Our pilot work indicates that prior to *Stones River Mystery*, many students have not learned much about molecules; they think that water is comprised of small units of water, or that water molecules are in water (see also Lee, Eichinger, Anderson, Berkheimer, & Blakeslee, 1993). Many also have the misconception that dissolved oxygen is a weaker form of oxygen—just like sugar dissolved in water is weaker than undiluted sugar—or, alternatively, that dissolved oxygen is a bubble in water.

Contrasting Cases for Phase II

In Phase II, students go through the same cycle of activities as in Phase I, except that they are focused on issues related to testing dissolved oxygen. Students first revisit the anchor to learn more about how and why scientists test dissolved oxygen. Teachers also do a "benchmark" lesson (Brown & Campione, 1994) where they introduce students to molecular models of water and dissolved oxygen. Then, once again students examine a set of contrasting cases. In this instance, the cases consist of tools that can be used to measure dissolved oxygen. Students are asked to review the tools and to justify their selection or rejection of each. They are encouraged to consult their text resources on dissolved oxygen whenever necessary.

The "bogus" tools in this set are designed to be foils for common misconceptions. As already noted, one misconception students have is that dissolved oxygen is weaker than regular oxygen. We included contrasts that motivate students to rethink this idea. For example, one item in the dissolved-oxygen catalog is Preservo, a chemical that stops oxygen from dissolving. The catalog also includes bogus testing tools that manipulate the water in ways that change the amount of dissolved oxygen. For example, the Agitator comes with a hand-held mixer. The mixer beats the water and causes bubbles of dissolved oxygen to form. The Agitator's manufacturer guarantees that counting these bubbles will provide an accurate measure of the amount of dissolved oxygen in the water. This item is designed to focus students on the size of molecules and the process of aeration. Another item, the Chem-Kit Probe, purports to contain a chemical that reacts with dissolved oxygen if the water sample is first heated to 212°. To reject this item, students will need to understand what happens to matter when it is heated.

Opportunities for Feedback, Reflection, and Revision in Phase II

Having studied the dissolved-oxygen items, students again use our internet site to input their "order" and get feedback about their decisions. Once again, the feedback suggests assumptions or concepts that students need to reconsider, and helpful resources to consult. Students are encouraged to consult particular chapters in their text resources. The feedback also suggests that they conduct some experiments. For example, the feedback recommends that students conduct an experiment to study the effects of temperature on dissolved oxygen. These experiments function as resources that help students better understand concepts related to dissolved oxygen and pollution.

The SMART WWWeb site for dissolved oxygen also contains other supports for reflection; they are designed to stimulate students to consider and reconcile other students' ideas about dissolved oxygen. There is a SMART Lab location where students can see and discuss other classes' choices of dissolved oxygen tools, and their reasons for selecting or rejecting tools. There is also a Kids Online location containing two online students' thinking related to dissolved oxygen tools. Each class submits online feedback to these "internet" students.

Students then revise their dissolved oxygen catalog "orders" using the above-mentioned resources, (i.e., feedback, the results from their experiments, and what they learned from their peers and by discussing SMART Lab and Kids Online). After revising their thinking, students again visit SMART WWWeb and make new choices of catalog tools and new justifications. They can again see summarized data from their class and other classes and see how the data have changed.

Is the Stones River Polluted?

As with the macroinvertebrate phase, the final activity in the dissolved oxygen phase is to conduct a dissolved-oxygen test of a sample of water from Stones River and interpret the results relative to normative data for that site on the river. This is the final piece needed to solve the challenge of whether Stones River is polluted. Students will discover that the river is seriously depleted of dissolved oxygen, and that the river is in trouble.

PHASE III OF THE RIVER CHALLENGE

Once students have determined that Stones River is polluted, they then return to the anchor video and see what was found by the students in the movie. The video students also find that the water is polluted, and they proceed to track down the source of the pollution. Eventually, the students in the movie discover the source of the pollution—vegetable and animal grease is leaking from barrels that have been illegally dumped along the river. The perpetrator is a local fast-food restaurant. At this point another challenge is posed to students. They are asked to decide how to clean up the pollution. This challenge constitutes Phase III.

Contrasting Cases for Phase III

Once students have determined that Stones River is polluted and move on to their next challenge, they should better understand dissolved oxygen, including the exchange of oxygen between plants and fish and macroinvertebrates, and how other factors such as temperature and turbidity influence the amount of dissolved oxygen. But they are not likely to have learned about bacteria, and consequently, have not fully explored the interdependencies of the river ecosystem. We therefore developed contrasting cases that motivate students to think about these issues. These cases are designed to help the students understand a model of the overall ecosystem by encouraging thought experiments about the implications of different models. Students are given the set of clean-up proposals and are asked to decide which plan they think is the best and why. They must also provide a rationale for not choosing each of the other proposals. These contrasting cases are designed to motivate students to think about the interrelation of living things in a river ecosystem, especially the role of bacteria, and how balance is lost and regained. The contrasts are designed to prompt children to think about what happens when grease is dumped in the river, and how bacteria are both part of the problem and part of the solution to cleaning up the river. For example, Decomposer Inc. describes how adding bacteria will help decompose the grease, whereas Recycle Kings advocates killing disease-ridden bacteria because grease is causing them to multiply, and so on. As students "run" their thought experiments about the likely chain of events, they identify gaps in their knowledge, such as whether bacteria are necessarily going to make things sick.

Opportunities for Feedback, Reflection, and Revision in Phase III

As with Phases I and II, students access SMART WWWeb to input and receive feedback on their tentative hiring decisions. In Phase III, the feedback comes from the SMART Better Business Bureau. Students learn whether the Bureau has received any complaints about the company, and what, if any, fraudulent claims the company has made (e.g., that fish eat grease, causing them to gain weight). Before making final hiring decisions, students are advised to read sections of their text resources and to conduct experiments to help them learn more. In addition, students discuss SMART Lab—in Phase III it contains other classes' hiring choices and reasons. Students also submit written feedback to students in Kids Online. Finally, students revise their hiring decisions, and use the SMART Better Business Bureau one last time to get feedback.

PHASE IV: GOING TO A LOCAL RIVER

Working with *Stones River Mystery* enables students to have a simulated experience with water-pollution monitoring and clean-up at the same time as they are immersed in the underlying river science. As a follow-up to these experiences, students also participate in an actual river project. In this project, students visit a local river, and conduct the water-quality tests that they learned about in the context of *Stones River Mystery*.

Elsewhere (e.g., Barron et al., in press; CTGV, 1997) we discuss why we prefer to combine problem-based learning (i.e., the use of simulated anchors and other resources) with project-based learning (i.e., opportunities to actually engage in tasks such as monitoring a river). Projects can be highly motivating experiences for students; they want to prepare as well as possible. Nevertheless, we and others find that learning outcomes in projects often fall short of what one might desire. Part of the problem is that the learning goals for these projects are often not well-articulated (see Barron et al., in press). Even when the goals are well-specified, students need scaffolds to help them think deeply about underlying concepts as they are preparing to do the project. Research conducted by Moore, Sherwood, Bateman, Brans-ford, and Goldman (1996) suggests that prefacing project activities with work on a related problem can significantly enhance the quality of students' project work. Students acquire the conceptual framework through their problem-based experiences that transfer to the project.

Students who participate in SMART understand that the problem-based work is preparatory to the project, and that it is a chance for them to gain the expertise that will enable them to perform well on the project. This is especially salient because the project is a high-stakes event for students: Students' project work is examined and used by an external audience if it meets prespecified criteria as to its quality. For example, after students conduct water-pollution tests at a local river, they prepare and present a report on their findings. Their presentations are videotaped and examined by our research personnel. If they are found to be valid, the tapes and reports are forwarded to our water-pollution-control agency for inclusion in their database on water quality.

Projects such as these are authentic both from the standpoint of the activities themselves (i.e., students do the same things that scientists do when they monitor water quality), and also from the standpoint of their evaluation and consequences. In the real world, water-quality data must be collected and interpreted appropriately so that scientists can help us pre-serve our environment. These are essentially the standards to which stu-dents were held. We speculate that this contributes to the high interest and sense of importance that students derived from their work. Students felt that they have done important work and were proud of their accomplish-ments. These feelings were reinforced by the response students received from the scientists who reviewed their video presentations and reports. The scientists related to us that they were very impressed by the quality of students' thinking and presentation skills, and at their own initiative, sent letters to this effect to students.

In previous research, we found that students' experiences in SMART are significant even after the project is long finished (Barron et al., in press; CTGV, 1997). Last year, we conducted interviews with a cohort of children who had participated in SMART the previous year. The interviewers—who were unfamiliar to the students—told students that they were interested in their ideas about school, in particular their impressions of fifth grade. The interviewer first asked a series of questions that were general in nature, for example, students' favorite and least favorite activities. They also asked: "What was the most important thing you did in fifth grade?", "Did you do anything in fifth grade that made you feel proud?", "Did you do anything in fifth grade where you used your creativity and imagination?", and "Did you do anything in fifth grade that you would like to do again?" "SMART" was the most frequent response given when students were asked about the most important thing they did, the most creative thing they did, and the thing they would like to do again. It was the second most frequent response to the question on what made them proud—the most frequent response was getting a good grade. Furthermore, it was not merely a select group of students for whom SMART was significant; almost 60% of the sample answered "SMART" to at least one of the four questions.

A SMART DESIGN EXPERIMENT

Our collaborators on SMART are a cadre of nine, fifth-grade teachers and their students from a middle school in Nashville, Tennessee. One of the teachers has been associated with the project since its inception; each year since then, we have added new teachers. The school in which we are working serves a disproportionate number of lower achieving students and is designated as school-wide Title I because virtually all students qualify for free or reduced lunch.

Teachers teach SMART each day in a 45-minute period that they have set aside for this purpose. They typically complete two or three modules, such as the *Stones River Mystery* module, over the course of a school year. Our initial development and research on SMART was conducted using anchors from our mathematical problem-solving series *The Adventures of Jasper Woodbury*. *Stones River Mystery* is our most recently developed module. We pilot-tested an abbreviated version of the module (we did not have enough time to include the third challenge in which students are asked to hire a company to clean up the pollution), and we are currently implementing the entire module.

Initial findings from our pilot work on *Stones River Mystery* follow. We also discuss data as it relates to SMART's supports for reflection; we discuss findings from an earlier study in which we examined the value-added of our resources for student learning, as well as students' conceptions and use of some of these features.

Learning in the Context of *Stones River Mystery*

Prior to and following *Stones River Mystery*, we gave students a test designed to measure their learning of the embedded science concepts. Table 13.1 contains the concepts we targeted and several sample test items. The test was comprised of both multiple-choice and open-ended items. We targeted concepts in two areas. First, we included questions designed to assess students' knowledge of molecules, namely, water and dissolved-oxygen

TABLE 13.1

Sample Items From Science Assessment

Molecules

Water molecules:

a. Make up water.

b. Are mixed in with water.

c. Are not part of water.

What is dissolved oxygen

a. Oxygen that is weaker than regular oxygen.

b. Oxygen that is part of a water molecule.

c. Oxygen that is in-between water molecules.

d. Oxygen that falls apart when wet.

e. Little bubbles in water.

When you heat water, which of the following things happen? (You can circle more than 1 answer.)

a. The molecules move faster and further apart, and some of the dissolved oxygen escapes into the air.

b. The water attracts oxygen to its surface, so the water gets more dissolved oxygen.

c. The molecules move faster and there is less room for dissolved oxygen.

d. Heating water does not do anything to the amount of dissolved oxygen.

Fish tanks have pumps that pump oxygen into the water. Rivers don't have pumps like fish tanks. How do rivers get oxygen? (You may circle more than one answer.)

a. There are lots of fish in rivers and they take the place of a pump by giving off oxygen.

b. Rivers do not need oxygen like fish tanks do.

c. When the river runs fast over rocks and water falls or splashes around, oxygen from the air gets mixed up in the water.

d. There are never enough fish or macroinvertebrates to use up all the oxygen so there is no need to get oxygen in the water.

e. There are lots of plants in rivers and they take the place of a pump by giving off oxygen.

Water Quality Testing

Why do scientists collect samples of macroinvertebrates from a river to help them find out if the water is polluted?

a. Microinvertebrates such as bacteria cause pollution.

b. If they collect a lot of macroinvertebrates in each sample, it means that the water is polluted.

c. If they collect a lot of crayfish in their sample, it means the water is polluted.

d. If certain types of macroinvertebrates are missing, the river is polluted.

Mr. Mayfield, a biologist, tested the river near his home. He found that dissolved oxygen was very low. He then sampled the macroinvertebrates. What would you predict about his sample?

a. There would probably be more macroinvertebrates than normal.

b. Many of the macroinvertebrates would be bacteria.

c. There would probably be many fewer types of macroinvertebrates than normal.

d. The level of dissolved oxygen would not help you predict anything about his sample.

Which macroinvertebrates are pollution tolerant?

a. Ones that do not need much oxygen or can store oxygen.

b. Ones that can eat bacteria without it killing them.

c. Ones that can live in water that has a lot of dissolved oxygen.

d. Ones that eat plants instead of other animals to survive.

molecules (e.g., "What is dissolved oxygen?", "What is water made of?", "What happens when you heat molecules?"). One misconception that students often have is that dissolved oxygen is a weaker form of oxygen, and consistent with this assumption, that it is a bad thing for the river. We included items and foils designed to identify this misconception. We also asked students to draw a picture of dissolved oxygen in water. We were particularly interested to see how students' models of these substances might change with instruction. For example, a common misconception of students is that molecules are in water instead of comprising water (Lee et al., 1993). We were interested to learn how our students would represent these molecular structures. Also related to molecules, we included questions that were designed to assess students' understanding of the effects of temperature and turbidity on dissolved oxygen and water because these factors are relevant to the context of river pollution (e.g., when substances that increase water temperature are discharged into rivers, the levels of dissolved oxygen decrease).

A second set of test questions involved students' understanding of the tests used to monitor water quality and why they are used. For example, we asked what determines the pollution tolerance of a macroinvertebrate, and how to predict what the dissolved oxygen levels might be if the water quality index was low.

Figure 13.6 contains the mean proportion of students correctly answering the multiple-choice questions related to molecules and water-quality testing. The largest pre-to-post change was on the water-quality testing items. At posttest, an average of 62% of the sample correctly answered these questions as compared with 33% at pretest. This is perhaps not surprising because the greatest amount of instructional time was devoted to thinking about water molecules and dissolved oxygen in the context of water-quality testing. Nonetheless, there were improvements on the molecule items as well. The largest changes were on the items that relate how heat and turbidity affect dissolved oxygen (i.e., heat causes dissolved oxygen and water molecules to move faster and farther apart, and some molecules to escape in the air; alternatively, turbidity causes oxygen to mix with and become trapped between water molecules).

Students' conceptions of dissolved oxygen improved as well. When we asked "What is dissolved oxygen" at pretest, students were likely to say one of two things: "It is a weaker form of dissolved oxygen" or "It is little bubbles in water." At posttest, neither of these were modal responses. Instead, the most frequent answer was "oxygen that is in-between water molecules."

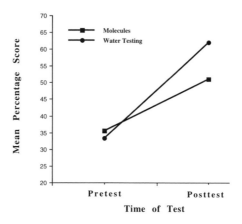

FIG. 13.6. Performance on assessment of concepts related to molecules and water quality testing.

Some students also responded with "oxygen that is part of a water molecule." Although incorrect, the latter response indicates that these students have some understanding of molecular structure. This interpretation is consistent with the findings from the item where we asked students to draw a picture of dissolved oxygen in water. At pretest, none of the students drew molecular representations. They drew pictures like those in Fig. 13.7a. At posttest, 35% of the students drew representations that were purely molecular and looked similar to those in Fig. 13.7b (i.e., both water and dissolved oxygen were represented as molecules), and an additional 15% drew pictures that were in part molecular (i.e., they drew representations that were micro-and macro-scopic). The drawings of the remaining students depicted bubbles in water. What is unclear from these representations is whether students understand that the bubbles are macroscopic. One possibility is that they drew bubbles so that the viewer could "see" the molecules.

Our results from the river project, although preliminary, are encouraging. We know from previous research in the domain of mathematics that problem-based learning using anchors is associated with greater learning gains than traditional instruction on the same content (CTGV, 1997; Pellegrino, Hickey, Heath, Rewey, Vye, & CTGV, 1991; Van Haneghan et al. 1992). We also know from our mathematics work that SMART resources (e.g., SMART Lab, Kids Online) enhance learning even more (Barron et al., 1995). Our pilot findings in the domain of science suggest that students

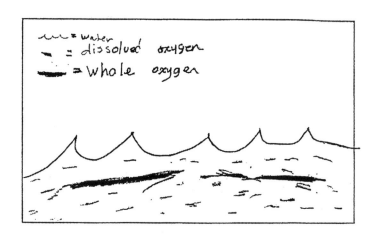

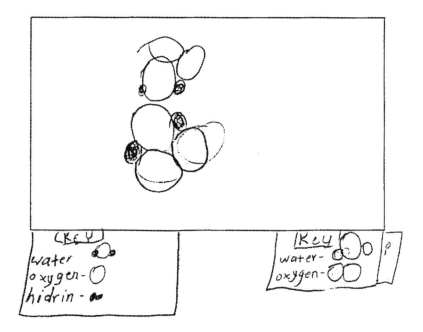

FIG. 13.7a (top) and b (bottom). Student's illustration of molecules at pretest and posttest.

can also learn important science content by participating in reflection and revision around meaningful problems and projects.

Changes in Monitoring

The foregoing results showed that SMART helped some students develop a deep understanding of some scientific concepts. But we still wanted to know whether there were changes in the ways the children monitored their own thinking and one another's thinking during the course of SMART. To this end, we video-taped groups of students as they made their initial and revised catalog choices. We hoped that the conversations would evolve into thoughtful discussions that attempted to identify key knowledge and cognition issues. The following is an example of the type of conversation that we had hoped for and found. In this case, the students were discussing their revised choices for the dissolved oxygen catalog. To help the reader notice how the students explicitly discuss knowledge and thinking issues, we have italicized their occurrences. In addition to typifying the type of reflection we found, we have chosen this protocol because it shows how the catalogs scaffolded the students' differentiation of important ideas. In this case, the students are aware that they are "helping" a river, but as a group, they had not yet distinguished between helping the river by monitoring it and helping the river by fixing it:

[In response to a question about whether to order Preservo]

S3:   No.

S2:   Why?

S3:   Because you don't want to change nothing.

S2:   Hold on. You might want this after you think about it.

S3:   No. I don't. You want to test the water, not save the oxygen.

S1:   But we do want dissolved oxygen. That's what you …

S4:   This is what you want to help out the river. Not if you are testing it.

S2:   Our last answer was no because we wanted to see how many dissolved oxygen is in the water.

S3:   How about this? You're not helping, you are testing the river not helping it right now.

S2: But we are trying to help it.

S3: But you got to test it first. See if it has to have any help at all.

S2: You won't even know if you need to help it when you test it.

S3: Yeah. *That's what I am thinking about.*

S1: That's what's hard about ...

S3: You have to test it before you can test it.

In general, we have found that over the course of SMART the students' conversations evolved so they became similar to the conversation just presented. The conversations were reflective and the students were explicitly attentive to their levels of understanding. Moreover, the students' abilities to discuss these matters without the support of an adult also improved. In the following protocol, we track a group of students as they work on their initial catalog order for macroinvertebrates, their revised macroinvertebrate catalog order, and then their revised order for the dissolved-oxygen catalog. Although we only show snippets of each protocol, the reduction in adult support was evident in the complete protocols: For the first macroinvertebrate order, the teacher took 20% of the turns; for the revised order, the teacher took 11% of the turns; and for the revised oxygen order, the teacher took 0% of the turns. Also, notice that in the first protocol, the students are merely "butting heads," in the second protocol they begin to justify their choices, and in the third protocol they are engaged in a give and take of reasoning.

(1) INITIAL ORDER FROM THE MACROINVERTEBRATE CATALOG

S3: In this it has two of the same thing and I don't know what they are talking about, because what if you are to put "no" on each one if they are the same thing?

Teacher: What?

S3: It has two nets. The same thing as that one. The same thing. What am I supposed to do, write the same thing? Two of the same thing. So what am I supposed to do. Write the same question?

Teacher: Ask them if they are the same. The first thing you need to do is to ask somebody in your group.

S3:   I already know they are the same.

Teacher: Well, you need to discuss it with your group. Do they think they are the same? Is there anything that they think are different?

S3   I am supposed to pick the one I want. Why I want that one and why I don't want it, if I didn't want it, and if I did want it?

Teacher: Do you want to help him?

All: No!

S1:   Ok, what did you say?

S2:   Yeah.

S3:   No. B.

S1:   No. B?

S3:   Yes, it says B.

All: Where?

S3:   Right here.

S1:   Okay.

S2:   Are these two the same?

S3:   Yes.

S2:   No, they are not.

S3:   Yes, they are.

S2:   No, they are not.

S3:   They are.

S1:   You are going to use up my eraser.

(2) REVISED MACROINVERTEBRATE ORDER

S1: This is the Hockmeister Dip Net, or whatever. 2 cm mesh, whatever. I said I wouldn't because it has big holes and the macroinvertebrates can slip out. I got one more. I got the Plastic Super Collector Cone, and I put that ...

Teacher: Let's don't talk about that.

S1: Ok. OK, Desiree. OK, then the next.

S2: OK, then.

S1: Which one was it—0.5 or the other?

S3: I agree with you [S1] because the macroinvertebrates can slip out.

S4: I agree with you, too, because the net, it can't be too big, but it can't be too small.

S5: I agree.

Teacher: So all of you agree?

S1: Okay, next.

(3) REVISED ORDER FROM DISSOLVED OXYGEN CATALOG

S1: But look, remember when we wrote the letters and we had to look at all that stuff again and it had said that it would not harm the animals and it says that it will keep the water from preserving so ... right here it says under Preservo ... it says that you know that fish and other animals and rivers need oxygen. So, what you are going to do is to keep it all from dissolving.

S2: [Reading] "Our miracle Preservo solution can solve your problem. One drop of Preservo will save the oxygen in 10 gallons of water without hurting anything that lives in the river." Do you understand that?

S4: Is it going to take the dissolved oxygen away or ...

S2: That's what I couldn't understand. It takes the dissolved oxygen away and then it says that it is not going to harm the animals, fish, and macroinvertebrates, but it is going to take the dissolved oxygen away and the macroinvertebrates need dissolved oxygen.

> S3: So, it will harm them.

> S4: It will kill them.

> S1: It is just trying to make us order that.

Teachers Impressions of the River Project

Comments from our collaborating teachers about SMART science were also encouraging. We asked them to compare their assessments of students' learning in the problem-to-project sequence with assessments of what had been learned the previous year when their students focused only on the river project without any problem-based preparation:

Teacher #1: The SMART River curriculum is very different [from the one used previously] and the difference showed when students went to the river. The focus in the SMART curriculum was on a balanced ecosystem. When the students went to the river, they looked for that balance. There was no focus in the other curriculum. It was a "humongous compilation of activities." Pollution in that setup came to mean outside contaminants, like trash and oil. With the SMART curriculum, pollution meant an ecosystem out of balance.

Teacher #2: The first year students went to the river they did tests for pH, macroinvertebrate Water Quality Index, and temperature, but they didn't know why they were doing these tests or what they meant. After SMART Science, they were much better prepared. They knew why they were doing the tests and could hypothesize about what might have caused possible pollution. These causes were not one step (e.g., Oil got in the water), but multiple step (e.g., Algae grew too much due to fertilizer, this blocked out sunlight, plants died causing dissolved oxygen to decrease).

Teacher #3: The process of justifying choices that students had to make in SMART opened their eyes to what they were supposed to be looking for. If they went to the river without doing the SMART curriculum, they would take the critter sample and think everything was fine because there were critters in there. Students wouldn't know they needed to look for different types, so the sampling would just reinforce wrong ideas. Students would think pollution was just trash.

An interesting aspect of these comments is that the teachers had been quite pleased with the previous river curriculum before they had completed the problem-to-project sequence. It was only after they had seen the big picture of what projects could become that they realized how much had been missing in their previous implementations of the river curriculum.

Students' Conceptions of the SMART Revision Cycle

The results just given suggest that the SMART resources are effective for promoting further learning of important concepts. We have also been interested to understand what students think about and how well they are able to negotiate the revision process because we know from baseline interviews that feedback and revision are not typical in their experience. To investigate students' understanding of the revision process, we conducted a series of structured interviews with a random sample of students from each of two classes participating in SMART. We interviewed them after each of two cycles of problem solving and revision. During each interview, we first asked students "Did you revise your work?" If the student answered in the affirmative, we followed up by asking "What did you change?" and "How did you know that you needed to change that?" Our purpose here was to find out which, if any, of the classroom resources were being used by students to help them revise.

All students indicated that they had done some revision and were able to specifically cite at least one change that they had made. Figure 13.8 contains their responses to the question "How did you know that you needed to revise that?" (Note that the percentages across categories do not sum to 100 because some students mentioned more than one information source.) Close to 50% of the students reported that they had made a particular change because of what they had read in the feedback sheet. Students also mentioned using a range of other resources, including the SMART programs, the anchor video, their peers, and their teacher.

Later in our interviews we directly asked students if they had used their feedback sheets and the SMART resources (in this case, video versions of Kids Online and SMART Lab). A large majority of students reported using their feedback sheets when specifically asked (75% and 90% in Interviews 1 and 2, respectively). Similarly, a large majority reported using the SMART resources (86% and 75% in Interviews 1 and 2, respectively).

Although our interviews suggested that the feedback had helped students revise, the teachers had questions about the extent to which students had used the feedback. They were concerned that the feedback was not specific enough to enable students to know what to do. As already mentioned, we deliberately designed the feedback in this way; we wanted to place some of the assessment responsibility in students' hands. However, we did not know

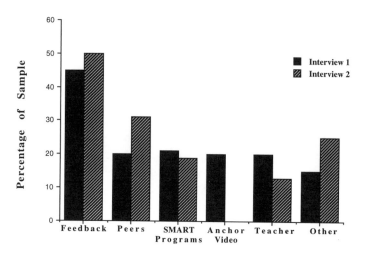

FIG. 13.8. "How did you know that you needed to revise?"

whether we had provided a sufficient scaffold for this to happen. This raised the question of whether the students' retrospective reports were accurate. Accordingly, we conducted another set of structured interviews focused on the feedback.

For these interviews, we randomly selected a new group of students. We first asked students "What did your feedback say?" All students were able to report one or more things that their feedback had indicated was in need of revision. (Note that these interviews took place 2 to 4 days after students had received their feedback.) Furthermore, when we examined students' actual feedback and compared them with what students had reported, students were accurate 77% of the time. Thus, although students did not necessarily report everything from their feedback, their reports were very accurate. These data indicate that students were reading and thinking about the feedback they had received, contrary to the teachers' impressions.

In our interviews, we also asked students to indicate what changes they had made in response to the feedback they had received. Forty-four percent of the time, students made revisions that were consistent with their feedback, and every student made at least one revision that corresponded to their feedback. Based on our interviews, it was clear that revision had been made very salient for students, and that the classroom was "information rich" in supporting this process. Furthermore, our interviews indicate that all students were able to use some aspect of their feedback to improve their work.

SUMMARY OF FINDINGS AND FUTURE DIRECTIONS

Our goal has been to describe a model for the design of learning environments that support metacognitive activities, such as monitoring learning and understanding, and selecting strategies to deal with the situation. Interviews with middle-school teachers indicate that many feel that their students fail to utilize the kinds of strategies that are usually recognized as metacognitive. Helping students learn to monitor, regulate their activities, and revise their work when needed are some of their major goals. For most of its life, the metacognitive literature has focused on characteristics of individual learners as the "active ingredient" for metacognitive activities. Recently, we and other researchers (e.g., Brown & Campione, 1994) have attempted to supplement this emphasis on individual cognition with an emphasis on social and environmental support for monitoring, reflection, and revision. Our SMART environments are examples of attempts to provide these kinds of support.

The particular example of SMART discussed in this chapter focused on the goal of helping students learn about interdependence and ecosystems in the context of river monitoring. We argued that the ability to monitor and guide one's learning requires students to have a clear mental model of the contexts in which they must ultimately use their knowledge. Teaching practices that leave students totally to their own devices place an undue burden on metacognition because they create a "Catch-22" with respect to novices (i.e., they cannot develop strong mental models until they learn, but they need such models to self-monitor and regulate their own learning). In contrast, too much teacher control robs students of opportunities to take responsibility for their own levels of learning, and to revise their thinking when necessary.

The SMART environment we discussed involved several types of support for metacognition. First, we used the anchor video Stones River Mystery to expose students to an example of their ultimate testing context (i.e., monitoring a river) at the very beginning of their instruction. This helped set the stage for exploring not only what is involved in monitoring rivers, but also how, why, and when to monitor them. We noted that the use of simulated anchors is much less expensive (in terms of both money and time) than actually taking students to the river. In addition, students can easily re-explore the anchor as needed. Second, we noted that showing an anchor was helpful but not sufficient for effective learning. Many features in the video are not noticed by novices, and many of the ideas necessary to communicate about interdependence cannot be shown simply as a movie. As a result, we created additional materials designed to help students (a) discover what they need to know; (b) make their thinking visible so that they could receive feedback; and (c) after receiving feedback, revise their previous plans.

The catalogs were designed to help students detect gaps in their knowledge and to communicate their thinking with one another. By specifically designing for particular contrasts, it is possible to help students notice features and dimensions that otherwise can be difficult for novices to notice. For example, the difference between the 2cm and .5mm Hockmeister Dip Nets helped the students focus on the question "Just how big are macroinvertebrates, anyway?" The contrast between the dip nets and the TetraBen Laser Counter helped students focus on the kinds of data they needed to collect about macroinvertebrates (e.g., simply count the total number or sort the invertebrates into different categories of pollution sensitivity). From a design standpoint, catalog items can be created that make certain types of contrasts more or less salient. For example, we have experimented with catalogs that have two types of laser counters—one that counts the total number of macroinvertebrates and one that counts different types of macroinvertebrates and states their pollution sensitivity. This makes the question "What kinds of data do we need on macroinvertebrates?" even more salient than in the original catalog we used.

Accompanying the catalog are resources that can help students acquire the knowledge needed to make catalog choices. Students initially treated the resources as linear texts that they read from beginning to end. Eventually they learned to define learning goals and use the index to determine where to read in the resources. It seemed clear to us that students had rarely had occasion to use text resources in this way and suggests that we may enhance students' metacognitive skills if we provide them with greater opportunities to participate in classroom activities that clearly support the use of particular strategies.

In addition to catalogs and resources, SMART provides multiple opportunities for feedback, reflection, and revision. For each phase of the river monitoring project, students could go to the Web for feedback and then revise their order. They also had opportunities to hear the ideas of "Kids Online" participants and to craft responses to these participants and see what they did with the information. The "Kids Online" provided models of evision that were especially salient and important to the children in the class. Ideally, these models are internalized and used more generally by students.

Multiple sources of data were used to assess the effects of the SMART intervention. Some focused on students' understanding of concepts such as interdependence and ecosystems; others involved analyses of changes in students argumentation and learning strategies over time. We were very pleased to see the kinds of changes that occurred. Ideally, we would have liked to have studied how students in SMART approached the goal of learning new sets of information about different subject matters. For example, could they gradually be weaned from the need to use catalogs of contrasting cases, seek feedback from and the web, and listen and respond to students on line? Due to time limitations, it was impossible for us to attempt a study of this type.

We were able to interview sixth-grade teachers with students who had been in SMART the previous year. Our interviews with them were not about SMART per se. They were about the kinds of strategies that they saw their children using. The sixth-grade teachers saw important differences in students who had and had not been involved in SMART in the fifth-grade. For example, for one assignment sixth graders worked in groups to solve a complex problem and then present their solutions. A sixth-grade teacher explained:

> ... The (SMART) groups were organized, they were able to present, they could tell you what the problem was, why they need to solve it, and then show the solution. And I don't think that would have happened in the first six weeks of school had it not been (for SMART).... I know it wouldn't have happened.

It seems probable to us that our SMART environments can be designed to provide even more support for metacognitive development. For example, we did not engage students in the kinds of structured self-assessment that was so successful in studies by researchers such as Lin (1995), and White and Frederickson (1995) in which students were explicitly prompted to engage in reflection. It is possible that the scaffolds and feedback support in SMART make it unnecessary to also engage in structured self-assessment. On the other hand, the addition of these kinds of activities might make the effects of SMART even stronger. This is a question deserving of further research.

ACKNOWLEDGMENTS

Preparation of this chapter was supported by National Science Foundation Grant NSF MDR-9252908. The opinions expressed are those of the authors and should not be attributed to the funding agency. Members of the Cognition and Technology Group who contributed to the research reported in this chapter are Helen Bateman, Kadira Belynne, Hank Clark, Chuck Czarnik, Joan Davis, Michael Gaines, Susan Goldman, Susan Hickman, Michael Jacobson, Phoebe Jacobson, Xiadong Lin, Taylor Martin, Cynthia Mayfield-Stewart, Ray Norris, Ashley Owen, Jim Pellegrino, Jay Pffafman, Bob Sherwood, and Carolyn Stalcup. We would like to thank the teachers and students with whom we collaborated on the work described in this paper.

REFERENCES

Barron, B. J., Schwartz, D. J., Vye, N. J., Moore, A., Petrosino, A., Zech, L., Bransford, J. D., & Cognition and Technology Group at Vanderbilt (in press). Doing with understanding: Lessons from research on problem- and project-based learning. *Journal of the Learning Sciences.*

Barron, B., Vye, N. J., Zech, L., Schwartz, D., Bransford, J. D., Goldman, S. R., Pellegrino, J., Morris, J., Garrison, S., & Kantor, R. (1995). Creating contexts for community-based problem solving: The Jasper Challenge Series. In C. N. Hedley, P. Antonacci, & M. Rabinowitz (Eds.), Thinking and literacy: The mind at work (pp. 47–71). Hillsdale, NJ: Lawrence Erlbaum Associates.

Bereiter, C., & Scardamalia, M. (1989). Intentional learning as a goal of instruction. In L. B. Resnick (Ed.), Knowing, learning, and instruction: Essays in honor of Robert Glaser (pp. 361–392). Hillsdale, NJ: Lawrence Erlbaum Associates.

Bransford, J. D. (1979). Human cognition: Learning, understanding, and remembering. Belmont, CA: Wadsworth Publishing.

Bransford, J. D. (1981). Social-cultural prerequisites for cognitive research. In J. H. Harvey (Ed.), Cognition, social behavior, and the environment (pp. 557–569). Hillsdale, NJ: Lawrence Erlbaum Associates.

Bransford, J. D., Arbitman-Smith, R., Stein, B. S., & Vye, N. J. (1985). Three approaches to improving thinking and learning skills. In R. Segal, S. Chipman, & R. Glaser (Eds.), Thinking and learning skills: Relating instruction to basic research (Vol. 1, pp. 133–206). Hillsdale, NJ: Lawrence Erlbaum Associates.

Bransford, J. D., Franks, J. J., Vye, N. J., & Sherwood, R. D. (1989). New approaches to instruction: Because wisdom can't be told. In S. Vosniadou & A. Ortony (Eds.), Similarity and analogical reasoning (pp. 470–497). New York: Cambridge University Press.

Bransford, J. D., & Stein, B. S. (1993). The IDEAL problem solver (2nd ed.). New York: Freeman.

Bransford J. D., Stein, B. S., Vye, N. J., Franks, J. J., Auble, P. M., Mezynski, K. J., & Perfetto, G. A. (1982). Differences in approaches to learning: An overview. Journal of Experimental Psychology: General, 111, 390–398.

Bransford J. D., Zech, L., Schwartz, D. L., Barron, B. J., Vye, N. J., & Cognition and Technology Group at Vanderbilt (in press). Design environments that invite and sustain mathematical thinking. In P. Cobb (Ed.), *Symbolizing, communicating, and mathmatizing perspectives on discourse, tools, and Instructional design.* Mahwah, NJ: Lawrence Erlbaum Associates.

Brown, A. L. (1975). The development of memory: Knowing, knowing about knowing, and knowing how to know. In H. W. Reese (Ed.), Advances in child development and behavior (Vol. 10). New York: Academic Press.

Brown, A. L. (1978). Knowing when, where, and how to remember: A problem of metacognition. In R. Glaser (Ed.), *Advances in instructional psychology* (Vol. 1). Hillsdale, NJ: Lawrence Erlbaum Associates.

Brown, A. L., Bransford, J. D., Ferrara, R., & Campione, J. (1983). Learning, remembering and understanding. In J. H. Flavell & E. M. Markman (Eds.), *Handbook of child psychology: Vol. 3 Cognitive development* (4th ed., pp. 77–166). New York: Wiley.

Brown, A. L., & Campione, J. C. (1994). Guided discovery in a community of learners. In K. McGilly (Ed.), *Classroom lessons: Integrating cognitive theory and classroom practice* (pp. 229–272). Cambridge, MA: MIT Press.

Brown, A. L., & Campione, J. C. (1996). Psychological theory and the design of innovative learning environments: On procedures, principles, and systems. In L. Schauble & R. Glaser (Eds.), *Innovations in learning: New environments for education* (pp. 289–325). Mahwah, NJ: Lawrence Erlbaum Associates.

Chi, M. T., Bassok, M., Lewis, P. J., & Glaser, R. (1989). Self-explanations: How students study and use examples in learning to solve problems. *Cognitive Science, 13,* 145–182.

Chi, M. T. H, deLeeuw, N., Chiu, M., & LaVancher, C. (1994). Eliciting self-explanations improves understanding. *Cognitive Science, 18,* 439–477.

Cobb, P. (1994). Where is the mind? Constructivist and sociocultural perspectives on mathematical development. *Educational Researcher, 23*(7), 13–20.

Cognition and Technology Group at Vanderbilt. (1997). *The Jasper project: Lessons in curriculum, instruction, assessment, and professional development.* Mahwah, NJ: Lawrence Erlbaum Associates.

Cole, M., & Griffin, P. (Eds.). (1987). *Contextual factors in education.* Madison, WI: Wisconsin Center for Education Research.

Flavell, J. H. (1976). Metacognitive aspects of problem solving. In L. B. Resnick (Ed.), *The nature of intelligence.* Hillsdale, NJ: Lawrence Erlbaum Associates.

Flavell, J. H. (1985). *Cognitive development.* Englewood Cliffs, NJ: Prentice-Hall.

Garner, W. R. (1974). *The processing of information and structure.* Potomac, MD: Lawrence Erlbaum Associates.

Gibson, J. J., & Gibson, E. (1955). Perceptual learning: Differentiation or enrichment. *Psychological Review, 12,* 306–355.

Greeno, J. G., Collins, A., & Resnick, L. B. (1996). Cognition and learning. In D. Berliner & R. Calfee (Eds.), *Handbook of educational psychology* (pp. 15–46). New York: Simon, Schuster & Macmillan.

Johnson-Laird, P. N. (1983). *Mental models.* Cambridge, MA: Harvard University Press.

Lave, J. (1988). *Cognition in practice: Mind, mathematics, and culture in everyday life.* Cambridge, England: Cambridge University Press.

Lee, O., Eichinger, D. C., Anderson, C. W., Berkheimer, G. D., & Blakeslee, T. D. (1993). Changing middle school students' conceptions of matter and molecules. *Journal of Research in Science Teaching, 30,* 249–270.

Lin, X. D. (1995, April). *Metacognitive considerations for technology-based learning environments: Importance of supporting students' reflections.* Paper presented at American Educational Research Association, San Francisco, CA.

McNamara, T. P., Miller, D. L., & Bransford, J. D. (1991). Mental models and reading comprehension. In R. Barr, M. L. Kamil, P. B. Mosenthal, & P. D. Pearson (Eds.), *Handbook of reading research* (Vol. 2, pp. 490–511). New York: Longman.

Moore, A., Sherwood, R., Bateman, H., Bransford, J. D., & Goldman, S. R. (1996). Using problem-based learning to prepare for project-based learning. In J. D. Bransford (Chair), *Enhancing project-based learning: Lessons from research and development.* Symposium conducted at the 1996 Annual Meeting of the American Educational Research Association, New York.

Newell, A., & Simon, H. A. (1972). *Human problem solving.* Englewood Cliffs, NJ: Prentice-Hall.

Pellegrino, J. W., Hickey, D., Heath, A., Rewey, K., Vye, N. J., & Cognition and Technology Group at Vanderbilt. (1991). *Assessing the outcomes of an innovative instructional program: The 1990–1991 implementation of the "Adventures of Jasper Woodbury"* (Tech. Rep. No. 91–1). Nashville, TN: Vanderbilt University, Learning Technology Center.

Pressley, M., Woloshyn, V., Lysynchuk, L. M., Martin, V., Wood, E., & Willoughby, T. (1990). A primer of research on cognitive strategy instruction: The important issues and how to address them. *Educational Psychology Review, 2,* 1–58.

Rogoff, B. (1990). *Apprenticeship in thinking.* New York: Oxford University Press.

Scardamalia, M., & Bereiter, C. (1985). Fostering the development of self-regulation in children's knowledge processing. In S. F. Chipman, J. W. Segal, & R. Glaser (Eds.), *Thinking and learning skills: Research and open questions* (Vol. 2, pp. 563–578). Hillsdale, NJ: Lawrence Erlbaum Associates.

Sherwood, R. D., Petrosino, A. J., Lin, X., Lamon, M., & the Cognition and Technology Group at Vanderbilt. (1995). Problem-based macro contexts in science instruction: Theoretical basis, design issues, and the development of applications. In D. Lavoie (Ed.), *Towards a cognitive-science perspective for scientific problem solving* (pp. 191–214). Manhattan, KS: National Association for Research in Science Teaching.

Van Haneghan, J. P., Barron, L., Young, M. F., Williams, S. M., Vye, N. J., & Bransford, J. D. (1992). The Jasper series: An experiment with new ways to enhance mathematical thinking. In D. F. Halpern (Ed.), *Enhancing thinking skills in the sciences and mathematics* (pp. 15–38). Hillsdale, NJ: Lawrence Erlbaum Associates.

White, B., & Frederiksen, J. R. (1995). *The ThinkerTools inquiry project: Making scientific inquiry accessible to students and teachers* (Causal Models Research Group Report 95–02). Berkeley: School of Education, University of California at Berkeley.

Whitehead, A. N. (1929). *The aims of education.* New York: MacMillan.

Zech, L., Vye, N. J., Bransford, J. D., Goldman, S. R., Barron, B. J., Schwartz, D. L., Kisst-Hackett, R., Mayfield-Stewart, C., & Cognition and Technology Group at Vanderbilt. (in press). An introduction to geometry through anchored instruction. In R. Lehrer & D. Chazan (Eds.), *New directions for teaching and learning geometry.* Hillsdale, NJ: Lawrence Erlbaum Associates.

14

The Metacognition of College Studentship: A Grounded Theory Approach

Michael Pressley
University of Notre Dame
Shawn Van Etten
University at Albany, State University of New York
Linda Yokoi
University of Maryland at College Park
Geoffrey Freebern
University at Albany, State University of New York
Peggy Van Meter
Pennsylvania State University

We are interested in how college students cope with the academic demands made on them—how they manage all of their courses at once! As metacognitive theorists, we come to this task with certain strong assumptions (Flavell, P. Miller, & S. Miller, 1993, chapter 7). We assume that studying and time management involve at least some use of strategies and are affected by student prior knowledge related to the content of courses. Metacognition, which is knowledge and beliefs about thinking and the factors affecting thinking, regulates the articulation of strategies and knowledge. Yes, some use of study strategies and application of prior knowledge during study probably are automatized and occur without conscious regulation, but a great deal of studying and academic self-management involves conscious decision making and self-regulation. When that is the case, students' knowledge and beliefs about when and where to use various strategies is a primary determinant of how students tackle academic demands. Motivation also plays a role, with student cognition very much a function of whether and when students expect to be rewarded for exerting academic effort (Borkowski, Carr, Rellinger, & Pressley, 1990; Dweck, 1986; Dweck & Leggett, 1988). Because studying does involve conscious decision making, we assume that students are aware of many of the factors affecting their motivation, with their conscious reward expectancies playing a large role in their academic decision making.

Of course, there is at least partial support for these assumptions. We are aware of research documenting metacognitive regulation of a variety of strategies adults use as they carry out academic reading and writing, with prior knowledge consistently interacting with and affecting strategy use (e.g., Flower et al., 1990; Pressley & Afflerbach, 1995). Self-regulated study, in particular, has been conceived as based largely on student study tactics and strategies (e. g., Zimmerman & Martinez-Pons, 1986, 1988, 1990). For example, in Zimmerman and Martinez-Pons (1986), high-achieving high-school students reported greater use of a variety of strategies than did low-achieving high-school students. Their strategies included organizing and transforming to-be-learned information; seeking information (e.g., from the library); notetaking; self-consequating (e.g., going to a movie as a reward for doing well on a test); rehearsing and memorizing; seeking assistance from someone else (e.g., peer, teacher, or other adult); and reviewing texts, notes, and tests. Zimmerman and Martinez-Pons (1990) reported that gifted elementary, middle-school, and high-school students indicated greater use of such self-regulation strategies than nongifted students. Zimmerman and Martinez-Pons (1988) also reported high correlations between high-school students' self-reported use of self-regulation strategies and students' strategy use as documented by teacher reports. Consistent with our perspective on motivation, a great deal of evidence has been generated in recent years that students have fine-grained beliefs about what they can do and what they cannot do (e.g., Marsh, 1992). These beliefs go far in determining academic tasks that students will attempt and those they will avoid (Bandura, 1995).

When we began the research discussed in this chapter, we were also aware that student studying and achievement depend, at least in part, on course characteristics. For example, Thomas, Rohwer, and their associates (Thomas, et al., 1993; Thomas & Rohwer, 1987, 1993) have studied high-school and college courses with respect to the demands made on students, the supports provided by instructors (e.g., feedback on tests, quizzes, and homework), and the compensations made by instructors (e.g., extra credit opportunities, exact test items provided before test). Although the results in their studies were extremely complicated, in general, more active study and greater learning were observed in demanding courses than in less demanding ones, especially when instructors provided supports for study. Active study and overall achievement were reduced when instructors provided compensations.

In reviewing the previous work on studying by college students, we felt some frustration. Even the most ambitious studies focused on student activity and achievement only in single courses, and then were concerned only with activities and achievement directly relevant to the focal course in the study. This seemed unnatural to us because it is the rare student who has the luxury of taking one course at a time. More typically, students are juggling multiple courses, and as they do so, they also juggle other responsibilities, including work and commitments to friends and families.

In addition, previous research assumed that the influences and pressures on students are objective ones (e.g., course demands are experienced as demands by all students). We felt that this was too strong an assumption, one not consistent with contemporary theory and research. Students interpret the forces acting on them, and their interpretations influence their behaviors. Thus, students' academic outcomes can be interpreted as reflections of their personal efforts, personal abilities, external factors, or luck (e.g., Weiner, 1979). Moreover, grades can be interpreted, in part, by the goal structure of a class, with grades more likely to be interpreted as indications of ability in highly competitive classes or rewards of effort when students are graded on the basis of improvement (e.g., Nicholls, 1989). Given the assumption that the forces operating on students are as much their own cognitive constructions as objective, we felt that the previous research on college studentship needed to be complemented by research that more certainly admitted student interpretations. We believe that systematic study of these interpretations might permit more complete understandings of student academic life than what has followed from the previous quantitative research.

METHODOLOGY

Students have many conscious understandings about their academic world (e.g., Thorkildsen & Nicholls, 1991). Such understandings can be tapped through interviews analogous to the ways knowledge engineers, who are designing artificial intelligence systems (i.e., expert systems), interview people about the decisions they make when confronting problems that an expert system must be programmed to solve (e.g., Diaper, 1989; Meyer &

Booker, 1991; Scott, Clayton, & Gibson, 1991). Social scientists sometimes consider such interviewing to be ethnographic interviewing (e.g., Mishler, 1986; Spradley, 1979).

This type of interviewing begins with open-ended questions, either to small groups of people or to individuals. The data are analyzed as they come in, with the researcher categorizing responses and relating the various responses as part of generating a theory about the phenomenon under study. There are clear gaps in the theory following early rounds of questions. The gaps inspire new questions, ones more focused than the original questions. The new questions are posed to new samples of participants. The responses are analyzed with the emerging theoretical model modified. New gaps are now apparent, and thus, new questions are generated and new participants interviewed. Cycles of questioning and analyses continue until no new conclusions emerge that require adding to the theoretical model (Strauss & Corbin, 1990). The investigator is constantly comparing new responses to conclusions that have emerged, attempting to identify both new information consistent with old information and responses that challenge the previous conclusions. Hence, the approach to analysis described here is referred to as the *method of constant comparison*.

In this type of interviewing, every effort is initially made not to provide response alternatives to participants, but rather to require participants to generate responses so that the results reflect their construal of the situation, in contrast to the researcher's a priori conception of the situation. This contrasts with other interview approaches, such as those used in previous studies of students' self-regulated learning. In those studies, participants only indicated whether they used processes identified a priori by the researcher, for example, by indicating agreement to statements such as, "I usually set out to understand thoroughly the meaning of what I am asked to read," or "I tend to choose subjects with a lot of factual content rather than theoretical kinds of subjects" (Ramsden, 1992, p. 52).

A grounded theory can be produced from ethnographic interviews, a theory induced from data, and hence, grounded in data. Such an inductive, qualitative approach especially makes sense early in a research program when the goal is exploration and discovery of directions that could be explored in more detail (i.e., the discovery of potential hypotheses for subsequent hypothetico-deductive research; Patton, 1990; Potter, 1996). Because that is the position we are in with respect to understanding how students cope with the many demands placed on them, we elected a qualitative, inductive approach. Analyzing interview responses with the method of constant comparison forces the researcher to find, in interviews, multiple supports for each tenet of the grounded theory. In addition, the researcher must continue collecting and analyzing interview data until the various tenets of the theory are meaningfully related to one another.

Thus, in three different studies to date, our tactic has been to interview college students about an issue that we felt would be revealing about their coping with academic demands. In the first study, Van Meter, Yokoi, and Pressley (1994) interviewed college students about their use of one important study strategy—notetaking. In the first phase of the study, students were asked to tell everything they knew about notetaking. As the researchers analyzed initial responses, they formulated more focused questions intended to stimulate student elaborations and extensions of ideas mentioned in the earlier interviews. Once Van Meter et al. (1994) reached the point when they were obtaining no new insights from students' responses to open-ended questions about notetaking, they engaged in a quantitative exercise to increase confidence in the conclusions emanating from the open-ended approach. Each of the claims made by students during open-ended interviewing was put in the form of a statement, and a large sample of students was asked to indicate their agreement with those statements. Only the claims that survived this quantitative check remained in the final model of student notetaking.

The final model emerging from the Van Meter et al. (1994) analysis specified great situational variability in when and how students take notes. For example, students are more likely to take notes when exams are driven by lecture content. The students also reported great variability in the quality of the notes they take as a function of the situation, with the styles of some lecturers being much more compatible with effective notetaking than other lecturers (e.g., notes are easier to take when lecturers are organized, provide good outlines, and stick with their outlines). Student studying was also reported as varying as a function of the quality of notes that could be taken in a class. Thus, students reported more cooperative study efforts (e.g., getting together to figure out notes taken) and more reading of textbook material when the style of the lecturer was not conducive with good notetaking. A summary of the model obtained by Van Meter et al. (1994) is contained in the Appendix[1]. The students in that study had a great deal to say about notetaking. Thus, they reported that notetaking serves a number of goals. They had detailed beliefs about how the content of notes varied depending on situational factors. They also reported a variety of ways that notes could be used after they were taken.

In the two studies conducted since Van Meter et al. (1994), students have been asked to provide information about issues bigger than notetaking. In one study (Van Etten, Freebern, & Pressley, 1997), students were asked to tell everything about preparing for exams; in the other study (Van Etten, Pressley, & Freebern, in press), students were asked to provide information about everything affecting their academic motivations as students. Not surprisingly, the theoretical models of exam preparation and factors affecting academic motivation were more complex than the students' theory of notetaking.

RECURRING THEMES IN THE THREE ETHNOGRAPHIC INTERVIEW STUDIES

As we expected, each of the three ethnographic interview studies that we conducted produced unique results. One of the most striking outcomes found in these studies, however, is that some recurrent themes occur in the students' comments. That these themes recur in responses to diverse questions about academic demands and coping suggests to us that they reflect salient features of students' metacognition about coping with academic demands in college—that these dimensions go far in revealing the most robust thinking in students' metacognitions about college studying.

The eight subsections that follow present the most salient of the recurring themes. Each of the recurring themes is illustrated with supportive data from the grounded theories of notetaking, exam preparation, and freshmen motivation. Although we provide some reminders in what follows that we are referring to student reports, readers should keep that in mind. (If we were to vigilantly qualify every statement using phrases like, "The students reported ... or claimed ... or contended ... ," the section would be a monotonous read.)

Achieving Good Grades as an Overarching Goal of Students

The importance of earning good grades came through in all three grounded theories: Students reported that obtaining good grades was their primary motivation for studying for exams; notetaking was shaped by students to include information that is likely to be tested, and hence, critical to determining the course grade; and information about the likely grade on a test affected study (e.g., there is less studying if students perceive they can get a good grade without studying or if they believe that a good grade is impossible no matter how much studying occurs). In many different ways across the three ethnographic interview studies, students indicated that they spent a great deal of time thinking about grades, with this attention to grades affecting their study. There were multiple indications about how grades obtained thus far constructively shape present behavior in a course (e.g., notetaking and seeking help in a course were reported as affected by exam grades).

To be certain, in all three studies students reported other goals as part of taking courses, such as learning or preparing for occupational roles. Even so, obtaining good grades as an overarching concern came up again and again. Students made it quite clear that all other goals were secondary.

Use of Strategies

Students reported a great deal of know-how with regard to being effective students. Their commentaries always included much information about strategies for meeting the demands placed on them.

With respect to notetaking, students reported using notetaking to increase attention during class, improve understanding and organization of course material, prepare for tests, and complete homework assignments. Students have very specific strategies concerning the content that should be included in notes. For example, lecture notes need to flag content redundant with text, material the professor stresses, content highlighted on the board or overhead, definitions and main points, and information not presently understood by the student. Notetaking strategies also include recording key terms that provide an outline of critical lecture points and using a personal shorthand to deal with the volume of material presented in lectures. Students vary on whether they attempt paraphrased versus verbatim notes depending on what they know about course demands (e.g., Will verbatim regurgitation on the test pay off in this course?).

With respect to test preparation, students have a variety of strategies for juggling competing demands and for managing their time to maximize grades. Such strategic management includes a variety of strategies for coping with reading demands in courses (e.g., prioritizing readings, selective reading of what is perceived as most important and informative, and skimming some material). Attending class is also viewed as a test-preparation strategy: Students recognize that class is a source of information about what is critical to know. Students juggle social, work, and academic commitments. They distribute their study by dividing test preparation into a series of subgoals, scheduling periods of intensive study, and taking advantage of study opportunities during the day (e.g., preparing flashcards that can be used for review while walking to classes). In addition, they vary their studying depending on the type of test that is anticipated.

In fact, students reported many different study strategies, including the following:

- Rereading assignments and notes.
- Rewriting lecture notes.
- Integrating notes from readings with class notes.
- Highlighting and memorizing key concepts, definitions, and formulae.
- Making flash cards for drill of important information. (Many students, however, seemed to be aware of the limited gains of such rote strategies, recognizing that such drilling does not lead to real understanding of material.)
- Making up rhymes, acronyms, songs, stories, and images to connect important ideas and remember the connections.
- Posing questions about the material.
- Relating information to prior knowledge to personalize understanding of it.
- Developing outlines, tables, figures, and graphs of important information.
- Reading related material.
- Studying old exams.
- Seeking help from textbooks, library sources, computer data bases, and mass media.
- Creating an overarching conceptual structure integrating ideas in text and lectures. (Although students recognized that they often did not engage in such integration because of the great deal of effort involved.)

Students have motivational strategies, too. They reported setting grade goals for themselves, ones they believed attainable with effort. Often, these are proximal goals (e.g., a particular grade on a next test), with students reporting that on a day-by-day basis, it is more motivating to focus on proximal goals than distal goals. Students reported that they resisted explaining their performances to themselves in terms of anything other than effort, recognizing that their effort was controllable but that other potential explanatory mechanisms (e.g., ability, task difficulty) are not controllable. Hence, their motivation is increased by believing in effort.

Strategies for Coping With Distractions

Students believe that there are many distractions that must be kept under control if they are to succeed academically, and they reported spending a lot of effort coping with them. Friends can distract in class and in the dorm, causing inattention to homework. Visceral needs also can distract, with students reporting distraction when hungry or tired. Family issues can interfere with schoolwork. In addition, if the physical setting is not conducive to study (e.g., quiet, well-lighted), it can be a major distraction.

In all three studies, students reported strategies for dealing with distractions. Thus, notetaking was seen as an approach for maintaining attentional focus in class. Students claimed that they explicitly attempted to eliminate distractions in their study environment and distractions that might undermine their motivation to study (e.g., selecting friends who are also oriented toward studying).

Strategy by Course-Demand Interactions

Students reported that the particular strategies they use are very much affected by course demands. Thus, if verbatim recall will be required on a test, students attempt to take verbatim notes. If the test stresses understanding, students paraphrase as they take notes.

In general, students reported that they study more for courses in their major, ones covering interesting material and material that they expect to be important for future use. Challenging material also demands more study time, especially if students perceive that they can cope with the material with reasonable effort. In contrast, students know that they can study less when they have high prior knowledge related to to-be-learned content.

Strategies for dealing with deadlines vary with the firmness of the deadline and its immediacy. Imminent deadlines motivate immediate study. Flexible deadlines lead students to defer flexibly deadlined tasks in favor of other tasks that are due at a firm date, especially if that firm date is in the immediate future.

Strategy by Course-Experience Interactions

Students reported changing their approach to courses as a function of experience and feedback in a course. Specifically, students reported adjusting their notetaking to the style of the lecturer and/or after learning the nature of the exams from taking an exam. Students contended that feedback providing information about how they could improve was especially helpful and motivating. Also, students shift study schedules as the actual demands in courses become apparent. At times, this potentially involves major changes (e.g., dropping one course to devote more time to another).

Strategy by Prior Knowledge Interactions

Students know that prior knowledge related to a course makes a course easier. Thus, it is easier to take notes when prior knowledge is high, and if prior knowledge is really high, there may be no need to take notes. Preparing for an examination takes less time when prior knowledge is high.

Instructor Characteristics That Affect Studying

The instructor really matters from the student's perspective. Notetaking varies depending on the speed of presentation of the instructor. Organized, clear lecturers who separate the points they are making during lecture permit better notetaking than disorganized, unclear lecturers whose points lack definition. If the lecturer is so bad that good class notes cannot be prepared, students may decide not to use class notes when they study, relying more on the text, past exams, a teaching assistant, or discussions with other students for information about what is critical to study for an exam.

Instructors who facilitate test preparation do the following:

- Provide plenty of advance warning about exams.
- Make well-prepared presentations in class.
- Make clear how reading and written assignments relate to course goals.
- Identify content that is especially critical to know.
- Interactive productively with the class (e.g., lots of questions and answers between students and professor, occurring in a relaxed and friendly manner).
- Are available for out-of-class consultation.
- Provide old tests for review that are informative about what is important in the class.
- Test only material covered in course.
- Provide helpful notes on especially critical content.
- Give tests that can be completed comfortably during the amount of time permitted for the test.
- Speak English well and without an accent.

Some professors are more motivating than others, according to students. Motivating instructors are those who are like the following:

- Seem eager, interested in the material, responsible, knowledgeable, democratic, and permit choices.
- Are empathetic and caring.
- Provide realistic encouragement.
- Provide challenging, but not overly difficult, assignments.
- Give timely feedback.

- Grade for effort and improvement rather than emphasize competition.
- Emphasize the learning process rather than grades.
- Provide a number of proximal goals rather than one distal goal (e.g., a huge paper at the end of the term).
- Treat students like adults.

Classmates and Peers Affecting Study

The participants in our study believe that other students affect their academic activities, motivations, and performances. In courses in which notetaking is difficult, students can get together to pool the bits and pieces of information they have derived from lectures. Study groups can help in eliminating misconceptions and expand understanding of concepts. A study group can provide helpful input about the right content to emphasize and about the level of preparation needed to do well on an exam. Study groups, however, can also be a waste of time if individuals do not come to the group prepared.

Classmates' enthusiasm for a course can increase a student's academic motivation. A class may be more comfortable when a friend is in it, although a friend in class also can be distracting (e.g., increasing the amount of fooling around during class). Peers sometimes encourage academic engagement (e.g., when peers study a lot, it encourages a student to study a lot) or discourage it (e.g., when peers party, it is tempting to party as well). Not having many friends in class can undermine motivation, with students diverting time that might have been invested in studying to seeking out companionship and increased social relations.

Summary

In our experience, if you get a group of students together to talk about college and its demands, the conversation will turn very quickly to a discussion of grades and the importance of maximizing them. The students know and claim to use a variety of strategies in the pursuit of good grades, including strategies aimed at keeping themselves on task. The students believe that the strategies vary with the characteristics and demands of courses and assignments, and that strategies change over the duration of a course as students come to understand what is required to do well. Although students believe that prior knowledge matters, it is discussed less than strategies, with study strategies believed to vary somewhat depending on student prior knowledge.

Students view the people in their world as important in determining how they cope with academic demands. Foremost are their professors, who vary greatly, with some professors doing much to facilitate student coping and others making learning difficult as they undermine student motivation. Although peers can distract, they can also be sources of a great deal of information and motivation that is needed by students.

CAN WE BELIEVE THE STUDENT REPORTS?

It may turn out that the students were telling much more about the demands made on them and how they cope than is actually the case (Nisbett & Wilson, 1977). If so, subsequent investigations aimed at evaluating the grounded theory we are generating should eliminate some of the tenets in the theory as presented in this chapter. That is, we have been developing grounded theories of specific aspects of student academic coping, which are contributing to the development of an overarching grounded theory of student coping, one that we expect to test further. Without a theory suggesting their potential role in studying and student coping, however, many of the variables that emerged from the analyses we have conducted would never have been considered. Thus, even if the students are wrong, we are confident that the grounded theory that we are developing will be heuristic.

The theory that is emerging is going to be credible to many scholars who think about students in higher education. Why? Although the theory includes claims not advanced previously, many of the specific claims made by the students in our studies are consistent with other data on studying and learning. This consistency should bolster confidence in the students' reports as summarized in our emerging grounded theory of studying and coping. Consider the following consistencies with previous conclusions:

- Examinations and grades are the pre-eminent motivators for many college students (e.g., Abouserie, 1994; Michael, 1991; Zitzow, 1984).
- The students in these studies recognized the value of prior knowledge (e.g., Anderson & Pearson, 1984) and personal interest (Hidi, 1990) in facilitating acquisition of content.
- Instructors who encourage improvement are more motivating than those who emphasize competition (e.g., Ames, 1992; Nicholls, 1989).
- The students reported the types of helpful supports that teachers can give their students, as described by Thomas, Rohwer, and their colleagues (Thomas et al., 1993; Thomas & Rohwer, 1987, 1993), such as tips about how to study

for an examination, clear presentations, and clarifications when students are confused.

- The students indicated how critical it is for them to know the format of an upcoming examination, which is consistent with demonstrations that knowledge of exam format shapes study and affects performance (Lundeberg & Fox, 1991).

- One of the best substantiated outcomes in the psychological literature is that distributed study improves learning relative to massed study (Dempster, 1988), with the students in this study clearly indicating the advantages of distributed study.

- The students' claims about cooperative learning are consistent with what is known about the group dynamics of cooperative learning. The students reported awareness that group study can reduce their individual efforts, permitting learning that would have occurred only through the individual student's more intensive and extensive study (Karau & Williams, 1993). From early childhood, students feel better about providing academic help to students who provide academic help to them (De Cooke, 1992). Students in our studies reported feeling better about helping those who were prepared for study group versus those who came unprepared.

In short, the students' perceptions made many points of contact with existing theory and research, and many of their claims were consistent with what is known about student learning and cognition. Just as striking was that the students in our studies made no salient claims that clashed with specific previous conclusions about student learning and motivation. These consistencies between the students' perceptions and known relationships between learning and behavior inspire confidence in the students' perceptions. Even so, the students' portrayal of academic coping is more complicated than any previous conception of college studentship known to us. Academic coping occurs over a very long term, involves balancing many demands, and is affected by many variables. These points are elaborated in the concluding section of this chapter.

WHAT DO THE RESULTS TO DATE MEAN?

Previous research on academic coping by college students focused on a relatively few variables that researchers felt may be telling about student studying, variables that have substantial, somewhat generalizable effects on student understanding, learning, and thinking. A broader perspective is emerging from the work we are doing, which was designed to capture the

full array of variables that students believe influence their studying: Students view studying as situationally variable and multiply determined.

How a student studies depends on many factors in interaction, with the
common denominator across situations being that getting good grades
matter. If the students are accurate in their perceptions, efforts to predict
student studying on the basis of course characteristics or learner style
characteristics alone may be misguided or at best capture only a very small
part of the picture. Even the most ambitious of previous conceptions of
student studying (e.g., Entwistle, 1987) alluded only to a fraction of the
variables cited as critical by the participants in this investigation.

What seems to be emerging is a contextualist model. The nature of
studying at any moment is a function of student competencies (strategies,
knowledge), student perceptions and understandings of course demands,
instructor characteristics, and peer supports and demands. That studying
seems to be so contextually determined has important implications for
future research. Predictive hypothetico-deductive testing will be challenging, for relationships between studying and learning variables are presumed
to vary depending on many factors in interaction. That is not to say that
the contextualist position developed here cannot be studied.

All contexts have both quality (i.e., an overarching meaning, a whole-
ness) and texture (i.e., details relating to one another that comprise the
quality). Quality can be defined in terms of temporal spread. Consistent
with this notion, the theory that is developing includes claims about the
long-term nature of academic coping, including how it is affected by previous
coursework and background (i.e., prior knowledge). Academic coping begins early in a term, perhaps during the first meeting of the class, and
continues to intensify as exams near, with performance early in courses
affecting subsequent academic motivation and study. That is, the students
believe that there are a variety of textural details that sum to specify the
quality of the long-term process of studying.

Quality is also defined by change. Consistent with this idea, the theory
emerging here is detailing how academic coping and motivations to cope
shift as a function of a number of other variables. For example, from the
data on hand, a good case could be made for examining whether students
shift their coping strategies as the quality of lecturing varies, demands in
other courses increase or decrease, and so on.

Research on contextualist perspectives is not intended to produce uni-
versal laws. It involves the study of individuals in context. Some contextualist investigators use factorial methods, in the analysis of variance sense, to
examine a number of factors at a time in a controlled fashion. The expec-

tation is that there will be higher-order interactions reflecting the specificity of behavior. This is a weak approach (Goldhaber, 1997), for there is the assumption that the higher-order interactions obtained will be stable and replicable, including over place and time. To the extent that the contextualist perspective is correct, that behavior and performance always depend on ever-shifting elements of context, this assumption is not justified.

Goldhaber (1997) contrasts the factorial approach with ethnographic and narrative analysis techniques, both of which are more sensitive to sociohistorical context and subtle variations in behavior and outcomes as a function of changing context. We believe that much might be learned by taking this anthropological perspective, by studying student exam preparation from within the student culture. The work we have done to date has involved a form of narrative analysis, in that students told us about their own perceptions and experiences. Even so, we were concerned in the work completed thus far with getting beyond the voices of individual participants to a more generalized perspective. Perhaps our future work should be more concerned with listening, analyzing, and interpreting individual students' whole stories of studying for exams (i.e., their personal interpretations of the entire process of preparing for exams). To date, we were concerned with generating a theory that might inspire specific tests. Armed with such a theory, we may now be in a better position to understand individual narratives of studying versus before we catalogued the strategies and other factors that hypothetically interact as part of coping with the many academic demands that students face.

We look forward to hypothetico-deductive tests of the theory that is emerging from our work (i.e., the theory sketched in this chapter), as we are aware of the many criticisms of interview studies. We keep in mind as we interview college students, however, that if it were not for an interview study (Kreutzer, Leonard, & Flavell, 1975), there probably would not be an area of cognitive psychology known as metacognition. We also keep in mind that the method of constant comparison that we use (Strauss & Corbin, 1990) is more conservative in many ways than previous interview approaches, with each conclusion emerging from our work based on a great deal of data-based support. The point of doing constant comparisons is to generate a theory that is worthy of the resources required to carry out hypothetico-deductive investigations because it is a theory grounded in a great deal of data. Perhaps some readers of this volume who might prefer quantitative, hypothetico-deductive approaches over qualitative approaches will take up the challenge of testing the theory reported in this chapter, a theory that we believe goes far in capturing and explaining the academic lives of many college students.

REFERENCES

Abouserie, R. (1994). Sources and levels of stress in relation to locus of control and self esteem in university students. *Educational Psychology, 14,* 323–330.

Ames, C. A. (1992). Classrooms, goals, structures, and student motivation. *Journal of Educational Psychology, 84,* 261–271.

Anderson, R. C., & Pearson, P. D. (1984). A schema-theoretic view of basic processes in reading. In P. D. Pearson (Ed.), *Handbook of reading research.* New York: Longman.

Bandura, A. (Ed.). (1995). *Self-efficacy in changing societies.* New York: Cambridge University Press.

Borkowski, J. G., Carr, M., Rellinger, E. A., & Pressley, M. (1990). Self-regulated strategy use: Interdependence of metacognition, attributions, and self-esteem. In B. F. Jones (Ed.), *Dimensions of thinking: Review of research* (pp. 53–92). Hillsdale, NJ: Lawrence Erlbaum Associates.

De Cooke, P. A. (1992). Children's understanding of indebtedness as a feature of reciprocal help exchanges between peers. *Developmental Psychology, 28,* 948–954.

Dempster, F. N. (1988). The spacing effect: A case study in the failure to apply the results of psychological research. *American Psychologist, 43,* 627–634.

Diaper, D. (Ed.). (1989). *Knowledge elicitation: Principles, techniques, and applications.* New York: Wiley.

Dweck, C. S. (1986). Motivational processes affecting learning. *American Psychologist, 41,* 1040–1048.

Dweck, C. S., & Leggett, E. L. (1988). A social-cognitive approach to motivation and personality. *Psychological Review, 95,* 256–273.

Entwistle, N. (1987). A model of the teaching–learning process. In J. T. E. Richardson, M. W. Eysenck, & D. W. Piper (Eds.), *Student learning: Research in education and cognitive psychology* (pp. 3–12). Milton Keynes, England: Open University Press.

Flavell, J. R., Miller, P., Miller, S. (1993). *Cognitive development* (3rd ed.). Englewood Cliffs, NJ: Prentice-Hall.

Flower, L., Stein, V., Ackerman, J., Kantz, M. J., McCormick, K., & Peck, W. C. (1990). *Reading to write: Exploring a cognitive and social process.* New York: Oxford University Press.

Goldhaber, D. (1997). *Why we are: Theoretical perspectives on human development.* Manuscript in preparation.

Hidi, S. (1990). Interest and its contribution as a mental resource for learning. *Review of Educational Research, 60,* 549–571.

Karau, S. J., & Williams, K. D. (1993). Social loafing: A meta-analytic review and theoretical integration. *Journal of Personality and Social Psychology, 65,* 681–706.

Kreutzer, M. A., Leonard, C., & Flavell, J. H. (1975). An interview study of children's knowledge about memory. *Monographs of the Society for Research in Child Development, 40*(1, Serial No. 159).

Lundeberg, M. A., & Fox, P. W. (1991). Do laboratory findings on test expectancy generalize to classroom outcomes? *Review of Educational Research, 61,* 94–106.

Marsh, H. W. (1992). Content specificity of relations between academic achievement and academic self-concept. *Journal of Educational Psychology, 84,* 35–42.

Meyer, M., & Booker, J. (1991). *Eliciting and analyzing expert judgment: A practical guide.* London: Academic Press.

Michael, J. (1991). A behavioral perspective on college teaching. *Behavior Analyst, 14,* 229–239.

Mishler, E. G. (1986). *Research interviewing: Context and narrative.* Cambridge, MA: Harvard University Press.

Nicholls, J. G. (1989). *The competitive ethos and democratic education.* Cambridge, MA: Harvard University Press.

Nisbett, R., & Wilson, T. (1977). Telling more than we can know: Verbal reports on mental processes. *Psychological Review, 84,* 231–259.

Patton, M. Q. (1990). *Qualitative evaluation and research methods* (2nd ed.), Newbury Park, CA: Sage.

Potter, W. J. (1996). *An analysis of thinking and research about qualitative methods.* Mahwah, NJ: Lawrence Erlbaum Associates.

Pressley, M., & Afflerbach, P. (1995). *Verbal protocols of reading: The nature of constructively responsive reading.* Mahwah, NJ: Lawrence Erlbaum Associates.

Ramsden, P. (1992). *Learning to teach in higher education.* London, England: Routledge.

Scott, A. C., Clayton, J. E., & Gibson, E. L. (1991). *A practical guide to knowledge acquisition.* Reading, MA: Addison–Wesley.

Spradley, J. P. (1979). *The ethnographic interview.* New York: Holt, Rinehart, & Winston.

Strauss, A., & Corbin, J. (1990). *Basics of qualitative research: Grounded theory procedures and techniques.* Newbury Park, CA: Sage.

Thomas, J. W., Bol., L., Warkentin, R. W., Wilson, M., Strage, A., & Rohwer, W. D., Jr. (1993). Interrelationships among students' study activities, self-concept of academic ability, and achievement as a function of characteristics of high-school biology courses. *Applied Cognitive Psychology, 7,* 499–532.

Thomas, J. W., & Rohwer, W. D., Jr. (1987). Grade-level and course-specific differences in academic studying. *Contemporary Educational Psychology, 12,* 344–364.

Thomas, J. W., & Rohwer, W. D., Jr. (1993). Proficient autonomous learning: problems and prospects. In M. Rabinowitz (Ed.), *Cognitive science foundations of instruction* (pp. 1–32). Hillsdale, NJ: Lawrence Erlbaum Associates.

Thorkildsen, T. A., & Nicholls, J. G. (1991). Students' critiques as motivation. *Educational Psychologist, 26,* 347–368.

Van Etten, S., Freebern, G., & Pressley, M. (1997). College students' beliefs about examination preparation. *Contemporary Educational Psychology, 22,* 192–212.

Van Etten, S., Pressley, M., & Freebern, G. (in press). An interview study of college freshman's beliefs about their academic motivations. *European Journal of Psychology in Education.*

Van Meter, P., Yokoi, L., & Pressley, M. (1994). College students' theory of notetaking derived from their perceptions of notetaking. *Journal of Educational Psychology 86,* 323–338.

Weiner, B. (1979). A theory of motivation for some classroom experiences. *Journal of Educational Psychology, 71,* 3–25.

Zimmerman, B. J., & Martinez-Pons, M. (1986). Development of a structured interview for assessing student use of self-regulated learning strategies. *American Educational Research Journal, 23,* 614–628.

Zimmerman, B. J., & Martinez-Pons, M. (1988). Construct validation of a strategy model of student self-regulated learning. *Journal of Educational Psychology, 80,* 284–290.

Zimmerman, B. J., & Martinez-Pons, M. (1990). Student differences in self-regulated learning: Relating grade, sex, and giftedness to self-efficacy and strategy use. *Journal of Educational Psychology, 82,* 51–59.

Zitzow, D. (1984). The college adjustment rating scale. *Journal of College Student Personnel, 25,* 160–164.

APPENDIX: OUTLINE OF FINAL RESULTS: COLLEGE STUDENTS' THEORY OF NOTETAKING[1]

Goals

(What the student hopes to achieve by taking notes: Although the overarching goal is doing well in courses, students formulate more specific goals before and during notetaking, with the possibility of multiple goals for a single notetaking situation or shifts in goals within and between notetaking situations.

A. Attention: Increases student attention to lecture.
B. Understanding: Increases student comprehension and memory of material presented in lecture.
C. Organization: Opportunity to connect ideas, provide structure, and/or generate a holistic representation of lecture content.
D. Study aid: Informs about solutions to practice problems and provides information relevant to written assignments.

Content/Structure of Notes

A. Content that is placed in notes:
   1. Content redundant with text.
   2. Material professor stressed.
   3. Content on board/overheads.
   4. Content cited on syllabus.
   5. Definitions, main points, important concepts, and ideas.
   6. Information not well understood or familiar.
   7. Guest lecturer and film content not noted, nor is content that is common knowledge.
B. Structure (Preferred methods vary from student to student, but approaches cited here are common):
   1. Key terms.
   2. Outline of some sort (e.g., flagging relationships between more and less important content).
   3. Personal shorthand.

---

[1]From Appendix A in P. Van Meter, L. Yokoi, & M. Pressley (1994). Copyright 1994 by the American Psychological Association. Adapted with permission.

C. Completeness of notes:
   1. Verbatim.
   2. Paraphrased.
      a. Attractive because demands less writing.
      b. Paraphrased notes sometimes constructed in class as test of under-
         standing of content.

Contextual Factors Affecting Notetaking

A. Lecturer style:
   1. Speed: slow to fast (relative to difficulty/novelty of material.
   2. Structure:
      a. On a continuum, from organized to disorganized.
      b. On a continuum, from clear to vague.
      c. On a continuum, from separated points to unclear separation of points.

Instructor can aid notetaking by providing and sticking to outlines or
by giving signals that indicate important information (e.g., by presenting important material on the board, lecturing more slowly, repeating
central ideas and/or announcing what is important). Less considerate
lecturers may prevent students from being able to use preferred
notetaking methods (e.g., they talk too fast to permit students to use
preferred notetaking strategies) or from developing notes that represent relationships between concepts (e.g., by presenting diagrams and
lecture simultaneously, being poorly organized, and/or deviating from
lecture outline presented to class). In such courses, students may
adjust their notetaking to match the instructor's style better or as their
understanding of the demands of the course increases.

B. Student knowledge and characteristics:
   1. Prior knowledge: Easier to take notes when lecture content is related to
      prior knowledge possessed by the learner. When prior knowledge is high,
      fewer notes are taken and there is greater selectivity, focusing on new
      information in the lecture. Occasionally, students are so knowledgeable
      about the lecture topic that no notes are taken. High prior knowledge is
      especially advantageous when the lecturer is poorly organized or rapid in
      presentation.
   2. Increasing know–how: Knowing how to take notes increases as a function
      of college attendance (more organized, selective, accurate).
   3. Some students more committed to creating complete notes than are
      other students.

C. Type of content and course demands:
   1. Verbatim notes often favored for more defined and specific content (e.
      g., definitions, names, dates, examples). Verbatim used if accountability
      system in course requires verbatim recall of well–defined points or para-
      phrasing might distort meaning. (Even so, some students prefer para-
      phrasing for most notes, including to capture well–defined, specific
      points.)
   2. Paraphrasing possible with familiar material and preferred for conceptual
      and ill–defined content, especially if learning of general principles is the
      demand in the course.

Post–Class Processing of Notes

A. Occasionally class notes not used:
   1. Notes student considers not to be good (e.g., perhaps because lecturer is
      hard to take notes from).
   2. Material already well known.
B. Notes are processed after class:
   1. Methods:
      a. Review.
      b. Rewrite (changing form and/or content, including elaborations, reor-
         ganizations).
      c. Recopy (rewriting without changing form or content).
   2. Factors affecting the extent notes are used:
      a. Used for homework assignments when lecture content is pertinent to
         it (e.g., worked examples).
      b. Notes used proportionately more for exam preparation in
         easy–to–take–notes courses.
      c. Notes combined more with other sources of information (e.g., text,
         past exams, TA consultation, student discussions), especially in diffi-
         cult–to–take–notes courses.
      d. Personalized aspects of notes important in conveying information to
         students, so that own–constructed notes are more useful than notes
         taken by others.

Epilogue

Linking Metacognitive Theory
to Education

John Dunlosky
University of North Carolina at Greensboro

In Cavanaugh and Perlmutter's (1982) classic critique of metacognition, they concluded that the "present state of metamemory is not good, [and] in its present form, metamemory has little value ... The future utility of metamemory depends on the success of definitional clarification, development of new and more precise methodologies, and expansion of research into new domains" (pp. 22–23). Less than 15 years after Cavanaugh and Perlmutter's critique, researchers have met the challenge to significantly broaden and strengthen research of metacognition. The current vitality of metacognitive research is evident from numerous examples within each chapter of this volume.

With respect to Cavanaugh and Perlmutter's call for definitional clarification, Hacker (chapter 1, this volume) provides a discussion of the historical development of three concepts that have become central to defining metacognition: metacognitive knowledge, monitoring, and control. One or more of these concepts are represented in each chapter of this volume. Metacognitive knowledge is knowledge about one's own declarative and procedural knowledge and has been widely investigated in various areas of child development (see also Dunlosky & Hertzog, chapter 11, this volume, for references relevant to the aging in adulthood literature). A major focus of research here has been to discover whether the development of metacognitive knowledge enhances cognitive skills (but see Siegler & Shipley, 1995, for an alternative to metacognitive knowledge as causal agent in cognitive development). Carr and

Biddlecomb (chap. 4, this volume) argue that the development of metacognitive knowledge occurs through interactions between a child's past experience, interactions with peers and teachers, and input from the
environment—all of which can facilitate learning. And García, Jiménez,
and Pearson (chap. 9, this volume) explain how successful bilingual readers
utilize metacognitive knowledge about one language to guide reading in
another.

Monitoring and control were brought to the forefront of cognitive
psychology by Miller, Galanter, and Pribram's (1960) Test-Operate-Test-
Exit unit and have since been given a central position in numerous models
of self-regulation (e.g., see Carver & Scheier, 1990; Koriat & Goldsmith,
1996; and Reder & Ritter, 1992, for a few not specifically represented in this
volume). Accordingly, it is not surprising that issues about theory of monitoring and control arise throughout this volume. These theoretical issues,
which often involve metacognitive knowledge, are the focus of the next two
sections of this epilogue. I then discuss how researchers are making progress
in solving applied problems by linking metacognitive theory to education
and conclude with a revision of Cavanaugh and Perlmutter's critique of
metacognition.

METACOGNITIVE MONITORING
AND CONTROL PROCESSES

Nelson and Narens (1990) describe monitoring and control as dominance
relations between a meta-level system and an object-level system (see Hacker,
chap. 1, this volume, for an illustrative discussion of this two-level model
within the context of monitoring comprehension of text material). Monitoring refers to the flow of information from an object-level system to a
meta-level system. That is, a meta-level system receives input from an
object-level system. By contrast, control refers to the flow of information from
the meta-level system to an object-level system. This flow of information
entails a meta-level system influencing processes at an object-level system.
This two-level model is general in that a person may monitor products of
processing that arise during the completion of any cognitive task (e.g., during
a learning task, analogical reasoning, problem solving, and so on), and control
may involve any number of self-initiated actions (e.g., continuing the same
processing, terminating processing, or initiating new processing).

Although typically not discussed using these terms, theory within a given
content area often involves describing the flow of information between a
meta-level system and an object-level system. Accordingly, a set of core

questions appears to drive research programs across content areas: How do (or can) people monitor their performance when they are involved in a cognitive task? How accurate are people at assessing on-going performance? And what are the roles of monitoring in the subsequent control of task-related behavior? As discussed next, chapters in this volume showcase advances in metacognition by delivering answers to these and other theoretical questions.

Monitoring

Several theoretical issues about metacognitive monitoring are highlighted by research on monitoring of text comprehension. A major issue in the metacomprehension literature is to understand why people's monitoring of text comprehension at times appears so poor. In particular, why do people often have difficulties detecting contradictions within a text? Why do they fail to detect that their naive beliefs about a topic are incompatible with scientifically accepted beliefs provided in the text? And why do people appear relatively inaccurate at assessing how well they have comprehended recently read material? Several chapters in this volume provide insight into understanding the nature of these aspects of metacomprehension, which include the limitations of metacognitive monitoring (Otero, chapter 7), the multidimensional nature of text predictions (Maki, chapter 6), and the irony of on-line monitoring of comprehension (Hacker, chapter 1). I discuss each of these in turn.

Otero's suppression hypothesis (for further elaboration, see Otero & Kintsch, 1992) suggests that inaccurate monitoring of comprehension results naturally from the operation of normal text comprehension. As a person reads a proposition that contradicts earlier information (either another proposition of the text or his or her own beliefs), the contradictory meaning of the proposition is activated and a negative link is constructed between this proposition and the earlier information. The final representation of these propositions, however, is established only after a phase of integration. During this integration phase, activation spreads between the propositional links to yield the final activation of propositions. As described by Otero, if one of the contradictory propositions is heavily weighted, integration of the propositional network will suppress the inconsistent meaning of the other proposition. Thus, the contradiction will not be represented in the final propositional network, and detecting the contradiction will prove impossible. However, if suppression does not occur during the integration phase of comprehension, the contradictory meanings may later be activated via working memory, which will increase the likelihood that the inconsistency will be detected.

This scenario highlights an assumption about metacognitive monitoring that is evident in much of the metacognitive literature and that constrains the general model of monitoring and control proposed by Nelson and Narens (1990). Namely, in the specific case of monitoring comprehension, an individual does not have direct access to the underlying activation of the contradictory meaning of an inconsistent proposition that occurs during the construction phase. More generally, the assumption is that the meta-level system does not have direct access to the underlying processes that occur within the object-level system (e.g., Ericsson & Simon, 1980, and see Koriat's, 1993, disconfirmation of direct-access views of monitoring). However, an individual does have access to products from object-level processes, such as information retrieved about the long-term representation of a text that is accessible after the integration phase.

In contrast to evaluating whether people detect inconsistencies in text, Maki focuses on a person's ability to judge his or her own comprehension of text. A method generally used in this literature is to have people read several texts and have them make a single assessment about how well they understood each, such as by having them predict their ability to correctly answer inferential questions about each text (for a review of this literature from a different perspective, see Weaver, Bryant, & Burns, 1995). As explained by Maki, the relation between predictions and subsequent performance is relatively low, again indicating poor metacomprehension.

Otero's theoretical perspective suggests that poor metacomprehension during reading results because of inadequate processing of textual meaning. Whereas this aspect of normal reading may contribute to the inaccuracy of text predictions, Maki emphasizes that text predictions are a joint function of several factors. Because only one of these factors involves monitoring of text comprehension, the inaccuracy of text predictions may be more indicative of other factors in assessing comprehension, such as the "inappropriate use of topic familiarity, incorrect judgments about level of learning, incorrect predictions about the amount of forgetting, or incomplete knowledge about the nature of the text" (Maki, this volume, p. 119).

An implicit lesson from this conclusion is that when researchers investigate metacognitive monitoring of any kind of task, they should not assume the methods provide process-pure measures of an individual's monitoring of the products of object-level processing (Dominowski, chap. 2, this volume). Metacognitive predictions are perhaps especially problematic because people need to map information that is monitored onto a rating scale, a transformation that may be based on a person's knowledge about how the output of monitoring relates to whatever is being judged (e.g., performance on inference questions, recall performance, etc.). Thus, inaccurate predictions may be due to inaccurate monitoring, inaccurate knowledge about how the output from monitoring relates to task performance, or to both. This observation, however, does not imply that investigating the accuracy of text predictions will be less informative than investigating people's detection of errors in text. On the contrary, understanding the multiple bases of text predictions will have important implications for education because a student's goal is not only to assess comprehension immediately after reading but also to assess whether comprehension of to-be-learned materials will be maintained well into the future. Most important, Maki provides a theoretical framework that brings order to this literature en route to a better understanding of the bases and accuracy of text predictions.

One difference between research discussed by Maki and that presented by Otero is whether a person is reading an error-free text or one that intentionally includes contradictory information. Hacker (chapter 1, this volume) explores the relevance of this potentially critical issue. Although Hacker's theoretical perspective is more akin to Otero's theory in that both emphasize the importance of utilizing theory of text comprehension to understand metacomprehension, the spirit of the former is more akin to research reviewed by Maki in that both focus on metacomprehension during comprehension of error-free text. In contrast to the literature on text predictions that are made after comprehension takes place, Hacker develops a model of metacomprehension that highlights the interplay between a person's current understanding of the text (i.e., model of the text) and on-going construction of the meaning of the text.

According to Hacker's general cognitive-metacognitive framework of text comprehension, a reader may fail to detect that a text is being miscomprehended for at least two reasons: either because monitoring is not engaged (which he explains using the mechanisms of Otero's suppression hypothesis described earlier) or "because readers construct a text that conforms with their metacognitive models of the text . . . rather than the actual text" (Hacker, this volume, p. 179). The latter is somewhat ironic because, according to Hacker's definition of monitoring (matching an internal meta-level model of the text with on-going construction of meaning at the object-level), the reader's monitoring can be accurate even though comprehension fails (i.e., the meta-level model of the text matches the object-level meaning of the text being constructed, but neither capture the intended meaning of the text). To investigate these compelling ideas, one will need to develop objective measures to operationalize readers' internal model of a text, their on-going construction of meaning, and when they engage in a comparison of the model with the constructed meaning.

As evident from this discussion, a person's assessments of his or her own cognition may appear to fail for numerous reasons. To add to this list, Vye et al. (chapter 13, this volume) describe the role that knowledge plays in assessing one's preparation for a cognitive activity:

> Anyone who has given speeches to different groups of individuals … knows the importance of being able to anticipate the kinds of questions they are likely to be asked at the end of their presentations. The better individuals can imagine (model) the situation in which one must use one's knowledge, the easier it is to assess one's level of preparation … The idea that monitoring is highly knowledge dependent creates a "Catch-22" for novices. How can they assess whether their learning activities are leading them in the direction of "adequate preparation" if they don't already have a clear mental model of their ultimate testing situation? (p. 309)

Put differently, assessing progress toward a goal will often involve comparing the output of monitoring to some standard of evaluation, which can be viewed as one's knowledge about what represents adequate performance for a particular task. In conjunction with the two-level model, standards of evaluation provide a powerful framework for localizing inadequacies of people's self-assessments. As an example, consider what are perhaps the most extreme deficiencies represented in this volume, namely, the psychological disorders described by McGlynn in which patients are often not aware of their severe impairments. McGlynn noted that the majority of schizophrenics in one investigation "vehemently denied that they were emotionally ill" (p. 237). Several metacognitive deficits may jointly contribute to this deficiency. Many individuals with schizophrenia may receive inaccurate information about the products of their underlying mental states, which corresponds to a disruption of the flow of information from a specific object-level system that underlies a disorder and the meta-level system (cf. Schacter's, 1989, model of consciousness). This disruption may correspond to an underlying neurological insult (e.g., to the frontal or parietal lobe) and could result in unawareness even when patients are provided with evidence to the contrary.

Another possibility is that some individuals who are prone to schizophrenia may lose sight of an appropriate standard of evaluation across time.

Because the onset of symptoms may be gradual, an individual may develop a new standard of evaluation in which the symptoms are not indicative of illness, or the individual may forget earlier standards of evaluation that better matched more normative thought. The idea here is that monitoring may be intact, but that a schizophrenics' standards of normalcy become inappropriate. Although this possibility may not fully account for the severity of individuals' unawareness, research linking social anhedonia to the likelihood of developing psychosis (e.g., Kwapil, Miller, Zinser, J. Chapman, & L. J. Chapman, 1997) suggests this mechanism may contribute. In particular, perhaps individuals who are prone to psychosis and who isolate themselves socially do not attain feedback from others that their initial psychotic-like experiences are abnormal.

In summary, several questions about monitoring link research across many domains: What are the bases of people's on-line monitoring? And what factors, if any, limit the accuracy of people's monitoring? Although I reviewed arguments from only a few contributors, chapters include most theoretical or empirical advances that provide at least partial answers to these interrelated questions. Piecing these advances together to form a unified theory of monitoring provides one of the greatest theoretical challenges for future research.

Control

Whereas metacognitive knowledge and monitoring have received growing attention in the literature since the mid-1960s, research of control processes within a metacognitive framework has received much less attention (but see Nelson, 1992, for some exceptions).[1] This is also reflected in this volume in that although both monitoring and control are mentioned in almost every chapter, the bulk of discussion does not focus on control. One possible reason for this lag between research on monitoring versus control is evident from the two-level model in which monitoring is fundamental to control: Information monitored from the object-level is utilized at the meta-level to make decisions about whether (and how) to control processes at the object-level. Thus, it seems reasonable that adequate explanations of control will first require at least some explanation of monitoring.

---

[1]A great deal of research has focused on control processes within cognitive, social, and life-span developmental perspectives. Some notable programs have included investigating dual-task performance, stop-signal inhibition, primary-versus-secondary control, regulation of emotions, to name only a few (for a review of others, see Karoly, 1993). Theory within each of these areas may include metacognitive components, although metacognitive metaphor may not be explicitly used. Even so, metacognitive research on control will benefit by considering theoretical issues and applied issues that have guided programs of research from these other perspectives.

The assumption that the functional role of monitoring is in controlling action and thought pervades this volume. Concerning problem solving, Davidson and Sternberg (chapter 3) state "selective comparison involves discovering a nonobvious relationship between new information and already acquired information ... The solver realizes that new information is similar to old information in certain ways [monitoring] and then uses this information to form a mental representation based on the similarities [control]" (p. 53). García et al. (chapter 9, this volume) describe how bilingual readers' comprehension of English text was related to their ability to detect cognates, which suggests "that the students were making use of cognate relationships in their English reading" (p. 200). For Winne and Hadwin (chapter 12, this volume), the functional role of monitoring in control is perhaps most evident. "If the student acts on evaluations, this is *control* by which elements in the collage of cognitive conditions may be altered; standards may be adjusted, added, or abandoned; and, operations of new kinds may be carried out" (p. 281). The link between monitoring and control is not only evident in theoretical statements like these, but it has also been demonstrated empirically in a variety of domains.

Thus, a major question about whether monitoring influences control has received an affirmative answer.[2] Also implicit in these quotations is that monitoring may have its largest influence on task performance vis-à-vis control. That is, merely monitoring and evaluating progress toward a goal may have a negligible influence on performance, but performance may be enhanced when monitoring is utilized in controlling subsequent actions and thought (for a discussion of when monitoring alone may directly influence performance, see Dominowski, chapter 2, this volume). For instance, as described by Dunlosky and Hertzog (chapter 11, this volume), older and younger adults appear equally accurate at monitoring on-going progress during learning; and yet, during self-paced study, older adults appear to underutilize the highly accurate output from monitoring. Other illustrations of adequate monitoring followed by poor control appear in this volume.

---

[2]An assumption often made is that people explicitly use the output of monitoring and evaluation to control subsequent processing, such as deciding to terminate studying, deciding which strategies to use to solve a problem, and so forth. Although such explicit monitoring and control processes may often occur, control may also be based on implicit processes that do not involve explicit monitoring. Most important for education, training people to explicitly use metacognitive processes when more implicit processing (or automatic processing) governs the control of action and thought may be detrimental to performance. These issues are not discussed further here because the explicit-vs-implicit nature of control processes were not a focus of this volume. Anyone interested may refer to discussions of these and related issues by Reder and Schunn (1996) and by Siegler and Shipley (1995).

Such illustrations lead to other questions about control that seem especially relevant to education: Is control of a given self-regulated task optimal? If not, what aspects are constraining success? And can people be taught to overcome those constraints to enhance performance? Several obstacles ensure that obtaining answers to these questions will not always be straightforward. For many kinds of tasks, it may be difficult to operationalize optimal self-regulation. In solving any kind of problem, even students who solve problems correctly may be viewed as suboptimal if they cannot do so in a timely manner. This is especially relevant to education, where classroom achievement is often assessed under timed situations. In attempting to learn difficult material, control may be optimal even when a student cannot master all of the material. Thus, because optimal self-regulation may often be a joint function of several factors, determining whether people are optimally regulating their learning may be at best difficult.

An alternative and common approach has been to identify conditions in which suboptimal performance is evident: students making a decision without fully considering the relative quality of alternatives (Vye et al., chapter 13, this volume), students missing inconsistencies in text (Otero, chapter 7, this volume), older adults' performing poorly on self-regulated tasks (Dunlosky & Hertzog, chapter 11, this volume), and novice writers leaving problems in their written text (Sitko, chapter 5, this volume). Thus, even though optimal regulation may not be defined in each of these situations, an assumption is that people here could change their regulation to enhance performance.

These examples also illustrate the importance of linking metacognitive theory to specific applications. In particular, there are many reasons why regulation may be suboptimal, and the reasons may differ as a function of the particular task. Thus, it is critical to link current theory of self-regulated action and thought to performance on a particular task, for example, note taking (Pressley, Van Etten, Yokoi, Freebern, & Van Meter, chapter 14, this volume), solving math problems (Carr & Biddlecomb, chapter 4, this volume) or learning a second language (Garcia et al., chapter 9, this volume). Developing these links will allow us to localize deficiencies in specific components of regulation, which will provide necessary insight into how to help people compensate for the deficits. An analytic approach has been an effective means for understanding human performance in many areas, and given recent advances in metacognitive theory, this approach may be especially useful in improving regulation that occurs across most aspects of student scholarship.

WHAT IS THE CURRENT UTILITY
OF METACOGNITIVE RESEARCH
FOR EDUCATION?

The previous discussion focuses mainly on theoretical questions about metacognition that appear in various domains of research. In each domain, researchers have also attempted to link theory to specific applications.[3] An interplay between theory and application is widespread throughout many areas of psychology and shows promise for yielding theory that will be most relevant to improving people's lives. Because metacognitive processes can play a central role in performing many tasks, metacognitive research arguably has much utility for educational applications. Few would disagree. However, even though theoretical advances are evident in almost every area of metacognition currently being investigated, some areas may require further development before they provide techniques that will have an immediate impact. In the remainder of this section, I describe how a few areas of metacognitive research may successfully link to education.

Comprehension Monitoring and Writing Processes

Theory pertaining to predictions of future performance (e.g., Dunlosky & Hertzog, chapter 11, and Maki, chapter 6, this volume) may at first appear lacking in relevance to education. For instance, one could argue that students are unlikely to make these kinds of predictions anyway, so what use is it to know how they make them? This criticism is misguided, however, because if students can be highly accurate in predicting how well they will comprehend text during an upcoming exam, training them to utilize this skill may help them to enhance their comprehension. Unfortunately, people are relatively poor at predicting their memory and comprehension of text (but see Weaver et al., 1995, for exceptions). Although Maki (chapter 6, this volume) discusses why people's predictive accuracy may be poor, current theory provides no prescription for how students should monitor their comprehension to attain high levels of predictive accuracy across a wide variety of materials. As long as future research is specifically designed to

---

[3]In an article for the Division 20 Newsletter (1995), Chris Hertzog and I described the metaphor of linkage as representing "a synergistic interplay between basic and applied research issues. Here research is focused on developing a progressive research program to address theory-based questions, with a major focus of the theory placed on real-life situations" (p. 9). Fisk and Kirlik (1996) explain how linking theory and application provide advances both in developing theory as well as in applying theory to enhance human behavior. As important, they also provide an excellent primer on how to successfully link theory and application by discussing "characteristics of practically relevant research programs" (see Fisk & Kirlik, 1996, pp. 3–8).

solve this applied problem, we remain optimistic that new theory will provide a solution.

Otero (chapter 7, this volume) provides an explanation of why people often fail to detect inconsistencies in a text. A critical step for education is to understand implications of his explanation with regard to helping students detect inconsistencies between their knowledge and a to-be-learned text or between two contradictory propositions within a text. Although the latter may not be viewed as a practically relevant goal for normal text comprehension (Hacker, chapter 1, this volume), prescribing how students can better detect inconsistencies in text may be critical in their efforts to adequately review and revise their writing. More specifically, Sitko (chapter 5, this volume) describes reviewing as "the process in which writers reexamine what has been written and compare it to their internal representation of intended text" (p. 96). When Otero's suppression hypothesis is applied to reviewing, a prediction is that writers will miss errors or inconsistencies in their text if they heavily weight the internal representation of their intentions. Heavily weighting this internal representation may suppress actual meaning of the text that is inconsistent with the intended meaning. That is, because writers may have a clearly formed intention of what they want to write, they may fail to detect prose that contradicts their intended meaning.

Although this indicates that having a clearly formed intention may ironically lead to errors in revision, this scenario also suggests a straightforward technique to improve revision skills. In particular, a person should not revise immediately after writing, but instead should delay revision until some time (perhaps several days) after writing. After this delay, the original intention will presumably be less heavily weighted, which will help writers detect problems in their text. This prediction parallels common wisdom to "put down that essay for a while before you rewrite" and has recently been empirically supported (Hacker, Dunlosky, Plumb, & Thiede, 1997). Finally, research on writing and revision provides an exemplar for the benefits of linking theory to application, because "the assumptions that underlie strategy training in writing are restatements of the [theoretical] model applied to instruction" (Sitko, chapter 5, this volume, p. 99).

Problem Solving

Having students provide explanations for what they are doing when solving a problem can enhance their performance. As argued by Dominowski (chapter 2, this volume), this kind of verbalization requires a student to provide metacognitive statements about his or her own problem solving, which results "in more flexible approaches to problem solving and the use of more complex and effective strategies" (p. 39). Note that what is critical here is not merely having students monitor what they are doing, but instead having them provide an explanation for what they are doing. Monitoring is still critical (i.e., without the ability to monitor information from working memory, metacognitive verbalization would not be possible), but explaining the output of the monitoring is what improves problem solving. Although these benefits of verbalization may not extend to all situations, this technique appears readily applicable to many kinds of classroom problem solving.

Davidson and Sternberg (chapter 3, this volume) also describe a variety of techniques that a student may be taught to improve his or her problem solving. As important, they not only outline various metacognitive skills that have been used to improve problem solving, but they also provide several questions for future research, such as "How do [metacognitive] processes work together on different types of problems? [And] how can use of the processes, separately and together, be enhanced?" (p. 64). These questions highlight the dual aims of practically relevant programs of research that are described throughout this volume. In particular, Fisk and Kirlik (1996) explain that "to have practical relevance, research should derive from real, practical problems, but the work also should be designed to incorporate, build on, and advance theory" (pp. 2–3). The idea here is to understand more fully the interaction between metacognitive processes (a theoretical aim) so as to enhance the effectiveness of those processes in the context of solving real-world problems (a practical aim).

Concerning both aims, Winne and Hadwin (chapter 12, this volume) provide a general framework that can be used to describe a student's self-regulated behavior within any academic activity. Student scholarship is viewed as a complex interaction between multiple metacognitive and cognitive processes (cf. Fig. 11.1 of Dunlosky & Hertzog, chapter 11, this volume). More specifically, the COPES model captures the recursive nature of self-regulated study by mapping possible interactions among the stages of study as well as the processes within those stages. This theory shows much promise in guiding research that is aimed at solving real-world problems that students commonly face.

Student Scholarship

A major obstacle for developing general theories of student scholarship is obtaining adequate descriptions of how students behave, which includes activities that occur in the dorm, in the classroom, and in interactions outside the class with faculty and peers. Understanding these aspects of student life is critical because they may influence whether students engage in activities that lead to effective self-regulated learning. For instance, teaching effective strategies to guide learning will not be useful if students are not motivated to use those strategies. Thus, understanding how a student's scholarship may be influenced by his or her environment and interactions with others may be critical for launching intervention programs that improve student scholarship.

Pressley et al. (chapter 14, this volume) overcome the obstacle just described by developing a theory of student scholarship that is grounded in students' reports of how they approach scholarship. Their methodology involves obtaining students beliefs about scholarship through open-ended interviews. By scanning the students' responses, one develops an appreciation of the multitude of factors that may influence students. With regard to students' theory of taking class notes, Pressley et al. (see also Van Meter, Yokoi, & Pressley, 1994) compiled over 30 factors that students believe influence how they take and use their notes in learning class-related materials. Not only do some of these factors coincide with those developed from other research, but it seems likely that many factors reported by Pressley et al. would not have been discovered without using their interview-based methods.

Perhaps most impressive in regard to improving student scholarship, the method used by Pressley et al. yields findings that have immediate implications for education. Their research resulted in over 15 recommendations for how instructors may facilitate students' preparation for an upcoming test! Given that Pressley et al. describe results from three studies that cover notetaking, exam preparation, and freshman motivation, their chapter is filled with too many viable implications for education to describe here. And even though their interview-based method may require an heroic effort to complete successfully, the bottom-line is that these efforts will provide a broad foundation for research programs aimed at improving student scholarship.

Working directly in the classroom setting, Vye et al. (chapter 13, this volume) adopt current theory of metacognitive monitoring and control to promote student scholarship. In contrast to training an individual student to use a metacognitive strategy to improve his or her own performance, their approach involves developing a social environment that will support a variety of metacognitive processes (see also Brown, 1997, for an overview of another successful program based on this collaborative-cultural approach). Two central aspects of their program appear readily applicable in the classroom. First, anchored instruction provides students with an in-depth understanding of a particular topic (versus a shallow overview of multiple topics). Second, through interactions with teachers and other students, students learn to utilize a variety of metacognitive resources (e.g., self-assessment and reflection) in trying to gain an in-depth understanding. The idea is not merely to learn about the particular topic to which the instruction is anchored, but to learn about how one should expertly pursue learning any topic. This approach will help students to become self-directed scholars and deserves attention at all levels of instruction.

CONCLUSION

Reflect upon the diversity of topics discussed in this volume: problem solving, reading comprehension, writing and revising, and note taking, to name a few. Each of these topics has been positively influenced by develop-ments in metacognitive research since Cavanaugh and Perlmutter (1982) wrote "Metamemory: A Critical Examination." Theoretical advances are providing solutions to applied problems, and attempts at solving applied problems have provided further insights into theory. Although Cavanaugh and Perlmutter may still disagree on the utility of some developments in the area of metacognition, the synergy that is occurring among domains high-lighted here and elsewhere is testimony for the following revision of Cavanaugh and Perlmutter's earlier conclusion: The current state of meta-cognition shows much promise; in its present form, metacognitive research has yielded theory that may substantially increase achievement across many domains. The continued utility of metacognition will depend on further refining theory that is readily generalizable to everyday applications.

ACKNOWLEDGMENTS

Thanks to Doug Hacker and Keith Thiede for their comments about a draft of this manuscript.

REFERENCES

Brown, A. L. (1997). Transforming schools into communities of thinking and learning about serious matters. *American Psychologist, 4*, 399–413.

Carver, C. S., & Scheier, M. F. (1990). Origins and functions of positive and negative affect: A control-process view. *Psychological Review, 97*, 19–35.

Cavanaugh, J. C. & Perlmutter, M. (1982). Metamemory: a critical examination. *Child Development, 53*, 11–28.

Ericsson, K. A., & Simon, H. A. (1980). Verbal reports as data. *Psychological Review, 87,* 215–251.

Fisk, A. D., & Kirlik, A. (1996). Practical relevance and age-related research: Can theory advance without application? In W. A. Rogers, A. D. Fisk, & N. Walker (Eds.), *Aging and skilled performance: Advances in theory and applications* (pp 1–15). Mahwah, NJ: Lawrence Erlbaum Associates.

Hacker, D. J., Dunlosky, J., Plumb, C., & Thiede, K. (1997, March). *Immediate versus delayed revision: Don't revise that essay just yet.* Paper presented at the annual meeting of the American Educational Research Association, Chicago, IL.

Hertzog, C., & Dunlosky, J. (1995) The cutting edge. *Adult Development & Aging News, 22,* pp. 3, 9, 15.

Karoly. P. (1993). Mechanisms of self-regulation: A systems view. *Annual Review of Psychology, 44,* 23–52

Koriat, A. (1993). How do we know that we know? The accessibility model of feeling of knowing. *Psychological Review, 100,* 609–639.

Koriat, A., & Goldsmith, M. (1996). Monitoring and control processes in the strategic regulation of memory accuracy. *Psychological Review, 103,* 490–517.

Kwapil, T. R., Miller, M. B., Zinser, M. C., Chapman, J., & Chapman, L. J. (1997). Magical ideation and social anhedonia as predictors of psychosis-proneness: A partial replication. *Journal of Abnormal Psychology, 106,* 491–495.

Miller, G. A., Galanter, E., & Pribram, K. H. (1960). *Plans and the structure of behavior.* New York: Holt.

Nelson, T. O. (Ed.). (1992). *Metacognition: Core readings.* Boston: Allyn & Bacon.

Nelson, T. O., & Narens, L. (1990). Metamemory: A theoretical framework and new findings. In G. H. Bower (Ed.), *The psychology of learning and motivation,* (Vol. 26, pp. 125–141). New York: Academic Press.

Otero, J., & Kintsch, W. (1992). Failures to detect contradictions in a text: What readers believe versus what they read. *Psychological Science, 3,* 229–235.

Reder, L. M., & Ritter, F. E. (1992). What determines initial feeling of knowing? Familiarity with question terms, not with the answer. *Journal of Experimental Psychology: Learning, Memory, & Cognition, 18,* 435–452.

Reder, L. M., & Schunn, C. (1996). Metacognition does not imply awareness: Strategy choice is governed by implicit learning and memory. In L. M. Reder (Ed.), *Implicit memory and metacognition* (pp. 45–77). Mahwah, NJ: Lawrence Erlbaum Associates.

Schacter, D. L. (1989). On the relation between memory and consciousness: Dissociable interactions and conscious experience. In H. L., Roediger, III & F. I. M., Craik (Eds.), *Varieties of memory and consciousness.* (pp. 355–389). Hillsdale, NJ: Lawrence Erlbaum Associates.

Siegler, R. S., & Shipley, C. (1995). Variation, selection, and cognitive change. In T. J. Simon & G. S. Halford (Eds.), *Developing cognitive competence. New approaches to process modeling* (pp. 31–76). Mahwah, NJ: Lawrence Erlbaum Associates.

Van Meter, P., Yokoi, L., & Pressley, M. (1994). College students' theory of notetaking derived from their perceptions of notetaking. *Journal of Educational Psychology, 86,* 323–338.

Weaver, C. A., Bryant, D., & Burns, K. D. (1995). Comprehension monitoring: Extensions of the Kintsch and van Dijk Model. In C. A. Weaver III, S. Mannes, & C. R. Fletcher (Eds.), *Discourse comprehension: Essays in honor of Walter Kintsch* (pp. 177–193). Mahwah, NJ: Lawrence Erlbaum Associates.

Author Index

A

Abouserie, R., 358, 362
Ackerman, B. P., 178, 182, 185, 188
Ackerman, J., 348, 362
Ackerman, P. L., 292, 302
Acredolo, C., 160, 160
Adams, M. J., 170, 175, 188
Adams, R. D., 226, 248
Adamson, R. E., 58, 65
Afflerbach, P., 348, 363
Ahlum-Heath, M. E., 36, 44
Ahwesh, E., 295, 303
Ainley, M. D., 292, 301
Alajouanine, T., 229, 244
Albertson, L. R., 168–169, 189
Albrecht, J. E., 148, 160
Alessi, S. M., 147, 160
Alexander, J., 8, 21, 72, 89
Alexander, P. A., 148, 160, 300, 301
Alexopoulos, G. S., 240, 244
Allwood, C. M., 42, 44
Alvermann, D. E., 150–152, 160–162, 164
Amador, X. F., 222, 237–239, 244–245

Ames, C. A., 358, 362
Anderson, C., 90
Anderson, C. W., 70, 324, 331, 345
Anderson, G., 117, 142, 146, 161
Anderson, H., 157, 164
Anderson, J. R., 48, 65, 287–288, 301
Anderson, L. M., 94, 101, 103, 114
Anderson, R. C., 50, 65, 205, 216, 358, 362
Anderson, R. I., 146, 148, 161
Anderson, T. H., 147, 160
Andreasen, N. C., 238–239, 244
Angel, R. W., 240, 246
Ankerhus, J., 225, 248
Anschutz, L., 261, 271
Anscombe, R., 236, 245
Anthony, H. M., 94, 101, 103, 114
Appelbaum, P. S., 238–239, 246
Apperson, L .S., 238–239, 246
Applebee, A. N., 98, 100–101, 110, 113
Arbitman-Smith, R., 310, 344
Arkes, H. R., 141, 142
Armbruster, B., 148, 173, 161
Armour-Thomas, E., 86, 89

Artzt, A. F., 86, 89
Ashby, W. R., 169, *189*
Atkinson, R. C., 5, *21*
Auble, P. M., 306, *344*
Auden, W. H., *44*
August, D. L., 171, 173, *188*
Ausubel, D. P., 149, *161*

B

Babinski, M. J., 222–223, *245*
Bäckman, L., 261, 263, 270, *273–274*
Baddeley, A. D., 226, *248*
Bain, B., 196–197, *216*
Baker, L., 50, *65*, 145–148, 152, *161*,
    165–166, 171, 173, 175, 185,
    188–189
Baldi, R., 259, 267, *271*
Baltes, P. B., 260, *272*
Bandura, A., 255, *271*, 348, *362*
Bandura, M., 255–258, 261–262, *272*
Bar-Tal, D., 157, *161*
Barnes, T. R. E., 237, *246*
Barre, J. A., 223, *245*
Barron, B. J., xiii, 20, 307, 311,
    327–328, 332, 344, 346, 372,
    375, 379
Barron, L., 332, *346*
Barston, J., 34, *44*
Bartko, J. J., 237, *245*
Bartlett, B. J., 262, *273*
Bartolomé, L., 199, *218*
Bassok, M., 31, *44*, 306, *345*
Bateman, H., 327, *345*
Beach, R., 103, *113*
Beal, C. R., 117, *142*, 146, *161*, 173,
    175–176, 180, 182, *189*
Bell, J. A., 16, *22*
Bell, M., 239, *246*
Bell, T., 73, *90*

Bellott, B. P., 256–257, *274*
Belmont, J. M., 4, 16, *21*
Ben-Zeev, S., 196, 202, *217*
Bendixen, L. D., 139, *144*
Benjamin, A. S., 270, *271*
Bennett-Levy, J., 226, *245*
Benson, D. F., 230, 240, 242, *248*
Benton, J. S., 231–232, *247*
Benton, S. L., 97, *113*
Berardi-Coletta, B., 36, 38–40, *44*
Bereiter, C., 93–97, 100–101, 103,
    105, 109, 112, *113*, *115*, 306,
    310, *344*, *346*
Berg, C. A., 293, *302*
Berger, P. A., 240, *246*
Bergman, P. S., 223, *247*
Berkheimer, G. D., 324, 331, *345*
Berman, K. F., 240, *246*
Berry, D. C., 35, 37–38, 42, *44*
Berry, J. M., 251, 254–255, 258–259,
    271, *274*
Berry, S., 117–119, 126, 132, 137,
    140, *143*, 145, *162*
Berti, A., 224–225, 230, 242, *245*
Bertschinger, H., 236, *245*
Best, D. L., 256–258, *271*
Bialystok, E., 193, *217*
Biddlecomb, B., xiii, 20, 367, *375*
Bienias, J. L., 261, *274*
Biggs, J. B., 292, *301*
Birch, H. G., 58, *65*
Bisanz, G. L., 14, *21*
Bisiach, E., 224–225, 230, 242, *245*
Bjork, R. A., 270, *271*, *273*
Blais, J., 295, *303*
Blakeslee, T. D., 324, 331, *345*
Blanchard-Fields, F., 249, *271*
Blankenship, S. E., 58, *68*
Blumer, C., 141, *142*

Bluth, G., 146, 163
Bohaska, L. A., 229
Bol, L., 348, 358, 363
Bonitatibus, G. J., 175, 189
Booker, J., 350, 363
Borkowski, J. G., 8, 10, 17, 20, 21, 72,
    90, 251, 253, 271, 274, 348,
    362
Bowen, B. A., 107, 113, 231–232, 247
Bower, A. C., 34, 44
Boyle, R. A., 156, 163, 287, 303
Bracewell, R. J., 8, 21, 94, 113
Bramblett, J. P., 256–257, 274
Brandt, D., 146, 163
Bransford, J. D., xiii, 20, 171, 175, 179,
    189, 306–311, 313, 327–328,
    332, 344–345, 372, 375, 379
Braverman, M. T., 73, 90
Briars, D. J., 49, 65
Briggs, P., 291, 301
Brigham, M. C., 266, 372
Brill, L., 182, 189
Brincones, I., 146, 148, 161
Britton, J., 100, 114
Broadbent, D. E., 37–38, 42, 44, 168,
    189
Brofenbrenner, U., 57, 65
Brooks, K., 32, 45
Brooks, L., 295, 303
Brosh, M., 157, 161
Brown, A. L., 7, 9, 16, 21, 50, 57,
    62–63, 65, 67, 85, 89, 94–95,
    100, 114–115, 148, 161, 165,
    173–174, 178, 189–190,
    306–307, 311, 324, 341,
    344–345, 379, 380
Brown, J. L., 156, 161
Brown, R., 173, 176, 185, 191, 285,
    295, 304

Bruck, M., 198, 217
Bruer, J. T., 111, 114
Bruyn, G., 234, 245
Bryant, D. S., 119, 126, 130, 132,
    135–136, 140, 144, 370, 376,
    381
Burgess, T., 100, 114
Burnett, R. E., 94, 110–112, 114
Burns, H. L., 103, 114
Burns, K. D., 370, 376, 381
Burton, A. M., 37, 45
Buss, R., 73, 90
Butler, D. L., 13, 21, 176, 191, 278,
    281, 289, 301
Butterfield, E. C., 4, 14, 16–17, 21,
    53–54, 56, 66, 165, 168–169,
    173–175, 189–190
Buyer, L. S., 36, 38–40, 44
Byers, J. L., 34, 44
Byrnes, J. P., 50, 62, 67, 292, 302

C

Cacioppo, J. T., 296, 302
Cadelle-Elawar, M., 87, 89
Caine, E. D., 234–235, 245
Caldeira, M. H., 159, 161
Calero-Breckheimer, A., 200, 217
Camp, C. J., 250, 254, 259–261,
    271–272
Campanario, J. M., 146, 152,
    154–157, 159, 161–163, 166,
    173, 190
Campione, J. C., 7, 16, 21, 50, 63, 65,
    306–307, 311, 324, 341, 345
Caprio-Prevette, M. D., 256–257, 271
Cardenas, C., 241, 247
Carey, L., 94, 98, 105, 114, 174, 189
Carpenter, P. A., 170–171, 173, 177,
    189–190

Carpenter, W. T., 237, 245
Carr, M., xiii, 8, 10, 20, 21, 72, 79, 89,
        253, 271, 348, 362, 367, 375
Carraher, D. W., 57, 65
Carraher, T. N., 57, 65
Caruso, M. J., 266, 268–269, 273
Carver, C. S., 251, 271, 294, 302, 368,
        380
Castell, M. A., 178, 189
Catrambone, R., 292, 302
Cavanaugh, J. C., 12, 17, 21, 250–251,
        261, 271–273, 367–368, 380,
        380
Ceci, S. J., 57, 65
Chapman, J., 373, 381
Chapman, L. J., 373, 381
Charalambous, A., 238, 247
Chi, M. T. H., 31, 44, 53–55, 65, 306,
        345
Chiu, M., 306, 345
Christensen, C., 141, 142
Cicerone, K. D., 243, 245
Clark, S. C., 238–239, 244
Clayton, J. E., 350, 363
Clement. J., 149, 161
Clift, R., 171, 173, 188
Cobb, P., 77, 90, 307, 345
Cohen, S., 297–298, 303
Cole, K. D., 257, 275
Cole, M., 230, 248, 307, 345
Collier, V., 215, 219
Collins, A., 156, 161, 170, 175, 188,
        307, 345
Collins, G. N., 226, 248
Commins, N. L., 204, 218
Conant, R. C., 169, 189
Confrey, J., 149, 161
Connor, L. T., 253, 264–268, 272
Cook, L., 146, 161

Corbin, J., 350, 361, 363
Cordón, L. A., 289, 302
Corkin, S., 226, 247
Cornoldi, C., 253, 273
Corsale, K., 18, 21
Corsini, D. A., 4, 21
Costa, E., 159, 161
Coulter, L., 233, 247
Covington, M. V., 287, 302
Crawford, J., 193–194, 217
Crisafi, M. A., 57, 65
Critchley, M., 225, 245
Crooks, T. J., 159, 161
Cross, D. R., 62, 67
Crouse, A., 290, 303
Crumpton, E., 237, 248
CTGV, xiii, 20, 307, 311–312, 314,
        327–328, 332, 344–346, 372,
        375, 379
Cuerva, J., 155, 158, 161
Culp, G. H., 103, 114
Cummins, J., 199, 215, 217
Cutting, J., 224, 245

D

Daiute, C., 103, 114, 186, 189
Dallob, P. I., 32, 44, 60, 65
Dalton, B., 186, 189
Damasio, A. R., 244, 245
Danielczyk, W., 231, 234, 245
Danielsen, U. T., 225, 248
Danks, J. H., 197–198, 218
Dansereau, D. F., 295, 303
Davidson, J. E., xiii, 8, 20, 22, 49,
        52–53, 58–59, 61, 65–66, 68,
        374, 378
Davidson, N., 59, 68
Davidson, R. E., 34, 44
Davila, R., 240, 248

Davis, S. W., 256, 258, *271*
Davis, T. B., 295, *302*
Davison, A. N., 231–232, *247*
Day, J. D., 50, 65, 289, *302*
De Cooke, P. A., 359, *362*
de la Rosa, D., 215, *217*
De Leeuw, N., 306, *345*
Dee-Lucas, D., 148, *161*
Delclos, V. R., 59–60, 66
Dempster, F. N., 294, *302*, 359, *362*
DeNisi, A., 289, *302*
Dennehey, D. M., 258, *271*
Deuser, R., 8, *22*, 52, 66
Deutsch, A., 73, *90*
Devolder, P. A., 266, *272*
Diaper, D., 349, *362*
Di Vesta, F. J., 36, 40, 44–45
Dixon, R. A., 250–251, 254–255, 258,
        265–266, *272*
Dodd, D. H., 293, *302*
Dominowski, R. L., xiii, 20, 28, 32,
        34–36, 38–40, *44*, 60, 65,
        370, 374, 377
Dorner, D., 39, *44*
Dorsey, J. F., 222, 224, *247*
Duguid, P., 156, *161*
Duit, R., 149, *163*
Duncker, K., 58, 66
Dunkle, M. E., 139, *144*
Dunlosky, J., xiii, 15, 20, *22*, 131–132,
        143, 173, 250, 253, 259,
        264–268, *272–273*, 367,
        374–378, *381*
Dunn, S., 103, *114*
Durgunoglu, A. Y., 193, 199–200, *218*
Dweck, C. S., 296, *302*, 348, *362*
Dyson, A. H., 111, *114*

E

Eaton, S., 103, *113*
Ebert, M. H., 234–235, *245*
Eichinger, D. C., 324, 331, *345*
Eisenberger, R., 298, *302*
Elbaum, B. E., 293, *302*
El-Dinary, P. B., 173, 176, 185, *191*,
        250, 260, 273, 285, 295, *304*
Elliot-Faust, D. J., 171, *191*
Elliott, E., 255–258, 261–262, *272*
Ellis, S., 51, 63, 66, 157, *161*
Emig, J., 95, *114*
Endicott, J., 237, *245*
Endtz, L. J., 225, *246*
Englert, C. S., 94, 101, 103, *114*, 185,
        191
Englser, C. S., 98–99, *115*
Entwistle, N. J., 159, *161*, 360, *362*
Epstein, W., 117–121, 126, 128,
        132–137, 140, *142–143*, 145,
        148, 152, *162*, 165, 173, 178,
        189
Ericsson, K. A., 7, *22*, 27–29, 32–33,
        38, *44*, 201, *217*, 370, *381*
Erlwanger, S. H., 88, *89*
Evans, J. St. B. T., 34, *44*
Evans, P., 285, 295, *304*

F

Fahy, T. J., 228, *245*
Feinstein, J. A., 296, *302*
Feldman, C., 196, 202, *217*
Feltovich, P. J., 54, 65, *67*
Fennema, E., 158, *162*
Ferrara, R., 306, *345*
Ferretti, R. P., 17, *21*
Ferris, S. H., 231–232, *247–248*
Ficzere, S. A., 176, *191*
Fisk, A. D., 376, 378, *381*

Fitzgerald, J., 98, 105, *114*
Flaherty, E. G., 32, *45*
Flaum, M., 237–239, *244–245*
Flavell, J. H., 2–5, 7–9, 14, *22*, 50, 59, 66, 69, 89, 94, *114*, 168, 171, 173, *188–189*, 251, *272*, 306, *345*, 347, 361, *362*
Fleece, A. M., 251, 265–266, *272*
Flor, D., 71, *90*
Florio-Ruane, S., 103, *114*
Flower, L., 93–95, 97–100, 103–105, 109–112, *114–115*, 174, *189*, 348, *362*
Floyd, M., 257, 263, *272*
Folds-Bennett, T., 8, *21*, 72, 89
Foley, J. M., 127, 129, 131, 133, 140, *143*
Folstein, M. F., 231, *247*
Foos, P. W., 295, *302*
Ford, M. L., 148, *162*
Fordyce, D. J., 228–229, *245*, *247*
Forrest-Pressley, D. L., 171, *191*
Fortsch, W., 237, *246*
Fox, P. W., 359, *362*
Fozard, J. L., 254, *274*
Franks, J. J., 171, 175, 179, *189*, 306, 310, 313, *344*
Frederiks, J. A. M., 231–232, *245*
Frederiksen, J. R., 343, *346*
Freebern, G., xiv, 20, 294, 352, *363*, 375, *379*
Freedman, S. W., 111, *114*
Freeman, K., 297–298, *303*
Freidrichs, A. G., 14, *22*
Freire, P., 215, *217*
Friedman, S., 235, *247*
Fry, P. S., 256–257, *271*
Fuller, D., 72, 89

G

Gabriesheski, A. S., 264, *273*
Gadamer, H. G., 177, 182, 186, *189*
Gagne, R. M., 36, *45*
Galambos, S. J., 198, *217*
Galanter, E., 368, *381*
Galda, L., 71, *90*
Gallagher, D., 257, *275*
Gallimore, R., 101, *115*
Gamas, W. S., 149, *162*
Gámez, A., 194, 213, *218*
García, G. E., xiii, 20, 193–194, 199–201, 203, 213–214, *217–218*, 368, 374–375
García-Arista, E., 156, 159, *161–162*
Garcia-Mila, M., 70, *90*
Gardner, H., 48, 51, 66
Gardner, M. K., 51, 68
Garner, R., 50, 66, 146, 148, 157–159, *162*, 173
Garner, W. R., 313, *345*
Garofalo, J., 70, 72–73, 89–90
Garrison, S., 307, 311, 332, *344*
Garrod, A. C., 175, *189*
Garron, D. C., 234, *248*
Gassel, M. M., 225, *246*
Gee, J. P., 215, *217*
Genesee, F., 198, *217*
Gentner, D., 57, 66
Gerlach, T. L., 135–136, *143*
Gernsbacher, M. A., 138, *142*, 176, *191*
Gertzog, W. A., 149, *163*
Ghatala, E. S., 16, 19, *22–23*, 133–134, 138, 140, *143–144*
Gibson, E. L., 313, *345*, 350, *363*
Gibson, J. J., 313, *345*
Gilbert, J. K., 149, *162*
Gilhooly, K. J., 30, *45*

Gillström, Å., 119, 126, 128, 130, 135, 138, 140, *142*

Givon, H., 103, 108, *115*

Glaser, R., 54–55, 65, 67, 306, *345*

Glasersfeld, E. V., 11, *22*, 74, 77, 89–90

Glass, G. V., 149, 152, *162*

Glenberg, A. M., 117–121, 126, 128, 132–137, 140, *142–143*, 145, 148, 152, *162*, 165, 173, 178, *189*

Glisky, E. L., 227–228, 246, *284*

Globerson, T., 103, 108, *115*

Glover, J. A., 97, *113*, 137–138, 140, *143*, 295, *302*

Goetz, E. T., 147, *160*, 200, *217*

Goldberg, T. E., 240, *246*

Goldhaber, D., 361, *362*

Goldin, S. E., 55, *66*

Goldin-Meadow, S., 198, *217*

Goldman, S. R., 307, 311, 327, 332, *344–346*

Goldsmith, M., 251, 253, 270, *272*, 368, *381*

Golinkoff, R. M., 212, *217*

Goncz, L., 198, *218*

Goodman, L. A., 123, *143*

Goodwin, C., 187, *189*

Goossens, L., 250, 259–260, 262–263, *274*

Gordon, B., 231–232, *247*

Gordon, E., 97–98, 105, *114*

Gordon, G. G., 223, *247*

Gorin, L., 148, *163*

Gorman, J. M., 222, 237–239, *244–245*

Graesser, A. C., 119, 126, 130–131, 135, 140, *143*, 170, 186, *189*

Graf, A., 266–267, *273*

Greene, T. R., 295, *272*, *303*

Greeno, J. G., 54, 56, *66*, 307, *345*

Gregory, D. J., 30, *45*

Griffin, P., 307, *345*

Guider, R. L., 257, *275*

Guindon, R., 154, *162*

Gunstone, R. F., 149, *162*

Gupta, L., 297, *304*

Gustafson, I., 231–232, *246*

Guthrie, J. T., xiv

Guzzetti, B. J., 149, 151–152, *162*

H

Hacker, D. J., xiii, 20, 165, 173–175, 186, *189–190*, 367–369, 371, 377, *381*

Hackler, E., 225, *246*

Hadwin, A. F., xiii, 20, 251, 374, 378

Hagen, J. W., 4, *22*

Hague, S., 151, *161*

Hakuta, K., 193–195, 197–198, *218*

Haladyna, T., 293, *302*

Hale, C. A., 251, *274*

Hall, V. C., 126, 131, 133–134, *144*, 148, 156, *164*, 286, *303*

Hamlett, K. W., 256, 258, *271*

Hammer, D., 147, *162*

Hamptom, B., 240, *246*

Hancin-Bhatt, B., 193, 199–200, *218*

Hanesian, H., 149, *161*

Hansen, J., 173

Hare, V. C., 300, *301*

Harrington, C., 60, *66*

Harris, J. E., xiv, 226, *248*

Harris, K. R., xiv

Hart, J. T., 4, 13–14, *22*

Hart, S. S., 87, *90*

Hartman, D. K., 177, 183–184, *190*

Harvey, D. J., 36, 40, *45*

Hawkins, J., 54, *67*

Hayes, J. R., 50–52, 54, 66, 93–95, 97–99, 103, 105–106, 109, 114–115, 174, 189
Hayes-Roth, B., 55, 66, 97, 114
Hayes-Roth, F., 97, 114
Heath, A., 332, 346
Heath, S. B., 194, 218
Hegarty, M., 51, 66
Heineken, E., 165, 173, 175, 190
Hekster, R. E. M., 225, 246
Heritage, J., 187, 189
Hertzog, C., xiii, 20, 140, 143, 250–251, 254–255, 258–259, 264–268, 272–273, 367, 374–376, 378, 381
Hess, T. M., 249, 271
Hesse, D., 181, 190
Hewson, P. W., 149, 163
Hickey, D., 332, 346
Hidi, S., 358, 362
Higgins, L., 94, 104, 112, 114–115
Holden, T., 241, 247
Holley, C. S., 32, 45
Holyoak, K. J., 54, 57, 66
Hopkins, K. D., 159, 161, 163
Hoyt, J. D., 14, 22
Hultsch, D. F., 140, 143, 255, 258, 272–273
Hunt, E. B., 51–52, 67
Hunt, R. D., 234–235, 245
Hynd, C. R., 151, 161–162

I

Ianco-Worrall, A. D., 196, 202, 218
Idol, L., xiv
Inhelder, B., 4, 22
Irving, M. H., 228, 245
Ives, E. R., 224, 248

J

Jackson, N. E., 53, 56, 66
Jacobs, J. E., 62, 67
Jagust, W. J., 233, 247
James, W., 13, 22
Jarvis, L. H., 197–199, 218
Jarvis, W. B. G., 296, 302
Jessup, D. L., 72, 79, 89
Jiménez, R. T., xiii, 20, 193–194, 199, 201, 213–214, 217–218, 368, 374–375
Joaquim, S. G., 253, 273
Johnson-Laird, P. N., 169, 190, 308, 345
Johnston, J., 168–169, 189
Johnston, P., 145, 164
Jonas, D., 138–140, 143
Jones, B. F., xiv
Joynt, R. J., 231–232, 246
Just, M. A., 170–171, 173, 177, 189–190
Justice, E. M., 72, 90

K

Kahn, R. L., 222–223, 231, 248
Kaiser, J., 223, 245
Kajer, W. K., 127, 129, 131, 133, 140, 143
Kallod, M., 138–140, 143
Kanfer, R., 292, 302
Kantor, R., 307, 311, 332, 344
Kantz, M. J., 348, 362
Kaplan, C. A., 30–31, 45, 58, 66
Karau, S. J., 359, 362
Karoly, P., 377, 381
Karpf, D. A., 34, 45
Kaszniak, A. W., 232–236, 246
Kellogg, R. T., 32, 45

Kempler, S., 241, 247
Keramari, E., 238, 247
Keren, G., 264, 272
King, A., 42–43, 45, 60–61, 66, 295, 302
King, W. L., 34, 44
Kingsley, P. R., 4, 22
Kinsbourne, M., 230, 246
Kintsch, W., 147–148, 153–154, 162–164, 170–172, 175–177, 179, 183, 190–191, 369, 381
Kirby, J. R., ix
Kirlik, A., 376, 378, 381
Kirschner, B. W., 98–99, 115, 185, 191
Kisst-Hackett, R., 307, 311, 346
Kliegl, R., 260, 272
Klopfer, D., 54, 67
Kluger, A. N., 289, 302
Kluwe, R. H., 8–10, 12, 16–17, 20, 22
Knight, S. L., 200, 218
Kodzopeljic, J., 198, 218
Koehler, P. J., 225, 246
Kogut, D., 87, 90
Kolko, G., 181, 190
Koriat, A., 251, 253, 270, 272, 368, 370, 381
Körkel, J., 295, 302
Korsakoff, S. S., 226, 246
Kotler-Cope, S., 250, 259, 272
Kotovsky, K., 51, 66
Kraft, R. G., 97, 113
Kramer, J. J., 260–261, 271
Kramer, N., 257, 275
Kraus, C., 148, 162
Kreupeling, W. J., 151, 163
Kreutzer, M. A., 361, 362
Kroll, M. D., 148, 162
Krug, D., 295, 302
Kruglanski, A. W., 157, 161

Kruindenier, J., 103, 114
Kruskal, W. H., 122, 143
Kucharski, L. T., 241, 248
Kuhn, D., 70–71, 90
Kulikowich, J. M., 148, 160
Kuperis, S., 176, 191
Kwapil, T. R. J., 373, 381

L

Lachman, M. E., 255–258, 261–262, 270, 272
Lai, C., 141, 142
Lambert, W. E., 195–196, 214, 218
Lamon, M., 312, 346
Landauer, T. K., 269, 273
Langer, J. A., 199, 218
Langer, K. G., 244, 246
Larkin, J. H., 54–55, 66, 148, 161
Larkin, J. M., 49, 65
LaVancher, C., 306, 345
Lave, J., 307, 345
Leal, L., 87, 90
Lee, O., 324, 331, 345
Leggett, E. L., 296, 302, 348, 362
Leiguarda, R., 232–233, 247
LeMare, L., 291, 304
Leonard, C., 361, 362
Leonesio, R. J., 253, 273
Leong, D., 58
Leopold, W. F., 195–196, 218
Lesgold, A., 54, 67
Lester, F. K., 70, 72–73, 89–90
Levin, J. R., 16, 19, 22–23, 133–134, 138, 140, 144
Levine, M., 34, 45
Lewis, P. J., 306, 345
Lewkowicz, C. J., 255–258, 261–262, 272
Liddle, P. F., 236–237, 246

Lin, X. D., 312, 343, *345–346*
Lin, I. F., 237, *246*
Lindhauer, B. K., 179, *190*
Lipson, M. Y., 62, 67, 150, *162*
Little, L. D., 119, 126, 130–131, 135, 140, *143*
Lockhead, J., 60, *68*
Lodico, M. G., 16, *22*
Lott, L., 257, 261, 263, *274*
Lovelace, E. A., 137, 140, *143*
Lucas, T., 199, *218*
Luchins, A. S., 58, *67*
Luchins, E. S., 58, *67*
Lundeberg, M. A., 359, *362*
Luria, A. R., 197, *218*
Lyerly, O. G., 230, *248*
Lysaker, P., 239, *246*
Lysynchuk, L. M., 306, *346*

M

Macedo, D., 215, *217–218*
MacLeod, C. M., 51–52, *67*
Magliano, J. P., 119, 126, 130–131, 135, 140, *143*
Mahendra, B., 235, *246*
Mahoney, G. J., 179, *190*
Maki, R. H., xiii, 20, 117–119, 121, 123, 126–127, 129, 131–140, *143*, 145, *162*, 165, *190*, 369–371, *376*
Malenka, R. C., 240, *246*
Mann, D. M. A., 231–232, *247*
Mannes, S. M., 179, *190*
Marcoen, A., 250, 257, 259–260, 262–263, *274*
Marinos, V., 238, *247*
Markell, K. A., 141, *144*
Markley, R. P., 260–261, *271*
Markham, L., 98, 105, *114*

Markman, E. M., 4, *22*, 50, 67, 117, *143*, 145, 147–148, 152, *162–163*, 166, 171, 173–175, 185, *190*
Marsh, H. W., 348, *362*
Martin, N., 100, *114*
Martin, V., 306, *346*
Martinez-Pons, M., 348, *363*
Marx, R. W., 156, *163*, 279, 287, 291, *303–304*
Mason, S. E., 139, *144*
Masterson, F. A., 298, *302*
Mathews, N. N., 51–52, *67*
Matsuhashi, A., 97–98, 105, *114*
Maw, C. E., 215, *217*
Mayer, R. E., 51, 66, 146, *161*
Mayfield-Stewart, C., 307, 311, *346*
Mazzie, C. A., 97, *115*
Mazzoni, G., 253, *273*
McAfee, O., 58
McCarthy, M., 231–232, *247*
McClelland, J. L. 170, 175, *191*
McCloskey, M., 149, *163*
McCormick, K., 348, *362*
McCutchen, D., 175–176, 180–181, *191*
McDermitt, M., 298, *302*
McDermott, J., 54–55, *66*
McDonald-Miszczak, L., 140, *143*, 258, *273*
McEvoy, C. L., 257, 261–262, *273*
McEvoy, J. P., 238–239, *246*
McGeorge, P., 37, *45*
McGlynn, S. M., xiii, 20, 221, 226–228, 230, 233–236, 242–244, 246, *248*, 372
McHugh, P. R., 231, *247*
McKitrick, L. A., 254, *271*
McKoon, G., 285, 288, 295, *302*

McLachlan, D. R., 227, 233, *248*
McLain, E., 87, 90
McLaughlin, B., 195, *218*
McLean, R., 103, 112, *115*
McLeod, A., 100, *114*
McNamara, T. P., 308, *345*
Means, M. L., 295, *303*
Meichtry, Y. J., 157, *163*
Melcher, J., 59, 68
Meregalli, S., 230, 242, *245*
Merriman, W. E., 197–198, *218*
Metcalfe, J., 250, 253, *273*
Meyer, B. 146, *163*
Meyer, B. J. F., 262, 270, *273*
Meyer, D. E., 59, 68
Meyer, M., 349, *363*
Meyers, M., 49, 67
Mezynski, K. J., 306, *344*
Michael, J., 358, *363*
Michalakeas, A., 238, *247*
Migliorelli, R., 232–233, *247*
Mikkelsen, B. H., 135–136, *143*
Millac, P., 228, *245*
Miller, A. T., 7, *22*
Miller, D. L., 308, *345*
Miller, G. A., 5, *22*, 368, *381*
Miller, G. E., 171, *191*
Miller, M. B., 373, *381*
Miller, P., 347, *362*
Miller, S., 347, *362*
Milner, B., 226, *247*
Miner, A. C., 253, *273*
Miramontes, O., 204, *218*
Mishler, E. G., 350, *363*
Mitchell, M. S., 230, *248*
Moely, B. E., 87, 90
Monk, C. A., 51, 66
Moon, J. R., 257, 261–262, *273*
Moore, A., 327, *345*

Moore, D., 146, *164*, 166, 173, *191*
Morgan, M., 292–293, *302*
Morin, L., 223, *245*
Morris, C. C., 119–121, 126, 128, 131–136, 140, *142–143*
Morris, D. L., 236, *246*
Morris, J., 307, 311, 332, *344*
Moscovitch, M., 227, 233, *248*
Mosenthall, P., 156, *163*
Moynahan, E., 17, *22*
Mukherjee, S., 241, *247*
Murphy, M. D., 264, 266, 268–269, *273*
Murray, H. G., 133–134, 138, 140, *144*
Muthukrishna, N., 8, 20, *21*
Myers, J. L., 154, *163*
Myslobodsky, M. S., 242, *247*

N

Nagy, W. E., 193, 199–200, 203, *217–218*
Narens, L., 2, *22*, 168–169, 190, 250–252, 266–267, *273*, 281, 286, *302*, 368, 370, *381*
Nathanson, M., 223, *247*
Neary, D., 231–232, *247*
Neely, A. S., 261, 263, 270, *273*
Nelson, T. O., 2, 14–15, *21–22*, 122, 131–132, *143*, 168–169, 190, 250–253, 266–267, *272–273*, 281, 286, *302*, 368, 370, 373, *381*
Nesbit, J. C., 297, *304*
Newell, A., 5, *22*, 49–50, 53, 67, 310, *345*
Nicholls, J. G., 7, *22*, 349, 358, *363*
Nickerson, R. S., 59, 67
Nielsen, J. M., 224, *247*
Nieto, S., 215, *218*
Nilsson, L., 231–232, *246*

Nisbett, R., 8, 23, 358, 363
Nist, S. L., 279, 303
Nold, E., 98, 109, 115
Nolen, S. B., 148, 163, 293, 302
Norman, D. A., 288, 303
Norris, L., 94, 110–112, 114
Norris, S. P., 32, 35, 45
Northen, B., 231–232, 247
Novak, J. D., 149, 161, 163
Nystrand, M., 101, 111, 115

O

Oakhill, J., 173
O'Brien, E. J., 148, 152–153, 160, 163
O'Donnell, A., 295, 303
Ohlsson, S., 32, 45
Oka, E. R., 158, 163
Olarte, S., 241, 247
Olson, D. R., 182, 190
Oltman, J. E., 235, 247
Ornstein, P. A., 18, 21
Ostertag, J., 173
Oswald, W. T., 241, 248
Otero, J., xiii, 20, 145–148, 152–159,
        161–163, 166, 173, 175–177,
        179, 183, 190, 369–371, 375,
        377, 381

P

Padrón, Y. N., 200, 218
Padrone, F. J., 244, 246
Palincsar, A., 62–63, 65, 67, 95, 115,
        165, 173–174, 185, 190
Papagno, C., 224–225, 245
Paris, S. G., 8, 10–11, 17, 20, 23,
        49–50, 62, 67, 158, 163, 179,
        190, 292, 302
Park, D. C., 261, 273

Patalano, A. L., 59, 68
Patricio, A., 159, 161
Patton, M. Q., 350, 363
Pea, R. D., 54, 67
Peal, E., 195–196, 214, 218
Pearson, P. D., xiii, 20, 152, 164, 173,
        177, 187, 190–191, 193, 199,
        201, 205, 213–214, 216–218,
        358, 362, 368, 374–375
Peck, V., 14, 21
Peck, W. C., 94, 112, 115, 348, 362
Peeck, J., 151, 163
Pellegrini, A. D., 71, 90
Pellegrino, J., 307, 311, 332, 344, 346
Penrose, A. M., 94, 111, 115
Perani, D., 224–225, 245
Perfetti, C. A., 175–176, 180–181, 191
Perfetto, G. A., 306, 344
Peristeris, A., 238, 247
Perkins, D. N., 59, 67, 288, 303
Perlmutter, M., 12, 21, 367–368, 380,
        380
Peterson, P. L., 73, 87, 90
Petracca, G., 233, 247
Petracchi, M., 232–233, 247
Petraglia, J., 94, 104, 114
Petrosino, A. J., 312, 346
Petty, R. E., 296, 302
Pfundt, H., 149, 163
Piaget, J., 4, 22
Pintrich, P. R., 156, 163, 287, 292,
        303–304
Pirie, J., 134, 138, 143
Plake, B. S., 97, 113
Pliskin, N. H., 240, 246
Plude, D. J., 269, 273
Plumb, C., 165, 173–175, 189–190,
        377, 381
Podd, M. H., 240, 246

Polkey, C. E., 226, *245*
Pollard, P., 34, *44*
Polya, G., 56, 67, 70, 90
Poon, L. W., 254, *274*
Popkin, S. J., 254, *274*
Posner, G. J., 149, *163*
Potter, W. J., 350, *363*
Powell, G. E., 226, *245*
Prata-Pina, E. M., 159, *161*
Pressley, M., xiv, 10, 16, 19–20, *21–23*, 69, 72, 90, 133–134, 138, 140, *143–144*, 171, 173, 176, 185, *191*, 250, 253, 260, 266, *271–274*, 285, 290, *294–295, 303–304*, 306, 346, 348, 351–352, 362, 375, 379, *381*
Pribram, K. H., 368, *381*
Prigatano, G. P., 222, 228–229, *247*
Pritchard, R., 200, *218*

Q

Quathamer, D., 165, 173, 175, *190*

R

Rabinowitz, H. S., 58, *65*
Rabinowitz, M., 297–298, *303*
Ramirez, J. D., 215, *218*
Ramsden, P., 159, *161, 164*, 350, *363*
Ranseen, J. D., 229
Raphael, T. E., 94, 98–99, 101, 103, *114–115*, 185, 187, *190–191*
Ratcliff, R., 285, 288, 295, *302*
Ratner, H. H., 145–146, *164*, 165, 173, *191*
Raviv, A., 157, *161*
Readence, J. E., 150, *161, 164*

Reder, M. L., 173, 251, 253, *273–274*, 368, 374, *381*
Redlich, F. C., 222, 224, *247*
Reed, B. R., 233, *247*
Rees, E., 54–55, *65*
Reis, R., 50, 66, 146, *162*
Reisberg, B., 231–232, *247–248*
Rellinger, E. A., 10, *21*, 36, 38–40, *44*, 251, 253, 271, *274*, 348, *362*
Resnick, L. B., 62, 67, 307, *345*
Rewey, K., 332, *346*
Reynolds, R. E., 278, *303*
Rhodes, N., 290, *303*
Rifkin, B., 54, *68*
Ritter, F. E., 251, *274*, 368, *381*
Robinson, H. A., 278, *303*
Roedel, T. D., 136, 139, *144*
Roen, D. H., 176, *191*
Rogers, T., 152, *164*, 173, 177, *191*
Rogoff, B., 60, 67, 307, *346*
Rohman, D. G., 95, *115*
Rohwer, W. D., Jr., 348, 358, *363*
Rönnberg, J., 119, 127–128, 130, 135, 138, 140, *142*
Rosch, E., 177, *191*
Roschelle, J., 187, *191*
Rose, F. C., 226, *247*
Rose, T. L., 260, *275*
Rosen, A. M., 241, *247*
Rosen, H., 100, *114*
Roueche, J. R., 229, *245*
Roush, W., 249, *274*
Rowell, J. A., 160, *164*
Rubba, P., 157, *164*
Rubinson, H., 54, *67*
Rumelhart, D. E., 170, 175, *191*, 288, *303*
Rusch, K. M., 141, *144*
Ryle, G., 8, *23*

S

Sabe, L., 232–233, *247*
Salomon, G., 103, 108, *115*, 288, *303*
Sánchez, G. I., 195, *218*
Sanders, R. E., 264, 266, 268–269, *273*
Sandifer, P. H., 230, *247*
Sandler, R., 241, *247*
Sanocki, T., 119–121, 126, 128, 132–136, 140, *142*
Santulli, K. A., 87, *90*
Saville-Troike, M., 204, *219*
Saylor, L. L., 251, 265–266, *272*
Scardamalia, M., 93–97, 100–101, 103, 105, 109, 112, *113*, *115*, 306, 310, *344*, *346*
Schacter, D. L., 221–222, 226–228, 230, 233, 242, 244, *246–248*, 372, *381*
Schallert, D. L, 300, *301*
Scheier, M. F., 251, *271*, 294, *302*, 368, *380*
Schenk, S., 148, *164*
Scher, H., 240, *248*
Schliemann, A. D., 57, *65*
Schmitt, F. A., 264, 266, 268–269, *273*
Schneck, M. K., 231, *248*
Schneider, W., 12, 15, 17, 19, *23*, 69, 72, *90*, 250, *274*, 285, *303*
Schoenfeld, A. H., 12–13, 17, 23, 59, 63, *67*, 73, 79–80, 84, *90*
Schommer, M., 129, 131, *144*, 286, 289, 290, *303*
Schooler, J. W., 32, *45*, 59, *68*
Schraw, G., 136, 139, *144*, 281, *303*
Schriver, K. A., 94, 98, 105–106, *114–115*, 174, *189*
Schultz, N., 146, *164*
Schunk, D. H., xiv, 148, *164*, 293, *303*
Schunn, C., 374, *381*

Schwartz, B. L., 253, 273
Schwartz, D. L., xiii, 20, 307, 311, 313, 327–328, 332, 344, 346, 372, 375, 379
Schwartz, L. K., 269, 273
Scogin, F., 257, 261, 263, 270, 272, 274
Scott, A. C., 350, 363
Seidman, L. J., 236, 248
Seifert, C. M., 59, 68
Serra, M., 119, 121, 123, 126–127, 131–135, 140, 143, 165, 190
Shapiro, L. J., 73, 90
Shaughnessy, J. J., 139–140, 144
Shaw, J. G., 5, 22
Shen, M., 196, 202, 217
Sherman, J., 158, 162
Sherwood, R. D., 310, 312–313, 327, 344–346
Shiffrin, R. M., 5, 21
Shimamura, A. P., 227, 248, 250, 273
Shipley, C., 367, 374, 381
Shirey, L. L., 278, 303
Shoulson, I., 231–232, 235, 245–246
Siegler, R. S., 50–51, 55, 63, 66, 68, 367, 374, 381
Sigal, M., 241, 247
Silver, E. A., 73, 90
Simon, D. P., 54–55, 66
Simon, H. A., 5, 7, 22, 27–33, 38, 44–45, 49–51, 53–56, 66–67, 201, 217, 310, 345, 370, 381
Simpson, M. L., 279, 303
Sims, N. R., 231–232, 247
Singer, M., 170, 189
Sinkavich, F. J., 139–140, 144
Sinnott, J. D., 249, 274

Sitko, B. M., xiii, 20, 94, 98–99, 106–107, 111, 115, 375, 377
Skoutas, C., 238, *247*
Slife, B. R., 73, *90*
Smagorinsky, P., 102, 109, *115*
Smith, A. D., 261, *273*
Smith, E. C., Jr., 36, *45*
Smith, E. E., 59, *67*
Smith, J., 260, *272*
Smith, J. M., 241, *248*
Smith, L. C., 150, *161, 164*
Smith, M. C., 148, *164*
Smith, M. E., 193, *219*
Smith, S. M., 58, *68*
Snowden, J. S., 231–232, *247*
Snyder, B. L., 133–134, 138, 140, *144*
Snyder, T. E., 149, 152, *162*
Sommers, N., 98, *115*
Spargo, E., 124, *144*
Spiga, R., 237, *246*
Spradley, J. P., 350, *363*
Spurlin, J. E., 295, *303*
Squire, L. R., 226–227, *248*
Stark, K. D., 73, *90*
Starkstein, S. E., 232–233, *247*
Steffe, L. P., 73, 77, 86, *90*
Stein, B. S., 306, 309–310, *344*
Stein, S., 285, 295, *304*
Stein, V., 348, *362*
Sternberg, R. J., xiii, 8, 20, 22, 51–53, 55, 57, 61, 66, 68, 374, 378
Stevens, D. D., 94, 101, 103, *114*
Stigsdotter, A., 261, *274*
Stinessen, L., 36, *45*
Storandt, M., 257, 259, 261, 263, 270, *274*
Strage, A., 348, 358, *363*
Stratman, J., 94, 98, 105, *114*, 174, *189*
Strauss, A., 350, 361, *363*

Strauss, D. H., 222, 237–239, *244–245*
Strauss, J. S., 237, *245*
Strike, K. A., 149, *163*
Stuss, D. T., 230, 240, 242, *248*
Suchman, L. A., 187, *191*
Suls, J. M., 32, *45*
Sunderland, A., 226, *248*
Surber, J. R., 129, 131, *144*
Swallow, J., 103, 112, *115*
Sweller, J., 292, *303*
Swett, M., 135, 138, 140, *143*, 145, *162*
Swing, S. R., 73, *90*
Symonds, C. P., 226, *247*

T

Taylor, D. W., 58, *65*
Teson, A., 232–233, *247*
Teuber, H. L., 226, *247*
Te Velde, J., 225, *246*
Tharp, R. G., 101, *115*
Theologou, A., 238, *247*
Thiede, K., 377, *381*
Thomas, E. L., 278, *303*
Thomas, J. W., 348, 358, *363*
Thomas, W. P., 215, *219*
Thompson, G. G., 195, *219*
Thompson, R. C., 127, 129, 131, 133, 140, *143*
Thompson, W. B., 139, *144*
Thorkildsen, T. A., 349, *363*
Tobis, J. S., 228, *246*
Tomer, A., 263–264, *274*
Tomer, R., 241, *247*
Trabasso, T., 170, *189*
Traxler, M. J., 176, *191*
Treat, N. J., 254, *274*
Tregar, B., 199, *219*

Tuckman, B. W., 296, 303
Tulving, E., 227, 233, 248
Tupper, D. E., 243, 245
Turner, L. A., 251, 274
Twadell, F., 203, 219

V

Vallar, G., 224–225, 245
van den Bosch, A. B., 151, 163
van Dijk, T. A., 148, 153–154, 162,
    164, 175–176, 191
Van Etten, S., xiv, 20, 294, 352, 363,
    375, 379
Van Haneghan, J. P., 332, 346
Van Meter, P., xiv, 20, 290, 294, 303,
    351–352, 363, 375, 379, 381
Van Putten, T., 237, 248
Van Ranst, N., 257, 274
Van Rossum, E., 148, 164
Varia, V., 241, 247
Varner, K. R., 138, 142
Vásquez, O., 199, 218
Verhaeghen, P., 250, 257, 259–263,
    274
Verhoeven, L. T., 199, 219
Vesonder, G. T., 14, 21
Victor, M., 226, 248
Viennot, L., 149, 164
Vilkki, J., 226, 248
Von Hagen, K. O., 224, 248
Vosniadou, S., 152, 164, 173, 177, 191
Voss, J. F., 295, 303
Voss, J. T., 14, 21
Vye, N. J., xiii, 20, 306–307, 310–311,
    313, 327–328, 332, 344, 346,
    372, 375, 379
Vygotsky, L. S., 26, 45, 101, 115, 187,
    191, 195, 219

W

Waas, G. A., 73, 90
Waggoner, D., 215, 219
Wagner, D. A., 54, 68
Wagner, R. K., 57, 68
Walczyk, J. J., 126, 131, 133–134, 144,
    148, 156, 164, 286, 303
Wallace, D. L., 94, 105, 110–112,
    114–115
Wang, Y., 54, 67
Warkentin, R. W., 348, 358, 363
Warrington, E. K., 225, 230, 246, 248
Waterman, L. J., 241, 248
Watts, D. M., 149, 162
Waxman, H. C., 200, 218
Weaver, C. A. III, 119, 126, 132,
    135–136, 140, 144, 165–166,
    173, 191, 370, 376, 381
Weaver, S. L., 255–258, 261–262, 272
Weil, E. M., 52, 68
Weinberger, D. R., 240, 246
Weiner, B., 349, 363
Weingartner, H., 234–235, 245
Weinstein, E. A., 222–223, 230–231,
    248
Weisberg, R. W., 32, 45
Weiss, J., 73, 90
Welch, D. C., 251, 255–257, 274
Wellman, H. M., 7, 14, 22–23, 76, 91,
    94, 114
Wertsch, J. W., 85, 91, 101, 115
West, R. L., 250–251, 254–259,
    262–264, 269, 271, 274
Whimbey, A., 60, 68
White, B., 343, 346
White, R. T., 149, 162
Whitehead, A. N., 310, 346
Wilder, L., 36, 40, 45

Wilkinson, A., 117, *143*, 148, 152,
    162, 165, 173, 178, *189*
Willanger, R., 225, 248
Willert, M. G., 127, 129, 131, 133,
    140, *143*
Willey, R. J., 176, *191*
Williams, D., 225, 246
Williams, K. D., 359, 362
Williams, S. M., 332, *346*
Willig, A. C., 215, *219*
Willis, S. L., 254, *274*
Willoughby, T., 306, *346*
Wilson, M., 348, 358, *363*
Wilson, R. S., 234, 248
Wilson, T., 8, *23*, 358, *363*
Winne, P. H., xiii, 13, 20, *21*, 251,
    278–279, 281, 286–287, 289,
    291, 294, 297–298, 300, *301*,
    303–304, 378
Winograd, P., 8, 10–11, 17, 20, *23*,
    145, *164*, 173
Wittgenstein, L., 177, 180, *191*
Woloshyn, V., 134, 138, *143*, 306, *346*
Wong, B. F., 199, *219*
Wong, B. Y. L., 176, *191*, 291, *304*
Wong, R., 291, *304*
Wood, E., 306, *346*
Woodruff, E., 103, 112, *115*
Woulters, C. A., 292, *304*
Wyatt, D., 285, 295, *304*

Y

Yale, C., 237, *248*
Yale, S. A., 222, 237–239, *244–245*
Yaniv, I., 59, 68
Yates, P. O., 231–232, 247
Yesavage, J. A., 260, *274–275*
Yokoi, L., xiv, 20, 290, 294, *303*,
    351–352, *363*, 375, 379, *381*
Young, C. J., 262, 273
Young, D. A., 240, 248
Young, M. F., 332, *346*
Yu, A., 196–197, *216*
Yu, S. L., 292, *304*
Yussen, S. R., 148, *164*
Yzaguirre, R., 215, *217*

Z

Zabrucky, K., 145–146, *164*, 165–166,
    173, *191*
Zarit, S. H., 257, *275*
Zech, L., xiii, 20, 307, 311, 313, 332,
    344, *346*, 372, 375, 379
Zechmeister, E. B., 141, *144*
Zellermayer, M., 103, 108, *115*
Zhou, Z., 87, 90
Zimlin, L., 175, *189*
Zimmerman, B. J., xiv, 348, *363*
Zinser, M. C., 373, *381*
Zitzow, D., 358, *363*
Zohar, A., 70, 90
Zook, K. B., 40, 45

Subject Index

A

Abstraction, 76–78, 88
Achievement, 97, 250–251, 348, 375, 380
Activities of daily living, 232–234
Alphabet search, 16
Alzheimer's disease (AD), 227, 231–234
Amnesia, 221, 224, 226–228
Anchored instruction, 310–313, 324, 326–327, 329, 332, 341, 380
Anchoring, 264–265
Anosodiaphoria, 222
Anosognosia, 221–225, 230–232, 242
Anton's syndrome, 222, 224
Artificial intelligence, 349
Attention allocation, 13
Attributional retraining, 255–257, 270

B

Benchmark lesson, 324
Bilingualism, 193–216, 368, 374–375
    additive, 214
    subtractive, 214
Biliteracy, 194, 201–202

C

Calibration, 145, 151, 165, 167
Cognates, 199–200, 203–204, 209, 211, 213, 216, 374
Cognitive conflict, 87, 149–150, 152, 156, 158
Cognitive development, 3–4, 20, 50, 74, 193, 195, 197–198, 214, 250
Cognitive restructuring, 256, 258
Collaboration, 71, 101, 103–105, 109–112, 311, 313, 357
Collaborative-cultural approach, 379
Comprehension, 5, 63, 120, 146, 157, 165–171, 178–180, 204, 207, 234, 270, 291, 306, 369, 371, 374, 376
    failures, 166–167, 171–174, 178, 188, 295, 371–372
    monitoring, 50, 117, 126–127, 145–152, 156–160, 165–167, 170–173, 175, 177–179, 182, 184–188, 205, 208–209, 211–212, 368, 370, 376
    monitoring standards, 146, 169–172, 186, 372–373
    problems, 145–147, 175, 178–179, 205, 208

Concurrent reports, 28–29
Consciousness, 7, 87, 222–223, 231
Construction-integration (CI),
    153–155, 176
Constructivism, 11, 69, 71, 74, 78, 80,
    86–88, 349
Contextualism, 360–361
Contrasting cases, 308, 313–316, 324,
    326, 342–343
Control (see Metacognition, control)
COPES, 279–286, 289, 294, 299, 301
Coping, 350–355, 358–361
Critical thinking, 35, 102, 104

D

Dementia, 223, 231, 233–236,
    241–242, 257
Denial, 221–222, 224, 230, 232, 236,
    244
Developmental psychology, 3, 42, 70,
    72–73, 85, 96–99, 107, 250,
    264–265, 267–268
Dialogue, 62, 101, 167, 186–187
Discovery technique, 79
Dissonance, 174
Domain familiarity, 119–126, 141
Dominance relations, 168, 368

E

Ease of comprehension, 126–128, 131,
    141
Ease of learning (EOL), 13, 286
Editing, 95–96, 98–99, 106, 113
Encoding, 48–50, 53, 60–61, 64, 178
Epistemic authority, 147, 149, 157–158
Epistemological beliefs, 147, 287,
    289–290, 293–294

Error detection paradigm, 117, 145,
    157, 166, 371
Ethnographic interviewing, 349–350,
    361
Evaluation, 38, 40, 59, 63–64, 70–73,
    75–76, 80, 84, 87, 94, 96,
    101, 104–105, 112–113,
    145–147, 156–159, 165–167,
    171–172, 183–184, 205, 281,
    284, 288, 374
Executive control (see Metacognition,
    control)
Executive processes, 9, 32
Expertise, 55, 97–100, 102, 105–107,
    113, 120–121, 285, 295, 328
External text base, 171, 175

F

Feedback, 32, 34, 98, 101–102,
    106–107, 134, 141, 181, 228,
    240, 243, 256, 262, 269, 284,
    294, 299, 317–321, 325, 327,
    339–340, 342–343, 355–356
Feeling of knowing (FOK), 13–14, 227
Forgetting, 119, 131–132, 141, 178,
    231–232, 257, 370
Free recall, 16–17, 130, 135
Frontal lobe, 226–227, 230, 232–234,
    236, 239–240, 242, 244, 372

G

Goal setting, 95, 97, 99, 103, 107,
    111, 171, 279, 283, 292–294,
    299, 364
Grounded theory, 350–352, 358,
    360–362

Group problem solving, 61–63, 86–87

H

Hemianopia, 224–225
Hemiplegia, 221–225
Hermeneutic inquiry, 180
Heuristics, 56, 296
Huntington's disease (HD), 231,
    234–235

I

Illusions of knowing, 129, 178–179
Imagery, 256, 260
Individual differences, 20, 30, 42,
    137–140, 254, 283, 289, 296,
    299
Inference, 29, 31, 34, 118, 120, 126,
    135–137, 140–141, 145, 148,
    154, 175, 177–178, 182, 186,
    188, 205–209, 211, 214, 279,
    282–283, 291
Instruction, 16, 20, 309, 318, 341,
    348–349, 358–359, 379
  bilingualism, 194, 199, 202, 212–215
  literacy, 210
  mathematics, 74, 78–80, 83, 85–89
  motivation, 356–357
  notetaking, 365
  problem solving, 51, 53, 56, 59–64
  reading, 376–377
  strategy, 98–100, 103, 105, 112–113
  test preparation, 133–134, 141–142,
      356
  text comprehension, 158–160, 187
  verbalization, 29, 33, 37, 41–42
  writing, 93–95, 98–103, 105–112, 377
Intelligence, 57, 62, 97, 194–196
Interdependence and threshold hy-
    pothesis theory, 199
Interpretation of text, 166, 174–188
Introspective methods, 98

J

Judgments of learning (JOL), 13, 15,
    131–132, 266–270, 286–287

K

Knowledge
  activated, 149–155, 158, 369
  conditional, 283, 285, 295–296
  declarative, 8–10, 94, 102, 159, 168,
      204, 250–251, 367
  domain-specific, 42, 48, 53, 55, 71,
      285, 290–292, 295, 297–298,
      307
  inert, 310
  metacognitive, 3, 5–6, 48–50, 60,
      62–64, 69–74, 79, 85–86,
      88–89, 100, 168, 194,
      211–212, 214, 251–254,
      262–263, 265, 269, 285,
      367–368, 373
  prior, 62, 74, 99–100, 106, 112,
      150–151, 156, 167, 172, 176,
      178–179, 181–185, 201,
      205–206, 208–210, 292, 299,
      301, 347–348, 354–358, 360,
      365
  procedural, 8–10, 94, 102, 157–158,
      168, 367
  process, 93–94
  product, 93–94
  strategic, 73, 78–80, 85, 88, 94
  telling, 96–97
  transforming, 96–97
Korsakoff's syndrome, 226–227

L

Language acquisition, 5, 193, 202
Learned industriousness, 298
Learner characteristics, 148, 158, 349
Letter-series completion, 16
Level of processing, 128–130
Lookbacks, 146, 171

M

Macropropositions, 154, 176
Magnetic resonance imaging, 244
Meaning making, 179–180, 182, 188
Memory, 132, 134, 154, 221, 224,
    226–228, 231–233
    complaints, 256, 259
    long-term, 9, 15, 27, 49, 153, 279, 295
    plasticity, 260–261
    self-efficacy, 249, 251–252, 254–259,
        263
    short-term, 15, 95, 99, 148, 153, 306
    strategies, 251–252, 255–257, 259–262,
        269
    working, 15, 27–28, 49, 95, 97, 99, 103,
        108, 152, 155, 171, 176–178,
        185, 279, 295, 306, 370
Mental map, 50
Mental model, 48, 51, 105, 107, 153,
    169, 172, 174, 178, 182–183,
    185–186, 308–309, 312–313,
    341–342, 372
Meta-level, 286–288, 291–292, 300
Metacognition
    control, 5, 7–12, 16–19, 32, 55, 94, 96,
        100–102, 105, 111, 113, 135,
        145, 147, 149, 156–159,
        165–175, 178–179, 182–188,
        250–251, 253, 255–256, 270,
        278, 281, 286–288, 291–292,
        294–301, 306, 341, 347–348,
        354–355, 367–370, 373–375,
        379
        editing, 288–289, 299–301
        toggling, 288–289, 295, 299–301
    deficits, 372
    definitions, 2–4, 8, 10–11, 29, 48, 94,
        250, 286, 306, 347, 367
    experiences, 3, 5–6
    monitoring, 31, 38, 40, 43, 54–55,
        59–61, 63–64, 70, 72–73, 80,
        82–87, 94–96, 100, 106, 111,
        113, 117, 165–171, 205, 250,
        252–254, 278, 281, 285–288,
        291–301, 306–309, 317, 334,
        341, 367–374, 379

comprehension (see Comprehension,
    monitoring)
deficit, 223, 227–228, 230, 234, 236,
    240–241, 244
direct access, 370
memory, 2–3, 5, 7–19, 250, 262–270
process-pure measure of, 370
utilization of, 252–253
skill, 3, 48–49, 54, 60, 63–64, 88, 306,
    308, 310, 342, 378
strategies, 5, 70, 87, 100, 168, 194,
    200–201, 205, 211, 379
training (see Instruction)
Metacomprehension, 117–118, 130,
    132, 135–137, 141, 145,
    165–166, 369–371
Meta-level, 368, 370–373
Metalinguistic awareness, 193–194,
    200
Metamemory, 2–5, 7, 140, 145,
    165–167, 367
Method of constant comparison, 350,
    361
Monitoring (see Metacognition, moni-
    toring)
Motivation, 10–11, 20, 94, 97, 172,
    221, 279, 299, 313, 317, 324,
    326–328, 347–348, 352,
    354–360, 379
Motivational orientations, 148, 281,
    283, 285, 292

N

Need for cognition, 296–297
Norm of study, 252–253, 255
Notetaking, 290, 301, 348, 351–357,
    364–366, 375, 379

O

Object-level, 286–288, 368, 370–373

P

Parkinson's disease (PD), 231, 234
Peer collaboration, 86–87, 101, 104, 106, 357–359
Perturbation, 75–76, 78, 84, 86–87
Pick's disease, 231–232
Picture association, 16
Planning, 7, 54–55, 58–60, 62, 64, 70–71, 73, 87, 95–97, 99–100, 102–105, 108–110, 112–113, 234, 279, 283–284, 292–293, 300
Positron emission tomography (PET), 244
Postdictions, 118–119, 133, 137–140, 142, 266
Practice tests, 133–134, 137
Prediction, 118–142, 165, 227–228, 308, 370, 376
    accuracy, 15, 118–142, 264–267, 270, 370–371, 376
    global, 133, 137, 264–266
    item-by-item (see JOLs, FOKs, EOL)
    test performance, 15, 118–142
    Prereading familiarity, 121–126
Problem solving, 5–6, 9, 11, 17, 25–27, 30–33, 36–43, 47–48, 50–54, 56–58, 62, 64, 69–70, 73–75, 79–80, 85, 97–98, 103, 106, 112, 147, 168, 306, 311, 313, 318, 332, 339, 343, 374–375, 377–378
    fixation, 58
    givens, 48, 52, 55, 60
    goals, 48, 52, 55–56, 60, 74–75
    incubation, 58
    insight problems, 32, 59, 61
    mathematical, 40–42, 51, 57, 61–63, 69–89, 329, 332, 375
    obstacles, 48, 60, 64
    selective combination, 52–53, 61
    selective comparison, 52–53, 61, 374
    selective encoding, 52–53, 61

well-structured problems, 60
Problem-based learning, 327–328, 332, 338
Procedural facilitation, 95, 101, 103, 105, 108–109
Production system, 287
Project-based learning, 327, 332, 338

Q

Questioning, 29, 38–43, 61, 63, 86, 88, 99, 110, 112, 133, 174, 182–186, 205, 207–209, 214, 354

R

Radical constructivism, 69
Reading, 145–160, 165–188, 198–216
    strategies, 194, 199–205, 210, 212–215
Reason giving, 33, 35–39, 42
Recall-judgment-recognition (RJR), 13
Reciprocal teaching, 62–64, 95
Reflection, 11, 48, 52, 69, 71, 73, 76–79, 85–86, 88, 98, 104–105, 111, 236, 243, 307, 311, 317–318, 321, 325, 327, 332, 334–335, 341–343, 349, 380
Reflective talk, 99, 104–105
Reflective thinking, 74, 83, 85–86
Regulation (see Metacognition, control)
Rehabilitation (see Training)
Rereading, 50, 72, 135, 145, 171, 184, 205, 208, 284
Resonance, 152, 155
Retrospective interviews, 98
Retrospective reports, 27–29, 339

Reviewing, 70, 95–96, 105–106, 284, 348, 377
Revising, 94–96, 98–102, 105–107, 109, 112–113, 184, 207, 211, 307, 310–311, 317, 321, 325, 327, 332, 334–335, 339–342, 377

S

Scaffolding, 101, 213, 294, 311, 313, 327, 332, 339, 343
Scheme theory, 74–80, 82–85, 87–88
Schizophrenia, 223, 236–243, 372–373
Seen judgments, 13
Self-appraisal, 10–11, 20
Self-assessment, 10, 13, 226–228, 234, 236, 307–311, 342–343, 372, 380
Self-efficacy, 10, 158
Self-management, 10–11, 17, 20, 53, 347
Self-monitoring (see Metacognition, monitoring)
Self-paced study (see Study)
Self-regulated comprehension, 167, 169, 172, 174–175, 178–188
Self-regulated learning, 88, 167, 250–252, 254, 259–260, 263, 269–270, 278, 281, 297, 299, 347–348, 350, 375, 379–380
Self-regulated study, 265–266, 268, 287–289
Self-talk, 98
Self-testing, 268–270
Semantic dimensions, 196
Serial recall, 13–14
Short-term memory (see Memory)

SMART environments, 311, 316–318, 325, 327–329, 332, 334–335, 338–339, 341–343
Social constructivism, 69, 71
Social context, 100, 104, 107, 111, 113, 156, 307
Social interaction, 9, 63, 70–71, 85–86, 97
Social support, 307, 320, 341
Sort-recall, 13–14, 16–19
Spacing effect, 294–295
Standards of evaluation (see Comprehension, monitoring standards)
Stereotypy, 58, 64, 229
Strategy, 48, 55, 62–63, 70–73, 76–78, 85, 87–88, 94, 96–97, 102, 104, 107–108, 110, 113, 130, 149, 152, 157, 159, 168–171, 174, 176, 306, 309, 316, 341, 343, 348, 353–355, 360–361, 379
  code-mixing, 203–204, 211
  reading, 62, 145–146, 156
  use, 5–7, 9–10, 12, 16–19, 40, 42, 62–63, 69–72, 78–79, 85, 101, 158–159, 347–348, 353–354, 356–357, 378
Studentship, 349, 352
Study, 250–253, 277–301, 347–349, 351–353, 355, 358–361, 378
  allocation, 13–15, 255, 267–269
  self-pacing, 253–254, 259, 268, 270, 374
  standards, 281–284, 286, 288, 291–292, 294–296, 298–300
  strategies, 253–254, 256, 259–260, 262, 266, 270, 278, 284, 294, 297–298
  tactics, 278–279, 282–290, 292, 294–300, 348, 354
  tasks, 279, 281, 283, 289, 291, 293, 296, 299–300

time, 14–15, 264, 268, 270, 347, 353, 355
Substitution tasks, 196
Summarizing, 107, 129–130, 171, 184
Suppression hypothesis, 153–155, 179, 369, 377

T

Tardive dyskenesia (TD), 240–241
Task appraisal, 251–252
Task-specific models, 169
Test preparation, 253, 352–353, 356, 361
Test-Operate-Test-Exit unit (TOTE), 368
Text retrievability, 126, 128–131
Think aloud, 26, 28–33, 38–40, 43, 60, 95, 98–99, 102, 106–107, 146, 184, 194, 201, 203, 207, 210, 213, 358, 361
Tip of the tongue, 13, 253
Topic familiarity, 119, 123–124, 126, 141

Training, 16–17, 38, 61–64, 227–229, 239–240, 243–244, 376–377
  memory, 250–252, 254–266, 268–270
Transfer, 10, 12, 16, 35–39, 43, 56–57, 60, 62–63, 71, 77, 199, 204–205, 211, 213–214, 216, 306, 310, 327,
Translating, 95–97, 100, 203–204, 209

V

Verbal report (see Think aloud)
Verbalize, 18, 26–33, 35–40, 43, 60, 84, 96, 377–378

W

Wernicke's aphasics, 229–230
Wisconsin Card Sorting Test (WCST), 240
Working memory (see Memory)
World Wide Web (WWW), 317–321, 325, 327, 342–343